THE PRIESTLY ELEMENT IN THE OLD TESTAMENT

BY

WILLIAM R. HARPER

THE PRIESTLY ELEMENT IN THE OLD TESTAMENT

AN AID TO HISTORICAL STUDY

FOR USE IN ADVANCED BIBLE CLASSES

BY

WILLIAM RAINEY HARPER

PROFESSOR OF SEMITIC LANGUAGES AND LITERATURES
IN THE UNIVERSITY OF CHICAGO

REVISED AND ENLARGED EDITION

Wipf & Stock
PUBLISHERS
Eugene, Oregon

Wipf and Stock Publishers
199 W 8th Ave, Suite 3
Eugene, OR 97401

The Priestly Element in the Old Testament
An Aid to Historical Study
By Harper, William R.
ISBN 13: 978-1-55635-218-8
ISBN 10: 1-55635-218-2
Publication date 1/24/2007
Previously published by University of Chicago Press, 1905

PREFACE TO THE THIRD EDITION.

THIS treatment of the Priestly Element in the Old Testament is intended to serve as a guide for students who wish to take up the questions relating to the subject from an historical point of view. The materials for a preliminary study of the various topics are gathered together, and arranged with suggestions as to order and method of procedure.

It is thought that the work proposed is within the reach of the more mature pupils in the Sunday school, although the needs of college and theological students have been kept especially in mind.

The general results of modern historical criticism have been taken as a basis for the work, since it is only from the point of view of history that these subjects may now be considered intelligently. Each special topic connected with the general subject of the Priestly Element furnishes a beautiful illustration of the growth and development of Israelitish and Jewish thought under the controlling influence of a conception of God which became more and more pure with the advancing centuries.

Four methods of treatment have been employed, each being deemed best adapted to the case in hand, viz.: in Chapter I, a systematic statement of the scope of the Priestly Element; in Chapters II–IV, an historical statement covering in barest outline the story of the Priestly Element *as a whole*, in its progress and development; in Chapters V–XI, a classified and comparative examination (indicated by questions and suggestions based upon the material presented) of the more important special factors which, taken together, constitute the Priestly Element; in Chapters XII–XIX, a critical examination of the literature produced by the Priests, and of its essential significance. The appendix on the vocabulary of worship will be found serviceable to those who wish to enter somewhat carefully into a consideration of the details. In Appendix B there will be found a classified list of the most important books, while in Appendix C the more valuable recent literature (since 1901) has been indicated.

Some experience in the use of this manual in the class-room seems to indicate that it furnishes an opportunity whereby both instructor and pupil may work with greatest freedom. It is not a text-book; nor is it merely a syllabus. It may be adapted to almost every possible method of teaching.

An effort has been made to indicate definitely and fully the more accessible literature on each topic. I wish to express my appreciation of the assistance rendered me by my colleague, Dr. John M. P. Smith, especially in the arrangement and verification of the scriptural references, and the references to the literature on the various topics. For obvious reasons the latter have been arranged chronologically, the literature in languages other than English being placed by itself.

In this more complete form (Chapters XII–XIX and the Appendixes, constituting the new matter added to the first edition) it is hoped that an outline has been prepared which will assist many students in their desire to gain a reasonable familiarity with a really large and complex subject.

William R. Harper.

February 22, 1905.

CONTENTS.

Part I.

THE GENERAL SCOPE OF THE PRIESTLY ELEMENT.

Part II.

THE HISTORY OF THE PRIESTLY ELEMENT IN THE OLD TESTAMENT.

Part III.

A COMPARATIVE STUDY OF THE LAWS AND USAGES OF WORSHIP.

Part IV.

THE LITERATURE OF WORSHIP—THE LEGAL LITERATURE.

Part V.

THE LITERATURE OF WORSHIP—THE HISTORICAL LITERATURE.

Part VI.

THE LITERATURE OF WORSHIP—THE HYMNAL LITERATURE.

Part VII.

THE PERMANENT VALUE OF THE PRIESTLY ELEMENT.

Appendixes.

CHAPTER I.

THE GENERAL SCOPE OF THE PRIESTLY ELEMENT IN THE OLD TESTAMENT.

§ 1. **Three Elements Enter into Religion.** — The religion of an individual or nation depends upon the prominence given to one or another of these elements:

(1) *Worship*, or, more technically, *cult*, a word which expresses the general attitude of the individual or group of individuals toward an outside higher world of supernatural or divine existence, and includes the outward acts that in various forms symbolize the inward thought. **Pss. 103:1; 150.**

(2) *Belief*, or, more technically, *creed*, a word which expresses the peculiar intellectual position entertained by an individual or group of individuals concerning certain facts supposed to be essential, and their explanation. **Deut. 6:4; John 3:36.**

(3) *Conduct*, or, more technically, *ethics*, which includes all the acts and feelings of man in so far as they are related to his duties to himself and to his fellows, and to the fundamental ideas of right and wrong. **Mic. 6:8; Isa. 1:16, 17; James 1:27.**

§ 2. **Three Great Channels of Revelation** are found in the Old Testament; through these, separately and together, there has come down to us a wonderful story of the interworking of God and man. These are:

(1) The *word* of the prophet, including the utterances through centuries of that unique order established to give to the Hebrew nation and to the world the "word" of God. **Jer. 18:18; Jer. 1:11.**

(2) The *counsel* of the sage, including the wise sayings and philosophical teachings (in the form of proverbs, riddles, essays, dialogues, etc.) found, for example, in the books of Proverbs, Job, and Ecclesiastes. **Jer. 18:18; Prov. 1:5, 25, 30; 8:14.**

(3) The *instruction* (or law) of the priest, which forms the subject of consideration in this and the following studies. **Jer. 18:18; Ps. 19:7.**

§ 3. **The Place of Worship is First of All to be Noticed.** — In ancient times because it seemed to men that *certain* *places* were more favored by the gods than were others, in modern times because men fancy that a certain environment is especially conducive to the spirit of worship, the *place* has always been a subject of greatest importance. The place was in early days something *connected with nature:*

1 Kings 14:23; 1 Chron. 21:29; Exod. 19:2, 3, 12.

(1) *High places*, or hills, were especially sought as being the abode of God.

Gen. 12:6; 13:18.

(2) *Trees* of a notable character are frequently referred to as connected with worship.

Gen. 16:13, 14.

(3) *Springs*, or *wells*, are places by the side of which angels were thought to dwell.

Gen. 31:44–54; Gen. 28:18–22.

(4) *Sacred stones* are mentioned as places to which the god came to meet his worshiper, and on which food was placed or libations of oil poured out.

In each of these places Jehovah had shown his presence, and it was for this reason that the hill or tree or spring or stone was sacred. (From Numb. 22:41 it is to be seen that this idea of sacred places was found among other nations; *cf.* also Isa. 16:12.)

The place was also often something of a more or less *artificial* character, as is seen in the use of—

Exod. 20:24–26; 1 Kings 7:48; 2 Kings 16:10–15; Exod. 27:1–8; 1 Kings 2:28–30.

(5) *The altar*, which was sometimes only of loose earth thrown up; at others, of unhewn stone; at still others, of gold and precious stones. This altar was the refuge and asylum of him who fled the hand of vengeance, the witness of vows, the place on which the sacrifice was laid.

Josh. 4:11; 1 Sam. 4:3–6; 2 Sam. 6:2–17; Exod. 25:10–21; Exod. 25:22.

(6) *The ark*, or *chest*, a sacred box in which certain sacred things were deposited; which was used in case of war, because it was thought to afford protection; and was designated as a place of communion with God.

2 Sam. 7:2–6; Exod., chap. 26; Exod. 33:7–9; Numb. 17:4, 12, 13.

(7) *The tent*, or *tabernacle*, a dwelling in which the ark was preserved, and around which the holiest associations clustered. Moses made most practical use of it, and it came to occupy an important place in Hebrew thought and tradition.

1 Kings 6:1, 2, 11–14, 37, 38; Ezek. 43:1–12; Hag. 1:4–14; Ezra 3:12, 13; 6:13–18.

(8) *The temple*, which with the progress of civilization (the establishment of courts and the building of palaces) took the place of the tent, as being more dignified than

a *tent*. There was (*a*) Solomon's temple, erected at a significant period of national development; (*b*) the temple of Ezekiel's vision, which was destined to play an important part in the history of Israel's religious thought; and (*c*) the second temple, erected with some disappointment, after the return from exile.

It is to be noted, once more, that communion with God is sought and obtained in connection with natural places (hills, trees, springs, stones) and with places constructed by man (altars, ark, tent, temple). It will be at a later time, when temples are destroyed, men are scattered, groups living here and there, when the realistic conception gives place to the idealistic, and the material to the spiritual, that synagogues and churches will spring into existence, and, thus in still another form, satisfy the inward craving of humanity for a *sacred place*, in which to offer worship to the unseen powers. **Exod. 3:2–5; Ps. 137.**

§ 4. **The Priest, or Minister** of worship, was the second necessity of worship, the first being the place. It was the *priest* who conducted the worship.

(1) His function was threefold: to carry the ark, to minister to Jehovah, to bless in his name. In the earliest times the need of having some such priest was felt, his presence being thought to be attended with peculiar blessing. **Deut. 10:8; Judg. 17:7–13; 18:3–6; Lev. 8:1–10.**

(2) The priest-idea became so strong in Israel that the nation itself was understood to be a nation of priests, or a priestly nation, set apart to minister to the other nations of the world. After the exile, kings ceased to sit on Israel's throne; and priests, under the form of a hierarchy, controlled the affairs of the nation. This fact shows how great a rôle the priest played in Israelitish history. **Deut. 14:2; Exod. 19:6; Ezra 7:21, 25, 26.**

(3) Besides the priests and prophets who served and spoke for Jehovah, there were at many times in Israel's history priests and prophets whose lives were devoted to the service of other gods. **1 Kings 18:19–22; 2 Kings 23:4, 5; Ezek. 8:15, 16.**

§ 5. **Sacrifice** was the most significant act of worship in ancient times.

Gen. 18:1-8; 1 Sam. 1:3-8; 9:23-25; 1 Chron. 16:1-3.

(1) At first this was a social meal, a banquet in which the offerer and his friends participated and to which the deity was invited. There are frequent references to such sacrificial meals in which the members of a family, or of a clan, or, indeed, of a whole nation took part. This meal was full of joy, sometimes boisterous. Those who participated were eating and drinking with the deity; it was a communion of the worshiper and his god.

Ps. 51:18, 19; Isa. 1:11-17; Lev., chaps. 1-7; 8-10; 11; 12-15; etc.

(2) In later times *sacrifice* became more formal, and gradually grew into an exclusively religious act. The prophets strongly denounced sacrifice in which the true spirit of worship was lacking, or which in itself, without a proper life, was thought to gain Jehovah's favor. The book of Leviticus is devoted to the subject of sacrifice, viz., the method, the kinds, etc., etc. This more formal and exclusively religious conception of sacrifice came to prevail universally in the last centuries of Israel's history.

(3) Several different kinds of *offerings* or sacrifice were distinguished, according as each expressed a particular purpose, or was presented by a particular method; among these were:

Gen. 8:20; Lev., chaps. 4, 9.

(*a*) *The burnt-offering*, which consisted of the burning of a whole animal of the proper kind upon an altar as an offering to Jehovah.

Lev. 3:1-6; Judg. 20:26.

(*b*) *The peace-offering*, which was also an animal sacrifice, but differed from the burnt-offering in that it provided for the giving of only the blood and certain specified parts of the animal to Jehovah, the rest being eaten by the sacrificial guests.

Gen. 35:14; Exod. 29:40, 41; Numb. 28:7.

(*c*) *The drink-offering*, which was a libation of wine, or oil, usually made in connection with other offerings.

Exod. 30:1, 7-9; Numb. 4:16.

(*d*) *The incense-offering*, in which fragrant spices were burned with the thought that the rising fragrance was acceptable to Jehovah.

Lev., chaps. 5, 7, 14; Numb. 6:12.

(*e*) *The trespass-offering*, which was made for the purpose of expiating offenses against Jehovah and man in which the damage could be estimated and covered by compensation; the blood of the animal was poured out to Jehovah, the fat was burned on the altar, and the rest was the perquisite of the priests.

(*f*) *The sin-offering*, which occupied a very important place in the cultus and of which the emphasis placed upon the shedding of blood is a conspicuous feature; the specifications for this part of the ritual are very complete and detailed.

Lev. 4:24-34; Lev., chap. 16; Numb., chap. 7; 15:27.

(*g*) *The wave-offering*, consisting of certain portions of the sacrifice that were given over to the priests and were waved by them before the altar as a token of the fact that they belonged to Jehovah, but had been given over by him to the priests.

Deut. 12:6-17; Numb. 15:19-21; Numb. 18:8-29; Exod. 29:27, 28.

(4) Great care was taken as to the materials which might enter into a sacrifice. These were in general flesh, fine flour or meal, incense, oil, wine, cakes of dough, salt. Here again important conceptions were associated with each of the materials, and regulations were enacted prescribing the exact character and amount of materials to be used.

Exod. 20:24; 29:40; 30:1; Lev. 2:1, 4, 13; 7:12; 23:13.

§ 6. **The Times of Worship** were an important item, for these were the feast occasions; these were often merely the social meals of a clan; or, in other cases, were connected with a pilgrimage. They had their origin in connection with the times of the moon and the seasons, arising, as they did, out of the pastoral or agricultural life. Men whose hearts have the same tendencies are drawn together, and in the act of association there is worship; for the more closely they are united, the nearer they may come to God. To know more of God is itself to worship him, and the highest form of worship is, perhaps, that which involves communion with others as well as with God.

1 Sam. 9:12, 13 22-24; 1 Sam. 1:3, 4.

(1) There were three great feasts, the first coming in the springtime, the second in the early summer, the third in the autumn. These correspond roughly to the more modern Easter, Pentecost, and Thanksgiving seasons.

Exod. 23:14-17.

(2) There were also special feasts and feast days, which in early times seem to have been of a joyous character.

Hos. 2:11.

(3) There were days, like the Day of Atonement, which were days of affliction rather than of joy.

Lev. 16:29-34.

Zech. 7:3-5; Esther 9:28-31.

(4) There were also fast days, as well as feast days, celebrating some great calamity.

§ 7. **Other Acts of Worship.**—In connection with and forming a part of worship were several specific acts, such as—

Gen. 24:12 ff.; 1 Sam. 1:10; 8:6; 1 Kings 8:23-53; Isa. 38:2, 3; Neh. 1:4-11; 2:4.

(1) *Prayer;* this was always implied in the act of sacrifice, but very frequently it was independent of sacrifice. If the deity is a person, and if he has real interest in his clan or tribe or people, he will surely listen to them, when in distress their heart appeals for succor; and also when in joy they express appreciation of some great favor which he has shown them. Abraham's prayer for the city in which his relatives dwelt is characteristic of the earliest and the latest periods of civilization, and is thoroughly typical of humanity.

Judg. 11:30-39; 1 Sam. 1:11; Judg. 13:3-7; Numb. 6:1-12.

(2) *The vow* was a kind of prayer, very common in ancient times, and, when once made, regarded as inviolable. It sometimes involved a simple gift; at other times, perhaps, as in the case of Jephthah, the sacrifice of a human life; and again, as in the case of the Nazirite, it signified setting apart to the service of God.

1 Kings 6:19; Exod. 28:30; Gen. 20:3; 28:10, 18.

(3) *The oracle* and *dream*, as methods of ascertaining the divine will, must be counted as acts of worship. In these methods, as in all the others, the Israelites did not differ from the other ancient nations in the midst of whom they dwelt.

Isa. 47:9; Jer. 27:9; Mal. 3:5; Dan. 2:2; Deut. 18:9-13.

(4) *Sorcery* was employed in many forms, for there were diviners, augurs, enchanters, charmers, consulters with familiar spirits, wizards, and necromancers; but acts of this kind were always forbidden.

Gen. 4:21; Amos 5:23; Isa. 30:29, 32; Jer. 48:36; Numb. 10:2, 31:6; Josh. 6:4 ff.; Pss. 137:2; 33:2; 2 Sam. 16:14; Exod. 15:20; Pss. 149:3; 150:4.

(5) *Music* and *dancing* were accompaniments of worship. If worship is the expression of the heart in communion with God, it must include melody and rhythm, sound and movement. Music has always formed a part of worship, and in many cases dancing has accompanied, not only festival, but worship.

§ 8. **Songs and Hymns of Worship.**—These furnish us, perhaps, the highest product of the priest-work; for, although much of the Psalter is prophetic in its character, by far the greater part is the high and holy expression of the soul of individual or nation in its deepest communion with God; and nowhere in all literature may religious songs of so tender and deep a character be found as in the Hebrew Psalter, the hymn-book of the Hebrew temple, the work of the Hebrew priest. These have been variously and quite minutely classified; but here reference may be limited to —

(1) Songs of thanksgiving, in which gratitude is expressed for great favors received from Jehovah and his praises are gladly sung. **Pss. 103; 134; 136.**

(2) Songs of petition and prayer, in which the poet pleads for the intervention of Jehovah in behalf of himself or of Israel, bringing deliverance from difficulty and danger, or restoration to divine favor. **Pss. 80; 88; 102.**

(3) Songs of penitential confession, in which the sinner pours out his confession of sin and guilt. **Pss. 51; 116; 130.**

§ 9. **Laws Regulating Worship and Life** were, likewise, largely formulated, promulgated, and executed by the priests. Legislation, therefore, in its stricter sense, was the function of the priests, rather than of the prophets or sages. The priest's work included something more than the various elements which enter into or are connected with what we would today call *worship*. In those days the religious life and the secular life were the same. Religion and politics were the same. This means that it was impossible to draw a line between religious life and ordinary life. The priest's work dealt with both. It had to do, consequently, with such matters as the treatment of one's neighbor's cattle, the treatment of birds, the building of a house. There were laws, for example, concerning the harvest, the oppression of the poor, the treatment of defectives, tale-bearing, etc., etc. These are a few examples only, taken from the great law-books, Exodus, Leviticus, and Deuteronomy. It is to be understood, of course, that these laws, as they were from time to time formulated, included the teachings of the prophets and sages, as they appeared and did their work and passed away. But in addition to these laws of sociological character there were the laws which regulated

Deut. 22: 1-12; Exod. 21: 1-35; 22: 1-27.

Lev. 19: 9-37; Exod. 23: 1-9.

Exod. 23:18, 19; Deut. 30:15-20; Lev., chap. 21.

the details of worship in all respects, *e. g.*, the priest, his dress, his maintenance, the offerings, their material, etc., etc. These more strictly come into consideration in connection with topics already discussed (*cf.* §§ 3, 7).

2 Chron. 5:2—7:2; *cf.* 1 Kings, chap. 8.

§ 10. **The History of Worship** was naturally written or compiled by priests, and thus constitutes a part of the priest-work of the Old Testament. The history of Israel, as we find it in the books of Samuel and Kings, had already been written (about 550 B. C.). This history was prepared from a wholly prophetic point of view. It was intended to teach prophetic lessons, especially those connected with the idea of the enormity of sin and its disastrous consequences. At a later date (about 300 B. C.) the priests undertook to traverse the field of sacred history, and in so doing used, to some extent, the same original sources. This *priestly history* is found in the books of Chronicles, Ezra, and Nehemiah. In these books the thought always uppermost is that of the *history of worship*. Its purpose was to assist in establishing regular service in the second temple, and to kindle in the hearts of the people a national life and spirit, and respect for the institutions of the national religion. The differences in matter, tone, and spirit between the prophetic and the priestly histories is easily seen by a comparison of the treatment which each gives to the same subject, *e. g.*:

1 Chron., chaps. 15, 16; *cf.* 2 Sam. 6:12-19.

2 Chron., chaps. 29-32; *cf.* 2 Kings, chaps. 18-20.

2 Chron. 35:1-19; *cf.* 2 Kings 23:21-23.

1 Kings, chap. 8.

(1) The dedication of the temple (*cf.* 2 Chron. 5:2—7:10).

1 Chron., chaps. 28, 29; *cf.* 1 Kings 1:32-40.

(2) The transfer of the ark to Jerusalem.

(3) The accession of Solomon.

1 Chron., chap. 21; *cf.* 2 Sam., chap. 24.

(4) The account of the plague in David's reign.

2 Sam. 11:2-27.

(5) The sin of David with Bathsheba, which is not mentioned in Chronicles.

1 Chron., chaps. 23-26.

(6) The organization of the priests and Levites and temple officials, which is treated in full in Chronicles, and not mentioned in Samuel and Kings.

It is proposed, after this general view of the work of the priests as a whole, to undertake to do five things in the following series of studies:

(1) To trace the history of worship from the beginning to the end of the Old Testament times, through the early, the middle, and the late periods.

(2) To classify and note the elements of worship in the Hebrew Psalter, the Christian's Book of Psalms.

(3) To analyze and present the essential points of interest in the histories which the priests themselves prepared, and which are found in the books of Chronicles, Ezra, and Nehemiah.

(4) To determine the great ideas which entered into and controlled the priest-work.

(5) To explain as far as it may be possible (*a*) the purpose and spirit of this *priest-element* as it appears in its various forms in Israelitish history and literature; (*b*) the permanent, as distinguished from the transitory, elements which it contained; (*c*) the contribution which it made to Christianity, or, in other words, its relationship to Christianity.

Part Second

THE HISTORY OF WORSHIP

II. History of Worship in the Earlier Old Testament Period.

III. History of Worship in the Middle Old Testament Period.

IV. History of Worship in the Later Old Testament Period.

CHAPTER II.

HISTORY OF WORSHIP IN THE EARLIER OLD TESTAMENT PERIOD.

§ 11. **Worship Alone Constituted Religion** in the earliest times. It was later that greater and greater emphasis came to be placed on *conduct* and *belief* (see § 1). A ceremony or religious rite was associated (in the various ancient religions) with some fact, or supposed fact, or legend, or myth. But it was the *rite* which constituted the religious element, and not any belief concerning the origin of the rite. "It made no difference what the worshiper believed concerning the ceremony, if only he performed it regularly and accurately." "What was obligatory or meritorious was the exact performance of sacred acts prescribed by religious traditions." It was the prophets and sages who introduced at the same time higher conceptions of God and higher conceptions of life.

See W. R. SMITH, *Religion of the Semites* (2d ed.), pp. 17–22; MENZIES, *History of Religion*, pp. 6–13, 64 f.; WELLHAUSEN, *Prolegomena to the History of Israel*, pp. 52–5.

§ 12. **A Semitic Period in the Development of Worship** preceded the earliest Hebrew worship, and formed the basis of it. It will be remembered that the Semitic family (1) gave to the world the two earliest civilizations of which we have knowledge, the Egyptian and the old Babylonian, and controlled the world's political history for forty or fifty centuries; (2) has been mediary, not only in the field of commerce and between man and man, but also, in that higher field of religion, between God and man, in that they have proved to be the religious teachers of the world, since through them have come the world's three highest faiths—Judaism, Christianity, and Mohammedanism.

See G. A. SMITH, *Historical Geography of the Holy Land*, pp. 28 ff.; W. R. SMITH, *op. cit.*, pp. 28–83; C. G. MONTEFIORE, *The Religion of the Ancient Hebrews* (Hibbert Lectures, 1892), pp. 22–30; J. F. MCCURDY, *History, Prophecy and the Monuments*, Vol. I, pp. 5–11; FRITZ HOMMEL, *The Civilization of the East*, pp. 25–7.

§ 13. **The Most Ancient Form of Semitic Religion**, the parent of all others, was that found in the old mother-home of Arabia. It was a religion well adapted to the condition of the people, who, at that time, were still in clans. The Hebrews, together with the Moabites, Ammonites, and Edomites, had "their root in a state of society when there was no large and orderly community, but only a multitude of small and restless tribes; when there was no written law, but only custom; and when there was no central authority to execute justice, but it was left to a man's fellow-clansmen to avenge his murder." In this time—

(1) *There was a god for each clan*, and this god was thought to be a very remote ancestor. To leave the clan meant to leave the god. This clan-god was closely connected with every undertaking of the clan, whether of peace or war; and his name everywhere was "Lord," "King," "Mighty One."

See MENZIES, *History of Religion*, pp. 74–6; W. R. SMITH, *Religion of the Semites* (2d ed.), pp. 35–9; D'ALVIELLA, *Origin and Growth of the Conception of God* (Hibbert Lectures, 1891), pp. 204–7.

(2) *The worship* of the clan-god was important, because every detail of life was dependent on his favor. His favor or anger was shown at certain spots, which thenceforward became *sacred places*, and here those who inquired of him would find him. The god could not, of course, be worshiped *anywhere outside* of the land which belonged to him; and if one left that land and entered another, he must at once transfer his worship to the god of the new land.

See MENZIES, *op. cit.*, pp. 160 f.; BUDDE, *Religion of Israel to the Exile*, pp. 53–5.

(3) *The present life* played a larger part than the future life; for, while the early Semites believed in the continued existence of the departed, they regarded them as destitute of energy, as "shades laid in the ground." "After death, it was held, even religion came to an end. A man must enjoy the society of his god in this life; after death he could take part in no sacrifice, and could render to God no thanks or service."

See MENZIES, *op. cit.*, p. 161; C. G. MONTEFIORE, *op. cit.*, pp. 454–7; R. H. CHARLES, *A Critical History of the Doctrine of a Future Life*, pp. 51–4.

(4) This explains, in some measure, *the rites of worship* which existed in these primitive times, viz.:

(*a*) *The sacrifice;* the man sought a sacred place (*i. e.*, a place where the god was likely to be found), killed an animal, put the blood of the animal on a stone; the god touched the blood, the man touched it, and this act was a renewal of the declaration that the man and the god were of the same blood, and that the covenant between them was renewed.

See MENZIES, *op. cit.*, pp. 65–8, 162; SCHULTZ, "The Significance of Sacrifice in the Old Testament," *American Journal of Theology*, Vol. IV, pp. 257–61; G. S. GOODSPEED, "The Atonement of Communion," *Biblical World*, Vol. XVII, pp. 96–106.

(*b*) *The feast or banquet;* at this the god was supposed to sit with his people and to receive his share of the animal just slain. In late times, when the god was thought to live above, his share was burned and he received the savor or smell of the sacrifice. The feast included dancing, and even gross kinds of indulgence. All was joyful. Happiness, reaching even to "orgiastic ecstasy," was universal.

See W. R. SMITH, *op. cit.*, pp. 253–8; SCHULTZ, *Old Testament Theology*, Vol. I, pp. 188 f.

§ 14. **Three Great Periods** are seen in the development of this primitive Semitic worship, as it appears in the Old Testament history. Two opinions exist as to whether the writing of the Pentateuch (or five books of the law) was practically finished in the days of Moses, or in the days of Ezra. **Josh. 24:2,3.**

See GREEN, *The Higher Criticism of the Pentateuch*, pp. 31–58; BRIGGS, *The Higher Criticism of the Hexateuch*, 1897, pp. 156–62; DRIVER, *Introduction to the Literature of the Old Testament* (6th ed.), pp. 82–98, 123–6, 135–59; CARPENTER AND HARFORD-BATTERSBY, *The Hexateuch*, Vol. I, pp. 17–23.

This question does not concern us here; for all students agree that, whatever may have been the date of *writing*, the date of *adoption* of the laws and ceremonies by the masses of the people is definitely announced in Scripture, viz.:

(1) *The Levitical law in all its fulness* and the Levitical ritual of worship were not adopted until the times of Ezra (440 B. C.). **Neh., chap. 8.**

(2) *The Deuteronomic law*, as laid down in Deuteronomy, did not come into force until Josiah's time (621 B. C.). It is clear that there was **2 Kings 22:8—23:3.**

(3) *An earlier legal code* and an earlier form of worship which served to connect the old Semitic worship with the Deuteronomic. This earliest of the three **Exod. 20:23—23:19.**

periods is first to be considered and presents itself in three different stages, viz.:

Gen. 47:1-10. (*a*) *The primitive Hebrew stage*—that which existed during the days of the patriarchs, and while Israel was still a nomadic people, wandering from place to place.

Judg. 1:1-4; 2:11-19. (*b*) *The Canaanitish stage*—that in which the primitive form came into contact with the corrupt and licentious practices of the Canaanitish religion; it was at this time that Israel was settling down to an agricultural life.

Hos. 11:1-4; 12:10, 11; Amos 2:10-12; Isa. 2:6-9. (*c*) *The prophetic stage*—that in which the prophets made heroic struggle against the corruption and idolatry of Israel, by pointing out a truer conception of God, the adoption of which affected both the conduct and the worship of the nation.

Josh. 24:3-7. § 15. **In the Primitive Stage of the Early Period the Worship** was, of course, only slightly different from that common Semitic worship described above. The people were still wandering about. Leaders had been raised up by God whose work would in time lead the people higher and higher toward a proper conception of God and of his worship. But, as the Old Testament so clearly shows, the people hung back; refused to follow the divinely appointed leaders; and only after fifteen hundred years of instruction finally acknowledged Jehovah to be the only God. The facts concerning worship are these:

Gen. 12:6-8; 13:4, 18; 26:24 f.; 32:22-32; 35:14 f. (1) *The place* selected for worship by the patriarchs was the place in which they pitched their tent; *e. g.*, Abraham worshiped at Shechem, and near Bethel; Jacob at Beersheba, and at Peniel, and at Bethel. *Trees*, *springs*, and *stones* are also mentioned.

Gen. 31:46. The *altar* must have been something very simple, consisting only of stones gathered together, or of earth thrown up.

Gen. 31:19, 34 f. *Teraphim*, or household gods, were found in Jacob's family. There seems not to have been an ark or chest in use.

Gen. 22:13; 27:25; 28:18; Exod. 24:4-8. (2) *The priest* was the leader, whoever he may have been, Abraham, Isaac, Jacob, or Moses. There was no class of priests.

(3) *The sacrifice* was a family meal, or a clan meal, *i. e.*, a banquet. It consisted of flesh, specially prepared; its savor was smelled by Jehovah; it was eaten by representatives of the deity. Gen. 26:28-30; Gen. 8:20, 21; Gen. 18:1-8.

(4) *The times* were irregular; sacrifice was offered at *any* time. There is no reference to the observance of dates marked by the *moon*, or of the *sabbath*. *Cf.* references given above.

(5) *Other acts of worship* are seen in —

(*a*) The *prayer* of Abraham for the deliverance of Lot, of Abraham's servant for guidance in the pursuit of his mission, and of Jacob for deliverance from Esau. Gen. 18:23-33; 24:12 ff.; 32:9-12.

(*b*) The *vow* of Abraham paid to Melchizedek; and that of Jacob made on his journey to Laban, the Syrian. Gen. 14:18-24; 28:20-22.

(*c*) The *dreams* of the patriarchs, which as methods of receiving communications from the deity are to be classed with acts of worship. Gen. 15:12-21; 28:10-18; 35:9-13; 37:5-10.

(*d*) The *cup* of divination of Joseph, and the *teraphim* (see p. 16). Gen. 44:1-5.

(6) *Songs and hymns*, *laws*, and *history-writing* had not yet taken formal shape; or, at all events, they have not come down to us in the form which existed in these early days. The present literary form of pieces like the "Blessing of Jacob," the "Song of Moses at the Red Sea," and the "Decalogue" comes from a time later than the settlement in Canaan. Gen. 49:1-26; Exod. 15:1-18; Exod. 20:1-17.

§16. **In the Canaanitish Stage of the Early Period** the worship was greatly changed. This was due partly to the change from nomadic to agricultural life, and partly to contact with *Canaanitish* forms of worship, which were peculiarly rich and fascinating. The name of the Canaanitish divinity, Baal, meant "lord." It is easy to see that the Israelite would feel that he was not doing justice to his God, if he did not pay him every possible honor, or at least the honors paid their gods by his neighbors, the Canaanites. Consequently much that was Canaanitish was now appropriated. Judg. 2:1-5.

(1) *Places and representatives;* here arise —

(*a*) The *high places*, all over the land, which soon became centers of corruption and licentiousness. Judg. 6:25-32; 1 Sam. 1:3.

Judg. 3:7; 6:25, 30; 9:6; 10:6.

(*b*) The *pillars* and the tree trunks, or Asherim, which were to be found at the high places and were taken over into the Jehovah-worship which was carried on at these places.

Judg. 20:27 f.; 1 Sam. 4:3 ff.

(*c*) The *ark* or *chest*, which was thought to represent the deity, and which the people carried with them when they went to battle, as in Eli's days.

Cf. Exod. 32:8, 19–24; Numb. 21:8 f.; 2 Kings 18:4.

(*d*) The image of the *serpent*, or of the *bull*, which was adopted, now and again, as the proper representation of deity.

1 Sam. 14:41; 28:3–6.

(*e*) The *Urim and Thummim*, which were carried in a pocket of the priestly ephod, were in use as a means of discovering the divine will with reference to any course of action.

Judg. 17:7; Judg. 18:3–5, 19, 20; Judg. 6:19; 13:19; 17:5; 6:25–27; 11:31, 39.

(2) The *priest* was sometimes a professional, bearing the name Levite, and cultivated a certain professional tone by which he was recognized as a Levite. He seems to have been more acceptable than the patriarch or oldest son, who in the past had performed priestly duties. The priest went about wherever he could find employment. But the old family priesthood still continued, and sacrifice was not restricted to any class of priests.

Judg. 6:19–21, 26–28; 13:16–23; 1 Sam. 1:3–5, 9, 13–15.

(3) *Sacrifice* was the same as before, an act of communion with the deity. The burnt-offering seems to have occupied a more prominent place.

1 Sam. 20:5, 6, 18, 24, 27, 29; Judg. 9:27; 21:19; 1 Sam. 1:3, 13.

(4) *Times and seasons.*—Now there arose feasts of the moon; the sabbath was also observed, probably as a time of rejoicing; there were also the Feasts of Harvest and Vintage, because Israel had now become an agricultural people. These feasts furnished opportunity for drunkenness and licentiousness.

(5) *Other acts.*—We read of the—

Judg. 13:8; 15:18; 1 Sam. 1:10, 12–17.

(*a*) *Prayers* of Manoah, Samson, and Hannah.

Judg. 11:30, 31, 35–40; 21:1, 7, 18; 1 Sam. 1:11.

(*b*) *Vows* of Jephthah and of Hannah, and of the tribes of Israel against Benjamin, because of its outrage upon the Levite's concubine.

Judg. 13:3–5, 9–21; 1 Sam. 3:1–18.

(*c*) *Visions* of Samson's parents, and of the child Samuel, during his sojourn in the temple at Shiloh.

1 Sam. 28:7–14.

(*d*) *Sorcery and witchcraft* in connection with Saul's attempt to learn the outcome of his contest with the Philistines.

(*e*) *Music and dancing* in connection with the yearly feasts at Shiloh, with the sons of the prophets, and, a little later, on the part of David. This was characteristic of the joyous spirit that permeated the religion of these times. **Judg. 21:19–21; 1 Sam. 10:5; 16:16–22; 18:6, 7, 10; 19:9.**

(6) *Songs and hymns* are seen in the exodus song, with its refrain; the song of Deborah; and the song of Hannah. **Exod. 15:1–21; Judg., chap. 5; 1 Sam. 2:1–10.**

(7) *Laws* were unquestionably taking form, under divine guidance, as the codification of custom. To what extent this was true is a matter of dispute between (*a*) those who believe that the Israelitish legislation, as it has come down to us, was the work of one generation, and of one man, Moses, and (*b*) those who believe that this legislation is the product of seven or eight centuries of history, although based upon and growing out of the work of Moses (*cf.* references to literature on § 14).

§ 17. **In the Prophetic Stage of the Early Period** great influences were at work to purge and purify the corruption which had entered into Israel's worship, and to teach a conception of God which, in itself, would lead to a higher type of worship. This period begins roughly with Samuel's work of reformation and closes just before Josiah's reformation (621 B. C.). The great names of the period are Samuel and David; Elijah, Elisha, and Jonah; Amos and Hosea; Isaiah and Micah; and, last of all, Zephaniah and Jeremiah, in whose days the reformation came. The details of this reformation belong to the second or middle period; but the preparation for the great changes wrought in 621 B. C. was made by the prophets of the preceding centuries. The actual practices of this sub-period were full of superstition. Let us first note what they were and then the attitude of the prophets toward them. **Amos, chap. 5; Hos., chap. 4; Isa., chap. 1.** **2 Kings 23:1–3.** **2 Kings 23:4–14.**

(1) *Places of worship.*

(*a*) *The high places* were still used in different parts of the country, as is seen in the cases of Samuel, whom Saul first met at the sacrifice on the high place; of Solomon, even when the temple had been built; of Jeroboam; of the people of Judah in Rehoboam's time and under later kings; and of Ahaz. **1 Sam. 9:12–14, 19, 25; 1 Kings 3:3, 4; *cf.* 11:7; 12:31 f.; 14:23; 2 Kings 2:3; 14:4; 15:4; 17:9, 11, 29, 32; 18:4; etc.**

1 Kings 14:23; 2 Kings 3:2; 10:27; 17:10; Hos. 3:4; 10:1, 2.

(*b*) *The pillars and Asherim* occupied even a larger place than before, continuing in general use until the reign of Josiah.

2 Sam., chap. 6; *cf.* 1 Chron., chaps. 13, 15, 16.

(*c*) *The ark* was transferred with great solemnity to Jerusalem, when that city became under David the nation's capital. This supreme act of worship was accompanied by music and dancing.

1 Kings, chaps. 5, 6; 7:13–8:66; *cf.* 1 Chron., chap. 17; 22:2–19; 2 Chron., chaps. 2–7.

(*d*) *The temple* was built by Solomon; this act was full of significance for the future history of worship. As the king had his palace, so Jehovah was to have his temple. The ceremonial would now be better organized; a basis was furnished for future development; priests and singers must be provided for regular service. While at this central place the worship would henceforth be conducted in a purer form, but at the same time with luxurious magnificence, the old routine continued in all its corruption throughout the country at large.

1 Sam. 28:1–25.

(*e*) *The spirit of Samuel,* called Elohim (*i. e.*, God), was thought to have been called forth after death by the witch of Endor, in order to speak with Saul at his request.

1 Kings 12:25–33; 2 Chron. 11:14, 15; Hos. 8:5, 6.

(*f*) *The calves* set up at Bethel and Gilgal were figures of Jehovah, intended to be worshiped by the Israelites of the north, in order that they might not be induced to go to Jerusalem for worship.

1 Kings 12:31–33; 2 Sam. 6:13, 14; 1 Kings 3:15; 1 Kings 2:26, 27; 2 Kings 11:4, 9, 12, 15, 17; 12:2; 2 Kings 16:12–16.

(2) *The priest* now became a more important personage; the professional element increased. The bond between those engaged in the same work was strengthened by association. The Levite was gaining ground, as over against the older patriarchal priest. The temple required professional service. Samuel was a priest, and in his time the monarchy took shape, which meant a separation of the state and church. With the royal sanction the priestly order was greatly strengthened; but the king maintained supremacy and, according to the old patriarchal idea, offered sacrifice as head. Since the priest was judge, he formulated decisions, which in later times were to become *law.*

1 Kings 8:62–65; Hos. 2:11; Exod. 23:18f.; 2 Kings 17:17.

(3) *Sacrifice* was offered, sometimes upon a great scale; the old idea of communion with God continued; and a great feature of the sacrifice was the element of

joy. The sacrifice might not be offered with leavened bread. The first-fruits of the ground were called for. Sometimes human sacrifice was offered.

(4) *Times* were now more definitely fixed. Exod. 20:8; Exod. 23:12; Hos. 2:11; 2 Kings 4:23; 11:5, 7, 9; 16:18.

(*a*) The *sabbath* was an established institution, whatever may have been its origin.

(*b*) The beginnings of a *sabbatical year* were made, in the custom of allowing the land to lie fallow every seventh year. Exod. 23:10, 11.

(*c*) Three agricultural *feasts*, with dates dependent upon the climate, were observed, viz.: the Feast of Unleavened Bread (Easter time), in celebration of the departure from Egypt; the Feast of Harvest, when the first-fruits were gathered; and the Feast of Ingathering, in the autumn. Exod. 23:14-17; Exod. 34:22, 23; 1 Kings 8:2; 12:32; Hos. 2:11.

(5) *Other acts.*

(*a*) *Prayers* continued to be offered, as in the case of Samuel at Mizpah, and on the occasion of the people's demand for a king; of David, after Nathan had made known to him Jehovah's purpose to establish his house in Israel, and on the occasion of the death of Bathsheba's child; of Solomon, at the time of the dedication of the temple at Jerusalem; of Elijah, for the restoration of the widow's son to life, and on Mount Carmel; and of Hezekiah, for deliverance from Sennacherib. 1 Sam. 7:5, 8, 9; 8:6; 12:23; 2 Sam. 7:18-28; 12:16; 1 Kings 8:22-54; 1 Kings 17:20-22; 18:36, 37; 2 Kings 19:15-19.

(*b*) *Vows* were still made, as, for example, in the case of Absalom, and of the Nazirites. 2 Sam. 15:7, 8; Amos 2:12.

(*c*) *Oracles and dreams* are seen in David's inquiry of Jehovah after the death of Saul, and before the battle with the Philistines in the valley of Rephaim; in Jehovah's message to David through Nathan; in Solomon's dream at Gibeon; in Ahab's consultation of the prophets before advancing upon Ramoth-Gilead; and in the use made of the brazen altar by King Ahaz. The visions of Amos and Isaiah may also be mentioned in this connection. 2 Sam. 2:1; 5:23, 24; 2 Sam. 7:4; 1 Kings 3:5 ff.; 22:5-28; 2 Kings 16:15; Amos 7:1-9; 8:1 ff.; Isa., chap. 6.

(*d*) *Sorcery* was practiced, for it was distinctly opposed by Saul and Samuel (although Samuel himself is said to have been called from the grave by a witch), and by later prophets. 1 Sam. 28:3-20; Isa. 8:19; 19:3; Mic. 5:12.

1 Sam. 10:5; Amos 5:23; 6:5; 2 Sam. 6:5, 14, 16; Isa. 30:29; 1 Kings 1:40.

(*e*) *Music and dancing* were greatly developed in connection with the feasts and the worship on the high places, and the regular services of the temple at Jerusalem which contributed much to the enrichment of the worship of Jehovah.

1 Sam. 18:7; 2 Sam. 1:19–27; 2 Sam. 3:33 f.; 18:33; 2 Sam., chap. 22 =Ps. 18.

(6) *Songs* were sung, sometimes of a secular character, as when the women of Israel praised the warlike deeds of Saul and David, and when David lamented the death of Saul and Jonathan, or that of Abner, or of Absalom; at other times of a religious character, as perhaps when David sang upon the occasion of his deliverance from Saul (but see § 19).

§ 18. **The Prophets' Attitude** toward the actual practice of the people, as it was conducted by the priests, was that of undisguised opposition. It is asserted many times that —

Amos 7:9; Hos. 10:8; Mic. 1:5; 1 Kings 14:22, 23.

(1) The high places were an occasion of sin, and aroused Jehovah's anger, and must therefore be destroyed. They were one of the most effective channels of corruption to the worshipers of Jehovah.

Hos. 4:6–9; 5:1; 6:9; Mic. 3:11; Zeph. 3:4.

(2) The priests were altogether corrupt and self-seeking; they were the leaders in sin, going to the farthest extremes of debauchery and licentiousness, and carrying the people down to destruction along with themselves.

Amos 4:4; 5:22; Hos. 4:13, 14; 12:11; 13:2;

(3) Sacrifice was displeasing to Jehovah, since the people were multiplying offerings with the thought that this was all that was necessary to secure Jehovah's blessing; whereas justice and mercy were alone pleasing to him.

Amos 5:21; 6:4–6; Hos. 2:11; Isa. 1:13, 14.

(4) Feast days and seasons had become occasions of orgiastic revelry and must be brought to an end. These were in large measure borrowed from the Baal-worship, and were not yet wholly purified.

Isa. 1:15; Mic. 3:4.

(5) Prayer was in vain, no matter how fervent and frequent, since it came from people whose hearts were evil, and their hands red with blood.

Isa. 8:19; 19:3.

(6) Sorcery and witchcraft were condemned and regarded as unworthy of a people whose worship should be given to Jehovah.

§ 19. **The Songs and Hymns of the Early Period** furnish one of the most difficult questions within the entire realm of biblical study. Modern scholars, for the most part, teach (1) that *the law* is the product of many centuries of history conducted by God in such a manner as to produce that law, the basis being found in the work of Moses; and (2) that to ascribe the whole to Moses permits no opportunity for *gradual* unfolding of the divine plan. So they teach (1) that most of the seventy-three psalms ascribed by tradition to David belong to a later age, when ideas of God were higher and purer than in David's times, and when the worship of God by leaders and people had become pure and spiritual; and (2) that to ascribe these psalms, or most of them, to David is to turn the history of Israel's religious thought wrong side foremost, and to presuppose in David's times a condition of spiritual life on the part of David and the people which could not have existed until centuries later. This very serious and important question may not be taken up here. It is to be noted, however, that in the case of the *psalms*, as in the case of the *law*, whatever may have been the date of origin, the people never reached a position in which they could use these psalms (with a few exceptions) as the expression of their spiritual communion with God, until (*a*) the prophets had preached long centuries, (*b*) the priests themselves had united to purge and purify a corrupt worship, (*c*) the city of Jerusalem was destroyed and the land laid waste, (*d*) the inhabitants were carried away into a foreign country, and (*e*) the nation was taught, once for all, what had many times been said, but never actually believed, viz., that there was *one* God, and *one only*. The psalms as a distinct part of the priests' work will receive further consideration in a later chapter.

See EWALD, *Commentary on the Psalms*, Vol. I, pp. 60–71; PEROWNE, *Book of Psalms* (second edition), Vol. I, pp. 1–21; MURRAY, *Origin and Growth of the Psalms*, pp. 127–43; CHEYNE, *The Origin and Religious Contents of the Psalter*, pp. 190–225; KIRKPATRICK, *The Psalms* (*Cambridge Bible*), Vol. I, pp. xxxi–xxxviii; DRIVER, *Introduction to the Literature of the Old Testament* (6th ed.), pp. 373–80; STANLEY, *Lectures on the History of the Jewish Church*, Lecture XXV; articles on "David" in HASTINGS' *Dictionary of the Bible* and CHEYNE'S *Encyclopædia Biblica*.

The views of some of the most important commentators concerning the number of psalms that may be assigned to David are:

(1) Binney, all, or nearly all, assigned by tradition.

(2) Olshausen, Lengerke, Cheyne, Baethgen, Duhm, Wellhausen, probably none.

(3) Hitzig, 3–19, except 5, 6, 14.

(4) Ewald, 3, 4, 7, 8, 11, 18, 19, 24, 29, 32, 101, and some fragments.

(5) Delitzsch, 3–19, 22–24, 25, 28–30, 32, 34, 36–39, 41, 51, 52, 54, 56–63, and some others doubtful.

(6) Perowne grants that some of those ascribed to David cannot have been written by him, but thinks that he "personally contributed more than any other individual" to the Psalter, and was the founder of a school of sacred poetry. Similarly also Kirkpatrick.

Exod. 20:1–17; Deut. 5:6–21; Exod. 34:10–28; Exod. 20:22—23:33.

§20. **The Laws of the Early Period** may be classified under three heads: the decalogue, in two editions; the small book of the covenant; and the larger book of the covenant. Before considering these separately, a few points may be suggested concerning them as a whole:

(*a*) However early or late they may have taken on their present literary form, they themselves certainly go back to the period of Israel's earliest history.

(*b*) They contain much material which, of course, had an existence long before the days of Moses; *e. g.*, there had been prohibition of murder and of stealing centuries before Moses.

(*c*) They reflect, in general, an early and, indeed, primitive stage of society; but this stage is the agricultural, and therefore later than the nomadic.

(*d*) They are arranged in groups of ten, or of five.

(1) *The decalogue.*

Exod. 20:1, 22; Exod. 24:12; Deut. 5:4; Acts 7:53; Gal. 3:19; Heb. 2:2.

(*a*) It is said to have had its origin in different ways; *e. g.*, as having been (1) spoken by God, (2) given through angels, (3) written by the finger of God.

Exod. 34:28, 29; Deut. 4:13; Deut. 5:2; 9:5; 10:4.

(*b*) It is given different names; *e. g.*, (1) the ten words, (2) the words of the covenant, (3) tables of the covenant, (4) covenant, (5) testimony, (6) two tables of testimony.

(*c*) It has two forms, viz., that in Exod. 20:1–17, and that in Deut. 5:6–21; and although both are said to have been engraved on stone, there are many differences; *e. g.*,

Exod. 20:8; *cf.* Deut. 5:12; Exod. 20:12; *cf.* Deut. 5:16; Exod. 20:17; *cf.* Deut. 5:21.

(1) the first word of the fourth commandment; (2) the reason assigned for observance of the fourth commandment, viz., the creation and rest of God in the one, the bringing of Israel out of Egypt in the other; (3) the two additional clauses in the one form of the fifth commandment; (4) the different order of the first two clauses and the addition of "his field" in the tenth commandment.

(*d*) It has been suggested that originally all the commandments consisted, like the sixth, seventh, and eighth, of one or two words, and that the remainder, *e. g.*, in the second, third, and fifth, was added at a later time.

(*e*) It is *divided* (1) *into ten words*, but the division is not clear, since the Lutheran and Romish churches combine the first and second as one and divide the tenth; (2) *into two tables*, but, here again, Jewish and Christian scholars, ancient and modern, fail to agree, three methods being advocated, according as the two tables contained, the first, three commandments, and the second, seven; the first, four, and the second, six; the first, five, and the second, five.

(2) *The small book of the covenant*, the laws of which may thus be grouped: (*a*) five on the duty of worshiping only Jehovah; (*b*) one on image-worship; (*c*) five on the offering of firstlings; (*d*) five on feasts; (*e*) four on sacrifices and offerings. These laws seem to have been written in groups of five or ten, groups (*b*) and (*e*) having lost part of their number. They are all directly concerned with worship.

Exod. 34:12–14; 34:17; 34:19, 20; 34:21, 18, 22, 23; 34:25, 26.

(3) *The large book of the covenant*, which contains: (*a*) five enactments on *worship*;[1] (*b*) five on rights of slaves; (*c*) five on slave concubines; (*d*) five on acts of violence. Then follows one (a fragment) on the reviling of father and mother. After that (*e*) five on personal injuries; (*f*) and (*g*) ten on injuries in connection with property, slaves, and cattle; (*h*) five on theft and damage to property; (*i*) and (*j*) ten on breaches of trust. Then follow three fragments on sexual crimes, *magic*, *sacrifice to other gods*. After that (*k*) five on the dealings with the weak and poor; (*l*) five on *reverence and offerings*. Then follow two on purity. After that (*m*) five on testimony. Then follow two on kindness. After that (*n*) five on justice, and (*o*) and (*p*) ten on *feasts and offerings*. In all there are sixteen groups of five, and eight fragments of groups, each of which probably consisted of five.

Exod. 20:23–26; 21:2–6; 21:7–11; 21:12–16; 21:17; 21:18–25; 21:26—22:1; 22:2–6; 22:7–17; 22:18–20; 22:21–27; 22:28–30; 22:31; 23:1–3; 23:4–5; 23:6–9; 23:10–19.

A study of the subjects given above, and a reading of the enactments, will show the early character of these laws as contrasted with those given in Deuteronomy and Leviticus. It is to be noted (1) that the greater part of

[1] In this classification the laws relating to worship are *italicized*.

this code is concerned with subjects which are not today thought of as religious, but that in early times there was no distinction between "religious" and "secular"—everything was religious; (2) that all the enactments concerning religion, in the narrower sense of the word, have to do with its objective features—feasts, sacrifices, offerings, ritual, etc.—all of which is included in *worship*. It is these enactments that lie back of the teaching of the prophets down to about 650 B. C.

In the next study it will appear that great and fundamental changes are to occur after 650 B. C. in all the regulations which concern the subject of worship and its allied subjects.

CHAPTER III.

THE HISTORY OF WORSHIP IN THE MIDDLE OLD TESTAMENT PERIOD

§ 21. **The Middle Old Testament Period** (see § 14 (2)) had for its most striking event the discovery and publication of the book of the law, known in these later times as *Deuteronomy*. It is impossible here, as in the history of any period, to draw sharp lines of separation. 2 Kings 22:8—23:3.

(1) Just *when* this middle period began cannot be fixed definitely. But this much is clear, that the work of the prophets (*cf.* § 18) in the years preceding 621 B. C. (*a*) pointed out the evils which had crept into the worship of the people; (*b*) presented such conceptions of God's justice, love, holiness, and unity as would furnish a basis for higher and more spiritual forms of worship than those which were already in existence; and this (*c*) prepared the way for something which, up to this time, the people could not appreciate. Amos 5:24; 9:7; Hos. 8:5, 6, 14; Isa. 1:12–17; 6:1–5; etc.

(2) Just *when* this middle period ended is likewise indefinite, but it is evident that after and out of this period there came a still higher form of worship, destined in God's providence (*a*) to endure through a period of great political and religious upheaval, and (*b*) to serve as the basis for a worship still higher in its ideals and in its spiritual character.

§ 22. **Three Distinct Stages May be Traced** in the history of the middle or Deuteronomic period. These may be classified as:

(1) *The pre-exilic stage*, which ended with the removal of the people from their land and with the destruction of the temple around which the whole system of worship centered. 2 Kings 25:8–21.

(2) *The exilic stage*, during which the people were in Babylon, away from all the familiar scenes of worship

and under the influence of an entirely new religious environment.

Ezra, chap. 1; 7:1-10. (3) *The post-exilic stage*, beginning with the return from exile, including the building of the second temple, and ending approximately with the visit of Ezra to Jerusalem.

§ 23. **The Deliverance of Jerusalem in Hezekiah's Day** (701 B. C.) had exerted a marked influence on worship. To Hezekiah is ascribed an important work as reformer,
2 Kings 18:4; *cf.* Isa. 36:7. in that he (1) removed the high places, (2) broke the pillars, (3) cut down the Asherim, (4) broke in pieces the brazen serpent that Moses had made, which, in his day, was wor-
Amos 7:9; Hos. 10:1, 2; Isa. 30:22; 31:7. shiped as a representation of God in Jerusalem. In so far as these things were accomplished, Hezekiah was acting in accordance with the commands of the prophets (see § 18). But it seems that the work was not as thoroughgoing as it might have been, since in Josiah's times,
2 Kings 23:13. seventy or eighty years later, the high places erected by Solomon near Jerusalem were still in existence. Hezekiah's reformation, however transient, was closely connected with the deliverance of Jerusalem from Sennacherib and the Assyrian army in 701 B. C. This invasion
2 Kings 18:13; *cf.* 18:33-35. had two results: (1) The outlying villages with their high places were destroyed and dishonored, and the country people came to see that the worship as practiced in the
2 Kings 19:20-37. high places was of no avail in times of great distress. (2) Jerusalem, the temple, and the God whose worship was conducted in the temple (a worship beyond question comparatively pure) were *delivered*, and thereby greatly honored, for the whole nation had therein a posi-
Deut. 12:2-19. tive experience of Jehovah's power. This paved the way for the exaltation of the temple-worship and the destruction of the worship in the high places, changes which together form the great characteristic of the middle period.

See W. R. SMITH, *The Prophets of Israel* (2d ed.), pp. 353-64; CORNILL, *The Prophets of Israel*, pp. 67 f.; DRIVER, *Isaiah, His Life and Times*, pp. 66-83; the article "Hezekiah" in HASTINGS' *Dictionary of the Bible*, Vol. II, p. 377; and the corresponding article (§ 1) in *Encyclopædia Biblica*, Vol. II.

§ 24. **Manasseh's Reign Brought a Great Reaction.**— This came about because (1) the prophetic party (that is, the party of reformers) pushed forward more rapidly than the people could follow, *e. g.*, (*a*) in destroying the objects and places of worship held in veneration by the people for many centuries, and (*b*) in holding up conceptions of God and of life which the people were still too ignorant and debased to appreciate; (2) the people were disappointed in the hope, raised by the prophets, that with Jerusalem's deliverance Assyria would perish, when, as a matter of fact, Assyria still remained powerful, subduing Egypt and taking tribute from Judah; (3) the people believed that this failure of their desires and the consequent adversity had their origin in the proposed reforms of the prophets, and that these very reforms (*e. g.*, the breaking down of the high places) were displeasing to Jehovah.

2 Kings 18:4; 2 Kings 19:19.

2 Chron. 33:11.

Cf. Jer. 44:15–19.

The reaction exhibited itself in (1) the murder of the prophets and their partisans; (2) setting up again the idols, and the Asherim; (3) giving permission to enchanters and augurs and witches and wizards to practice their arts; (4) encouraging human sacrifice; (5) introducing the worship of other gods even within the temple itself, *e. g.*, the host of heaven—the chariots of the sun being placed within the temple.

2 Kings 21:16; Jer. 2:30.
2 Kings 21:3–5.
2 Kings 21:6.

2 Kings 21:6; 23:10; Mic. 6:6, 7.
2 Kings 21:3, 4; 23:11, 12.

§ 25. **The Discovery of the Deuteronomic Law** followed a generation or so of prophetic silence. This silence was occasioned by persecution, and had for its result the production of a work which, in itself, summed up prophecy and furnished the text-book of worship for a long time to come. While the mouth of the prophet was closed, his pen worked. In this work the lessons of Manasseh's reaction were taken into account; for the new order of worship, while revolutionary in some aspects, was, after all, an evolution from that which preceded it. The new cult went as far as possible in retaining old usages and old ceremonies, thus avoiding the difficulties occurring in connection with the earlier attempts at reformation. Many other things were learned anew from the experience of the reaction, *e. g.*,

Deut. 4:15–19; Deut. 6:14, 15; Deut. 17:14–20.

Deut. 15:19; Deut. 16:16.

Deut. 12:2-4. the demoralizing influence of the high places, and the necessity of purging and purifying the ritual. These were incorporated in the written document.

See CHEYNE, *Jeremiah, His Life and Times*, pp. 62–4; CORNILL, *op. cit.*, pp. 80–82; DRIVER, *A Critical and Exegetical Commentary on Deuteronomy*, pp. xlix–lxii.

No opportunity, however, presented itself under Manasseh or Amon for the promulgation of this book. It was put away in the temple. In Josiah's reign, (1) when the hearts of the people were being turned to Jehovah by the terror aroused in connection with the
Jer. 1:1, 2; Zeph. 1:1. Scythian invasion; (2) when Jeremiah and Zephaniah were preaching with all the vigor of the older prophets;
2 Kings 22:1, 2. (3) when Josiah, a young man, was turning his face in the
2 Kings 22:3-8. direction of the true God; (4) when the temple was being cleansed and repaired, in order that Jehovah might be thereby honored—*then* this book, the book of Deuteronomy, was discovered, brought to the king, read to him, and read again to the people. The immediate circumstances of this discovery are described in some detail; *e.g.*:
2 Kings 22:8-10. (1) The book was found by Hilkiah, the high-priest, and given by him to Shaphan, the scribe, who read it, took it
2 Kings 22:11-14. to King Josiah, and read it to him. (2) The king was greatly grieved as he listened and realized how far short of the demands of this book the religious life of Israel had fallen. He at once sent a delegation of leading men to Huldah, a prophetess, to inquire Jehovah's will con-
2 Kings 22:15-20. cerning the book. (3) She declared that the judgments it contained would fall upon Israel because of their desertion of Jehovah and their worship of other gods, but that Josiah would reign in peace because of
2 Kings 23:1-3. his faithfulness to Jehovah. (4) Upon hearing this, Josiah called a great meeting of all the people, read the newly found book to them, and caused them to join him in a covenant with Jehovah to conform to Jehovah's requirements as laid down therein. Thereupon the work of reform was begun throughout the land.

§ 26. **The Results of the Finding of Deuteronomy** are very fully given us in the sacred narrative. These results constituted what is called Josiah's reformation, and included:

(1) The destruction of the *high places and altars* throughout the land. 2 Kings 23:8, 12, 13, 15, 19.

(2) The breaking down of the *pillars and Asherim.* 2 Kings 23:6, 14.

(3) The removal of the *teraphim* and other *idols.* 2 Kings 23:24.

(4) The destruction of the *horses and chariots of the sun.* 2 Kings 23:11.

(5) The deposition and destruction of *idolatrous priests* and of the *priests of the high places.* 2 Kings 23:5, 8, 9, 20.

(6) The abolition of *human sacrifice.* 2 Kings 23:10.

(7) The observance of the *Feast of the Passover.* 2 Kings 23:21–23.

(8) The prohibition of *sorcerers and wizards.* 2 Kings 23:24.

(9) The purification of worship involved in doing away with the *Sodomites.* 2 Kings 23:7.

Two things may be said: (*a*) There is nothing essential commanded in Deuteronomy which Josiah did not try to do; (*b*) every single act of the reformation will be found commanded in Deuteronomy.

× § 27. **The Teaching of Deuteronomy** on the more important points of worship may be briefly summarized as follows:[1]

(1) *Object of worship.*—Jehovah only is to be worshiped; all idols and other objects of worship must be destroyed. Deut. 6:4; 10:20; 13:6–11; 17:2–5; 16:21 f.; 7:5, 25

(2) *Place of worship.*—Worship is permitted only at one central sanctuary, viz., the temple at Jerusalem. All local shrines are to be destroyed. Deut. 12:2–7, 11, 17 f., 26–28.

(3) *Priests.*—These now become a distinct class, the tribe of Levi being set apart to perform the priestly function. There are, of course, more Levites than are needed for priests; these are to be teachers and judges. The duties of the Levites at the local sanctuaries being abolished, many of them are naturally without means of support, and special provision has to be made for them in the law. Deut. 10:8, 9. Deut. 18:1–8.

(4) *Sacrifice.*—The continuance of sacrifice is taken for granted, but every sacrifice is to be offered at the central sanctuary. All firstlings are, as before, especially designated as sacrifices to Jehovah. Deut. 12:13 f.; 15:19 f.

[1] For an examination of this book as a code of laws, see pp. 155–69.

(5) *Days and seasons.*— Set times of worship are
Deut. 5:12–15. appointed to be observed: (*a*) The *sabbath* is preserved
Deut. 15:1–18. unchanged. (*b*) The *sabbatical year* becomes established,
and is extended to the cancellation of all debts owed by
Hebrews to their fellow-countrymen and to the release
Jer. 34:1–20. of all Hebrew slaves. There was an unsuccessful attempt
to enforce this provision with reference to slaves in the
Deut. 16:1–15. reign of Zedekiah. (*c*) Three annual *feasts* are fixed, as
before, in connection with the agricultural seasons; but,
like all other acts of worship, they are to be celebrated at
Jerusalem. New elements appear in the fixing of the
duration of the Feast of Tabernacles at seven days, and
of Pentecost at one day, and in the connection of the
Passover with the exodus from Egypt. No reference is
made to *feasts of the moon.*

Deut. 14:3–21. (6) *Other acts of worship.*— (*a*) A list of *clean and*
unclean animals is given; this classification probably
Deut. 23:21–23. had a religious basis; (*b*) faithfulness in the performance
Deut. 14:28f.; 26:12. of *vows* is enjoined; (*c*) a *triennial tithe* is imposed which is
Deut. 18:10–12; 23:17f.; 14:1. to be given to the Levite, the widow, and the poor; (*d*)
perverted acts of worship, such as *human sacrifice, sorcery,*
Deut. 9:20, 26–29. etc., are prohibited; (*e*) *prayers* of Moses are recorded.

See Cheyne, *op. cit.*, pp. 64–7; Driver, *A Critical and Exegetical Commentary on Deuteronomy*, pp. xix–xxxiv; article "Deuteronomy" (§§ 27–32) in *Encyclopædia Biblica*, Vol. I; and corresponding article (§ iv) in Hastings' *Dictionary of the Bible*, Vol. I.

§ 28. **The Full Significance of the Deuteronomic Principles, the Spirit with which These are Presented, and the Great Changes Wrought by Their Adoption** are difficult to appreciate. Some of these points may be noted:

Deut. 6:4; 4:28; 10:17. (1) The fundamental idea is that there is but one
god worthy to be called God; other gods are wood
and stone.

Deut. 4:32–36; *cf.* Exod. 19:6. (2) With such a God dealing directly with the nation,
Israel's life must be high and holy; for otherwise it will
be unworthy.

Deut. 12:2–7. (3) There shall be only one place of worship, and
that the temple in Jerusalem; in this way the licentious
nature-worship can be done away with.

Deut. 10:8. (4) The conduct of worship must be guarded, and

consequently it is placed under the control of a special tribe, the Levites.

(5) The method of presentation is a wonderful one, being twofold, prophetic and priestly; viz., (*a*) exhortations of the most "sweetly impressive" character, full of spiritual strength; (*b*) laws, many of them dating from the earliest times, others from a later period; some of them apparently arbitrary in their tone, others full of the reasons which should lead to their observance.

Deut. 4:1–13; 6:1–25; etc.

Deut. 5:6–21.

Deut., chaps. 12–26.

(6) The spirit throughout is the spirit of love, and is akin to that exhibited in the book of Hosea. "The primal love of Jehovah to Israel fills the foreground of each writer's discourse, and all human relationships within the Israelitish community are rooted in this."[2] But this love is no sentimental love; Israel's God is a God of justice as well as of love.

Deut. 7:7–10; Deut. 10:12–15.

Deut. 6:17–19; Deut. 10:18.

(7) The restriction of worship to *one* place is "tantamount to a suppression of religion in the whole country outside of Jerusalem."[3] How can the country people now consult Jehovah? The neighboring altar to which the fugitive might flee and be safe is done away with, and distant cities of refuge are only a partial substitute; while the function of the altar as a place to which the people might come and receive judgment is given to the gates of the cities and to the temple at Jerusalem. Israel in the country must now live without God, with whom before he had lived so closely.

Deut. 14:22–27.

Deut. 19:1–13.

Deut. 16:18; 17:8–13.

(8) The feasts are beginning to be denaturalized; that is, they are losing their agricultural significance, and are to be more and more closely associated with historical events — the Feast of Unleavened Bread, with the flight from Egypt; the Feast of Weeks, with the giving of the law on Sinai; the Feast of Tabernacles, with the journey in the desert. Religion is a matter of fixed days and seasons, rather than an everyday affair.

(9) The setting apart of priests, and the placing of

See article "Feasts" (§§ 9, 10) in *Encyclopædia Biblica*, Vol. II; WELLHAUSEN, *Prolegomena to the History of Israel*, pp. 91 f.; CORNILL, *op. cit.*, p. 86.

[2] CHEYNE, *op. cit.*, p. 66.

[3] CORNILL, *op. cit.*, p. 85.

all worship in their hands, thus compelling the people to make use of them, while beforetime the use of a priest was voluntary, draws the line sharply between laity and clergy. The priest changes his function; for he is now preëminently a sacrificer, while before he consulted the oracle and announced the divine will.

Deut. 18:3; 21:5; 26:3, 4; Deut. 17:9, 12; 20:2-4; 24:8.

(10) The significance of the sacrifice is greatly changed. Sacrifice being lawful only at the one central sanctuary, it was offered for the most part only in connection with the three great yearly festivals when all Israelites were required to be at Jerusalem. The popular, joyous aspect of it as a banquet and as an offering of joy and thanksgiving, made frequently and in connection with any suitable occasion, now begins to disappear, and a more and more solemn and expiatory character is given to all sacrifice.

Deut. 14:24 f.; 16:16.

(11) What is it henceforth to be religious? To do the thing laid down in a book. The day that saw Deuteronomy accepted, its ritual of worship adopted, and its teaching concerning priest and sacrifice recognized—that day saw the beginning of the *death* of prophecy. It was, of course, the prophets' own work; but they had established the agency by which, later, they themselves would be strangled; because from this time forward the *voice* of the prophet is unnecessary.

Deut. 4:40; 6:1-9, 24, 25; 7:11; 8:1, 6, 11; 30:10.

See Cornill, *op. cit.*, p. 89.

(12) The adoption of Deuteronomy signified the separation of church and state. This was necessary, for the state is soon to die—within thirty-five years. This separation made it possible for the church to live, after the death of the state.

See Cornill, *op. cit.*, p. 88.

(13) The act of Josiah and his people in accepting Deuteronomy was the first step toward the canonization of Holy Scripture—the first step in a long line of similar events which have given us the Bible with our modern conceptions of inspiration.

(14) *In a word*, worship, whether viewed narrowly or broadly, is henceforth *almost* a new thing. The Israelitish religion seems to have been revolutionized. Of course,

a closer study shows that all this was evolution, not revolution; the prophets had prepared the way; the prophets and priests worked together. A priest found the book and gave it to the king, and the priests received through this book privileges they had never before enjoyed.

See BUDDE, *Religion of Israel to the Exile*, pp. 171–9.

§ 29. **A Second Reaction** followed after thirteen years of successful work on the part of Jeremiah and Josiah.

(1) Jeremiah at the beginning of the reformation had preached the contents of this book throughout the villages of Judah, sometimes incurring the opposition and persecution of his friends. **Jer. 11:1–6, 18–23.**

(2) The times that followed for thirteen years were quiet and prosperous; the king and the people lived before God and received his blessing.

(3) Perhaps during this time the work of the sages began to flourish. *Cf.* **Prov., chaps. 1–9; Jer. 18:18.**

(4) Assyria was losing ground; Necho of Egypt (608 B. C.) began to encroach upon the Assyrian territory. Josiah met him at the battle of Megiddo and was slain. The reformation failed. The people believed the king's death was a divine punishment for changing the forms of worship in their religion. The opposing party gained control, and then followed the series of events which resulted, in a few years, in the downfall of the kingdom. **2 Kings 23:29; 2 Chron. 35:20–24. 2 Kings 23:36 f.; 24:8 f.**

§ 30. **The Significance of the Babylonian Exile in its Relationship to Worship** cannot easily be overestimated. Its effect upon some of the principal ideas and institutions may be noted here:

(1) *Object of worship.*—The removal to Babylonia involved the leaving behind of all idolatrous objects of worship, or their confiscation or destruction by the conqueror. The leaders of Israel's religious life looked upon idolatry as one of the chief causes of the exile. The removal from the land with which Jehovah had always been associated to a land which was the dominion of another god also involved either an acknowledgment of the power of this foreign god, or else the maintenance **2 Kings 25:13–17. Ezek. 6:11–14; 8:3–18. Isa. 40:12–31; 44:9–20; 45:5–7; 46:5–7.**

of a belief in Jehovah's supremacy and universality. That this higher conception of Jehovah prevailed is clear from the fact that we hear nothing of idolatry after the return from the exile, and especially from the teachings of Isa., chaps. 40–66.

Isa. 45:18–22; 48:12; Isa. 51:12, 13.

(2) *Place of worship.*—The temple being destroyed, and all the familiar scenes of worship being left behind, together with all material and external reminders of Jehovah's presence, the worshipers were necessarily led to a more spiritual conception of God. Moreover, absence from the temple developed an ability to do without the temple services which was in part responsible for the origin of synagogues.

Ezek., chaps. 40–48.

Isa. 61:6.

(3) The occupation of the *priests* was gone, in so far as it was dependent upon the temple. The book of Ezekiel furnishes an illustration of one phase of priestly activity during these days. The thought of Israel as a nation of priests appears.

Isa. 43:22–24; 56:7.

(4) *Sacrifice* could no longer be offered, but it did not lose any of its importance in the thought of the people.

Isa. 56:2, 4, 6; 58:13; 66:23.

Isa. 58:3–5.

(5) *Times and seasons.*—(*a*) The *sabbath*, being an institution which was independent of the temple, could still be kept, and it received much emphasis during and after this period. Sabbaths were also observed by the Babylonians. (*b*) *Feasts*, which had always been occasions of joy, could no longer be observed legally, and emphasis was laid on (*c*) *fasts*, which were of an exactly opposite character and were not dependent upon the temple.

Isa. 63:15—64:12; 56:7.

Isa. 52:1, 11.

Isa. 65:1–7, 11; 66:3, 4.

(6) *Other acts of worship.*—(*a*) In the absence of all the regular public means of worship, those who worshiped "in spirit and in truth" naturally had frequent recourse to *prayer*. The future temple is thought of as a house of *prayer*. (*b*) The recognition of the captivity as a punishment for sin led to an exalted conception of Jehovah's holiness and to the laying of great emphasis upon ceremonial *cleanness*. (*c*) It is probable, however, that many became apostates from the Jehovah-worship and took up the worship of their conquerors.

Cf. Ezek. 10:9–22.

(7) *The influence of the Babylonian worship* on Israel's ritual is evident in succeeding ritualistic legislation, as

also in some of Ezekiel's imagery. Jehovah through the exile again brought Israel into contact with a great religion, as he had already done in the case of Baalism. Just as Israel had learned some truths through Baalism, and to some extent had enriched the cultus of Jehovah thereby, so was she to do through the agency of Babylon's worship.

§ 31. **The Priest-Prophet of the Captivity, Ezekiel,** occupied an important place in the further development of the ritual of worship. His place may only be touched upon here. With prophetic idealism, legalist though he was, his vision pictured a future temple, a future service, and a future priesthood, as follows:

(*a*) *The temple.*—While the temple of Solomon had been virtually a part of the royal palace, the new temple is to be wholly separate from the royal dwellings and from all other ordinary habitations; for it is the earthly habitation of the most holy God, who had abandoned **Ezek. 45:1-8.**
the former city and temple because of their profanation by sin and uncleanness. To prevent any such profanation of Jehovah in future

the sacred "oblation," the domain of the priests, Levites, **Ezek. 48:7-23.**
prince, and city, is placed in the center of the restored tribes, Judah on one side of it and Benjamin on the other. In the midst of this oblation is the portion of the priests, that of the Levites lying on one side, and that of the city on the other. In the middle of the priests' portion stands the temple. This is a great complex of buildings, around which on all sides lies a free space or suburbs. Then comes a great wall surrounding the whole buildings, forming a square of five hundred cubits. Within this wall is an outer court, and within this an inner court. . . . . In this inner court stands the altar, and to the back of it the temple house. The house has also a graduated series of compartments increasing in sanctity inwards—an outer apartment or porch, an inner or holy place, and an innermost, where the presence of Jehovah abides.[4]

(*b*) *The priests.*—The sons of Zadok only are to be **Ezek. 44:4-16.**
priests; all other Levites are to be subordinate ministers, performing the more menial tasks of the sanctuary.

[4] DAVIDSON, *The Book of Ezekiel* (Cambridge Bible), p. 290.

Foreigners are not to be permitted to enter the temple, as heretofore, to perform any tasks. The distinction between clergy and laity is clearly marked; none of the latter — not even the prince — may enter the inner court of the temple. The sanctity of the priests as the ones ministering in the presence of Jehovah is strongly emphasized and guarded in many ways, such as the requirement that they wear special garments while discharging their sacred functions. They live upon their share of the sacrifices of the people.

Ezek. 44:17–28. Ezek. 44:29, 30.

(*c*) *Sacrifice* occupies an important place in the ritual. The various kinds mentioned are: (1) the *sin-offering*, which is much emphasized; (2) *burnt-offerings*, which are numerous; (3) the *trespass-offering*, which was a variety of the sin-offering; (4) the *meal-offering;* (5) the *peace-offering;* (6) the *continual burnt-offering* made every morning. Special places are provided for the cooking of the offerings that are to be eaten by priests and people.

Ezek. 43:18–26; 42:13; 44:27. Ezek. 43:27; 44:11. Ezek. 42:13. Ezek. 46:13–15. Ezek. 46:19–24.

(*d*) *Times and seasons.*—The old times are all to be observed, viz., the *sabbath*, the *new moons*, and the three *feasts*, the Passover receiving special notice.

Ezek. 44:24. Ezek. 45:17—46:11.

§ 32. **The Priestly Character of the Prophetic Work of These Times** appears most strongly. This means that the priest-work was gaining ground, while the prophetic work was losing ground. But it will be noted that (*a*) a new situation was coming in which the priest-work would be more greatly needed; and (*b*) the priest-work had taken into itself all that had been contributed by the prophets. It is true, therefore, that not the priest-work pure and simple, but the priest-work as strengthened by, and as containing, the truth proclaimed through prophets, was the power that now held the forefront.

This priestly element is seen —

Jer. 1:1.

(1) In the priestly birth and character of the prophet Jeremiah, whose home was at Anathoth, one of the headquarters of the priests.

Deut., chaps. 12–26.

(2) In the priestly character of a large portion of the book of Deuteronomy.

Deut. 18:5; *cf.* Judg. 17:7–13.

(3) In the position now occupied by the priests as compared with their former position.

(4) In the priestly character and service of Ezekiel. **Ezek. 1:3; chaps 40–48.**

§ 33. **The Return of the People from the Babylonian Exile** introduced an entirely new situation. It was one, however, in which for eighty years (538–458 B. C.) the book of Deuteronomy and its regulations were supreme. It was a time of discouragement; the high hopes of the returning exiles were dashed to the ground in the presence of desolated homes, wasted lands, failure of crops, loss of political independence, and the destruction of Jerusalem. The struggle against these adverse conditions seems to have absorbed most of their energies during the first years after the return, the requirements of worship being largely neglected. We may note the attitude toward some of the principal institutions. **Ezra 2:64 f.** ***Cf.* Hag. 2:15–19.**

(*a*) *The temple.*—Partly because of opposition on the part of certain enemies, but chiefly on account of discouragement and indifference, the foundation of the temple was not laid until December, 520 B. C., eighteen years after the return, and the work was not finished until 516 B. C. Because of the poverty of the people, this new temple fell far short of the splendor of the old. The religious leaders were convinced that prosperity and glory could come to Israel only if the temple were first restored. This shows how large a place it had come to occupy in religious thought and practice. **Ezra 5:2; Hag. 2:18; Ezra 6:15.** **Hag. 2:3; Ezra 3:12.** **Ezra 5:1, 2.** **Hag. 1:9, 10.**

(*b*) *The priest* was gaining more and more importance in the life and worship of the people. Of the returning exiles a large proportion consisted of priests and other temple servants. There seems to have been developing the distinction between priests and Levites which was to become fixed later. That the distinction was not yet clearly made is evident from the fact that the two titles appear to be synonymous in some passages, just as they are in Deuteronomy. One priest had already achieved prominence as the leader of his brethren, and he appeared side by side with the prince in all important concerns, and was superior to him in religious affairs. A high standard was set up for the priests by Malachi, and their corruption was severely denounced. **Ezra 2:36–39.** **Ezra 6:18, 20.** **Ezra 8:20; 10:5; Mal. 3:3.** **Zech. 3:1–9; 6:11–13; Hag. 1:1, 12; 2:2, 4.** **Mal. 2:5–9; 3:3.**

Mal. 3:8, 9. Tithes for the support of the priests were still in force, but were reluctantly paid.

Ezra 3:2, 3. (*c*) *Sacrifice* was at once renewed at Jerusalem upon the return from exile, if, indeed, it had ever wholly ceased. One of the earliest acts was the erection of an altar of burnt-offering upon the site of the former temple, that the regular sacrifices might be offered to Jehovah. These sacrifices were probably those provided for in Deuter-
Mal. 1:7, 8, 12–14; Mal. 3:8. onomy (*cf.* § 27 (4)) and earlier laws. Malachi denounces those who bring maimed, imperfect, and polluted offerings, and insists upon the best of everything as an offering to Jehovah.

(*d*) *Times and seasons.*—These probably continued the same as they had been under the Deuteronomic law.
Ezra 3:4, 5; 6:19–22; Zech. 7:1–7; Zech. 8:18, 19. Specific mention is made, in the literature that comes from these days, only of the Feast of the New Moon, the Feast of Tabernacles, the Passover, and of four fasts which had been observed every year since the beginning of the exile.

Ezra 3:10, 11. (*e*) *Other acts of worship.*—(1) *Music* and *singing* are mentioned in connection with the laying of the founda-
Mal. 1:14. tion stone of the temple. (2) *Vows* were still made.
Mal. 3:5. Neh. 1:4–11; 2:4; etc. (3) *Sorcery* was not even yet wholly uprooted. (4) That the habit of *prayer* was not discontinued is clear from Nehemiah's statements concerning himself at a little later time.

§ 34. **The Priestly Character of the Prophetic Work** of these later years is seen in —

Hag. 1:8–10; Zech. 1:16; 4:9; 6:12–15. (*a*) The emphasis laid upon the necessity of building the temple as a prerequisite to the enjoyment of Jehovah's favor. This is the main theme of Haggai's prophecy.

Zech. 3:1–10; 4:2, 3; 6:11; 7:1–7; 8:18, 19. (*b*) The prominence given to priestly interests in the utterances of Zechariah, who speaks of the temple, the high-priest, fasts, feasts, etc.

Mal. 1:6–14; 2:1–9; Mal. 3:1–4; 3:8–10; Mal. 4:4. (*c*) The large place given to matters pertaining to worship in the book of Malachi, which probably comes from the very end of this period. The main interest of the author seems to be centered in an effort to reform the ritual and those who have charge of it.

§ 35. **The Songs and Hymns of the Middle Period** are very numerous. Their spirit may be gathered from the following examples:

(1) Songs celebrating the deliverance of Jerusalem, as in the days of Hezekiah. Pss. 46; 48.

(2) Songs describing the wickedness of the times, as in the days of Manasseh. Pss. 36; 54; 64.

(3) Songs depicting the destruction of Jerusalem and the going into captivity. Pss. 80; 31.

(4) Songs expressing the sense of loneliness and wretchedness experienced during the exile. Pss. 137; 22; 69; 88.

(5) Songs celebrating the joy and gladness of the return from exile. Pss. 126; 115.

(6) Songs of the second temple, written particularly for congregational worship. Pss. 106; 107.

It is to be noted concerning the songs thus classified—

(*a*) That those of earlier date were considerably modified in the later days when the use of songs in congregational worship was more thoroughly established.

(*b*) That it is exceedingly difficult to fix exactly the date of many psalms because of the lack of historical indications; *i. e.*, references to historical events.

(*c*) That many psalms which seem to express individual experiences and aspirations are really congregational in their character; *i. e.*, they were written to express the feelings of a community.

(*d*) That a fuller treatment of this part of the element of worship will be presented later (see chap. xviii).

CHAPTER IV.

THE HISTORY OF WORSHIP IN THE LATER OLD TESTAMENT PERIOD.

§ 36. **The Later Old Testament Period** in the history of worship is the story of *Judaism*, that is, the Jewish religion, which was the daughter of the Hebrew religion. The period, rightly considered, (1) *begins* with the Babylonian exile (§ 30), for at that time were set in motion the great ideas, and the modifications of old ideas, which finally made up Judaism; but (2) the time in which the distinct *establishment* and substantial development of Judaism took place falls within the two centuries of *Persian supremacy* (538–332 B. C.); while (3) the century and a half from 332 B. C. to 165 B. C., the period of *Greek influence*, had for its great achievement the final testing and rounding-out of Judaism.

See KENT, *A History of the Jewish People during the Babylonian, Persian and Greek Periods*, pp. v–vii; WELLHAUSEN, *Prolegomena to the History of Israel*, pp. 500 f.

§ 37. **Some of the Most Striking Characteristics** of this period are these:

(1) It is the *last* division of the Old Testament period. Is it a climax or an anti-climax? Is it a step higher in the development of the true religious conception, or is it a step lower than has hitherto been taken?

Cf. Ezra 1:5. (2) It is prevailingly *priestly* in its character, for (*a*) a king no longer sits on Judah's throne; (*b*) the prophet's voice and authority are now largely a thing of the past; while (*c*) it is the high-priest who occupies the place of supremacy alike in church and state. In Israel's earliest days the king acted as priest; now the priest acts as king.

Zech. 3:1–7; 6:11.

(3) It is distinctly an *ecclesiastical* situation which presents itself to our view; in fact, we are studying the history of a *church*, not that of a state.

Neh., chap. 8. (4) In view of all this, it is natural enough to find that the great event which characterized this period, the event which the sacred historians chronicled with especial emphasis, was the promulgation of *the Levitical law* by Ezra. With this we may compare the giving of the Deuteronomic law, in its relationship to the middle period (§ 28).

§ 38. **The Situation Culminating with the Building of the Temple, 516 B. C.,** presents the following, among other, elements which may be taken as directly growing out of the exile and *leading up* to this later period:

(1) Jeremiah's teaching of *individualism*, which emphasized the fact that each individual sustained a distinct personal relation to Jehovah in addition to his relation to him as a part of the nation. Each man is responsible for his own sins and for those only, and his acceptance with God depends upon himself alone. Jer. 31:29-34; Ezek., chap. 18; Deut. 24:16.

(2) Ezekiel's teaching of the *new community*, a new city in which no government will be needed, for there will be no crime and no injustice. God will be judge. He will bestow upon the people all that they need. The city will have no obligation to provide for the welfare of the people. God will fight Israel's battles, and Israel's only work will be to bury the corpses of the slain. What, now, will prince and people do? *Engage in worship, continual worship.* The only object of care will be the temple and its materials; the only taxes will be church taxes. This is Ezekiel's vision of the kingdom of God on earth. Ezek., chaps. 40-48. Ezek. 39:1-16; *cf.* Isa. 65:17-25; Ezek. 17:25-30.

(3) There is general recognition of the idea that Israel's religion, and, indeed, its national existence, was not dependent upon a monarchy, nor, indeed, upon any particular form of government. Ezek., chap. 18; Zech. 8:20-23.

(4) There exists a more general readiness to accept the teachings of the prophets, which at the time of their utterance were unheeded or rejected. Zech. 1:1-6; 7:1-7; *cf.* Joel 2:28, 29.

(5) The necessity for meeting together in small groups for worship, and the nature of the exercises possible under the circumstances, viz., public reading of scripture and prayer, are leading to the organization of *synagogues.* Ezek. 8:1; 20:1-3; *cf.* Ps. 74:8.

Exod. 20:23—23:33. (6) With the book of the Covenant (§ 20), and the book of Deuteronomy (§ 25) which had become the adopted code of religious life, and the more recent and more elabo-
Ezek., chaps. 40-48; rate program of worship suggested by Ezekiel (§ 31), all
cf. Isa. 51:17-20. in existence, and all rendered *impossible of observance* by the circumstances of the people, there is seen to be a great indefiniteness and uncertainty in the situation, which, while confusing, signified most clearly that the "Law" was not yet finished, and prepared the minds of the people for the more *definite and final* formulation still to be made.

Cf. Ezra 1:2-4; Ezra 6:1-12; Ezra 7:11-26; Neh. 2:1-9. (7) The broad and generous *policy of Cyrus* and his successors on the Persian throne, a policy of state and religion very different from that of preceding history, as well as from that of still later times, made possible in the way of progress and growth what otherwise would have been impossible.

Jer. 24:1-10. (8) The higher character of the Babylonian Jews, and the special circumstances of their environment, as distinguished from that of the Jews who remained in Judah, forms an important factor in the movement toward national *exclusiveness* which is henceforth to be so prominent.

Hag. 2:6-9; Zech. 2:9-13. (9) The expectations, publicly announced, of Haggai and Zechariah that in the political upheavals of the day (*i. e.*, the revolts of the Babylonians in 519 and 515 B. C. against the Persian rule) deliverance and glory would come to Israel; the embassy of four Jews from Babylon, bringing gifts of silver and gold which are made into a
Zech. 6:9-12. crown for Zerubbabel (not Joshua); and the fact that
Zech. 3:8. Zerubbabel had been given the name Branch or Sprout—all this points to the suggestion that there were many who still expected a descendant of David to sit upon Israel's throne; but the hope was impossible of realization because (*a*) the whole trend of events was toward the priestly rule, and (*b*) perhaps the Persian authorities may have interfered to prevent an act which would certainly have led to treason,
Ezra, chap. 5; *cf.* Neh., chap. 6. just as they did in the case of the building of the walls.

See CHEYNE, *Jewish Religious Life after the Exile*, p. 15; KENT, *op. cit.*, pp. 147 f.

(10) The residence in Babylon brought the Jews into close touch with an elaborate system of sacrifice, the most important characteristic of which was the *propitiatory* idea. This is significant in view of the fact that henceforward the greatest possible emphasis will be placed upon sacrifice as an *atonement*, and upon prayer for *forgiveness*. Lev., chap. 16; Neh. 1:4-11.

See PAUL HAUPT, "Babylonian Elements in the Levitical Ritual," *Journal of Biblical Literature*, Vol. XIX, pp. 55-81; JASTROW, *Religion of Babylonia and Assyria*, p. 668.

(11) Because in Babylon there was no chance to offer sacrifice, such a thing being utterly inconceivable, *fasting* came into great prominence, since "by denying themselves their ordinary food they gave expression to the intensity of their feelings, and at the same time laid before Jehovah a gift which could be presented at any time and at any place." Isa. 58:3 ff.; Ezra 8:21; Neh. 1:4; Joel 1:14; Zech. 7:3-5.

See KENT, *op. cit.*, p. 43; BENZINGER, article "Fasting," § 6, in *Encyclopædia Biblica;* STANTON, article "Fasting," §§ 1*b* and 3, in HASTINGS' *Dictionary of the Bible;* CHEYNE, *op. cit.*, pp. 9-11.

(12) It was, likewise, because in Babylon the great feast days could not be properly or regularly observed, that greater and greater attention was given to the observance of the *sabbath*, for this could be done anywhere. The nature of the observance was probably much influenced by the customs in vogue in Babylon. Ezek. 20:12-24.

(13) The removal to another land, and residence in that land, took away the narrow conception of a national god which had always existed among the masses; and now the time has come when first the people as such will accept the great and fundamental doctrine of *one god, i. e., monotheism*. But Jehovah, in becoming the creator of the world, and the ruler of the universe, will not seem to be in as close touch as formerly with his people. He will be holy, in the sense of being separated. He will be higher and more majestic; less familiar and more dignified, because *greater*. Isa. 44:6. Isa. 40:28. Isa. 40:12-17.

See MONTEFIORE, *Religion of the Ancient Hebrews* (= Hibbert Lectures, 1892), pp. 228, 268 f.; SCHULTZ, *Old Testament Theology*, Vol. I, pp. 175 f.; DAVIDSON, article "God," § IV, (4), in HASTINGS' *Dictionary of the Bible*.

(14) According to the manner in which the individual Israelites meet these new and strange conditions they Neh. 13:15–28. will divide themselves into two classes: (*a*) those who break away from their old religion because of inability to adopt a larger faith and a broader conception of God, or because of personal advantage gained by giving up the Mal. 3:16–18. old; and (*b*) those who, in spite of calamity and misapprehension, maintain themselves steadfast and true. This means a purging of the people, the growing *stronger* of those who are strong, and the weeding out of those who are weak.

See KENT, *op. cit.*, pp. 221 f.; MONTEFIORE, *op. cit.*, pp. 291 ff.

Hag. 2:3; Ezra 3:12, 13. (15) When it was realized quite clearly that the promises of the prophets were not to be fulfilled at the time of the return from exile, there was disappointment Mal. 2:17. and despair on every side. Some became indifferent to Isa. 59:9–15. God, for they put on *him* the blame for their disappointment. Others, the more devout, took the blame upon *themselves.* With full faith in God's ability to do the things which he had promised, they reasoned in their hearts that this glorious future must have failed of realization because of Israel's sin; yes, because of their own unworthiness this glory was being postponed. They *Cf.* the prophet who speaks in Isa. 42:18–25. reasoned further: We, who have sinned and have thus made it impossible for the great day of deliverance to be ushered in—*we* must change our ways; we must become *Cf.* Ps. 15. more holy; we must increase our piety; our lives must be of such purity *that God will be compelled to keep his promises.* It was this situation and this interpretation of it that prepared the way for "the legalism and the salvation by works of the later Judaism."

See CORNILL, *Prophets of Israel*, pp. 155–9.

§ 39. **A Great Reaction Came after the Building of the Temple in 516 B. C.,** which lasted nearly three-quarters of a century. Concerning this it will be noted—

Neh. 5:1–12; Mal. 3:5; Mal. 2:10. (1) That, in all probability, only a few of the Babylonian Jews had yet returned;[1] the weak, narrow, and

[1] The question of dates, always a more or less difficult one, is in this case especially difficult. *Cf.* KENT, *op. cit.*, pp. 196 ff.; H. E. RYLE, *Ezra and Nehemiah* (Cambridge Bible), pp. xxxviii–xlv; CHEYNE, *op. cit.*, pp. 36–81; C. C. TORREY, *The Composition*

selfish elements were in control; the rulers were greedy of gain, oppressing the poor.

(2) There was in the community a strong tendency toward skepticism. The so-called "scorners" were in the majority, and included in their number not only rulers but priests, and these openly expressed doubts as to all the religious practices and opinions of the times, *e. g.*, (*a*) weariness of the routine of sacrifice; (*b*) what real benefit comes from serving God? (*c*) why not just as well worship the heathen gods? (*d*) what difference does it make whether a man does right or wrong? **Mal. 1:13. Mal. 3:14, 15. Mal. 2:17.**

(3) Under these circumstances the condition of worship was greatly degraded. This was seen in—

(*a*) The complaint of the priests as to the weariness of their occupation. **Mal. 1:13.**

(*b*) The low character of the high-priests, who were among the most guilty. **Neh. 13:4-9, 28.**

(*c*) The readiness of the people to cheat Jehovah in their sacrifices. **Mal. 1:6-14.**

(*d*) The attitude of the priests in general toward the entire service, including the sacrifice, so that the whole ceremonial came into contempt. **Mal. 1:8; 2:8,9.**

(*e*) The failure of the people to pay their tithes, so that the support of the entire system was about to fail. **Mal. 3:8-12.**

(*f*) The marriage of the priests into families of outside nations who served other gods. **Neh. 13:23-28; Mal. 2:10-16.**

(4) But there still remained the company of "faithful ones," who feared Jehovah, and were called "the just," "the poor and needy" (*cf.* above, § 38, (14), (15)). **Mal. 3:16-18; Pss. 69:32-36; 101:6; 113:7.**

§ 40. **Nehemiah's Coming (44 B. C.) Was a Great Event** in the history of Judaism.

(1) His work as a reformer and upbuilder of Jerusalem included— **Neh. 1:1—7:5; 12:27-43.**

(*a*) The rebuilding of the walls of Jerusalem as a protection against attack, and as a means of separating the Jews from their heathen neighbors. **Neh. 2:12—6:15.**

and Historical Value of Ezra-Nehemiah, pp. 51–65; W. H. KOSTERS AND T. K. CHEYNE, article "Ezra" in *Encyclopædia Biblica;* L. W. BATTEN, article "Nehemiah" in HASTINGS' *Dictionary of the Bible.*

Neh., chap. 11. (*b*) The repopulating of Jerusalem by bringing in Jews from the surrounding country to dwell there.

Neh. 13:23-28; Neh. 13:1-3. (*c*) The prohibition of marriages with heathen peoples and the driving out of all foreigners from the Jewish community.

Neh., chap. 5. (*d*) The restoration to its original owners of all property that had been acquired by mortgages and usury, and the remission of all interest.

Neh. 13:15-22. (*e*) The institution of a stricter observance of the sabbath, which had heretofore been freely violated.

Neh. 13:10-13; Neh. 10:32-39. (2) But in addition to all this he turned his attention to the temple and its service. Finding that this was being neglected because the Levites were under the necessity of working in the fields for their support, he took steps to secure the regular payment of the tithes, and appointed faithful officials to distribute them to the Levites. He also made regulations for the proper observance of sacrifices, offerings, and feasts.

§41. **The Work of Ezra,** in all probability, followed that of Nehemiah, the latter having by his masterful skill prepared the way (*cf.* §40). The steps in his eventful career may be summarily classified as follows:

Ezra 7:1-9; 8:21-23. (1) The *journey* took place in the seventh year of Artaxerxes, occupied a period of four months, and was made without military escort, since Ezra refused to manifest distrust in Jehovah's protection by asking the aid of Artaxerxes.

Ezra 7:15-23; 8:24-34. (2) The *gifts* said to have been offered by Artaxerxes and his princes for the temple at Jerusalem and its service, together with the requisition made by the king upon the governors of the western provinces and the free-will offerings of the Babylonian Jews themselves, were of great value, and were faithfully guarded and handed over to the temple officials.

Ezra 7:14-27. (3) The immediate *purpose* was to establish more securely and develop more elaborately the facilities for worship in the temple. Matters relating to the service and to the temple seem to have occupied the entire time and attention of the reformers for a couple of months after their arrival.

§ 42. **The Formal Adoption of the Law** took place at a public assembly of all the people. The method of procedure was in general the same as that used when the Deuteronomic law was publicly adopted by the nation (see § 25). The law was first read aloud in the hearing of the people. This produced a sense of sin and shortcoming on the part of all, and was followed by public confession. After this a solemn covenant was entered into by all the people to observe the requirements of the new law, and this covenant was signed by the representatives of the people, viz., the princes, priests, and Levites. **Neh., chaps. 8–10.**

§ 43. **The Law as Thus Proclaimed and Accepted**—

(1) Is described in Nehemiah as—

(*a*) Prohibiting marriages with the surrounding heathen. **Neh. 10: 30.**

(*b*) Providing for a strict observance of the *sabbaths* and *holy days*. **Neh. 10: 31.**

(*c*) Enforcing the observance of the *sabbatical year*, with the accompanying remission of all debts. **Neh. 10: 31.**

(*d*) Imposing an annual *tax* of one-third of a shekel per capita for the support of the services of the temple, including the offerings. **Neh. 10: 32, 33.**

(*e*) Arranging for the *wood to be furnished* for the burnt-offerings at stated intervals. **Neh. 10: 34.**

(*f*) Enjoining the bringing of all *first-fruits* and *firstlings* to the priests at the temple. **Neh. 10: 35–37.**

(*g*) Requiring that the people give *tithes* to the Levites in the various cities, and that the Levites bring a tithe of these tithes to the temple at Jerusalem. **Neh. 10: 38.**

(*h*) Calling for a hearty support of the temple and constant faithfulness to it. **Neh. 10: 39.**

(2) Contains regulations unknown to Deuteronomy, *e. g.*, the requirement that the land lie fallow every sabbatical year; the tax of one-third of a shekel for the temple services; the arrangement for the provision of fire-wood; and the law concerning tithes, which departs widely from the Deuteronomic law. **Neh. 10: 31*b*; *cf.* Deut., chap. 15; Neh. 10: 38; *cf.* Deut. 14: 22–29; 26: 12–15.**

(3) Was substantially the body of regulations found in Exod., chaps. 25–31; 34 : 29—40 : 38; Leviticus, and Numbers; in other words, the so-called *Levitical code.*

See KENT, *op. cit.*, p. 212; CHEYNE, *op. cit.*, pp. 72 f.; MONTEFIORE, *op. cit.*, pp. 315 ff.; J. ESTLIN CARPENTER AND G. HARFORD BATTERSBY, *The Hexateuch*, Vol. I, pp. 137–41; WELLHAUSEN, *op. cit.*, pp. 404–10.

§44. **The Significance of This Important Event** lies in the following points:

Cf. Neh. 10:30, 31 with 13:15-24; Ezra 9:1.

(1) The immediate connection of these new regulations with the times. They grew out of the effort to improve the existing moral and religious condition of the people, and they contain the principles that formed the basis of the work of reform.

(2) The fact that, although some additions remained still to be made to this code, it was substantially complete.

(3) The adoption and incorporation into this code of the important teachings of the prophets. It presented in the concrete and tangible form of specific precepts the great general truths that the prophets had long endeavored to inculcate. It presented truth and duty objectively, and thus met with a greater immediate success than the prophets' work had ever achieved.

Cf., e.g., Lev. 16:1—17:9; 22:1—24:9; 25:11—26:2.

(4) The overwhelming preponderance of material in the code relating to service or worship.

Lev. 14:10-32; 22:17-33; Exod. 29:38-42.

(5) The place occupied in it by sacrifice, and the emphasis (see §38, (10)) placed upon the idea of propitiation and forgiveness.

Neh. 10:37, 38.

(6) The great advance made by the priests and Levites; their support is no longer a matter of fitful charity, as it was under the Deuteronomic law, but is made a standing obligation upon the people, over the discharge of which the priests and Levites themselves are given control.

§45. **Another Important Headquarters for Worship, the Samaritan Temple on Mount Gerizim,** grew out of this priestly reformation. The Samaritans were a mixed race, whose ancestors were the poorer Israelites left behind after the deportation of the more influential classes to Assyria at the time of the fall of Samaria, and the Babylonian colonists who were brought to Israel in place of the deported captives. Their religion was thus naturally a corrupt mixture of Israelitish and Babylonian ideas and practices. They seem to have been influenced by Josiah's reformation, at least to the extent of regarding Jerusalem

2 Kings 17:6, 24-41; *cf.* 25:11, 12.

as the only lawful place of worship. Hence, when the **Ezra, chap. 4.**
effort to rebuild the temple was begun, the Samaritans sought to have a part in the work; but, being denied this privilege by the stricter Jews, they seem to have used their influence to obstruct the work. Nehemiah's atti- **Neh. 2:18-20.**
tude toward them was one of uncompromising opposition. They, for their part, opposed and hindered him greatly **Neh. 4:1-23; 6:1-19.**
in his work of rebuilding the walls of Jerusalem. The **Neh. 13:28.**
climax of Nehemiah's hostility to them was reached when he expelled the grandson of the high-priest from Jerusalem because he had married the daughter of Sanballat, one of the Samaritan princes. The new law, adopted when feeling was at such a pitch, of course gave the Samaritans no part in the worship at Jerusalem. Consequently they withdrew and built a temple for themselves on Mount Gerizim. In all probability many Jews who had contracted heathen marriages went over to the Samaritan community, to which they were so closely bound by family ties, and thus the community of the faithful was freed from many troublesome elements.

See MONTEFIORE, *op. cit.*, pp. 351 f.; CHEYNE, *op. cit.*, pp. 25–35; WELLHAUSEN, *op. cit.*, p. 498; GUTHE, article "Israel," §65, in *Encyclopædia Biblica.*

§46. **The Last Century of Persian Rule** (425–332) witnessed —

(1) The return of many Jews from the lands in which they had been scattered; for this return, like the first entrance into Canaan, was very gradual.

(2) The growing influence of those who thus returned as over against that of those who had remained.

(3) Great opportunity at first for free growth and expansion because of the weakness of the government of Persia.

(4) Serious calamity, later, because of the contest between Egypt and Persia, a contest in which the Jews were compelled to take part, and in which they suffered as perhaps never before in their history. From psalms **Pss. 74; 79.**
of this period we learn that the enemy entered Jerusalem and the temple itself, in which they set up their heathen standards and committed ruthless acts of vandalism, even setting the temple on fire. Not satisfied

with this, they burned all the synagogues of the land and slaughtered the people mercilessly, so that blood ran like water in the streets of Jerusalem.

See EWALD, *History of Israel*, Vol. V, pp. 165–206; CHEYNE, *Introduction to the Book of Isaiah*, pp. 357–63; W. EMORY BARNES, article "History of Israel," § 10, in HASTINGS' *Dictionary of the Bible;* GUTHE, article "Israel," § 66, in *Encyclopædia Biblica;* KENT, *op. cit.*, pp. 224–8.

§ 47. **The Religio-Political Organization of Judaism,** which had thus become crystallized, considered as to its outer form, was a *hierarchy*, a government by priests; for—

Exod. 28:1–39; Lev. 16:1–3, 17. (1) The chief ruler was the high-priest, who had despotic authority over the people, was robed in the royal purple, and alone represented the people before Jehovah in the holy of holies.

(2) The ruling aristocracy was made up of priests, many of them related to the high-priest.

Numb. 18:1–7. (3) The servants of the priests and the sanctuary were the *Levites.*

(4) The religious and civil functions are performed by one class, the priests. There is now no nation; it is a church.

Ezra 7:6, 10–12, 21; Eccles. 12:11. (5) The *scribes* come forward in response to the need of the times. Since the regulations concerning life and worship were now fixed and written down, there arose a demand for copies of the written law for the use of synagogues and individuals. The scribes who prepared these copies, being naturally better educated than the great majority of the people and spending most of their time in the study of the law, soon came to be looked to as peculiarly well-fitted to interpret the law to those less conversant with it.[2]

See MONTEFIORE, *op. cit.*, pp. 392–6.

§ 48. **The Place and Acts of Worship are Adjusted to the New Situation.**

Pss. 76:1, 2; 79:1. (1) The *temple* more and more came to be the center of the whole religious system. The thought of it as the place where Jehovah especially manifested his presence gave it a peculiar sanctity, so that none but the holy

[2] The scope of the activity of the scribes is well set forth in a saying ascribed to Simon the Just (300–290 B. C.): "Our fathers have taught us three things, to be cautious in judging, to train many scholars, and to set a fence about the Law."

people might enter its precincts. The worst crime of which an enemy could be capable was desecration of the temple. But, while emphasis was thus laid upon the temple, there was growing up alongside of it the *synagogue* with a function of a different kind. These were organized wherever there were a few Jews settled who wished to study the law. They especially supplied the religious needs of the many Jews scattered in many lands who were unable to make frequent visits to Jerusalem in order to participate in the splendid worship of the temple. While the temple services centered about sacrifices and offerings, the service of the synagogue centered in the reading and interpretation of the law. **Ps. 74:8.**

See MONTEFIORE, *op. cit.*, pp. 390 f.

(2) *Sacrifice* now took on more and more a propitiatory character, being looked upon chiefly as atonement for sin. The most minute regulations were made as to the details of every sacrifice, the manner in which the offering must be laid upon the altar, the disposition to be made of the fat and the blood, the garments to be worn by the officiating priest, etc. It seems as though the temple services must have been a constant succession of sacrifices. **Lev. 6:24—7:9; 16:1–34; Numb., chaps. 28; 29.**

(3) *Times and seasons* received more attention than ever before. The *sabbath* was particularly insisted upon as a sign of the covenant between Jehovah and his people. The penalty for performing any work on the sabbath was death. **Lev. 19:3; Exod. 31:12–17.**

(4) The *sabbatical year* was now made wider in scope, so as to include the land itself which was to be allowed to lie fallow. Furthermore, every fifty years an additional *year of jubilee* was to be celebrated, thus making two sabbatical years in succession. At this time all Hebrew slaves were to be released, and all land bought during the preceding forty-nine years was to revert to its original owners. **Lev. 25:1–7. Lev. 25:8–55.**

(5) The *feasts* provided for were the *Passover* and *Feast of Unleavened Bread*, the *Feast of Tabernacles*, the *New Moon*, the *Feast of Weeks*, the *New Year's Feast*, and the *Day of Atonement*. They were all definitely dated **Lev. 23:4–8, 33–36, 39–44; Numb. 28:11 ff., 26 ff.; Lev. 23:15 ff.; Numb. 29:1–6; Lev., chap. 16.**

by month and day, and thus were still farther removed from their agricultural origin. The Feast of Tabernacles was now celebrated in remembrance of the fact that the Israelites dwelt in tents during their journey in the wilderness. There was little difference in the manner of celebrating the various feasts—the most characteristic feature of them all is the endless sacrifices that accompanied them. They were all to a large extent of an expiatory nature; nevertheless it was felt necessary to devote one day per year to the special work of expiation, viz., the Day of Atonement.

(6) The public *fasts* which had been observed during the exile in commemoration of the exile and of the disasters connected with it were not incorporated into the new law, but seem to have come to an end in Zechariah's time. That fasting in general was highly esteemed as a means of propitiating Jehovah, and frequently practiced when occasion seemed to demand it, is clear in view of the place given to it in the regulations for the Day of Atonement, and the references to it in Joel and Nehemiah.

Lev. 23:32; Numb. 29:7; Joel 1:14; 2:12, 15; Neh. 1:4; 9:1.

(7) *Other acts of worship.*—Constant recourse was had to *prayer* on the part of pious Jews. The chief objects of prayer seem to have been deliverance from dangers, help in trouble, and forgiveness of sin with resulting bestowal of blessings.

Ezra, chap. 9; Neh. 1:4–11; 2:4; 5:19; 6:9, 14; 9:5–38; 13:22.

That *singing and music* occupied a large place in worship is clear from the allusions to the singers in connection with the dedicatory exercises held when the wall of Jerusalem was completed, and from the large number of psalms that come from this period (see § 50).

Neh. 7:1; 11:23; 12:27–29, 42, 45–47.

Soothsaying and magic seem to have been still practiced, but were prohibited by the law, as was also *necromancy.*

Lev. 19:26, 31; Lev. 20:6, 27.

Vows were recognized and provided for by the law.

Lev. 22:18, 21, 23; 27:1–8.

§ 49. **The Full Significance of This New Régime** is hard to grasp. The comfort afforded by it to the people cannot be questioned. This strange system, which seems to us, in our love of freedom, so distasteful, was, after all, the highest result yet achieved in the development of Israel's religion. It was based upon the doctrines

Ps. 84:1, 2.

of the prophet-priests, viz., individualism and solidarity. Its keynote was *monotheism*. Its God was a God whose supreme attribute was holiness, and who expected in every individual of the sacred community a holiness like his own. The underlying thought was the overwhelming *sense of sin*. Now, for the first time, the preaching of the prophets through all the centuries has found its place in the hearts of the people. The prayers are prayers of confession. God has grown greater, and man more humble in the sight of God. God is the God of the whole world. Israel is a company of individuals in a sacred community. Every act of life must be holy. The religious feeling is deeper than ever before and more universal. Men are anxious. The people, burdened as they are with their anxiety, smitten as they are in their consciousness of sin, humbled by their ideal of God, take upon themselves the severest yoke ever placed by religion upon the neck of man. A service worthy of this supreme God must be regulated in its most minute details. The service everywhere presents the thought of sin. Sacrifice is now the great act, and is no longer accompanied by gladness and joy. It represents purification from sin. It is "the chief symbol, and the great mystery of their faith." To be holy one must wash; one must touch no unclean thing; one must not eat what is unclean; one must observe the sabbath, the day of God; and all these acts of worship cultivated the spirit of exclusiveness. Then followed that haughty spirit. "Man who would go up to the hill of Jehovah must now be the one who has not eaten shellfish or pork, nor opened his shop on the sabbath, nor touched a dead body, nor used a spoon handed him by a gentile without washing it." We know the outcome of all this, as it is shown us in the New Testament, but "it kept the people separate from the world and constant to their faith, and made them endure the greatest temptations and the severest persecutions, and so enabled them to preserve the precious treasure committed to them until the time should come when the world was to receive it from their hands."

Lev. 19:1-4; 20:26; 22:15, 16, 31-33.

Pss. 106:6-47; 130.

Lev. 4:1—6:7.

Lev., chap. 15; Lev., chap. 11; Exod. 31:12-17.

Lev. 21:1-24.

See CHEYNE, *op. cit.*, pp. 73–81; KENT, *op. cit.*, pp. 213 f., 249 ff.; MONTEFIORE, *op. cit.*, pp. 465–552; WELLHAUSEN, *op. cit.*, p. 497.

§50. **The Psalms of the Second Temple are now Written,** and one fails to see the deeper meaning of all this if he forgets that in this period the *greatest number* of the
Pss. 118; 121; 67. psalms were written. The old prophetic ideas, which the people in the times of the prophet had refused to accept, are now a part of the people's creed and are sung by
Pss. 95; 46. them with joyous hearts in the congregation. Sacred
Pss. 122; 138; 145; 148–150. song becomes preëminently an act of worship. The worship of Jehovah in this act is as joyous and as delightful as it may be sad and grewsome in the act of sacrifice.
Pss. 143:10; 139; 125. In these very days, when such emphasis is laid upon the letter of the law, the service of song teaches that to obey Jehovah and to trust in him, to surrender one's self absolutely to him, is the end of all religion. Whatever may be the experience of life, it finds expression in these psalms; whether it be "penitence, intellectual perplexity,
Pss. 102; 91; 130; Pss. 109; 116; 123. domestic sorrow, feebleness, loneliness, the approach of death, the excitement of great events, the agony of persecution, or the quiet contemplation of nature." For each experience there is expression, and the heart-utterances which formed a part of the worship of this period, sung, to be sure, in the midst of the bleating of the lambs which are being slaughtered for the sacrifice, have proven to be the most satisfying utterances for the soul, in its deepest communion with God, which have ever reached the heart of man. The ritual may have been narrow, but the heart of every Jew was free. He was restrained outwardly, but no such restraint hindered him in the working of his mind and heart. Here was contradiction, to be sure, but contradiction no greater than is found in the tendency to substitute the synagogue for the temple, which now exhibits itself in spite of the exclusiveness that was the end and the result of the Levitical system.

§51. **The Greek Period of Influence, 332–165 B. C.,** added nothing essential to the content or form of service. It furnished the test of Judaism for which the work of Ezra and Nehemiah had been an unconscious preparation. In the crisis through which the true religion was to pass the form given to it by these men was of inestimable value. In the words of Cornill:[2]

That the development of Judaism took this special direction was a necessity of the history of religion.

For the heaviest struggle of Judaism still awaited it; the struggle against Hellenism. One hundred and twenty-five years after Ezra, Alexander the Great destroyed the Persian empire and made the Greeks the sovereign people of the eastern world. Through this a profound transformation was begun, which spread with startling rapidity and irresistible might, and led finally to the denationalizing of the East. That which the Assyrian had undertaken by brute force the Hellenes surmounted by the superior power of mind and culture. Greece destroyed the nationalities of the East by amalgamating them with itself and conquering them inwardly. Only one eastern nation withstood the process of dissolution, yea, more, absorbed into itself the good of Hellenism, and thus enriched and strengthened its own existence; and that was the Jewish. If it were able to do this, it was because Ezra and Nehemiah had rendered it hard as steel and strong as iron. In this impenetrable armor it was insured against all attacks, and thus saved religion against Hellenism. And, therefore, it behooves us to bless the prickly rind to which alone we owe it that the noble core remained preserved.

With this we may close our rapid survey of the *history* of the development of Israel's *worship*. In the light of this survey we shall next consider the more important special divisions included in it, viz., the laws, the histories, and the psalms.

[2] *Op. cit.*, pp. 162 f.

PART THIRD

COMPARATIVE STUDY OF THE LAWS AND USAGES OF WORSHIP

CHAPTER V.

THE LAWS AND USAGES CONCERNING THE PRIEST, CONSIDERED COMPARATIVELY.

§ 52. **To Speak of the History of Worship, as It is Presented in the Old Testament,** is to take for granted (1) that there were periods, (2) that these periods differed from each other to a greater or less extent, and (3) that there was either growth or decay, or perhaps both. The brief survey, just finished, distinguished three such periods, each with its peculiar characteristics, and presented what seemed to be a striking case of development, *i. e.*, growth from a lower and less complicated form of worship to one higher and more complicated. These periods were called early, middle, and later.

§ 53. **Each Period Had a Lawbook or Code of Legislation Peculiar to Itself,** viz.: (1) the *Covenant* Code (§ 14, (3)) for the early period, (2) the *Deuteronomic* Code (§ 27) for the middle period, and (3) the *Levitical* Code (§ 43) for the later period. Injunctions concerning nearly every topic relating to worship are found in each of these codes. These injunctions are sometimes couched in language almost the same; in other cases there are to be noted differences (additions or variations) of an important character; in still other cases they are quite contradictory. These differences, it is clear, exist because through succeeding centuries the people (*a*) changed their place of abode, *e. g.*, from the desert to Canaan, from Canaan to Babylon, and back again; (*b*) changed also their form of life, passing from the nomadic to the agricultural, and from the agricultural to the more centralized or city life; (*c*) changed their form of government, passing from a tribal form to the monarchical, and from that to a theocratic or hierarchical form; (*d*) came into contact with different nations, from whom much was learned, *e. g.*, the Canaanites, the Assyrians, the Babylonians, the Persians, and the Greeks; (*e*) were given great leaders, lawgivers, kings, and prophets, through whom, from time to time, new and better ideas of God and worship were taught.

Now, the different codes named above, as they severally appear and are adopted by the nation, reflect the onward and upward movement of the people toward the great goal of the nation's history, the time when Jesus Christ shall come and teach as men had never taught before. These codes, then, are different expressions of the usage and law of successive epochs. To understand any special topic connected with worship, one must examine systematically what each code contains on that topic. This is the *comparative study* of the laws relating to worship.

§ 54. **The Constructive Study of a Subject is Possible Only on the Basis of the Comparative Study.**—It is not the earliest usage in a particular case, *e. g.*, a distinction between the priest and the laity, nor the latest, that gives us a true idea of Israelitish thought and custom; it is, rather, the latest as growing out of and including, not only the earliest, but all the intervening steps between the two. At no one time did growth or decay stop; and it is only when we have the whole process before us that we begin to understand its significance.

§ 55. **Side by Side with the Codes We Find in the Hexateuch Also Histories** which refer frequently to customs of worship. It is interesting to note that each code is imbedded in a separate history; *e. g.*, (*a*) the Covenant Code is a part of a great *prophetic* history beginning with the creation and continuing down to the times of the Judges; (*b*) the Deuteronomic Code (Deut., chaps. 12–26) is a part of a history which is found, not only in the earlier part of Deuteronomy, but also in some places in Joshua, and elsewhere; while (*c*) the Priest Code is also closely connected with a history which begins with Gen. 1:1 and continues through Numbers. In studying the subject of worship, it is of interest to note what is said in these histories concerning each subject considered.

§ 56. **The Later Histories** contained in the books of Ezra, Nehemiah, and Chronicles give especial attention to the subject of worship. Just as the history in the books of Samuel and Kings is written from the prophetic point of view, that in these later books is written from the priestly point of view (see § 10), and hence gives much information concerning the institutions of worship as they existed at the time these books were written.

§ 57. **The Prophets Were Always Deeply Interested in Matters of Worship**; sometimes, as opponents of the ideas and practices existing in their day, they were trying to introduce new and better ideas; at other times, as allies of the priesthood, they were striving to awaken the zeal of the nation in behalf of the worship of Jehovah. In either case their writings contain much that is of value in a study of the development of Israel's ideas concerning worship.

§ 58. **The Priest Code, Manifestly, Is the Great Source of Information** upon the subject of worship, because (*a*) it contains the fullest presentation of each subject; (*b*) it is from the hands of the priests themselves, who were most deeply interested; and (*c*) it presents the latest stage of growth. But this Priest Code is itself a growth, and contains at least four strata of material, each of which represents a different age and stage of development. These are:

1. The Holiness Code, contained in Lev., chaps. 17–26, a body of laws which, as the name implies, lays especial emphasis upon the thought of the holiness of God and the necessity of corresponding holiness on the part of his people.

2. A collection of priestly teachings in reference to various sacrificial and ritualistic matters.

3. A set of miscellaneous materials, such as genealogical lists, elaborations of laws, and illustrative narratives.

4. A historical narrative from the creation up to the settlement in Canaan, which forms the basis of the P document, the three preceding elements having been incorporated into it.

See DRIVER, *Introduction to the Literature of the Old Testament*, 6th ed., pp. 126–59; ADDIS, *The Documents of the Hexateuch*, Vol. II, pp. 169–91; J. E. CARPENTER AND G. HARFORD-BATTERSBY, *The Hexateuch*, Vol. I, pp. 121–57.

§ 59. **The Priest of Early Times,** that is, as described in (*a*) the Covenant Code; (*b*) the historical material of J and E; (*c*) the pre-Deuteronomic portions of Judges, Samuel, and Kings; and (*d*) the pre-Deuteronomic prophetic utterances.[1]

1. The only allusion in the Covenant Code.[2]

Exod. 20:26.

[1] On the date, character, contents, and limits of these various documents see DRIVER, *Introduction to the Literature of the Old Testament;* also J. E. CARPENTER AND G. HARFORD-BATTERSBY, *The Hexateuch;* W. E. ADDIS, *The Documents of the Hexateuch;* BRIGGS, *The Higher Criticism of the Hexateuch;* HOLZINGER, *Einleitung in den Hexateuch;* WELLHAUSEN AND CHEYNE, article "Hexateuch" in *Encyclopædia Biblica;* F. H. WOODS, article "Hexateuch" in HASTINGS' *Dictionary of the Bible;* KUENEN, *An Historico-Critical Inquiry into the Origin of the Hexateuch;* WELLHAUSEN, *Prolegomena to the History of Israel*, pp. 228–391; STEUERNAGEL, *Allgemeine Einleitung in den Hexateuch* (=*Handkommentar zum Alt. Test.*, I. Abtheilung, 3. Band, pp. 249–86); W. R. HARPER AND W. H. GREEN, "The Pentateuchal Question," in *Hebraica*, Vol. V, pp. 18–73, 137–89, 243–91; Vol. VI, pp. 1–48, 109–38, 161–211 241–95; Vol. VII, pp. 1–38, 104–42; Vol. VIII, pp. 15–64, 174–243.

For a discussion of these questions from a different point of view see especially W. H. GREEN, *The Hebrew Feasts; cf.* also BISSELL, *The Pentateuch, Its Origin and Structure;* W. H. GREEN, *The Higher Criticism of the Pentateuch* and *Moses and the Prophets.*

[2] The following references are from the J document: Gen. 8:20 f.; 12:8; 22:13 Exod. 33:7–11; 19:22; 32:25–29; 4:14–17; 32:1 ff.; and the following from the E document: Exod. 20:26; 24:4–8; Deut. 33:8–11; 10:6; Josh. 24:33.

2. Non-priests frequently do priestly work.
   Gen. 8:20 f.; 12:8; 22:13; Exod. 33:7–11; 24:4–8; Judg. 13:19; 1 Sam. 7:1; 13:8–14; 2 Sam. 6:14–18; 1 Kings 18:30–38.
3. The story of Micah's priest.
   Judg., chaps. 17 and 18.
4. The consecration of the priest.
   Exod. 19:22; Judg. 17:5, 12; 1 Sam. 7:1.
5. The service rendered by the priest.
   1 Sam. 4:4; 7:1; 1 Kings 1:34; 1 Sam. 21:1–9; Hos. 4:6; Mic. 3:11; Isa. 28:7.
6. Priests were consulted as soothsayers.
   Judg. 18:5, 6; 1 Sam. 23:6–13; 30:7 ff.
7. The tribe of Levi.
   Exod. 32:25–29; Deut. 33:8–11.
8. Aaron and his descendants.
   Exod. 4:14–17; 32:1 ff.; Deut. 10:6; Josh. 24:33.
9. The sons of Eli and their behavior.
   1 Sam. 1:3; 2:22–25; 4:4; 1 Kings 2:27.
10. Elijah and the priests of Baal.
    1 Kings 18:19–40.
11. The prophets' estimate of the priest.
    Hos. 4:6–9; 5:1; 6:9; Amos 7:10–17; Mic. 3:11; Isa. 28:7.
12. The priest's dress and equipment.
    1 Sam. 2:18; Judg. 17:5; 18:14, 20; 1 Sam. 23:6, 9–12; 30:7, 8.
13. The priest's maintenance.
    Judg. 17:10; 18:4; 1 Sam. 2:12–17; 2 Kings 12:16.
14. The high-priest.
    2 Kings 12:10 (?).

§ 60. **Questions and Suggestions.**

1. What is the significance of the lack of any reference to *priest* in the Covenant Code (see § 15, (2))?

2. What connection is there between this lack of reference and the fact that laymen in early times acted as their own priests? Is there evidence that in cases where non-priests offered sacrifice they were doing so (*a*) through regularly appointed priests, or (*b*) by special divine authority?

3. Consider from the story of Micah's priest (*a*) the character of the times, (*b*) the existence of idolatry, (*c*) the place of the priest (*cf.* § 16, (2)).

4. How early and in what way were priests set apart or consecrated?

5. Formulate a list of the various functions performed by the priest in those days.

6. To what extent did people consult the priest about the ordinary affairs of life? *Cf.* the case of Samuel (1 Sam. 9:6 ff., 19 f.).

7. With what events and in what connection do the references to the tribe of Levi in this period appear?

8. Trace the line of Aaron as it is indicated down to later times. What, according to the tradition, was Aaron's official relation to Moses?

9. From the story of Eli's sons, point out (*a*) the basis of their right to be priests, (*b*) their functions as priests, (*c*) the various ways in which they abused their office.

10. Consider, in the story of Elijah and the priest-prophets of Baal, (*a*) the significance of the large number of prophets of Baal, (*b*) the non-priestly character of Elijah.

11. Enumerate, one by one, the shortcomings of the priests which are criticised by the prophets, and consider whether this state of things owed its existence (*a*) to a growing formality and emptiness of the Israelitish religion, or (*b*) to the influence exerted on the Israelitish religion by the neighboring religion, which was very sensual in its character, or (*c*) to the fact that now for the first time the prophets are holding up these high ideals, the priest-practice in Israel, as among other nations, having always been upon a low plane.

12. Consider the references to the priests' dress and equipment, and explain particularly the ephod, the Urim, and Thummim.[3]

13. What evidence is there that the priest in this period had any special perquisites or any regular maintenance?

14. How much may fairly be inferred as to the functions and authority of the high-priest in this period?

[3] See the article "Ephod," by G. F. MOORE, in *Encyclopædia Biblica;* the article "Ephod," by S. R. DRIVER, in HASTINGS' *Dictionary of the Bible;* VAN HOONACKER, *Le Sacerdoce lévitique*, pp. 370 ff.; KÖNIG, *Religious History of Israel*, pp. 107 ff.; G. F. MOORE, *Judges*, p. 381; KÖNIG, *Hauptprobleme*, pp. 59–63; FOOTE, "The Biblical Ephod," in *Johns Hopkins University Circulars*, May, 1900. On "Urim and Thummim" see SMITH'S *Dictionary of the Bible* (1893); KIRKPATRICK, *The First Book of Samuel* (Cambridge Bible Series), pp. 217 f.; KALISCH, *Exodus*, p. 544; WELLHAUSEN, *Prolegomena to the History of Israel*, pp. 394 f.; W. R. SMITH, *The Old Testament in the Jewish Church*, 2d ed., p. 292, note 1; T. WITTON DAVIES, *Magic, Divination and Demonology*, p. 75; RYLE, *Ezra and Nehemiah* (Cambridge Bible Series), p. 33; NOWACK, *Lehrbuch der hebräischen Archäologie*, Vol. II, pp. 93 f.; BENZINGER, *Hebräische Archäologie*, pp. 382, 407 f.; BAUDISSIN, *Die Geschichte des alttestamentlichen Priesterthums untersucht*, pp. 26 f.; STADE, *Geschichte des Volkes Israel*, Vol. I, pp. 156, 471–3, 505 f., 517 f.

§ 61. **Constructive Work.**—Upon the basis of the material considered, write a paper on "The Priest in Early Israelitish History," observing the following suggestions: (1) include only what can be corroborated by references to the literature of this period (see above); (2) use great caution in making general statements upon the basis of few facts; (3) remember that much may be gained by ascertaining what did *not* exist.

§ 62. **The Priest of the Deuteronomic Period,** that is, as described (*a*) in the laws of Deuteronomy, (*b*) in the Deuteronomic portions of the books of Samuel and Kings, and (*c*) by the prophets of the Deuteronomic period.[4]

1. The Levites, that is, the priests, become a distinct class.
   Deut. 10:8; **18:1**; 1 Sam. 2:28; Jer. 1:18; 8:1; 13:13; 23:33 f.; 26:7 f., 11, 16; 28:1, 5; 33:21; 34:19.
2. The service rendered by "the priests the Levites."
   Deut. 10:8; **21:5**; 33:8–10; **26:3 ff.**; **27:14**; **17:18**; 31:9; **17:8, 9, 12**; **19:17**; **20:2**; **24:8**; Jer. 18:18.
3. The prophets' estimate of the priest.
   Jer. 2:8; 5:31; 6:13; 14:18; 23:11; 32:32; Zeph. 3:4.
4. A later view of the wickedness of Eli's sons.
   1 Sam. 2:27–36.
5. The relative authority of priest and prophet.
   Jer. 29:25 f.; 5:31; 20:1 ff.; 11:18–23; *cf.* 1:1.
6. Differences of rank within the priestly order.
   2 Kings 23:4, 8, 9; Jer. 52:24; 29:25 f.; 19:1; **Deut. 18:6 f.**
7. Maintenance of "the priests the Levites."
   Deut. 10:9; **12:12**; **18:1–8**; **14:27, 29.**
8. Residence of priests.
   Deut. 18:6, 7; Jer. 1:1; *cf.* 11:21, 22; 32:6 ff.; Jer. 29:1.
9. Priests consulted as soothsayers.
   Deut. 33:8.

§ 63. **Questions and Suggestions.**

1. Consider the circumstances which, ordinarily, would encourage the building up of a special priest class. What connection existed between the centralization of worship in Jerusalem (§ 27, (2); *cf.* Deut., chap. 12) and the growth of a special class of priests? What is implied in the constantly recurring phrase "the priests the Levites"

[4] References printed in **bold-face** type are from the code of laws contained in Deuteronomy.

(*cf.* Deut. 17 : 18; 18 : 1; 21 : 5; 27 : 9; 31 : 9)? Does it mean (*cf.* Deut. 10 : 8) that all priests were Levites and all Levites priests?

2. Formulate the different functions which together made up the service of "the priest the Levite," distinguishing between regular and special functions. Consider the difference between the work of the prophet, the wise (man), and the priest (Deut. 18 : 18; Jer. 18 : 18).

3. What, according to the prophets, is the priest's attitude toward Jehovah and the true religion?

4. Compare the later view (1 Sam. 2 : 27–36) of the wickedness of Eli's sons with the former (1 Sam. 2 : 12–17, 22–25), note the points of change, and consider to what extent this is in harmony with Deuteronomic representations.

5. Recall the authority of the prophet (*a*) in the days of Saul, David, Solomon; (*b*) in the days of Elijah and Isaiah; and (*c*) consider to what extent, in the days of Jeremiah, the prophet had lost authority, while the priest had gained it.

6. Indicate the extent to which differences of rank had come to exist among the priests, and the significance of this fact.

7. Enumerate very accurately the sources of income and maintenance which were enjoyed by "the priests the Levites."

8. Were there special places of residence assigned to "the priests the Levites"? Did priests own property?

9. Is there anything additional to be said about the use of Urim and Thummim?

§ 64. **Constructive Work.**—Upon the basis of the material considered, write a paper on "The Priest in the Middle Period of Israelitish History"—that is, the so-called Deuteronomic period—discussing particularly (*a*) the class system, (*b*) the higher position now occupied, (*c*) the functions, (*d*) the maintenance provided by law.

§ 65. **The Priest as Described by Ezekiel.**

1. Ezekiel himself was a priest.
   Ezek. 1 : 3; 4 : 14.
2. Priesthood was limited to the sons of Zadok.
   Ezek. 44 : 15 f.; 40 : 46; 43 : 19, 24–27; 44 : 6–31; 48 : 11.
3. The priest's dress.
   Ezek. 42 : 14; 44 : 17–19.
4. Special "holiness" was required of priests.
   Ezek. 4 : 14; 44 : 20–22, 25–27, 31.
5. Service rendered by priests.
   Ezek. 44 : 11, 14, 15, 16, 23 f.; 40 : 46; 43 : 21, 24, 27.

6. Residence of priests.
   Ezek. 48:10–14; 42:13 f.; 46:19–24.
7. Maintenance of priests.
   Ezek. 42:13 f.; 44:28–30.

§ 66. **Questions and Suggestions.**

1. Consider the significance of the fact that Ezekiel, and also Jeremiah, Haggai, Zechariah, and Malachi—all the later prophets—were priests. Note that Ezekiel preached his visions of Israel's glorious future after the fall of Jerusalem. Consider the circumstances which led him to foresee and proclaim a system so exclusively *ecclesiastical.*

2. What limitation of the priesthood does he introduce, and why? In what respect is this an advance upon the Deuteronomic usage?

3. Consider the regulations made concerning the priest's dress; what was their purpose?

4. Enumerate the particular requirements made of the priests which were intended to mark their holiness, and show, in each case, how this was to be secured. In what sense is the word "holy" to be understood?

5. Indicate in what particulars the service required of the priest in Ezekiel's code differs from that of the Deuteronomic Code (§ 62, (2)); and show the principles underlying these changes.

6. What was to be the place of the priests' residence, and its extent? The meaning of the word "oblation"?

7. Prepare in detail a list of the items mentioned which should serve as the maintenance of the priest. Is there any variation from those mentioned in Deuteronomy?

§ 67. **Constructive Work.**—Prepare a paper showing how the priest, as seen in Ezekiel's vision, differed from the priest of the Deuteronomic times.

§ 68. **The Priest of the Later Period,** that is, as described (*a*) in the laws of the Levitical Code, (*b*) by the priestly prophets, and (*c*) in the priestly histories, *e. g.*, Ezra, Nehemiah, and Chronicles.[5]

1. Distinction between priests and Levites everywhere presupposed.
   Numb. 4:1–15, 19; 8:14–26; 18:1–7; 17:1–11; 25:10–13; 1 Chron. 6:49–53.
2. Special holiness required of priestly class.
   Lev. 21:1–9, 17–23; 22:1–8; 10:6; Exod. 30:19.
3. Service rendered by priests.
   Lev. 10:8–11; Numb. 4:4–14, 16; Lev. 16:32; 6:20–22; Hag. 2:11–13; Mal. 2:4–7; **Numb. 18:1–7; 27:21;** 2 Chron. 19:8, 11.

[5] References to the Levitical Code are in **bold-face** type.

4. Service rendered by Levites.
Numb. 4:1–3, 15, 21–33; 2:17; 3:23–26, 29–32, 35–38; 18:1–7; 3:5–10; Ezra 6:20; Neh. 11:15–18, 22; 1 Chron. 6:31–48; 15:2; 23:27–32; 26:20–32; 2 Chron. 5:4 f.; 19:8, 11.

5. Influence and numbers of priestly class.
Lev. 16:32; Numb. 4:19, 27 f., 33; 3:1–4; 4:34–49; 35:25–34; Hag. 1:1, 12, 14; Zech. 3:1–10; 6:9 ff. (?); Ezra 1:5; 2:61–63, 70; 3:2, 8–13; 5:2; 6:16; 7:7, 13, 16; 8:15–20, 29 f.; Neh. 11:15–18, 22; 12:1–26; 3:20, 22, 28; 5:12; 1 Chron. 6:1–47; 9:10–34; 23:1–24.

6. Place and work of the high-priest.
Numb. 35:25–34; Lev. 16:4–32; 6:22; Exod. 29:9; Numb. 27:21; Zech. 3:1–10; 6:9 ff. (?); Neh. 13:4, 28–30.

7. Consecration of high-priest.
Lev. 21:10–15; 6:20–22; 8:12, 14–36; Exod., chap. 29; Lev., chap. 9; Numb. 20:23–29.

8. Dress of priests.
Neh. 7:70–73; **Lev. 6:10 f.; 8:1–9, 13, 30; Exod., chap. 28; 39:1–31; 40:13 f.**

9. Residence of priests.
1 Chron. 6:54–81; Josh. 21:1–42; **Numb. 35:2–8;** Neh. 11:3; **Numb. 2:17; 3:23–26, 29–32, 35–38.**

10. Maintenance of priests.
Lev. 27:30–33; chap. 7; Numb. 3:4648; Ezra 7:24; Neh. 12:44–47; 13:10–14; Numb. 18:20 f., 24–31.

11. Courses of priests and Levites.
Ezra 6:18; 1 Chron. 24:1—26:19; 2 Chron. 5:11 f.; 8:12–15.

12. Prophets' estimate of the priests.
Hag. 2:11–13; Zech. 3:1–10; 6:9 ff.; Mal. 1:6–10; 2:4–9; 3:3; Isa. 61:6; 66:21; Joel 1:9, 13; 2:17.

§ 69. **Questions and Suggestions.**

1. Is there anywhere (*cf.* Neh. 11:20) in the post-exilic literature a passage in which the words "priest" and "Levite" are synonymous? *Cf.* Deut. (§ 62, (1)), and consider (*a*) the circumstances which have led to this differentiation, (*b*) its significance, and (*c*) the great change which has taken place since the time when everyone might be his own priest (*cf.* §§ 58, (2); 15, (2)).

2. What special limitations were imposed upon the priests (Aaron's sons) to secure their holiness?

3. Enumerate carefully the kinds of service expected of the priests

(Aaron's sons), and note how it differs from that required in Deuteronomy of "the priests the Levites."

4. Enumerate the kinds of service required of the Levites, and note the extent to which this service was in older times the work of "the priest the Levite."

5. What are the facts concerning the numbers of the priestly classes in this later period? Are they larger or smaller? Is their influence greater or less? What is the full significance of these facts?

6. What part has the high-priest played in the priestly work of earlier times? What is his place and work at this time?

7. What are the details of the consecration of the high-priest, and their interpretation?

8. Is more care now given to the peculiar dress of the high-priest? If so, in what details, and for what reason?

9. What special places are set apart for the residence of priests? Consider from various points of view the cities of refuge, noting especially the absence of any reference to them as Levitical cities in Deuteronomy (19:1–13).

10. What additions appear to the sources of income of the priests and Levites? Can the priests any longer be classed with the fatherless and widow as in Deut. 14:28, 29?

11. What is to be understood by the classification of the priests and Levites into courses and divisions?

12. How did the prophet, although himself a priest, estimate the priests of his times?

§ 70. **Constructive Work.**—Upon the basis of material in § 69 write a paper on the priest in later Israelitish history, noting especially such points as indicate changes in comparison with preceding periods.

§ 71. **Literature to be Consulted.**

STANLEY, *Lectures on the History of the Jewish Church*, Lecture XXXVI (1865); S. I. CURTISS, *The Levitical Priests* (1877); WELLHAUSEN, *Prolegomena to the History of Israel* (1878), pp. 121–51; KUENEN, *National Religions and Universal Religions* (Hibbert Lectures, 1882), pp. 314–17; GREEN, *Moses and the Prophets* (1883), pp. 78–83, 127–31; KALISCH, *Commentary on Leviticus*, Part I, pp. 559–659; SCHÜRER, *History of the Jewish People in the Time of Christ* (1886), Second Division, Vol. I, pp. 207–305; W. R. SMITH, article "Priest" in *Encyclopædia Britannica* (1889); MONTEFIORE, *The Religion of the Ancient Hebrews* (Hibbert Lectures, 1892), pp. 65–70, 116–18, etc.; SCHULTZ, *Old Testament Theology* (1892), see *Index;* KITTEL, *History of the Hebrews* (1892), see *Index;* E. H. PLUMPTRE, article "Priest" in SMITH'S *Dictionary of the Bible*, 2d ed. (1892); DRIVER, *Deuteronomy* (International Critical Commentary, 1895), see *Index;* MENZIES, *History of Religion* (1895), pp. 70, 183; BRIGGS, *Higher Criticism of the Hexateuch* (1897), p. 104; PICK, "The Jewish

High Priests Subsequent to the Return from Babylon," in *Lutheran Church Review*, 1898, pp. 127–42, 370–75, 655–64; JASTROW, *Religion of Babylonia and Assyria* (1898), see *Index;* TOY, *The Book of the Prophet Ezekiel* (Polychrome Bible, 1899), pp. 193 f.; W. R. HARPER, "The Priestly Element in the Old Testament as Seen in the Laws," *Biblical World*, Vol. XIV (1899), pp. 258–66; DUFF, *Old Testament Theology* (1891–1900), see *Index;* G. A. COOKE, article "Levi" in HASTINGS' *Dictionary of the Bible* (1900); MCCURDY, *History, Prophecy and the Monuments* (1895–1901), see *Index;* WALKER, "The Levitical Priesthood," *Journal of Biblical Literature*, 1900, pp. 124–37; BERLIN, "Notes on Genealogies of the Tribe of Levi in 1 Chron. 23–26," *Jewish Quarterly Review*, Vol. XII (1900), pp. 291–8; LAIDLAW, "The Priest and the Prophet," *Expository Times*, 1900; H. M. CHADWICKE, "Ancient Teutonic Priesthood," *Folk-Lore*, Vol. XI (1900), pp. 268–309; ADAMS, *The Mosaic Tabernacle: Studies in the Priesthood and the Sanctuary of the Jews* (1901).

GRAF, "Zur Geschichte des Stammes Levi," in MERX, *Archiv für wissenschaftliche Erforschung des Alten Testamentes*, Vol. I (1867), pp. 68–106, 208–36; MAYBAUM, *Die Entwicklung des altisraelitischen Priesterthums* (1880); SMEND, *Der Prophet Ezechiel* (1880), pp. 360–62; KITTEL, "Die Priester und Leviten," in *Theologische Studien aus Würtemberg*, Vol. II (1881), pp. 147–69; Vol. III, pp. 278–314; KUENEN, *Historisch-kritische Einleitung in die Bücher des Alten Testaments* (1885), Vol. I, pp. 281 ff.; STADE, *Geschichte des Volkes Israel* (1887), Vol. I, pp. 152 ff., 468 ff.; BAUDISSIN, *Die Geschichte des alttestamentlichen Priesterthums* (1889); H. VOGELSTEIN, *Der Kampf zwischen Priestern und Leviten seit den Tagen Ezechiels. Eine historisch-kritische Untersuchung* (1889); KUENEN, "Die Geschichte des Jahwepriesterthums und das Alter des Priestergesetzes" (1889), in *Gesammelte Abhandlungen*, pp. 465–500; SMEND, *Lehrbuch der alttestamentlichen Religionsgeschichte* (1st ed. 1893, 2d ed. 1899), see *Index;* BENZINGER, *Hebräische Archäologie* (1894), pp. 405–28; NOWACK, *Lehrbuch der hebräischen Archäologie* (1894), Vol. II, pp. 87–130; MARTI, *Geschichte der israelitischen Religion* (1897), pp. 44 ff., 50, 72, etc. H. BOURY, *Les Prêtres d'Israel* (1898); HUMMELAUER, *Das vormosaische Priesterthum in Israel* (1899); VAN HOONACKER, *Le Sacerdoce lévitique* (1899), and "Les Prêtres et les Lévites dans le livre d'Ezékiel," *Revue biblique*, 1899, pp. 177–205.

See also the commentaries of Delitzsch, Dillmann, Holzinger, and Gunkel on Genesis; of Dillmann, Holzinger, and Baentzsch on Exodus; of Dillmann and Baentsch on Leviticus; of Steuernagel and Bertholet on Deuteronomy; and of Davidson, Bertholet, and Kraetzschmar on Ezekiel.

§72. Supplementary Topics.

1. Consider that the Psalter was the songbook of the temple, and from an examination of Pss. 78:64; 99:6; 105:26; 106:16, 30 f.; 110:4; 115:10, 12; 118:3; 132:9, 16; 133:2; 134:1–3; 135:19 f. formulate the thought relating to the *priest* which is found in the Psalter.

2. Why do no direct references to the work and life of the *priest* occur in the Wisdom Literature, *i. e.*, in Job, Proverbs, Ecclesiastes, and Song of Songs?

3. Consider briefly the subject of *the priest* in New Testament writings, *e. g.*, Matt. 2:4; 8:4; 12:4 f.; 16:21; 20:18; 21:15; 26:3; 27:1; Mark 2:26; Luke 1:5, 8, 9; 10:31; 17:14; John 1:19;

Acts 4:1, 36; 6:7; Heb. 2:17; 3:1; 4:14 f.; 5:1, 5 f., 10; 6:20; chap. 7; 8:1, 3 f.; 9:6 f., 11, 25; 10:11, 21; 13:11; 1 Peter 2:5, 9; Rev. 1:6; 5:10; 20:6; etc., and indicate such points of difference, as compared with the position and work of the priest in the Old Testament, as seem most important.

4. Compare roughly the place of the priest among the Egyptians, the Greeks, and the Romans, and note points of similarity and difference as compared with that of the priest among the Hebrews.

See W. R. SMITH, article "Priest" in *Encyclopædia Britannica*; the articles "Pontifex" and "Sacerdos" in HARPER'S *Dictionary of Classical Literature and Antiquities;* MARTHA, *Les Sacerdoces athéniens.*

5. Consider the original meaning and exact usage of the words for priest, in Hebrew כֹּהֵן, Greek ἱερεύς, Latin *sacerdos.*

Cf. W. R. SMITH, article "Priest" in *Encyc. Brit.*, Vol. XIX, p. 746; NOWACK, *Hebr. Arch.*, Vol. II, pp. 89 f.; WELLHAUSEN, *Skizzen und Vorarbeiten*, Vol. III, pp. 130 f.

6. Consider the place of the priest among the Assyrians, the Arabs, and the Canaanites, who were closely related Semitic nations, and note points of similarity and difference as compared with his place among the Hebrews.

See especially JASTROW, *Religion of Babylonia and Assyria* (*Index*); W. R. SMITH, *Religion of the Semites* (*Index*); MCCURDY, *History, Prophecy and the Monuments* (*Index*); HAUPT, "Babylonian Elements in the Levitic Ritual," *Journal of Biblical Literature*, Vol. XIX, pp. 55–81; SAYCE, *Babylonians and Assyrians: Life and Customs*, pp. 249 ff.; L. W. KING, *Babylonian Religion and Mythology*, pp. 210 ff.

7. Consider the conception which existed among the Israelites that their nation was a kingdom of priests (*cf.* Exod. 19:6), the basis of this conception, the extent to which it was held, the influence which it exerted, and its connection with other Israelitish ideas, *e. g.*, with the idea of God, with the idea of the Day of Jehovah, and with their conception of their relation to the world.

8. Consider, in general, what may be called the *outside functions* of the priest, *i. e.*, those functions which were not distinctly priestly; *e. g.*, his place in war, Deut. 20:2; Numb. 10:1–9; 1 Sam. 4:4, 11; in education, Lev. 10:11; Neh. 8:2, 9, 13; in administration of justice, Deut. 17:8 f., 12; 19:17; 21:5; in prophecy, Deut. 33:8; Jer. 1:1; Ezek. 1:3; 4:14.

9. From a study of the books of Maccabees prepare a statement showing what were the place, the function, the character, the influence, the dress, the place of residence, and the maintenance of the *priesthood* about 165 B. C.

See, *e. g.*, 1 Macc., chap. 2; 3:45–51; 4:38, 42 f.; 5:6 f.; 7:9, 14 ff., 20–25, 33–38; 10:20 f., 32; 11:23–27, 57 f.; 12:5–23; 13:36 ff., 42; 14:20, 23, 27–49; 15:1 f., 6, 21, 24; 16:11 ff., 24; 2 Macc. 1:15 ff., 19–36; 2:17; 3:1, 9, 15 f., 21, 32–36; 4:7 ff., 24, 29; 11:3; 14:3, 7, 13; 15:12.

10. Take up more seriously the general relation of the priest to the prophet; *e. g.*, (*a*) Was there an early time and a later time when the two offices were not clearly distinguished? (*b*) What were the circumstances, in each case, which led to this lack of distinction? (*c*) How far may the priest be said always to have been engaged in struggle with the prophet? (*d*) What was the relation of each to the other (1) in order of time, (2) in order of thought?

11. Consider the significance of the priest as a mediator between God and the people. What influences led to the idea that this class of men could obtain access to God more readily than other men? What was the relation between the growth of the idea of priestly mediation and the acceptance of larger ideas of God?

CHAPTER VI.

THE LAWS AND USAGES CONCERNING THE PLACE OF WORSHIP, CONSIDERED COMPARATIVELY.

§ 73. **The Place of Worship in the Early Period,** that is, as described in (*a*) the Covenant Code, (*b*) the historical material of J and E, (*c*) the pre-Deuteronomic portions of Judges, Samuel, and Kings, and (*d*) the pre-Deuteronomic prophetic utterances (see § 59, note 1).

1. The only reference in the Covenant Code.[1]
   Exod. 20:24 ff.
2. The patriarchs had sanctuaries in various places, according to convenience.
   Gen. 8:20; 12:6–8; 13:18; 26:24 f.; 28:17, 22; 35:14; Judg. 20:18, 26 ff.; 21:4.
3. A tent of meeting was used as the place for seeking God.
   Exod. 33:7–11; Numb. 11:16 f., 24 f.; 12:4–10; 1 Kings 2:28–30.
4. There was a chest or ark which contained articles emblematic of the divine presence.
   Numb. 10:33–36; Josh., chap. 3; Judg. 20:27.
5. There were local shrines, at which offerings were made.
   Exod. 3:1; **20:24**; Numb. 23:1–6, 14–17; Judg. 6:18–26; 13:15–23; 20:18, 26 ff.; 21:4; 1 Sam. 1:3, 21; 2:14; 3:1–21, 10:8; 14:35; 1 Kings 3:4; 18:30–38; Deut. 27:5–7.
6. In course of time a temple was built for the worship of Jehovah.
   2 Sam. 7:1–7; 24:21–25; 1 Kings 6:1–38; 2 Kings 12:4–16; 15:35*b*; 18:15 f.
7. The altar was used as a place of refuge, and as such was sacred.
   1 Kings 2:28–30.
8. The prophets make reference to places of worship.
   Amos 2:8; 3:14; 4:4; 5:5; 7:9, 13; 8:14; 9:1; Isa. 1:12; 6:1, 4; 8:14; Hos. 4:13, 15; 8:1; 9:4, 8, 15; 10:8; 12:11; Mic. 3:12.

§ 74. **Questions and Suggestions.**

1. Consider, in reference to Exod. 20:24–26, (*a*) the meaning of the emphasis laid on *earth* as the material for the altar; (*b*) the reason

[1] The following are J-references: Gen. 8:20; 12:6–8; 13:18; 26:24 f.; 35:14; Exod. 33:7–11 (?); Numb. 11:16 f., 24 f.; Josh., chap. 3 (in the main); Numb. 23:1–6, 14–17 (?). The following are E-references: Gen. 28:17, 24; Exod. 20:24 ff.; Numb. 12:4–10; 10:33–36; Exod. 3:1; Deut. 27:5–7.

for objection to stone as a material; (*c*) the reason for objection to steps; and (*d*) the general primitive character of the whole regulation. (*Cf.* § 15.)

2. What connection was there between this primitive form of the altar and the custom of the patriarchs to build an altar wherever they pitched their tents? (*Cf.* § 15 (1).)

3. Consider the occasions on which reference is made to the tent of meeting, and note the uses made of it.

4. Was the use made of the ark or chest one which elevated Israel, or one which, upon the whole, encouraged a low conception of God?

5. Was there anything to indicate that this or that place should be used as a shrine or place of worship? Was there danger that in the use of these widely scattered shrines corrupt practices might be introduced? (*Cf.* § 18 (1).)

6. What were the political and social factors that were connected with the building of the temple? What immediate effects upon worship might be expected to follow? (*Cf.* § 17 (1) (*d*).)

7. On what principle did the use of the altar as an asylum or place of refuge rest? Was this a usage among other nations?[2]

8. What impression does one gather from the references made by the prophets to places of worship?

§ 75. **Place of Worship in the Middle Period,** that is, as described in (*a*) the laws of Deuteronomy, (*b*) the utterances of the Deuteronomic prophets, and (*c*) the Deuteronomic histories.

1. All local sanctuaries are prohibited.[3]
   Deut. 12 : 2–4, 13, 17; 16 : 5; 2 Kings 23 : 1–20.
2. Jerusalem is the only authorized place for worship.
   Deut. 12 : 5–8, 11, 12, 14, 18, 26 f.; 14 : 23–26; 15 : 19 f.; 16 : 2, 5–7, 11, 15 f.; 26 : 2; 1 Kings 12 : 25—13 : 6; 21 : 7; 22 : 3–8.
3. The temple at Jerusalem becomes the supreme court of justice.
   Deut. 17 : 8 ff.
4. The ark is the receptacle of the two stone tables of the law.
   Deut. 10 : 1–5, 8.
5. The prophets' teaching concerning the temple.
   Jer. 7 : 1–5, 10–15; 12 : 7; 17 : 12, 26; Zeph. 3 : 4; Hab. 2 : 20.

[2] *Cf.* W. R. SMITH, *Religion of the Semites*, 2d ed., pp. 148 f.; G. F. MOORE, article "Asylum" in *Encyclopædia Biblica;* J. G. FRAZER, "The Origin of Totemism and Exogamy," *Fortnightly Review*, April, 1899; STENGEL, article "Asylon" in *Realencyclopädie der classischen Alterthumswissenschaft;* BARTH, *De Asylis Graecis.*

[3] References in **bold-face** type are from the code of laws contained in Deuteronomy.

6. The destruction of Solomon's temple.
   2 Kings 25:9, 13–16.

§ 76. **Questions and Suggestions.**

1. Consider the *circumstances* which, in the course of centuries, led to the prohibition of local sanctuaries. What was to be gained by this revolution in practice? (*Cf.* § 28 (3).)

2. What must have been the sociological changes which followed the centralization of worship in one place, *e. g.*, its effect on commerce; on the general intelligence of the people; on the relative position of men and women; on habits of life? (*Cf.* § 28 (7).)

3. What would naturally follow such a change of practice in the relative desirability of city and country life, and what would be the effect upon Jerusalem as the center of political and judicial life?

4. Consider the material of which the chest was made and the use to which it was put.

5. Note how in this period the temple had fallen into disrepute in the opinion of the prophets, and why this happened.

6. Consider the details and the significance of the destruction of Solomon's temple.

§ 77. **The Place of Worship in Ezekiel.**

1. There is evidence of the existence of irregular altars.
   Ezek. 6:3, 4, 6, 13.
2. The temple at Jerusalem is represented as the only lawful sanctuary.
   Ezek. 20:40.
3. The temple is desecrated by those who profane its use.
   Ezek. 8:3–18; 23:38 f.; 44:6–8.
4. Feeling toward those who took part in the destruction of the temple.
   Ezek. 25:3.
5. The future temple.
   Ezek. 37:26–28; 40:5—43:17; 44:9; 45:3; 46:1–3; 46:19–24; 48:8 f., 21.

§ 78. **Questions and Suggestions.**

1. Consider the fact that at so late a time as that of Ezekiel there still existed irregular altars, and what was involved in this fact.

2. Note Ezekiel's statement as to the proper place of worship in the future (*cf.* § 31 (*a*)).

3. What were the prophet's feelings as to the abuse of the temple in his times?

4. Consider the relation of Ezekiel's temple (*i. e.*, the temple of his vision) to that of Solomon, (*a*) architecturally, (*b*) in the prominence it is to occupy in the routine of worship.

§ 79. **The Place of Worship in the Later Period,** that is, as described (*a*) in the laws of the Levitical Code, (*b*) by the priestly prophets, and (*c*) in the priestly histories, *e. g.*, Ezra, Nehemiah, Chronicles.

1. Worship may be conducted only at one central sanctuary.[4]
   Lev. 17:1–9; Exod. 29:42–45; 2 Chron. 11:16; Neh. 8:16; *cf.* Isa. 19:19.
2. Ancient sanctuaries are condemned.
   Lev. 26:27–31; Josh. 22:9–34; Isa. 27:9; 1 Chron. 21:28 f.; 2 Chron. 1:1–5; 32:12; 33:17.
3. Description of the tabernacle and its furnishings.
   Exod. 25:8—27:19; 35:4—40:38; Numb. 8:1–4; **Exod. 27:20 f.; Lev. 24:1–4;** Numb. 7:1–83.
4. Description of the ark.
   Exod. 25:10–22; 37:1–9; 2 Chron. 1:1–5.
5. The building of Solomon's temple.
   1 Chron. 17:1 ff.; 21:15 ff.; 21:28 f.; 22:6 ff.; 23:1 ff.; 28:1–3 11–21; 2 Chron. 2:1—5:1; chaps. 6 and 7.
6. The building of the second temple.
   Ezra 1:2 ff.; 2:68; 3:8–13: 5:2–5; 5:6 ff.; 6:3 ff., 14 ff.; 7:19–23
7. A later view of the place of the tabernacle in religious life.
   Numb. 9:15–23.
8. Later views of the place of Solomon's temple in Israel's worship.
   2 Chron. 20:28; 24:4–15; 27:2 f.; chap. 29.
9. The sanctuary as the place of God's self-manifestation.
   Exod. 25:22; 29:43; Numb. 16:41 ff.; Mal. 3:1; Numb. 7:89.
10. The altar of burnt-offering.
    Lev. 1:10 ff.; 6:9–13; Numb. 16:36–40; 7:84–88.
11. The prophets' attitude toward the sanctuary.
    Isa. 56:7; 60:7; Hag. 1:2–4, 7 f.; 2:3, 9; Zech. 1:16; 4:9; 6:12–15; 8:9; 14:16 ff.; Mal. 3:1; Mic. 4:1–4; Joel 1:9, 13 f. 16; Dan. 8:11; 9:17; 11:31.
12. Holiness of the sanctuary.
    Lev. 26:2; 19:30; 8:10 f.; Numb. 3:31 f.; 4:4–15; Neh. 6:10 f.; 13:4 ff.; 2 Chron. 33:4, 7, 15; 36:17; Dan. 8:11; 9:17; 11:31.

[4] References to the Levitical Code are in **bold-face** type.

§ 80. **Questions and Suggestions.**

1. Note that what was represented as a matter of reform in the middle period, viz., the restriction of worship to a single central sanctuary, now appears as a fundamental principle, everywhere taken for granted.

2. Consider the attitude of writers of this period to the sanctuaries which had existed in earlier times.

3. Note (*a*) the great detail with which the tabernacle is described; (*b*) the elaborate character of the tabernacle from an artistic point of view; and consider whether this description is to be taken (1) literally, a tent of this kind having actually existed in the earliest times, or (2) as a piece of splendid idealization, similar in some respects to Ezekiel's vision. What is involved in each of these propositions?

4. What, in general, was the ark, and what, in particular, was the purpose it was intended to serve?

5. Compare the references in Chronicles to the building of Solomon's temple with those in Kings (§ 73 (6)), and classify the results of the comparison.

6. Consider in the case of the second temple (*a*) the date of its erection; (*b*) its relative size and character in comparison with the first; (*c*) the special circumstances under which it was built.

7. What was the later view of the place of the tabernacle in Israel's religious life, as seen in Numb. 9: 15–23?

8. Consider later views also as to the place of Solomon's temple in Israel's worship.

9. To what extent was Israel's God believed to use the sanctuary as a place for manifesting his presence?

10. What was the altar of burnt-offering and its peculiar function?

11. How did the later prophets regard the sanctuary and its service?

12. What is meant by the *holiness* of the sanctuary, and in what did this consist?

§ 81. **Literature to be Consulted.**

JAMES FERGUSSON, article "Temple" in SMITH'S *Dictionary of the Bible* (1863); EWALD, *The Antiquities of Israel* (3d ed. 1866, transl. 1876), pp. 117–30; KUENEN, *The Religion of Israel* (1869 f., transl. 1874 f.), Vol. I, pp. 96–100, 241 f., 256–60, 305 f., 328 ff., 334–9, 390–95; OEHLER, *Old Testament Theology* (1870, transl. 1883), pp. 250–58; EDERSHEIM, *The Temple, its Ministry and Services as They Existed in the Time of Jesus Christ* (1874); TYLOR, *Primitive Culture* (1874), see *Index, s. v.* "Sacred Springs, etc.;" WELLHAUSEN, *Prolegomena to the History of Israel* (1878), pp. 17–51; CONDER, *Palestine Exploration Fund Quarterly Statement*, 1882, pp. 75 ff.; W. R. SMITH, *The Prophets of Israel* (1st ed. 1882, 2d ed. 1895), see *Index, s. v.*

"Sanctuaries;" H. P. SMITH, "The High Place," *The Hebrew Student*, 1883, pp. 225–34; CONDER, *Heth and Moab* (1883), chaps. vii, viii; PERROT AND CHIPIEZ, *History of Art in Phœnicia* (1885); E. C. ROBINS, *The Temple of Solomon* (1887); CONDER, *Syrian Stone Lore* (1887), pp. 42 f., 70; KITTEL, *History of the Hebrews* (1888–92, transl. 1895), see *Index, s. v.* "High Places," "Temple;" ROBERTSON, *Early Religion of Israel* (1889), see *Index, s. v.* "Sanctuaries," "Tabernacle," "Temple," etc.; W. R. SMITH, article "Temple" in *Encyclopedia Britannica* (1889); W. R. SMITH, *Religion of the Semites* (1st ed. 1889, 2d ed. 1894), pp. 140–212; H. SULLY, *The Temple of Ezekiel's Prophecy* (1889); PERROT AND CHIPIEZ, *History of Art in Judæa* (1890); J. POLLARD, "On the Baal and Ashtoreth Altar Discovered . . . . in Syria," *Proceedings of the Society of Biblical Archæology*, 1891, pp. 286 ff.; DUFF, *Old Testament Theology* (1891–1900), see *Indexes, s. v.* "Altar," "Place," "Sanctuary," etc.; SCHULTZ, *Old Testament Theology* (1892), see *Index, s. v.* "Sanctuary," "Tabernacle," "Temple," etc.; C. BALLING, *Jerusalem's Temple* (1892); MONTEFIORE, *Religion of the Ancient Hebrews* (1892), see *Index, s. v.* "High Places," "Temple;" J. STRONG, "The Tabernacle," *Biblical World*, Vol. I (1893), pp. 270–77; MENZIES, *History of Religion* (1895), see *Index, s. v.* "Temples;" MCCURDY, *History, Prophecy and the Monuments*, Vols. I–III (1895–1901), see *Index, s. v.* "Temple;" DRIVER, *Deuteronomy* (1895), pp. xliii–li; W. G. MOOREHEAD, *Studies in the Mosaic Institutions* (1896), pp. 31–90; TRUMBULL, *The Threshold Covenant* (1896), pp. 1–164; WIEDEMANN, *Religion of the Ancient Egyptians* (1897), pp. 200–206; H. B. GREENE, "Hebrew Rock Altars," *Biblical World*, Vol. IX (1897), pp. 329–40; A. BÜCHLER, "The Fore-Court of Women and the Brass Gate in the Temple of Jerusalem," *Jewish Quarterly Review*, 1898, pp. 678–718; J. A. SEISS, "The Great Temples at Baalbec," *Lutheran Church Review*, 1898, pp. 271–93; JASTROW, *Religion of Babylonia and Assyria* (1898), see *Index, s. v.* "Temples;" G. C. M. DOUGLAS, "Ezekiel's Temple," *Expository Times*, 1898, pp. 365 ff., 420 ff., 468 ff., 515–19; A. S. KENNEDY, article "Altar" in HASTINGS' *Dictionary of the Bible* (1898); C. SCHICK, "Remarks on the Tabernacle Controversy," *Palestine Exploration Fund Quarterly Statement*, 1898, pp. 241–3; EM. SCHMIDT, "Solomon's Temple," *Biblical World*, Vol. XIV (1899), pp. 164–71; A. H. SAYCE, *Babylonians and Assyrians: Life and Customs* (1899), pp. 246 ff.; W. E. ADDIS, article "Altar" in *Encyclopædia Biblica* (1899); W. C. ALLEN, article "High Place" in HASTINGS' *Dictionary of the Bible* (1899); BENSON AND GOURLAY, *The Temple of Mut in Asher, etc.* (1899); T. F. WRIGHT, "Was the Tabernacle Oriental?" *Journal of Biblical Literature*, 1899, pp. 195–8; TH. G. SOARES, "Ezekiel's Temple," *Biblical World*, Vol. XIV (1899), pp. 93–103; S. I. CURTISS, "The High Place and Altar at Petra," *Palestine Exploration Fund Quarterly Statement*, 1900, pp. 351–5; L. W. BATTEN, "The Sanctuary at Shiloh," *Journal of Biblical Literature*, Vol. XIX (1900), pp. 29–33; G. ALLEN, "Sacred Stones," *Fortnightly Review*, January, 1900; STIBITZ, "The Centralization of Jehovah Worship in Israel," *Reformed Church Review*, January, 1900; JOHN ADAMS, *The Mosaic Tabernacle: Studies in the Priesthood and the Sanctuary of the Jews* (1901); G. F. MOORE, article "High Place" in *Encyclopædia Biblica* (1901).

BÄHR, *Der salomonische Tempel, mit Berücksichtigung seines Verhältnisses zur hebräischen Architektur überhaupt* (1848); MERZ, article "Tempel" in *Real-Encyklopädie für protestantische Theologie und Kirche* (1st ed. 1854–68, 2d ed. 1877 ff.); BALMER-RINCK, *Des Propheten Ezechiel Gesicht vom Tempel* (1858); KAMPHAUSEN, "Bemerkungen über die Stiftshütte," *Theologische Studien und Kritiken*, 1858, pp. 97–121;

1859, pp. 110–20; FRIES, "Zu Kamphausen's Bemerkungen über die Stiftshütte," *Theologische Studien und Kritiken*, 1859, pp. 103–10; POPPER, *Der biblische Bericht über die Stiftshütte* (1862); RIGGENBACH, "Die mosaische Stiftshütte: Selbstanzeige," *Theologische Studien und Kritiken*, 1863, pp. 361–8; H. PIERSON, *De heilige steenen in Israel* (1864 ff.); H. OORT, "De heiligdommen van Jehovah te Dan en te Bethel vóor Jerobeam I.," *Theologisch Tijdschrift*, 1867, pp. 285–306; DUHM, *Die Theologie der Propheten* (1875), pp. 312–20; BAUDISSIN, *Studien zur semitischen Religionsgeschichte*, Vol. II (1878), pp. 143–269; KÜHN, "Ezechiel's Gesicht vom Tempel der Vollendungszeit," *Theologische Studien und Kritiken*, 1882, pp. 601–88; KOHLBRÜGGE, *Die Stiftshütte und ihre Geräthe* (1882); STADE, "Der Text des Berichtes über Salomos Bauten, I Kö. 5–7," *Zeitschrift für die alttestamentliche Wissenschaft*, 1883, pp. 129–77; SMEND, "Ueber die Bedeutung des jerusalemischen Tempels in der alttestamentlichen Religion," *Theologische Studien und Kritiken*, 1884, pp. 689–740; SCHÜRER, article "Tempel Salomo's" in RIEHM'S *Handwörterbuch des biblischen Alterthums* (1884); H. PAILLOUX, *Monographie du temple de Salomon* (1885); STADE, *Geschichte des Volkes Israel* (1887 f.), Vol. I, pp. 325–43, 446–67; Vol. II, pp. 45 ff., 113–28, 245–51; WELLHAUSEN, *Reste des arabischen Heidenthums* (1887), pp. 42–60, 98–105, 113, 171; TH. FRIEDRICH, *Tempel und Palast Salomos u. s. w.* (1887); O. WOLFF, *Der Tempel von Jerusalem und seine Maasse* (1887); H. L. SCHOUTEN, *De tabernakel Gods heiligdom by Israel* (1888); C. CHIPIEZ ET G. PERROT, *Le temple de Jérusalem et la maison du Bois-Libanon, restitués d'après Ezechiel et le livre des Rois* (1889); F. V. ANDRIAN, *Der Höhenkult asiatischer und europäischer Völker* (1891); PIEPENBRING, "Histoire des lieux de culte et du sacerdoce en Israel," *Revue de l'histoire des religions*, Vol. XXIV (1891), pp. 1–60, 133–86; E. DE BROGLIE, "La loi de l'unité de sanctuaire en Israel," *Compte rendu du congrès scientifique international des catholiques*, 1892, 2d sect., pp. 69–89; MARTI, *Geschichte der israelitischen Religion* (1897), pp. 27–31, 98–103; SMEND, *Lehrbuch der alttestamentlichen Religionsgeschichte* (1st ed. 1893, 2d ed. 1899), pp. 128–38; BENZINGER, *Hebräische Archäologie* (1894), pp. 243–9, 364–404; NOWACK, *Lehrbuch der hebräischen Archäologie* (1894), Vol. II, pp. 1–86; DILLMANN, *Handbuch der alttestamentlichen Theologie* (1895), see *Index, s. v.* "Tempel;" H. A. POELS, *Le sanctuaire de Kirjath-Jearim* (1895); S. A. FRIES, *Den israelitiska kultens centralisation* (1895); E. SCHURÉ, *Sanctuaires d'Orient, Égypte, Grèce, Palestine* (1898); AUG. FREIHERR VON GALL, *Altisraelitische Kultstätten* (1898); B. A., "Die heiligen Stätten in Palästina," *Beilage zur Allgemeinen Zeitung* (1898), No. 221; F. TOURNIER, "Notes sur les temples païens de furvière à l'époque romaine," *L'Université catholique*, 1899, pp. 361–92; BASSET, "Les sanctuaires du Djebel Nefousa," *Journal asiatique*, 1900; MEINHOLD, *Die Lade Jahves* (1900); ERNST SELLIN, *Studien zur Entstehungsgeschichte der jüdischen Gemeinde nach dem babylonischen Exil*, Vol. II (1901), pp. 44–56; B. STADE, "Die Kesselwagen des salomonischen Tempels, 1 Kö. 7:27–39," *Zeitschrift für die alttestamentliche Wissenschaft*, Vol. XXI (1901), pp. 145–90; K. BUDDE, "Die ursprüngliche Bedeutung der Lade Jahwe's," *ibid.* (1901).

§ 82. Supplementary Topics.

1. Consider the following citations from the book of Psalms: 5:7; 11:4; 20:2; 22:25; 24:3; 26:6–8, 12; 27:4–6; 28:2; 29:9; 36:8; 40:9; 42:4; 43:3 f.; 46:4; 48:1 f., 8 f.; 51:18 f.; 52:8; 55:14; 61:4; 63:2; 65:1, 4; 66:13; 68:15–17, 24, 29; 69:9;

73:17; 74:2 ff.; 76:2; 77:13; 78:54, 58, 60, 68 f.; 79:1–13; 84; 87; 92:13; 93:5; 96:6–8; 99:9; 100:4; 102:13 ff.; 114:2; 122; 125:1; 127:1 (?); 132; 134; 135:1 f.; 138:2; and formulate a statement concerning *the place of worship* as it stands related to the idea of worship as expressed in the Psalter.

2. Examine the allusions to *the place of worship* found in the apocryphal books, *e. g.*, 1 Macc. 4:36–59; 5:1, 68; 6:7, 18, 26, 51, 54; 7:33–38; 9:54–57; 10:41–44; 11:37; 13:3, 6; 14:15, 48; 16:20; 2 Macc. 1:8, 15 ff., 18, 32–34; 2:1 ff., 17–19, 22; 3:2, 12, 14 ff.; 4:14; 5:15–21; 6:2–5; 8:17; 9:16; 10:1–8, 26; 13:8, 23; 14:4, 31–33, 36; and note any important modifications which seem to have been made.

3. Consider *the place of worship* as it is referred to in the New Testament, *e. g.*, in Matt. 4:3; 6:2, 6; 9:35; 12:4–6, 9; 13:54; 21:12–14, 23; 23:16–22, 35; 24:1 ff., 15; 26:61; 27:5; Mark 1:21–29; 3:1; 5:22, 35 ff.; 6:2 ff.; 11:15 ff., 27; 12:41 ff.; 13:1 ff., 9; 14:58; Luke 1:8–23; 2:22 ff., 41 ff.; 4:16, 20, 28, 33, 38, 44; 6:6; 8:41, 49; 13:10; 19:45 ff.; 21:1–6, 37 f.; 22:52 f.; John 2:13–22; 4:19–24; 7:14, 28; 11:55 ff.; 16:2; Acts 1:13 f.; 2:1 ff., 46; 3:1 ff.; 4:1; 6:13 f.; 9:1 f., 20; 13:14 f., 43; 14:1; 16:16; 17:1 ff., 10, 17; 18:4, 8, 19; 19:8 f.; 20:7 ff.; 21:26 ff.; 22:19; 25:8; 28:30 f.; 1 Cor. 8:10; 16:19; Eph. 2:19–22; 1 Tim. 3:15; Philem., vs. 1; Heb. 8:1 f.; 9:1–12, 24 f.; 10:19 f.; 12:18 ff.; 13:10 ff.; Rev. 8:3; 9:13; 11:1 f., 19; 14:15, 18; 15:5–8; 21:3, 22; and formulate the points of difference which appear.

4. Study the origin and development of the synagogue, noting (*a*) its relation to the temple, (*b*) the different character of its services as compared with those of the temple, (*c*) its origin in response to a great religious need, and (*d*) its historical significance as the forerunner of the church, the Christian place of worship. See, *e. g.*, Ezek. 8:1; 20:1–3; Ps. 74:8; Matt. 9:35; 12:9; Mark 5:35; 6:1 ff.; Acts 9:1 ff.; 13:13 ff.; 14:1; 17:1, etc.[5]

5. Study the causes which led to the building of the Samaritan

[5] See article "Synagogue" in *Encyclopædia Britannica;* E. H. PLUMPTRE, article "Synagogue" in SMITH'S *Dictionary of the Bible;* SCHULTZ, *Old Testament Theology*, Vol. I, pp. 428 ff.; MONTEFIORE, *Religion of the Ancient Hebrews* (see *Index*, *s. v.* "Synagogue"); SCHÜRER, *History of the Jewish People in the Time of Christ*, Div. II, Vol. I, pp. 52–83; EDERSHEIM, *Life and Times of Jesus the Messiah*, Vol. I, pp. 430–50; FERGUSON, *The Synagogue Service in the Time of Christ;* KENT, *A History of the Jewish People* (see *Index*).

temple on Mount Gerizim. Was this movement a source of strength or of weakness to the Jewish community in Jerusalem? What was the attitude of Jesus toward the Samaritan temple? See, *e. g.*, Ezra, chap. 4; Neh. 2:18–20; 4:1–23; 6:1–19; 13:28; John 4:19–24 (*cf.* § 45).

6. Consider the causes which have led to the change of view as to the function of the place of worship seen in the fact that originally a temple was looked upon as the abode of the deity, while now it is regarded primarily as a meeting-place for worshipers.

7. Make a special study of Hezekiah's reform (see 2 Kings 18:3–7, 22; *cf.* 2 Chron. 29:3—31:20; 32:12), considering (1) the question concerning the age of the narratives; (2) the preparation for such a reform prior to Hezekiah's time; (3) the suggestion that the reform followed, rather than preceded, Sennacherib's invasion; (4) the probable relation of Isaiah to the reform movement; (5) the influence of such an attempt in preparing the way for a later reform.

See W. R. SMITH, *Prophets of Israel*, p. 363; STADE, *Geschichte des Volkes Israel*, Vol. I, pp. 607 f., 623; RENAN, *History of the People of Israel*, Vol. II, p. 518; CHEYNE, *Introduction to the Book of Isaiah*, p. 365; WELLHAUSEN, *Prolegomena to the History of Israel*, p. 23; STADE, *Zeitschrift für die alttestamentliche Wissenschaft*, Vol. III, pp. 8 ff.; VI, pp. 170 ff.; KITTEL, *History of the Hebrews*, Vol. II, pp. 355 ff.; CHEYNE, article "Hezekiah," HASTINGS'S *Dictionary of the Bible;* MCCLYMONT, article "Hezekiah," *Encyclopædia Biblica;* and the commentaries on Kings by KITTEL, BENZINGER, and SKINNER.

CHAPTER VII.

THE LAWS AND USAGES CONCERNING SACRIFICE, CONSIDERED COMPARATIVELY.

§ 83. **Sacrifice in the Early Period,** that is, as described in (*a*) the Covenant Code, (*b*) the historical material of J and E, (*c*) the pre-Deuteronomic portions of Judges, Samuel, and Kings, and (*d*) the pre-Deuteronomic prophetic utterances (see § 59, note 1).

1. Kinds of offerings.[1]
   Gen. 28:18; 35:14; Exod. 8:20 f.; 10:24 ff.; 18:12; 20:24; 24:5; Judg. 6:26; 1 Sam. 10:8; 21:6; 1 Kings 3:4; 12:26–33; 2 Kings 16:12 f.; Isa. 1:11–13; Hos. 4:13; 9:4; 11:2.
2. Materials of sacrifice.
   Gen. 4:3; 15:9 ff.; 8:20 ff.; 22:1–13; 28:18; 35:14; Exod. 20:24; Numb. 23:1–4, 14; Judg. 13:16–19; 6:18–24, 26; 1 Sam. 7:9 f.; 21:6; 1 Kings 8:5.
3. Manner of sacrifice.
   Exod. 34:25; 23:18; Numb. 23:1–4, 14; 1 Sam. 2:13–17; 2 Sam. 6:13; 1 Kings 18:30–38; 2 Kings 16:12 f.
4. Occasion and purpose of sacrifice.
   Gen. 46:1*b*; Exod. 23:15*c*; 34:20*c*; Numb. 23:1–4, 14; Judg. 6:18–24; 13:16–19; 1 Sam. 1:3 ff.; 6:15; 7:9 f.; 11:15; 20:29; 2 Sam. 6:13, 17 f.; 24:22–25; 1 Kings 8:5; 18:30–38.
5. Sacrifice was often a social or family meal.
   Gen. 18:1–8; 31:54; Exod. 18:12; Numb. 22:40; Deut. 27:6*b*, 7; 1 Sam. 1:3 ff.; 9:12 f.; 16:2, 5; 20:29.
6. Human sacrifice was not unknown.
   Gen. 22:1–13; Hos. 13:2(?).
7. Sacrifice to idols was common.
   Exod. 32:6; 1 Kings 12:26–33; 2 Kings 5:17(?); 10:19, 24 f.; Hos. 4:13; 11:2.
8. The priest was given a share of the sacrifice.
   1 Sam. 2:13–17.

[1] The following are J-references: Gen. 4:3; 8:20 ff.; 18:1–8; 35:14; Exod. 8:20 f.; 34:20*c*, 25; Numb. 23:1–4, 14 (?); Deut. 27:6*b*, 7 (?). The following are E-references: Gen. 15:9 ff.; 22:1–13, 28:18; 31:54; 46:1*b*; Exod. 10:24 ff.; 18:12; 20:24; 23:15*c*, 18; 24:5; 32:6; Numb. 22:40.

9. The prophets' attitude toward sacrifice.
Amos 4:4 f.; 5:22–25; Hos. 3:4; 4:13, 19; 6:6; 8:13; 9:4; 11:2; 13:2; Isa. 1:11–13; 34:6.

§ 84. **Questions and Suggestions.**

1. What were the various kinds of offerings made in this period? What significance attached to each kind — for example, what was the meaning of the burnt-offering? of the peace-offering? of the passover offering? Consider to what extent (*a*) sacrifice in this period was equivalent to a social meal; (*b*) the eating of meat was a sacrificial act; (*c*) the spirit of joy accompanied the act.

2. Note the kinds of material used in sacrifice, for example, the flesh of animals (what animals? animals of what age?), oil, wine, meal. What was the reason underlying the use of each of these kinds of material?

3. Why was leavened bread not to be used in connection with a sacrifice? Why was no part of the sacrifice to be left over until the morning of the following day? What points concerning sacrifice may be noted in connection with Balaam's sacrifice (Numb. 23:1–4, 14, 27–30)? Consider the custom of the priests in Samuel's time, and what it involved. Study Elijah's sacrifice on Gilgal, and note the bearing of the details on the subject.

4. Upon what occasion, and under what circumstances, were sacrifices offered? What purpose lay in the mind of the offerer? What was sought for in the act?

5. When sacrifice was only a social or family meal, what was the religious element? Was the deity ever thought to partake of the meal? Was the deity ever supposed to be related to the family? What was the connection between this social act and the spirit of joy which, in early times, seems to have characterized the act of sacrifice?

6. Consider the willingness of Abraham to sacrifice his son Isaac, and what was involved in this willingness? Explain to yourself the custom of human sacrifice; how could it have arisen? what wrong ideas did it rest upon?

7. Note some of the instances in which sacrifice was offered to idols. Since the idols were believed to represent deities, either that of Israel or those of other nations, was this not something clearly to have been expected?

8. Note that in this period the priest, whatever other kind of support he may have received, was given a share of the sacrifice.

9. Formulate a statement containing the substance of the prophet's

attitude toward sacrifice; and consider whether the prophet was opposing (*a*) the act of sacrifice itself; or (*b*) a cold, indifferent, hypocritical spirit, with which men in those days had become accustomed to offer sacrifice; or (*c*) the feeling, which had become quite general, that sacrifice was enough to gain Jehovah's pleasure, that this was all that he expected, and that this, without reference to conduct, constituted religion.

§ 85. **Constructive Work.**— Prepare a statement on *sacrifice in the early period*, embodying the material presented above.

§ 86. **Sacrifice in the Middle Period,** that is, as described in the laws of Deuteronomy, in the Deuteronomic prophecies, and in the Deuteronomic portions of the books of Samuel and Kings.

1. Kinds of offerings.[2]
   Deut. 12 : 4–7, 16; Mic. 6 : 6–8; Jer. 17 : 26; 33 : 11, 18.
2. Materials of sacrifice.
   Deut. 16 : 2–4; Mic. 6 : 6–8; Jer. 6 : 20; Isa. 43 : 23 ff.; 1 Sam. 2 : 27.
3. Manner of offering.
   Deut. 12 : 27; 16 : 7; Jer. 33 : 18; 1 Sam. 2 : 27.
4. Occasion and purpose of offerings.
   Deut. 16 : 2–4; 1 Sam. 3 : 14; Jer. 33 : 11.
5. Social element in sacrifice.
   Deut. 12 : 4–14; 1 Kings 3 : 15.
6. Slaughter and sacrifice are no longer synonymous terms.
   Deut. 12 : 15, 20–28.
7. Priest's portion of the sacrifice.
   Deut. 18 : 3, 4; 1 Sam. 2 : 28, 36.
8. Human sacrifice still existed.
   Mic. 6 : 6–8.
9. Prophets' attitude toward sacrifice.
   Zeph. 1 : 7, 8; Mic. 6 : 6–8; Jer. 6 : 20; 7 : 21 f., 29; 17 : 26; 33 : 11, 18; 46 : 10; Isa. 43 : 23 f.

§ 87. **Questions and Suggestions.**

1. Note in Deut. 12 : 4–7 (*a*) the kinds of offerings mentioned (including tithe, heave-offering, free-will offering), and (*b*) the spirit of rejoicing in which these offerings are to be made. Consider in Mic. 6 : 6–8 (*a*) the possibilities of sacrifice (including that of one's own child), (*b*) the purpose of sacrifice, and (*c*) the requirement of Jehovah.

2. Consider the materials used in sacrifice, as mentioned in passages

[2] References in **bold-face** type are from the code of laws contained in Deuteronomy.

cited above, and note any variations in comparison with those used in the earlier age.

3. Consider (*a*) the use made of the blood; its pouring on the altar; (*b*) the roasting of the flesh; (*c*) the eating of the flesh; (*d*) the employment of men "to burn meal-offerings and to do sacrifice."

4. Consider the connection of the Passover with the going-up of Israel out of Egypt, (*a*) in relation to time (was there not a spring feast celebrated by the ancient nations before the exodus?); (*b*) in relation to ceremony (why was unleavened bread to be used?); (*c*) in relation to the purpose of the act. Was the sacrifice intended to purge or purify from sin? Was sacrifice intended also to be an expression of gratitude for some favor already received?

5. Is the social element still to be seen in this period, that is, does the family or clan meal, with all its social accompaniments, constitute a sacrifice?

6. What new distinction has arisen as between the slaughter of animals and the act of sacrifice? Wherein does the distinction consist? What led to the making of the distinction? What, naturally, will follow as a result of making this distinction?

7. Note (*a*) the particular portions of each animal sacrificed, which are assigned as the portion of the priest, that is, for his maintenance; (*b*) the additional perquisites he receives in the way of grain, oil, wine, and meal; and (*c*) the ground for these gifts.

8. What evidence is there that in this period human beings are still used for sacrifice?

9. Consider the attitude of the prophets of this period toward sacrifice, and determine (see §84, 9) the real meaning of this attitude.

§88. **Constructive Work.**—Prepare a statement which will contain, in some detail, the differences between the usages of the middle period in respect to sacrifice, and those of the early period.

§89. **Sacrifice as Presented by Ezekiel.**

1. Kinds of offerings.
   Ezek. 40:39; 42:13; 46:12; 45:13–17; 20:40.

2. Materials of sacrifice.
   Ezek. 44:15; 46:4–7.

3. Manner of sacrifice.
   Ezek. 40:38–43; 44:11, 15; 46:4–15, 24.

4. Occasion and purpose of sacrifice.
   Ezek. 46:4–15; 43:18–27; 45:13–25.

5. Sacrifice was still thought of as a banquet.
   Ezek. 39:17–20; 46:24.
6. Sacrifice was still offered to idols.
   Ezek. 20:28–31.
7. Human sacrifice.
   Ezek. 16:20 f.; 23:39.
8. Priests retained a share of the sacrifice.
   Ezek. 42:13.

§ 90. **Constructive Work.**—Consider the various allusions to sacrifice in Ezekiel, under the topics suggested above, and prepare a statement covering (*a*) the points of resemblance and difference in comparison with the facts of the early and middle periods; (*b*) the more formal and official character with which sacrifice seems to be invested by Ezekiel; (*c*) the exceedingly elaborate system of sacrifice provided for, *e. g.*, in 46:4–15; (*d*) the fact that, notwithstanding all this, the earlier idea of sacrifice as a banquet still exists (39:17–20; 46:24).

§ 91. **Sacrifice in the Later Period**, that is, as described in (*a*) the laws of the Levitical Code, (*b*) by the priestly prophets, and (*c*) in the priestly histories, *e. g.*, Ezra, Nehemiah, Chronicles.

1. Kinds of offerings.[3]
   Lev. 7: 1, 11; **6: 9, 14, 25; 8: 22; 23: 10*b*, 11, 13; Exod. 25: 30; 30: 7; Numb. 15: 19; 5: 11–31.**
2. Materials of sacrifice.
   Lev. 1: 1–3, 10, 14; 2: 1, 4 f., 7, 11, 13–15; 3: 1, 3 f., 6 f., 9 f., 12, 14 f., 16 f.; 5: 6 f., 11; 6: 1–7, 15, 19 f.; 7: 3–5, 11 ff.; 9: 1–4; 12: 6–8; 14: 10, 49; 24: 5–9; Numb. 15: 1–21; Exod. 29: 1–3, 22 f., 38–42; Numb., chap. 28; Exod. 30: 34–38; Lev. 22: 18–25, 27 f.; 23: 10*b*–14.
3. The fat and blood are regarded as especially sacred.
   Lev. 7: 22–27; 8: 15, 23 f.; 9: 19–21; 17: 6; etc.
4. Manner of sacrifice.
   Lev. 1: 3–9, 11–13, 15–17; 2: 1 f., 4–16; 3: 1–17; 4: 1–35; 5: 8 f., 12; 6: 1–7, 8–13, 14–18, 19–23, 24–30; 7: 1 ff., 11–21; 8: 14–30; 9: 8–11, 12–14, 15–24; 14: 10–32, 49–53; 16: 3–28; 24: 5–9; Numb. 5: 11–31; 19: 1–22; Exod. 29: 10–42; 30: 7–10; Lev. 22: 29 f.; 19: 5–8.
5. Occasion and purpose of sacrifice.
   Lev. 4: 1–3, 13 f., 20, 22–28, 31, 35; 5: 1–6, 13–15, 17–19; 6: 1–7, 30; 9: 7; 12: 6–8; 14: 20, 31, 53; 15: 13–15, 28–30; 23: 10*b*–21; Numb. 5: 11–31; 15: 17–21, 22–28; 19: 1–22; chap. 28; Exod. 30: 7–10.

[3] References to the Levitical Code are in **bold-face** type.

6. The priests' share of the sacrifice.
   Lev. 2 : 3, 10 ; 5 : 13 ; 6 : 16–18, 26, 29 ; 7 : 6–10, 14, 28–38 ; 8 : 31 ; 10 : 12–20 ; Numb. 5 : 5–10 ; Exod. 29:27–32 ; Numb. 18 : 8–20.
7. All slaughter is sacrificial.
   Lev. 17: 1–9.
8. Few references to idolatrous sacrifices.
   Lev. 17:7.
9. Attitude of the prophets toward sacrifice.
   Isa. 19 : 21 ; 56 : 7 ; 66 : 3 ; Mal. 1 : 7–9 ; 3 : 3–5 ; Joel 1 : 9, 13 ; 2 : 14 ; Dan. 9 : 27.
10. Sacrifice is given a large place in the later histories.
   1 Chron. 15 : 26 ; 16 : 1 ; 21 : 26 ff.; 29 : 21 f.; 2 Chron. 1 : 5 ; 2 : 4 ; 5 : 6; 7 : 4 ff.; 8 : 12 f.; 11 : 16 ; 13 : 11 ; 15 : 11 ; 24 : 14 ; 29 : 20–36 ; 30 : 15 ff.; 31 : 2 ff.; 33 : 16 f.; Ezra 3 : 2 ff.; 6 : 17 ; 7 : 17 ; 8 : 35 ; 10 : 19 ; Neh. 10 : 33 f.; 12 : 43 f.
11. Prominence of the idea of sin in connection with sacrifice.
   Lev. 4: 35 ; chap. 16 ; 9: 3 ; 10: 16 ff.; Numb. 15: 22–31 ; 19 : 1–9.

§92. **Questions and Suggestions.**— How much in detail the various topics concerning sacrifice in the later period shall be taken up will be determined in some measure by one's archæological interests. In any case, these topics deserve consideration because of their sociological, as well as their religious, bearing :

1. Prepare a list of the kinds of offerings, viz., burnt-offering, peace-offering, sin-offering, etc., including vows, the offering involved in Naziritism, the offering of purification. From the passages describing each, and from a study of the name (in English and, if possible, in Hebrew), differentiate these various offerings from each other and determine what was distinctly characteristic in each case. Consider, now, whether any principle of classification exists ; *e. g.*: (*a*) Are they, in each case, voluntary or obligatory? (*b*) Are they, in each case, self-dedicatory, eucharistic, or expiatory? Suggest any other possible bases for classification.

2. Take up, one by one, the materials which might be used in sacrifice, noting, (*a*) in reference to animal offerings : (1) the particular animals which were deemed acceptable ; (2) the possible explanations of the selection of these animals with the rejection of others ; (3) whether the distinction between clean and unclean animals[4] was in any way connected with the choice for sacrifice ; (*b*) in reference to vegetable

[4] *Cf.* Lev., chap. 11 ; Deut. 14 : 3–21 ; and see G. A. SIMCOX, article "Clean and Unclean," § 8, in *Encyclopædia Biblica*, and chap. x.

offerings: (1) the particular vegetables authorized; (2) the reason or reasons for this selection; (*c*) the character of offerings worthy of being accepted; (*d*) other possible gifts outside of animals and vegetables, *e. g.*, one's hair,[5] one's virginity,[6] one's blood;[7] (*e*) objects connected more or less closely with sacrifice, *e. g.*, wine, incense, salt, oil, blood, fat, leaven, honey; (*f*) the meaning or significance of each kind of material as employed in sacrifice.

3. Note the particularly important emphasis placed upon the use of the blood and fat, and consider what was involved in this, and the principle underlying it.

4. Study, in detail, the method of sacrifice, viz., (*a*) the ceremonial of the animal sacrifice which included (1) the circumstances connected with the presentation of the victim, *e. g.*, the laying on of hands, the time, the place, (2) the slaughter, (3) the use made of the blood, (4) the flaying of the animal and its dissection, (5) the burning, (6) the washing, (7) the waving and heaving, (8) the sacrificial meal; (*b*) the ceremonial, in similar fashion, of the vegetable offering; (*c*) the ceremonial of the drink-offering; (*d*) the distinction involved between burning the offering and eating it; (*e*) the distinction involved between consuming all and only a portion.

5. Study the occasion and purpose of sacrifice as it appears in the later period, considering (*a*) how far it is *national*, *i. e.*, offered for the nation as a whole (*cf.* Exod. 29:38–42; Numb. 28:9—29:6); (*b*) how far it is *official*, *i. e.*, offered for certain officers of the state, the priest, or the ruler (*cf.* Numb. 4:22–26); (*c*) how far it is *individual*, *i. e.*, offered for the ordinary man as an individual; (*d*) how far it is *festal*, *i. e.*, associated with feasts, *e. g.*, the Passover, the Feast of Harvest; (*e*) how far it is *extraordinary*, *i. e.*, connected with special rather than regularly recurring events; (*f*) how far it is *local* or *centralized*, *i. e.*, offered where one chanced to be, or at some place selected from all other places, and authorized as the proper and only proper place; (*g*) how far it is, in this period, a gift or offering, rather than the payment of a demand or of something due.

6. Put together the various elements which made up the priest's

[5] See Lev. 19:27; 21:5; *cf.* Jer. 7:29, and W. R. SMITH, *Religion of the Semites*, 2d ed., pp. 323–35.

[6] *Cf.* 1 Kings 14:24; 15:12; 22:47; 2 Kings 23:7; NOWACK, *Hebräische Archäologie*, Vol. II, pp. 132 f.; W. R. SMITH, *Religion of the Semites*, pp. 454 ff.; FRAZER, *Golden Bough*, Vol. II, pp. 225 ff.

[7] *Cf.* Ps. 50:13; W. R. SMITH, *Religion of the Semites* (see *Index*, *s. v.* "Blood"); H. C. TRUMBULL, *The Blood Covenant.*

due, and consider whether (*a*) upon the whole he was properly repaid for his services, (*b*) he deserved any longer to be classed with the widow and orphan, as in Deuteronomy.

7. Note that all slaughter of animals for purposes of eating is sacrificial; that every animal must be formally presented at the appointed place; and that punishment is to be inflicted upon those who do not recognize this fact.

8. Observe that offerings to idols have almost fallen into disuse.

9. Consider the attitude of the later prophets toward sacrifice; are they hostile? or indifferent?

10. Make a list of the events narrated in the later histories with which sacrifice is connected, and note (*a*) how large a place sacrifice is given; (*b*) how much more frequently the priest-writers recount the act of sacrifice than do the prophetic writers of Samuel and Kings; (*c*) the significance of this in connection with the greater importance attached to sacrifice in this later period.

11. Consider (*a*) the intimate connection, whether expressed or implied, between all this detail of ceremonial and the idea of *sin;* (*b*) the intimate connection between the idea of sin thus expressed and the conception of God which had come to exist in this period; (*c*) the suggestive fact that, side by side with this objective expression of the appreciation of sin and of longing for communion with God, there should have been written so many of the psalms, which express subjectively and spiritually the same idea.

§93. **Constructive Work.**—Prepare a statement which will present in the form of a summary the essential differences between the later and preceding periods in reference to sacrifice, including (*a*) the chief points of practice, and (*b*) the essential principles involved.

§94. **Literature to be Consulted.**

J. H. KURTZ, *Sacrificial Worship of the Old Testament* (1863); ALFRED BARRY, articles "Sacrifice," "Sin-Offering," "Meat-Offering," "Burnt-Offering," etc., in SMITH'S *Dictionary of the Bible* (1863); EWALD, *The Antiquities of Israel* (3d ed. 1866, transl. 1876), pp. 23–111; KALISCH, *Commentary on Leviticus* (1867–72), Part I, pp. 1–416; Part II, pp. 9, 217 ff., 290 ff.; KUENEN, *Religion of Israel* (1869 f., transl. 1874 f.), Vol. I, pp. 236 f.; OEHLER, *Old Testament Theology* (1870, transl. 1883), pp. 261–323; TYLOR, *Primitive Culture* (1874), see *Index, s. v.* "Sacrifice;" SAYCE, "On Human Sacrifice among the Babylonians," *Transactions of the Society of Biblical Archæology,* Vol. IV (1876), pp. 25–31; E. PARK, "On the Question of the Divine Institution of Sacrifice," *Bibliotheca Sacra,* 1876, pp. 102–32; A. CAVE, *The Scriptural Doctrine of Sacrifice and Atonement* (1877); WELLHAUSEN, *Prolegomena to the History of Israel* (1878), pp. 52–82; R. COLLINS, "An Essay on Sacrifice," in *The Pulpit Commentary on Leviticus* (1882), pp. i–xiv; ALFRED CAVE, "The Levitical Sacrifices

Literally Considered," in *The Pulpit Commentary on Leviticus* (1882), pp. i–xxxi; H. C. TRUMBULL, *The Blood Covenant* (1885), see *Index, s. v.* "Sacrifice;" LEIGHTON, *The Jewish Altar* (1886); A. HOVEY, "Shekkar and Leaven in Mosaic Offerings," *Old Testament Student*, 1886, pp. 11–16; H. CROSBY, "The Sacrifices," *Old Testament Student*, 1886, pp. 249 f.; W. R. SMITH, article "Sacrifice" in *Encyclopædia Britannica* (1887); SAYCE, *Religion of the Ancient Babylonians* (Hibbert Lectures, 1887), pp. 77–82; F. GARDINER, "On the Reason for the Selection of Certain Animals for Sacrifice," *Journal of the Society of Biblical Literature and Exegesis*, 1888, pp. 146–50; W. H. WARD, "On Some Babylonian Cylinders, Supposed to Represent Human Sacrifices," *Proceedings of the American Oriental Society*, May, 1888, pp. xxviii–xxx; KITTEL, *History of the Hebrews* (1888–92, transl. 1895), see *Index, s. v.* "Sacrifice;" W. R. SMITH, *Religion of the Semites* (1st ed. 1889, 2d ed. 1894), pp. 213–340; ROBERTSON, *Early Religion of Israel* (1889), see *Index, s. v.* "Sacrifice;" P. A. NORDELL, "Old Testament Word-Studies: 7. Sacrifice and Worship," *Old Testament Student*, Vol. VIII (1889), pp. 257 ff.; W. M. RODWELL, *The Mosaic Sacrifices in Lev. I–III* (1890); SCHULTZ, *Old Testament Theology* (1892), see *Index, s. v.* "Sacrifice;" DUFF, *Old Testament Theology* (1891–1900), see *Indices* to Vols. I and II; TH. E. SCHMAUCK, "The Paschal Lamb," *Lutheran Church Review*, 1891, pp. 127–63; C. J. BALL, "Glimpses of Babylonian Religion. I: Human Sacrifices," *Proceedings of the Society of Biblical Archæology*, Vol. XIV (1892), pp. 149–53; MONTEFIORE, *Religion of the Ancient Hebrews* (1892), see *Index;* H. B. TRISTRAM, "Sacrifices in Babylonia and Phœnicia," *Sunday School Times*, 1894, No. 1; H. C. TRUMBULL, *Studies in Oriental Social Life* (1894), see *Index, s. v.* "Sacrifice;" A. HARPER, "The Prophets and Sacrifice," *Expositor*, 1894, pp. 241–53; T. K. CHEYNE, "The Date and Origin of the Ritual of the Scapegoat," *Zeitschrift für die alttestamentliche Wissenschaft*, 1895, pp. 153–6; PH. J. HOEDEMAKER, "The Atonement Money," *The Thinker*, 1895; A. A. BERLE, "The Real Meaning of Semitic Sacrifice," *Bibliotheca Sacra*, 1895, pp. 342–6; MENZIES, *History of Religion* (1895), see *Index, s. v.* "Sacrifice;" TRUMBULL, *The Threshold Covenant* (1896), see *Index, s. v.* "Sacrifice;" WIEDEMANN, *Religion of the Ancient Egyptians* (1897), see *Index, s. v.* "Offerings;" JASTROW, *Religion of Babylonia and Assyria* (1898), see *Index, s. v.* "Sacrifices;" A. FAIRBANKS, "The Significance of Sacrifice in the Homeric Poems," *The New World*, June, 1898, pp. 335–48; A. F. SCOT, *Offering and Sacrifice: An Essay in Comparative Customs and Religious Development* (1899); TRUMBULL, *The Covenant of Salt* (1899), pp. 83–96; BOYS-SMITH, "Sacrifice in Ancient Religion and in Christian Sacrament," *Expository Times*, December, 1899; January, 1900; S. R. DRIVER, article "Offer, Offering, etc.," in HASTINGS' *Dictionary of the Bible* (1900); GAST, "Idea of Sacrifice as Developed in the Old Testament," *Reformed Church Review*, January, 1900; HERMANN SCHULTZ, "The Significance of Sacrifice in the Old Testament," *American Journal of Theology*, Vol. IV (1900), pp. 257–313; DAVIS, "The Sin-Offering," *Bible Student*, February, 1900; EDWARD DAY, *The Social Life of the Hebrews* (1901), pp. 39–46; MCCURDY, *History, Prophecy and the Monuments* (1895–1901), §§ 738, 1006 f., 1014; D. MCKENZIE, *Exposition of Old Testament Sacrifice* (1901).

V. THALHOFER, *Die unblutigen Opfer des mosaischen Cultus* (1848); HENGSTENBERG, *Die Opfer der heiligen Schrift* (1852); RIEHM, "Ueber das Schuldopfer," *Theol. Studien und Kritiken*, 1854, pp. 93–121; S. W. RINCK, "Ueber das Schuldopfer," *Theol. Studien und Kritiken*, 1855, pp. 369–81; A. STOECKL, *Das Opfer, nach seinem Wesen und seiner Geschichte* (1860); OEHLER, revised by VON ORELLI, article "Opferkultus des A. T.'s," *Real-Encyklopädie für protestantische Theol. und Kirche* (2d ed., 1883); MENANT, "Les sacrifices sur les cylindres chaldéens," *Gazette archéologique*, 1883, Nos. 7–9; FRANZ DELITZSCH, article "Opfer" in RIEHM'S *Handwörterbuch des biblischen Alterthums* (1884); WELLHAUSEN, *Reste des arabischen Heidenthums* (1887), pp. 110–28; STADE, *Geschichte des Volkes Israel* (1887 f.), Vol. I, pp. 492–8; Vol. II, pp. 253–64; L. GLAHN, "Soningen i den gammeltestamentlige Offerkultus," *Festskrift Borcks Colleg.*, pp. 281–3 (1889); FRIEDR. NITZSCH, *Die Idee und die Stufen des Opferkultus* (1889); C. PIEPENBRING, "Histoire des lieux de culte et du sacerdoce en Israel," *Revue de l'histoire des religions*, 1891, pp. 1–60, 133–86; TH. NAVILLE, *Les sacrifices lévitiques et l'expiation* (1891); A. SCHMOLLER, "Das Wesen der Sühne in der alttestl. Opferthora," *Theol. Studien und Kritiken*, 1891, pp. 205–88; SMEND, *Lehrbuch der alttestl. Religionsgeschichte* (1st ed. 1893, 2d ed. 1899), pp. 138–45; NOWACK, *Lehrbuch der hebräischen Archäologie* (1894), Vol. II, pp. 203–75; BENZINGER, *Hebräische Archäologie* (1894), pp. 431–64; P. SCHANZ, "Der Opferbegriff," *Theol. Quartalschrift*, 1894, pp. 179–222; G. A. SIEGRIST, *L'idée du sacrifice dans l'A. T.* (1894); DILLMANN, *Handbuch der alttestl. Theologie* (1895), see ***Index, s. v.*** "Opfer;" STADE, "Die Eiferopferthora," *Zeitschrift für die alttestl. Wissenschaft*, 1895, pp. 166–78; KAMPHAUSEN, *Das Verhältnis des Menschenopfers zur israelitischen Religion* (1896); MARTI, *Geschichte der israelit. Religion* (1897), pp. 103–7, 225–31; LÉVI, *La doctrine du sacrifice dans les Brahmânas* (1898); G. DE ALVIELLA, "La théorie du sacrifice et les recherches de Robertson Smith," *Revue de l'université de Bruxelles*, April, 1898; M. LAMBERT, "Le mot דשן," *Journal asiatique*, Vol. XI (1898), pp. 326 f.; C. SCHMIDT, *Die Entwickelung der alttestamentlichen Opferidee* (1899); A. LOISY, "Notes sur la Genèse. VI: Le sacrifice d'Isaac: Gen. 22:1–19," *Revue de l'histoire et de la littérature religieuses*, 1899, pp. 458–62; P. VOLZ, "Die Handauflegung beim Opfer," *Zeitschrift für die alttestamentliche Wissenschaft*, 1901; LEFÉBURE, "Le sacrifice humain d'après les rites de Busiris et d'Abydos," *Sphinx*, **Vol. III, No. 2**; CHWOLSON, *Die Ssabier und der Ssabismus*, (1856), Vol. II, pp. 142–55.

§ 95. **Supplementary Topics.**

1. Study the principal references to sacrifice found in the Psalter, *e. g.*, Pss. 4:5; 20:3; 40:6; 50:5, 8–14, 23; 51:16 f., 19; 54:6; 56:12; 66:13, 15; 96:8; 106:28, 37 f.; 107:22; 116:17; 118:27; and consider (*a*) the attitude in general of these song-writers; (*b*) how far they have spiritualized the subject; (*c*) the relationship between the Levitical ceremonial and the spirit of the Psalms.

2. What did the sage have to say about sacrifice? *Cf.* Job 1:5; 22:27; 42:8 f.; Prov. 7:14; 15:8; 21:27; Eccles. 9:2.

3. From an examination of the books of Maccabees — *e. g.*, 1 Macc. 5:54; 7:33; 11:34; 12:11; 2 Macc. 1:8, 18, 23, 26, 31; 2:9 ff.; 3:3, 6, 32; 4:14; 6:7; 9:16; 12:43; 13:23; 14:31 — determine the spirit in which sacrifices were offered during the Maccabæan period, and note any changes that present themselves.

4. Consider the subject of sacrifice as it appears in the epistle to

the Hebrews, *e. g.*, Heb. 5 : 1–3 ; 7 : 26 f.; 9 : 6 ; 10 : 18, 26 ; 11 : 17 ; 13 : 10–16.

5. Consider the meaning and usage in the several documents of the various Hebrew words for sacrifice, viz., זֶבַח ; מִנְחָה ; עֹלָה ; שְׁלָמִים ; אָשָׁם ; קָרְבָּן ; חַטָּאת ; תּוֹדָה ; נְדָבָה ; נֶסֶךְ ; אִשֶּׁה ; תְּרוּמָה ; תְּנוּפָה ; כָּלִיל.

Cf. S. R. DRIVER, article "Offer, Offering, Oblation," in HASTINGS' *Dictionary of the Bible.*

6. Compare the usages relating to sacrifice among the Egyptians, Greeks, and Romans, and note points of similarity and difference as compared with the usages of the Hebrews.

See W. R. SMITH, article "Sacrifice" in *Encyclopædia Britannica.*

7. Compare the usages relating to sacrifice among the Assyrians, the Arabs, and the Canaanites, and note points of similarity and difference as compared with the usages of the Hebrews.

See especially PAUL HAUPT, "Babylonian Elements in the Levitic Ritual," *Journal of Biblical Literature*, Vol. XIX, pp. 55–81 ; JASTROW, *Religion of Babylonia and Assyria* (*Index, s. v.* "Sacrifice"); W. R. SMITH, *Religion of the Semites;* L. W. KING, *Babylonian Religion and Mythology*, pp. 210 ff.; A. H. SAYCE, *Babylonians and Assyrians*, pp. 245–9.

8. Consider the question of the *origin* of sacrifice.

See W. R. SMITH, article "Sacrifice" in *Encyclopædia Britannica;* A. F. SCOT, *Offering and Sacrifice: An Essay in Comparative Customs and Religious Development.*

9. Prepare a definition of sacrifice which may be considered biblical.

10. Consider the teachings inculcated by sacrifice, and whether these teachings (*a*) constituted the purpose and end of the Jewish service, or (*b*) pointed to something beyond and above.

11. Consider the relation of sacrifice, as it is represented in the Old Testament, to the Christ of the New Testament.

CHAPTER VIII.

THE LAWS AND USAGES CONCERNING FEASTS, CONSIDERED COMPARATIVELY.

§ 96. **The Feasts of Early Times,** that is, as described in (*a*) the Covenant Code; (*b*) the historical material of J and E; (*c*) the pre-Deuteronomic portions of Judges, Samuel, and Kings; and (*d*) the pre-Deuteronomic prophetic utterances (see § 59, note 1).[1]

1. The Feast of Unleavened Bread.[2]
   Exod. 34 : 18 ; 23 : 15 ; 13 : 3–10.
2. The Feast of Weeks.
   Exod. 34 : 22 ; 23 : 16*a*.
3. The Feast of Tabernacles.
   Exod. 34 : 22*b*; 23 : 16*b*; 1 Kings 8 : 2, 65 f.; 12 : 32 ; Judg. 9 : 27 ; 21 : 19 ff.
4. There were three feasts at which attendance was required by law.
   Exod. 34 : 23 f.; 23 : 14–17; 1 Kings 9 : 25 ; 1 Sam. 1 : 3.
5. The feasts were connected with agriculture.
   Exod. 23 : 15 f.; 34 : 22 ; Judg. 21 . 19 ff.
6. The feasts were always of a joyous and social character.
   Exod. 32 : 5 f.; Judg. 21 : 19 ff.; 1 Sam. 1 : 3, 7, 13 ff.
7. A feast often involved a pilgrimage to some shrine.
   Exod. 10 : 9 ; Judg. 11 : 40 (?) ; 1 Sam. 1 : 3, 7 ; 2 : 19.
8. The Passover.
   Exod. 34 : 25 ; 12 : 21–27.
9. The Feast of the New Moon.
   Hos. 5 : 7 (?); 1 Sam. 20 : 5 f.; 18 : 24 ff.; 2 Kings 4 : 23.
10. Special feasts were held, *e. g.:* the Feast of Sheep-Shearing; the Feast of Jephthah's Daughter.
    1 Sam. 25 : 2 ; 2 Sam. 13 : 23 ; Judg. 11 : 40.
11. Idolatrous feasts.
    Exod. 32 : 5 ; 1 Kings 12 : 32 f.; 2 Kings 10 : 20.
12. Attitude of the early prophets toward the feasts.
    Amos 5 : 21 ; 8 : 10 ; Hos. 2 : 11 ; 5 : 7 (?); 9 : 5 ; 12 : 9 ; Isa. 1 : 13 f.

[1] The following references are from J : Exod. 34 : 18–25 ; 12 : 21–27 ; 13 : 3–10 ; 10 : 9 ; the following are from E : Exod. 23 : 10–17 ; 32 : 5.

[2] References in **bold-face** type are from the Covenant Code.

§ 97. **Questions and Suggestions.**

1. Consider, in connection with the Feast of *Unleavened Bread*, (*a*) the duration; (*b*) the date (to what part of our year did Abib correspond?); (*c*) the nature and significance of "unleavened bread;" (*d*) the meaning of the phrase, "none shall appear before me empty;" (*e*) the association of this feast with the exodus from Egypt, and the point of connection; (*f*) the seeming identification of two entirely different things, viz., the Passover (see below) and the Feast of Unleavened Bread.

2. Consider, in connection with the Feast of *Weeks*, (*a*) other names for the same feast, viz., Harvest, First-Fruits (Pentecost, *cf.* Acts 2:1; 20:16; 1 Cor. 16:8); (*b*) the duration (*cf.* Deut. 16:9–12); (*c*) the date; (*d*) the connection of this feast with the close of the grain harvest; (*e*) the fact that there is no historical mention in the Old Testament of its observance (but *cf.* 2 Macc. 12:32 and the New Testament passages indicated above).

3. Consider, in connection with the Feast of *Tabernacles*, (*a*) other names, viz., Booths (Deut. 16:13), Ingathering; (*b*) the duration (*cf.* Deut. 16:13–15); (*c*) the date, late in the autumn; (*d*) the connection of this feast with the completion of the harvest of fruit, oil, and wine; (*e*) the lack of any specific regulations in the earlier legislation; (*f*) the fact that historical mention is made of only this feast among the three great feasts (1 Sam. 1:1 ff.; 1 Kings 12:32; 6:38); (*g*) the fact that this feast seems to have had its origin among the Canaanites (Judg. 9:27); (*h*) the important religious significance involved in the idea that the deity was the *lord* of the land and the dispenser of its fruits.

4. Consider, in reference to these meetings for festal purposes, (*a*) the number; (*b*) the distribution of these throughout the year; (*c*) the class of persons who were expected to be present; (*d*) the meaning of the phrase "appear before the Lord;" (*e*) the guarantee given of safety upon the journeys involved in attending the feasts; (*f*) the custom in Solomon's times. Are any places mentioned as the seats of a festival?

5. To what extent were these feasts of an agricultural character, that is, connected with agricultural pursuits, *e. g.*, harvest, ingathering of fruit, etc.? or how far were they solar feasts, that is, connected with certain seasons of the year? What was the usual time for harvest in Palestine? When did the end of the Jewish year come, and with what feast was it connected? Consider the connection of the feast at Shiloh with the vineyards near at hand. What particular characteristics

are associated with agricultural as distinguished from historical feasts? Would the climate, for example, to some extent determine the date? Would the harvest feast take place at the same time in localities in which there was a difference of two or three weeks in the period of the ripening of grain? What kind of feasts would be expected among people leading a pastoral life, as distinguished from an agricultural life? If these feasts are of agricultural origin, could Israel have observed them before becoming an agricultural people, that is, before settling in Canaan?

6. Are not harvest and vintage feasts generally occasions for joy? Are not eating and drinking and dancing the usual accompaniments of a feast? How far did the idea that the deity was sharing in the festivities contribute to the joyousness of the occasion? Did not the eating, etc., contribute to this end? Was not the very purpose a joyous one? Was there yet any conception of God or sin such as would interfere with this interpretation? Was there, at this time, any feeling of the need of an atonement?

7. (1) Does a man ordinarily feast by himself? (2) If the social element is important, would it be necessary to have places at which many might conveniently come together? Would this not necessarily involve a pilgrimage? (3) Consider the use of sacred places, like Shiloh, for such meetings. (4) What would be the social and political influence of such pilgrimages?

8. Consider (1) whether the *Passover*, although forming a part of the Feast of Unleavened Bread, is not treated independently of that feast; (2) whether, in its very nature, it is not pastoral (that is, of nomadic origin), rather than agricultural; (3) the meaning of the name "Passover;"[3] (4) the time of year in which it was observed; (5) the evidence in Exod. 7:16; 10:24, that the Hebrews observed a spring festival with offerings from their flocks before the days of Moses; (6) the original significance of the Passover, viz., a sacrificial meal in which those who partook united themselves more closely and came into closer communion with their God—all this, for greater security; (7) the connection of this very early festival at a later time (*a*) with the historical event of the exodus, and (*b*) with the Feast of Mazzoth.

[3] *Cf.* article "Passover" in HASTINGS' *Dictionary of the Bible;* J. MÜLLER, *Kritischer Versuch über den Ursprung des Pesach-Mazzothfestes;* NOWACK, *Hebräische Archäologie*, Vol. II, pp. 147 ff., 172 ff.; BENZINGER, *Hebräische Archäologie*, pp. 470 ff.; RIEDEL, *Zeitschrift für die alttestamentliche Wissenschaft*, Vol. XX, pp. 319–32; STADE, *ibid.*, pp. 333–7; C. H. TOY, "The Meaning of פֶּסַח," *Journal of Biblical Literature*, Vol. XVI, pp. 178 f.

9. Is the Feast of the *New Moon* agricultural, or rather astronomical? Is it recognized in the earlier legislation? Consider (1) its wide observance among Semitic peoples;[4] (2) its association with ancient family sacrifices; (3) its connection with the sabbath; (4) its possible use by prophets as a time for religious assembly; (5) its mention by the prophets (see below); (6) its great antiquity.

10. Consider the Feast of *Sheep-Shearing:* (1) Was not this, like the Feast of the New Moon, a pastoral rather than an agricultural feast? (2) Was it recognized in legislation? (3) Could it be observed elsewhere than in a cattle-producing portion of the country? (4) How late in Israel's history does it appear to have come down? (5) Did it ever take on any special religious significance? (6) What, in general, did it celebrate? Consider the mourning-feast in connection with the devotion of Jephthah's daughter to a life of perpetual virginity, and compare the similar cases in other history.[5]

11. Notice how special feasts are celebrated in addition to those which became authorized, as in the case of (1) Aaron and the calf, (2) Jeroboam at Bethel, (3) Jehu in honor of Baal.

12. Consider now the place occupied in the religious life by these feasts, and their influence: (1) To what extent did the feasts constitute the religion of the people? (2) How far would men postpone religious observances until the time of a feast? (3) How much store did the ordinary Israelite set by the feasts? Would the threat of their extinction disturb him? (4) In what way would such feasts serve to develop national feeling? to provide an education for the people? to encourage the spirit of unity? (5) To what extent would these assemblies serve to increase facilities for business transactions? (6) Is there any evidence that, in this period, the people as a whole (*cf.* later times) engaged in a great feast or festival? Or is it rather the custom of families and households? (7) What did the prophet say of the religious value of the feasts? To what did he make objection? (*a*) the lack of heart manifested? (*b*) or the fact that they were held in honor of other gods? or (*c*) the fact that the people thought the holding of these feasts to constitute the whole of religion, and neglected all that seemed pure and good in a religious life?

[4] *Cf.* MORRIS JASTROW, JR., *Religion of Babylonia and Assyria,* see *Index, s. v.* Moon," "Zag-muk," "Festivals," etc.; I. ABRAHAMS, article "New Moon" in HASTINGS' *Dictionary of the Bible.* See also HOMMEL, *Aufsätze und Abhandlungen* (1900), pp. 149–65.

[5] *Cf.* GOLDZIHER, *Mythology among the Hebrews,* pp. 96 ff., 104; STADE, *Geschichte des Volkes Israel,* Vol. I, p. 68; G. F. MOORE, *A Critical and Exegetical Commentary on Judges,* pp. 304 f.

§ 98. **Constructive Work.**—Prepare a tabular statement which will present in systematic form the facts concerning the feasts of the earlier period, as follows: (1) name, (2) origin, (3) date, (4) duration, (5) characteristic ritual, (6) meaning of name, (7) religious significance.

§ 99. **Feasts of the Deuteronomic Period,** that is, as described (*a*) in the laws of Deuteronomy, (*b*) in the Deuteronomic portions of the books of Samuel and Kings, and (*c*) by the prophets of the Deuteronomic period.[6]

1. Passover and Feast of Unleavened Bread are now combined.
   Deut. 16 : 1–8.
2. Feast of Weeks.
   Deut. 16 : 9–12.
3. Feast of Tabernacles.
   Deut. 16 : 13–15; 31 : 10 f.
4. All feasts must be held at the one central sanctuary.
   Deut. 16 : 5–7, 11, 16; 31 : 11.
5. The law still requires attendance at three feasts.
   Deut. 16 : 16 f.
6. Feasts are still occasions of joy.
   Deut. 12 : 8 ; 14 : 26 ; 16 : 11, 14 f.; 24 : 11 ; Isa. 9 : 3.
7. Feasts are still on an agricultural basis.
   Deut. 16 : 9, 13 ; *cf.* 16 : 1.
8. Attitude of the prophets toward feasts.
   Nah. 1 : 15 ; Jer. 51 : 39 ; Lam. 1 : 4, 15 ; 2 : 6 f., 22.
9. Josiah's Passover.
   2 Kings 23 : 21–23.

§ 100. **Questions and Suggestions.**

1. Concerning the Feast of the *Passover and Unleavened Bread*, consider (1) that the two feasts, distinct in origin, are now observed together; (2) the association of the Passover with the exodus; (3) the connection of this rite with that of the firstlings (Deut. 15 : 19 ff.); (4) the duration; (5) the lack of any designation of the day of the month; (6) the significance of the unleavened bread, and its historical connection; (7) the treatment of any remaining flesh; (8) the place at which this feast shall be observed; (9) the change in ritual and conception which takes place in the case of the Passover feast, and the reason for this; (10) the circumstances leading to the coalescence of the two feasts.

[6] References in **bold-face** type are from the code of laws contained in the book of Deuteronomy.

2. Concerning the Feast of *Weeks*, notice (1) that the time is fixed in connection with that of the Feast of Unleavened Bread, viz., seven weeks, the fiftieth day; (2) the duration; (3) the persons who are to be invited to the feast; (4) the place; (5) the joyous character; (6) the historical reminiscence suggested.

3. Concerning the Feast of *Tabernacles*, consider (1) the name and its origin (*cf.* 1 Sam. 1 : 8); (2) the time (no particular day designated); (3) the persons who are to participate; (4) the duration; (5) the place; (6) the motive; (7) the joyous character.

4. Consider the meaning of the constantly recurring phrase, "in the place which Jehovah thy God shall choose to cause his name to dwell there;" is it (1) a place, at one time in one locality, at another time in another locality, and consequently, in the course of time, are several places thus designated? Or (2) is it one central place for all time, viz., Jerusalem? (3) Consider some of the consequences which would follow such centralization; *e. g.*: (*a*) Would the feast thus transferred to Jerusalem continue its agricultural or pastoral character? (*b*) If a particular day is fixed, could the harvest feast any longer be connected with the harvest, which, on account of difference of climate, occurred at widely separated dates? (*c*) Would the historical be likely to supplant the natural interpretation of the feast? (*d*) Would the original ritual also lose its significance? (*e*) Could the firstlings actually be taken to Jerusalem to be sacrificed? (*f*) Could the head of a family take the entire family and dependents to Jerusalem? (*g*) Would he sell his own animal or grain, and then go to Jerusalem and buy (Deut. 14 : 24–26)? Would this affect commerce? (*h*) Could a man, in this case, arrange a sacrificial meal in Jerusalem and have his family and friends with him, as in the village or country? (*i*) Would not this lead to an entire change in the feeling connected with the observance of the feast? Would the observance become more general and less individual, more formal and serious, and less joyous?

5. Although the law still required attendance at these feasts, is it possible to suppose that any considerable proportion of the people could leave their homes and their work, and go to Jerusalem three times in a year? Would this have the effect of depriving these people of religious privileges?

6. Although the feasts are represented as still continuing their joyous character, could the old feeling actually have existed under the new régime, cut off as the worshiper was from friends and family, lost as he must have been in the great crowds gathering at Jerusalem?

7. Although feasts are still nominally on an agricultural basis (*cf.* the names, the method of determining the date, etc.), will it be possible for the agricultural character to be long maintained in view of (1) the detachment of the feasts from the exact season (one time being fixed for the entire country, although the harvest took place at different dates on account of climate); (2) their association with historical events and the emphasis thus placed on the idea of commemoration; (3) the necessary sale of one's own effects, and the purchase of others for the purpose of the feast?

8. Upon the supposition that the prophets themselves had to do with the formulation of the policy presented in Deuteronomy, and in view of the opinions expressed by Amos, Hosea, and Isaiah, what may we understand to have been their general position on the subject of these feasts and festivals? Did they represent the feasts as being an essential element in the religious life? Did they wish to see them modified in their character? Was it for this reason that they joined with the priests in those reforms, recorded in Deuteronomy, which in the end largely revolutionized the whole system? Did they think that the people were placing a false value upon these feasts in comparison with a pure and simple life?

9. Upon the acceptance of the book of Deuteronomy by Josiah and his people in 621 B. C., (1) what attitude was taken by the king toward the various corrupt forms of worship which existed at that time (*cf.* Deut. 23:4–20)? (2) What was the command issued as to the observance of the Passover? Does this mean that it had fallen into disuse? If so, how is such disuse to be explained? (3) What was the character of the Passover observed on this occasion?

§ 101. **Constructive Work.**—Write a statement covering three points: (1) the feasts which now no longer seem to be observed, and the reasons; (2) the modifications which have come to exist in the feasts transmitted from the earlier period, and an explanation of these modifications; (3) the progress, if any, which has been made in the adaptation of the ceremonial of worship (so far as it concerned feasts) to the religious life; or, to use the form of a question, was Israel in a better or worse position for the cultivation of the religious life, with the changes which had now come about?

§ 102. **Constructive Work.**—From Ezek. 36:38; 45:17, 18–21, 22–25; 46:1, 3, 6 ff., 9, consider (1) whether, in general, Ezekiel has much to say upon the subject. Is this because his development lies along other lines, or because the development has already reached its highest point? (2) Is there evidence (if so, what?) that the Deuteronomic system of feasts is accepted? (3) In what cases are definite dates now given, in which, hitherto, the time has been left undesignated? (4) What, now, is the relation of the Feast of the Passover to that of Unleavened Bread? (5) Present the evidence, if any is to be found, that the feasts have now lost their joyous character. (6) Is the centralization of worship involved in the arrangements which Ezekiel proposes?

§ 103. **The Feasts in the Later Period,** that is, as described (*a*) in the laws of the Levitical code, (*b*) by the priestly prophets, and (*c*) in the priestly histories, viz., Ezra, Nehemiah, and Chronicles.[7]

1. Feast of the Passover and Unleavened Bread.
   Lev. 23:4–8; Numb. 28:16–25; 9:1–14; Exod. 12:1–20, 43–50; 2 Chron. 8:13; 30:13–27; 35:1–19; Ezra 6:19–22.
2. Feast of Weeks.
   Lev. 23:15–21; Numb. 28:26–31; 2 Chron. 8:13.
3. Feast of Tabernacles.
   Lev. 23:34–36, 39–44; Numb. 29:12–38; 2 Chron. 5:3 ff.; 7:8–10; 8:13; Ezra 3:4; Neh. 8:13–18.
4. Feast of the New Moon.
   Numb. 28:11–15; 1 Chron. 23:31; 2 Chron. 8:13; 31:3; Ezra 3:5; Neh. 10:33.
5. Feast of Trumpets.
   Lev. 23:23–25; Numb. 29:1–6; 10:10.
6. Definite dates are fixed.
   Lev. 23:5, 6, 23, 27, 34, 39; Numb., chaps. 28, 29; Esther 9:21.
7. Agricultural significance is wholly lost.
   Lev. 23:42 f.
8. Celebration of feasts at Jerusalem is taken for granted.
   Zech. 14:16–19; 1 Chron. 23:31; 2 Chron. 35:1–19.
9. Sacrifices are multiplied in connection with feasts.
   Numb., chap. 29; 15:3; 2 Chron. 2:4; 30:24; 35:7–9.
10. Attitude of the prophets toward feasts.
    Zech. 14:16–19; Joel 1:14; 2:15.
11. Thought of sin predominant in feasts.
    Lev. 23:19; chap. 16; Numb. 28:15, 22, 30; 29:5, 11, 16, 19, 22, 25, 28, 31, 34, 38; Exod. 30:10.
12. Day of Atonement.
    Lev. 23:27–32; chap. 16; Numb. 29:7–11; Exod. 30:10.

[7] References in **bold-face** type are from the Levitical code of laws.

13. Feast of Purim.
Esther 8:17; 9:15–32.

§ 104. **Questions and Suggestions.**

1. In the later regulations and references relating to the Feast of the *Passover and Unleavened Bread*, note (1) the new phrases, "set feasts," "holy convocations," "appointed seasons;" (2) the exactness with which the date is fixed; (3) the absence of "servile work;" (4) the burnt-offering, and the meal-offering prescribed, the sin-offering which accompanies, and all this beside the continual burnt-offering; (5) that in time (*cf.* Exod. 12:1–20) the opinion comes to prevail that the Passover had been established before the exodus "in order that Jehovah might spare the firstborn of Israel, not because he had spared them;" (6) the restrictions placed upon participation in the Passover (Exod. 12:43–50); (7) the observance according to Chronicles (2 Chron. 30:13–27) of the Feast of Unleavened Bread in Hezekiah's times; (8) Josiah's Passover (2 Chron. 35:1–19); (9) Ezra's Passover; (10) the place of all these observances; (11) their general character; (12) that the offerings have the nature of fixed dues, rather than of voluntary gifts.

2. In the references to the Feast of *Weeks*, note (1) that the same general characteristics appear as in the case of the Feast of Unleavened Bread (see above); (2) that after the fall of Jerusalem it becomes a feast commemorating the giving of the law on Sinai, and is no longer considered a nature feast.

3. In the references to the Feast of *Tabernacles*, note (1) the same points as were considered above in the case of the preceding feasts, viz., fixing of date, multiplication of various kinds of offerings for each day, no servile work, etc.; (2) the chronicler's account of Solomon's observance of this feast in connection with the bringing up of the ark (2 Chron. 5:3 ff.); (3) Solomon's dedication of the temple in connection with this same feast (2 Chron. 7:8–10); (4) the observance in connection with the beginning of the second temple (Ezra 3:4); (5) the dwelling in booths in Ezra's time (Neh. 8:13–18).

4. The system of feasts now includes more definitely the Feast of the *New Moon*, concerning which it may be noted, (1) that a regular ceremonial is instituted; (2) that frequent mention is made of it in connection with the sabbath. Consider (3) what has led to this larger emphasis.

5. Consider, in the case of the Feast of *Trumpets*, (1) its connection with the sabbatical system;[8] (2) the provisions given for its

[8]See chap. ix.

observance; (3) the general provision for the blowing of trumpets with various feasts.

6. In all the cases presented consider (1) the fact that now the exact day of the month is prescribed; (2) the significance of this fact, as compared with the looser designations of earlier regulations.

7. In all the cases presented consider (1) the fact that the agricultural significance has been lost; (2) the fact that, even in the case of the Feast of Tabernacles (the last of all to receive this treatment), a historical meaning has been suggested and adopted; (3) the significance of these facts as seen in the routine of the ceremonial and the general character of the feasts.

8. Consider (1) whether, although no explicit statement occurs in the legislative material covering the point, it is not everywhere taken for granted that all feasts shall be celebrated at one place, viz., Jerusalem; and (2) whether this is not the understanding of the prophets and historians of the period.

9. Consider, in the case of all the feasts, (1) whether the largest emphasis is not now placed upon the sacrifice; (2) whether, in fact, with the great multiplication of sacrifices, everything else is not practically ignored; (3) the influence of this upon the people; (4) the explanation of it.

10. What appears to have been the attitude of the later prophets toward these feasts? Is there any longer indifference, lack of appreciation, or hostility? Why has this change of attitude come about? Does Judaism (Israel's religion after the exile) adopt an entirely new policy in reference to feasts, as compared with prophetism (Israel's religion before the exile)? Were the prophets of this period really priests, and, in consequence, in sympathy with everything priestly? Had prophecy now died?

11. Is it a fact that the idea of *sin* is now everywhere prominent? that, indeed, this idea is the controlling idea? that, therefore, confession instead of rejoicing is the order of the day? If this is the fact, how is it to be explained?

12. Concerning the *Day of Atonement*, one may undertake to answer the following questions: (1) Was it observed in the early or middle period, or did its observance arise only in the later period? (2) Is there any connection between it and Ezekiel's days of atonement (45:18–20)? (3) Or with the days of fasting held in commemoration of national calamities mentioned in Zech. 7:35; 8:19? (4) Or with the day of fasting (the twenty-fourth day of the month) mentioned in

Neh. 9:1? (5) What was the fundamental idea in this observance? Was propitiation thought of as being made in behalf of the individual or of the nation? Were the sanctuary and the land also included? (6) What evidence does the ritual furnish as to the fundamental idea? (7) What is the meaning of the phrases "sabbath of solemn rest," "afflict your souls" (Lev. 16:31)? (8) What conception of God gave rise to the idea of sin involved in this institution?

13. In the case of the Feast of *Purim* consider (1) its origin and occasion; (2) its date; (3) the question of its connection (*a*) with a Persian feast, (*b*) with a Babylonian feast; (4) the meaning of the name; (5) the method of observance.[9]

§ 105. **Constructive Work.**—Prepare a statement which will show the more important differences in the observance of the feasts between the usage of the middle period and that of the later period.

§ 106. **Literature to Be Consulted.**

A, P. STANLEY, *Lectures on the History of the Jewish Church*, Vol. I, Appendix iii = *The Samaritan Passover* (1862); S. CLARK, article "Passover," SMITH'S *Dictionary of the Bible* (1st ed. 1863, 2d ed. 1893); EWALD, *Antiquities of Israel* (3d ed. 1866, transl. 1876), pp. 348–80; SCHULTZ, *Old Testament Theology* (1st ed. 1869, 5th ed. 1896, transl. 1892), Vol. I, pp. 359–69; II, 87–100, 402 ff.; KUENEN, *Religion of Israel* (1869 f., transl. 1874), Vol. I, pp. 242–5, 262–7; II, pp. 28–30, 89–94, 253 f., 271–3; III, pp. 148–53; OEHLER, *Old Testament Theology* (1st ed. 1873, transl. 1883), §§ 140, 141, 144–6, 150, 153–6; EDERSHEIM, *The Temple: Its Ministry and Services* (1874), pp. 144–300; W. R. SMITH, article "Passover and Feast of Unleavened Bread," *Encyclopædia Britannica* (1875); WELLHAUSEN, *Prolegomena to the History of Israel* (1878, transl. 1885), pp. 83–120; W. R. SMITH, *The Old Testament in the Jewish Church* (1st ed. 1881, 2d ed. 1892), pp. 240, 269; IDEM, *Prophets of Israel* (1st ed. 1882, 2d ed. 1895), see *Index, s. v.* "Feasts;" EDERSHEIM, *Life and Times of Jesus the Messiah* (1st ed. 1883), see *Index, s. v.* "Dedication," "Feasts," "Passover," etc.; W. H. GREEN, *The Hebrew Feasts in Their Relation to Recent Critical Hypotheses Concerning the Pentateuch* (1885); E. SCHÜRER, *History of the Jewish People in the Time of Christ* (1885, transl. 1890), *passim;* PIEPENBRING, *Theology of the Old Testament* (1886, transl. 1893), see *Index, s. v.* "Feast," "Passover," etc.; SAYCE, *Religion of the Ancient Babylonians* (Hibbert Lectures, 1887), pp. 64–9; DOUGHTY, *Travels in Arabia Deserta*, Vol. I (1888), pp. 50–84, 190–214; W. R. SMITH, *Religion of the Semites* (1st ed. 1889, 2d ed. 1894), pp. 252–8; ROBERTSON, *Early Religion of Israel* (1889), pp. 363, 372, 378, 385, 397, 401; W. ST. CHAD BOSCAWEN, "The

[9] *Cf.* MORRIS JASTROW, JR., *Religion of Babylonia and Assyria*, pp. 686 ff.; ZIMMERN, *Zeitschrift für die alttestamentliche Wissenschaft*, Vol. XI, pp. 157–69; DE LAGARDE, *Purim—Ein Beitrag zur Geschichte der Religion;* SAYCE, *Proceedings of the Society of Biblical Archæology*, Vol. XIX, pp. 280; JENSEN, *Wiener Zeitschrift für die Kunde des Morgenlandes*, Vol. VI, p. 70; C. H. TOY, "Esther as a Babylonian Goddess," *New World*, Vol. VI, pp. 130–45; ALEXANDER KOHUT, *American Journal of Semitic Languages and Literatures*, Vol. XIV, pp. 192 f.

Babylonian and Jewish Festivals," *Babylonian and Oriental Record*, Vol. IV (1890), pp. 34–8; C. J. BALL, article "Festivals," SMITH'S *Dictionary of the Bible* (2d ed. 1893); H. C. TRUMBULL, *The Blood Covenant* (1893), see *Index, s. v.* "Feasting;" *idem, Studies in Oriental Social Life* (1894), see *Index, s. v.* "Feast;" *idem, The Threshold Covenant* (1896), pp. 203–12, 266; H. B. TRISTRAM, *Eastern Customs in Bible Lands*, (1894), pp. 69–86; SAYCE, *Proceedings of the Society of Biblical Archæology*, Vol. XIX (1897), pp. 280 f.; E. E. HARDING, article "Feasts and Fasts," HASTINGS' *Dictionary of the Bible* (1898); S. R. DRIVER AND H. A. WHITE, article "Day of Atonement," HASTINGS' *Dictionary of the Bible* (1898); A. KOHUT, "The Talmudic Records of the Persian and Babylonian Festivals Critically Illustrated," *American Journal of Semitic Languages and Literatures*, Vol. XIV (1898), pp. 182–94 (*cf. Revue des études juives*, Vol. XXIV, pp. 256–71); MORRIS JASTROW, JR., *Religion of Babylonia and Assyria* (1898), see *Index, s. v.* "Festivals;" C. H. TOY, "The Meaning of פֶּסַח," *Journal of Biblical Literature*, Vol. XVI (1898), pp. 178 f.; I. BENZINGER AND T. K. CHEYNE, article "Day of Atonement," *Encyclopædia Biblica* (1899); W. W. FOWLER, *The Roman Festivals of the Period of the Republic* (1899); WARREN, "Dates on Which Paschal Full Moons Occur," *Palestine Exploration Fund Quarterly Statement*, October, 1900; FAIRBANKS, "Festival Epidauria at Athens," *Classical Review*, November, 1900; FRAZER, "The Saturnalia and Kindred Festivals," *Fortnightly Review*, October and November, 1900; DUFF, *Old Testament Theology*, Vol. II (1900), see *Index, s. v.* "Feasts;" I. ABRAHAMS, article "New Moon," HASTINGS' *Dictionary of the Bible* (1900); I. BENZINGER, article "Feasts," *Encyclopædia Biblica* (1901); WILLIS, *The Worship of the Old Covenant*, pp. 190–214; WATSON, *Cambridge Companion to the Bible*, pp. 411–17; FARNELL, *The Cults of the Greek States*, Vol. II, pp. 648 f.; MCCURDY, *History, Prophecy and the Monuments* (1895–1901), see *Index, s. v.* "Feasts."

J. SPENCER, *De legibus Hebraeorum ritualibus* (2d ed. 1686), III, Diss. viii; J. MEYER, *De festis Hebraeorum* (1724); F. C. BAUR, "Ueber die ursprüngliche Bedeutung des Passahfestes und des Beschneidungsritus," *Tübinger Zeitschrift*, 1832, I, 40–124; IDEM, "Der hebräische Sabbath und die Nationalfeste des mosaischen Cultus," *ibid.*, 1832, III, 123–92; VATKE, *Die Religion des Alten Testamentes* (1835), Vol. I, pp. 492–8; J. F. L. GEORGE, *Die älteren jüdischen Feste* (1835); H. EWALD, in *Göttingischer Gelehrter Anzeiger*, 1835, pp. 2025 f.; 1836, pp. 678 f.; H. EWALD, in *Jahrbücher der biblischen Wissenschaft*, Vol. IV, pp. 131 f.; VIII, p. 223; IX, pp. 257 f.; F. HITZIG, *Östern und Pfingsten* (1837); BÄHR, *Symbolik des mosaischen Cultus* (1839), Vol. II, pp. 664 ff.; H. EWALD, "De feriarum hebraearum origine et ratione," *Zeitschrift für die Kunde des Morgenlandes*, Vol. III (1840), pp. 410–41; H. HUPFELD, *De primitiva et vera festorum apud Hebraeos ratione ex legum Mosaicarum eruenda* (1851–65); REDSLOB, *Die biblischen Angaben über Stiftung und Grund der Passahfeier* (1856); W. SCHULTZ, "Die innere Bedeutung der alttestamentlichen Feste," *Deutsche Zeitschrift für christliche Wissenschaft und christliches Leben*, 1857, pp. 23–30; JOH. BACHMANN, *Die Festgesetze des Pentateuch auf's neue kritisch untersucht* (1858); DILLMANN, article "Feste," SCHENKEL'S *Bibel-Lexicon* (1869); H. OORT, "De groote Verzoendag," *Theologisch Tijdschrift*, Vol. X (1876), pp. 142–65; D. HOFFMANN, in BERLINER'S *Magazin*, 1876, pp. 1 ff.; IDEM, *Abhandlungen über die Pentateuch-Gesetze*, Vol. I (1878); IDEM, in *Magazin für die Wissenschaft des Judenthums*, 1879, pp. 99 ff.; FRANZ DELITZSCH, in *Zeitschrift für kirchliche Wissenschaft und kirchliches Leben*, Vol. I (1880), pp. 173–83, 621 ff.; KUENEN, in *Theologisch Tijdschrift*, Vol.

XVII (1883), pp. 207–12; MÜLLER, *Kritischer Versuch über den Ursprung des Pesach-Mazzothfestes* (1883); ADLER, "Der Versöhnungstag in der Bibel, sein Ursprung und seine Bedeutung," *Zeitschrift für die alttestamentliche Wissenschaft*, Vol. III (1883) pp. 178–85; ORELLI, articles "Passah," "Pfingstfest," *Realencyklopädie für protestantische Theologie und Kirche* (2d ed. 1883); FRANZ DELITZSCH, article "Passah,' RIEHM'S *Handwörterbuch des biblischen Alterthums* (1884); RIEHM, article "Feste,' RIEHM'S *Handwörterbuch des biblischen Alterthums* (1884); ORELLI, article "Versöhnungstag," *Realencyklopädie für protestantische Theologie und Kirche* (2d ed. 1885); DE LAGARDE, "Purim; ein Beitrag zur Religionsgeschichte," *Mittheilungen*, Vol. II (1887), pp. 378 ff.; IV, p. 147, note 1; WELLHAUSEN, *Reste des arabischen Heidentums* (= *Skizzen und Vorarbeiten*, Vol. III, 1887), pp. 75–98; B. STADE, *Geschichte des Volkes Israel* (1887 f.), Vol. I, pp. 497–503; II, pp. 182, 258–60; I. BENZINGER, "Das Gesetz über den grossen Versöhnungstag, Lev. XVI," *Zeitschrift für die alttestamentliche Wissenschaft*, Vol. IX (1889), pp. 65–88; RIEHM, *Alttestamentliche Theologie* (1889), pp. 121–3; H. ZIMMERN, "Zur Frage nach dem Ursprunge des Purimfestes," *Zeitschrift für die alttestamentliche Wissenschaft*, 1891, pp. 157–69; SMEND, *Lehrbuch der alttestamentlichen Religionsgeschichte* (1st ed. 1893, 2d ed. 1899), see *Index*, *s. v.* "Feste;" W. NOWACK, *Lehrbuch der hebräischen Archäologie* (1894), Vol. II, pp. 138–203; I. BENZINGER, *Hebräische Archäologie* (1894), pp. 464–78; EERDMANS, "Der Ursprung der Ceremonien des Hosein-Festes," *Zeitschrift für Assyriologie*, Vol. IX (1894), pp. 290 f.; S. KARPPE, "Mélanges de critique biblique et d'assyriologie," *Revue sémitique*, Vol. II (1894), pp. 146–51; DILLMANN, *Alttestamentliche Theologie* (1895), see *Index*, *s. v.* "Feste," "Passah;" K. MARTI, *Geschichte der israelitischen Religion* (1897), see *Index*, *s. v.* "Feste," "Pesach," "Laubhüttenfest," etc.; F. BUHL, "Gottesdienstliche Zeiten im Alten Testament," *Realencyklopädie für protestantische Theologie und Kirche* (1899); SCHAEFER, *Das Passah-Mazzoth Fest* (1900); ERBT, *Purimsage in der Bibel* (1900); MOSSA, "Bedeutung des Passahfestes," *Saat auf Hoffnung*, 1900, No. 2; RIEDEL, "Miscellen 5. 6.: פֶּסַח, בצאת השנה," *Zeitschrift für die alttestamentliche Wissenschaft*, Vol. XX (1900), pp. 319–32; B. STADE, "Nachwort zu Lic. W. Riedel's 5. Miscelle: פסח," *ibid.*, pp. 333–7; C. BROCKELMANN, "Das Neujahrsfest der Jezîdîs," *Zeitschrift der Deutschen Morgenländischen Gesellschaft*, Vol. LV (1901), pp. 388 ff.

§ 107. **Supplementary Topics.**

1. Consider the few references to the celebration of feasts and feast days in the Psalter, viz., Pss. 4:7; 81:3; and note especially the so-called Psalms of Ascents, viz., 120–134, and their use in worship.[10]

2. Put together the references to feasts in the books of Maccabees, viz.: 1 Macc. 1:39, 45; 4:52–59; 7:49; 10:34; 13:50–52; 2 Macc. 1:9, 18; 2:9, 16; 6:6 f.; 7:42; 8:33; 10:5–8; 12:31 f.; 15:36; and make such a statement as the material thus examined will warrant.

3. Consider the principal references to feasts in the New Testament, viz.: Matt. 26:2, 5, 17 ff.; 27:15; Mark 14:1 f., 12, 14, 16;

[10] *Cf.* WELLHAUSEN, *The Book of Psalms — A New English Translation*, p. 210; KIRKPATRICK, *The Psalms, Books II, III* ("Cambridge Bible"), p. xxv; MURRAY, *Origin and Growth of the Psalms*, pp. 292–5; PEROWNE, *Book of Psalms*, Vol. I, pp. 86 f.; SMITH, "The Songs of the Ascent," *Expository Times*, November, 1900.

15:6; Luke 2:41 f.; 22:1–15; 23:17; John 2:13, 23; 4:45; 5:1; 6:4; 7:2–14, 37; 10:22; 11:55 f.; 12:1, 12, 20; 13:1, 29; 18:28, 39; 19:14; 1 Cor. 5:7; Heb. 11:28.

4. Take up for critical study the principal Hebrew words used to designate the feasts, viz.: פֶּסַח, חָג, חג שבעות, חג הקציר; חג האסיף; חג הסכות; חדש; מצות; פורים; etc.

5. Compare, in a very general way, the usage concerning feasts among the Egyptians, the Greeks, and the Romans, and note points of similarity and difference.[11]

6. Consider the place of feasts among the Assyrians, noticing especially the great number of them and the many points of similarity existing between the usages of Assyrian feasts and those of Hebrew feasts, *e. g.*, the pervading spirit of joyousness, the agricultural connection of some of them, the similarity between the feast of Zagmuk and the Jewish New Year's festival, and the Babylonian origin of the Feast of Purim.[12]

7. Study the Hebrew feasts in their relation to (*a*) the Arabic feasts or pilgrimages, (*b*) the Canaanite agricultural feasts.[13]

8. Consider comparatively the three great factors entering into and controlling the origin and development of feasts, viz., the element involved in a nomadic or pastoral life, that in an agricultural life, and that in a city life.

9. Consider (1) the conception of God which had come to be supreme in Israel after the exile, viz., holiness; (2) the relation of this conception to the teaching concerning sin prevalent in the same period; and (3) the influences of these conceptions upon the development of the feast system.

[11] See W. W. FOWLER, *The Roman Festivals of the Period of the Republic;* FAIRBANKS, "Festival Epidauria at Athens," *Classical Review*, November, 1900; FRAZER, "The Saturnalia and Kindred Festivals," *Fortnightly Review*, October and November, 1900; WIEDEMANN, *Religion of the Ancient Egyptians* (1897), see *Index, s. v.* "Festivals."

[12] *Cf.* especially MORRIS JASTROW, JR., *Religion of Babylonia and Assyria*, see *Index, s. v.* "Festivals."

[13] See SNOUCK HURGRONJE, *Het Mekkaansche Fest;* DOUGHTY, *Travels in Arabia Deserta;* WELLHAUSEN, *Reste des arabischen Heidentums;* and other literature cited in § 106.

CHAPTER IX.

THE LAWS AND USAGES CONCERNING THE SABBATH AND KINDRED INSTITUTIONS, CONSIDERED COMPARATIVELY.

§ 108. **The Sabbath and Kindred Institutions in the Early Period,** *i. e.*, as described in (*a*) the Covenant Code, (*b*) the historical material of J and E, (*c*) the pre-Deuteronomic portions of Judges, Samuel, and Kings, and (*d*) the pre-Deuteronomic prophetic utterances (see § 59, note 1).[1]

1. The law of the sabbath.[2]
   Exod. 34 : 21 ; 20 : 8–11 ; **23 : 12.**

2. Customs connected with the sabbath.
   2 Kings 4 : 23 ; 11 : 5, 7, 9.

3. Attitude of the prophets toward the sabbath.
   Amos 8 : 5 ; Hos. 2 : 11 ; Isa. 1 : 13.

4. The law of the sabbatical year.
   Exod. 23 : 10 f.; 21 : 2–11.

§ 109. **Questions and Suggestions.**

1. Consider, in examining the statements made concerning the sabbath, (1) why the sabbath is the only religious institution mentioned in the decalogue; (2) the first word, *remember*, and compare the first word in Deut. 5 : 12, *observe*. (3) Was either of these in any sense a warning equivalent to "take care," "be on the lookout for"? (4) What is the logical relation of the fourth commandment to the third, second, and first? Does this consist in its having originally had to do with the deity, as do the preceding? (5) Are there other variations between the two forms of the commandment given in Exod., chap. 20, and Deut., chap. 5? What are the variations? How shall we explain the existence of any variations at all? Is it possible that Exod. 20 : 9–11 and Deut. 5 : 13–15 are later additions made at different times to an earlier form, which, as in the case of the sixth, seventh, and eighth commandments, consisted of only two or three words,

[1] The following references are from E: Exod. 20 : 8–10; 23 : 10–12; 21 : 2–11; the only reference in J is Exod. 34 : 21.

[2] References in **bold-face** type are from the Covenant Code.

"Observe (or remember) the sabbath day to keep it holy"?[3] (6) What was involved in the command *to keep it holy?* (7) What may be said of the antiquity of the sabbath? Was it probably observed by the Hebrews in Egypt? (8) Was it originally connected with the new moon? (9) What are the chief considerations offered to show that it was originally a day for securing the good-will of the deity, *i. e.*, a day on which Jehovah rested *from his anger*, and was, therefore, more easy to propitiate; a day, however, which might prove to be unfavorable, but which might be changed to a favorable day by doing or not doing certain things?[4] (10) What, if this view is adopted, would be understood in particular to be the meaning of the word *rest?* of the word *observe?* (11) How did such strong emphasis come to be placed upon the idea of cessation from labor?

2. In respect to the usages which connected themselves with the sabbath, consider (1) the custom of visiting the man of God on the sabbath; (2) the custom of dividing the temple guard according as it came in or went out on the sabbath; (3) other early (?) customs, codified in later times, *e. g.*, remaining inside the house (Exod. 16:29), kindling no fire (Exod. 35:3), no gathering of wood for the fire (Numb. 15:32–36), no baking or cooking (Exod. 16:23). (4) So far as the *early* records are concerned, are there any other ideas than those of cessation from labor and of humanitarian motive?

3. What is to be gathered from the few allusions to the sabbath made by the prophets? (1) What are the people desiring to make of the sabbath, according to Amos? What restraint is evidently upon them? (2) Does Hosea's statement seem to place the sabbath in the same category with days of rejoicing and mirth? (3) What is the significance of the frequent association (as in Isa. 1:13) of the sabbath with the new moon?

4. Consider (1) regulations relating to the release of Hebrew servants after six years of labor; did this imply a regularly recurring seventh year in which all servants were released? Had this anything to do with a sabbatical year? (2) The regulations prescribing that the crop of every seventh year shall be given to the poor and the beasts; does the regulation say that all land was to lie fallow in the

[3] This is the view held, for example, by EWALD, *History of Israel*, Vol. II, p. 159; DILLMANN, *Exodus*, p. 201; *Speaker's Commentary*, p. 336; DRIVER, *Introduction, etc.*, p. 34; BRIGGS, *Higher Criticism of the Hexateuch*, pp. 181–7; MARTI, *Geschichte der israelitischen Religion; et al.*

[4] JASTROW, *American Journal of Theology*, Vol. II, pp. 312–52.

same year? Was this the recognition of a sabbatical year? (3) The motives underlying these regulations.

§ 110. **Constructive Work.**— Prepare a statement which will indicate the most important factors entering into the significance of the sabbath, and its characteristics as it appears in the earliest period.

§ 111. **The Sabbath and Kindred Institutions in the Middle Period,** *i. e.*, as described in the laws of Deuteronomy, in the Deuteronomic prophecies, and in the Deuteronomic portions of the books of Samuel and Kings.[5]

1. The law of the sabbath in the Deuteronomic decalogue.
   Deut. 5:12–15.
2. The attitude of the prophets toward the sabbath.
   Jer. 17:19–27; Isa. 56:2, 4, 6; 58:13, 14; 66:23; Lam. 1:7; 2:6.
3. The law of the sabbatical year.
   Deut. 15:1–18; 31:10.
4. Release of slaves in Jeremiah.
   Jer. 34:8–17.

§ 112. **Questions and Suggestions.**

1. Consider now in detail the Deuteronomic version of the sabbath law, including (1) the word *observe*, (2) the reference to Jehovah's former command (vs. 12), (3) the provision for the rest of the servants, (4) the reason given for the observance of the sabbath, viz., the deliverance from the bondage of Egypt; is this an implication that the sabbath was not observed by the Israelites in Egypt? How is it to be reconciled with the reason given in Exod. 20:11? (5) the effect upon the observance of the sabbath of the centralization of worship at Jerusalem; would this not take away the ritualistic observance and emphasize the humanitarian idea?

2. In an examination of the prophetic and historical allusions to the observance of the sabbath, consider (1) the small number of such references; is there any satisfactory reason? (2) the several items said by Jeremiah to have been commanded by Jehovah, viz., (*a*) as to burdens, (*b*) as to work, (*c*) as to hallowing the day; (3) the attitude of the people (Jer. 17:23); (4) the promises and threats in reference to its observance (Jer. 17:24–27); (5) the position assigned to the sabbath in connection with the observance of the covenant (Isa. 56:2, 4, 6); (6) the meaning of the phrases *from doing thy pleasure*, and *call the sabbath a delight* (Isa. 58:13), and the rewards offered; (7) the sabbath

[5] References in **bold-face** type are from the code of laws contained in Deuteronomy.

as a time, like the new moon, for worship (Isa. 66 : 23); (8) the forgetting of the sabbath in the exile.

3. Consider, in comparison with the regulations cited above (§§ 108, 4; 109, 4), the Deuteronomic regulations concerning (1) the year of release of debts: (*a*) to whom it shall and shall not apply; (*b*) does it mean that the debt, if not paid, will be forgiven or become outlawed; or that no interest will be exacted during this seventh year; or that no proceedings will be taken against the debtor during that year? (*c*) the reward promised; (*d*) the motive for this law; (*e*) does it imply an advanced commercial development? (*f*) is the year a fixed seventh year? (*g*) would it encourage or discourage business? (2) the regulations for the release of the Hebrew servant, noting the slight variations from the law given in Exodus; (3) whether Deuteronomy has any regulation concerning the rest of the land (*cf.* Exod. 23 : 10 f.); (4) the reading of the law prescribed for the Feast of Tabernacles during the year of release at the end of every seven years.

4. Consider the points involved in the story of the release of slaves in Jeremiah's time.

§ 113. **Constructive Work.**—Prepare a brief statement showing the nature of the changes which are being made, and the general trend.

§ 114. **The Sabbath as Described by Ezekiel.**

1. The purpose of the sabbath.
   Ezek. 20 : 12, 20.

2. The sabbath a *holy* day.
   Ezek. 44 : 24.

3. General profanation of the sabbath.
   Ezek. 20 : 13–24; 22 : 8, 26; 23 : 38.

4. Special worship and sacrifices for the sabbath.
   Ezek. 45 : 17; 46 : 1–5, 12.

5. The year of liberty.
   Ezek. 46 : 17.

§ 115. **Questions and Suggestions.**

1. What, according to Ezekiel, was the original purpose which the sabbath was to subserve? Compare the purpose also of the statutes (Ezek. 20 : 11), and the way in which both statutes and sabbaths had been treated by Israel.

2. What, in Ezekiel's time, was meant by *hallowing* or *keeping holy* the sabbath?

3. What was meant by *profaning* and *hiding the eyes from* the sabbath? Did the Israelites simply ignore it, or did they intentionally do that which brought it into disrepute?

4. Note the special character of the offerings indicated in Ezekiel's scheme for the sabbath day. What was the significance of this? Consider how the sabbath is still associated with the new moon.

5. Note the contents of the single reference in Ezekiel to the year of release or liberty.

§ 116. **Constructive Work.**—Summarize the position of Ezekiel, and indicate the relation of Ezekiel's attitude on this question to his general place in prophecy.

§ 117. **Sabbath and Kindred Institutions in the Later Period,** *i. e.*, as described in (*a*) the laws of the Levitical Code, (*b*) by the priestly prophets, and (*c*) in the priestly histories, viz., Ezra, Nehemiah, Chronicles.

1. The law of the sabbath.[6]
   Lev. 23 : 3 ; Exod. 31 : 12–17 ; 35 : 1–3.

2. Special days observed as sabbaths.
   Lev. 23 : 7 f., 24–32, 39 ; 16 : 29–31 ; Numb. 28 : 11–15, 18, 25 f. ; 29 : 1, 7, 12, 35.

3. Reasons assigned for the observance of the sabbath.
   Gen. 2 : 2 f. ; Exod. 20 : 11 ; **31 : 12 f., 17.**

4. Special offerings made on the sabbath.
   Lev. 23 : 38 ; Numb. 28 : 9 f. ; 1 Chron. 23 : 31 ; 2 Chron. 2 : 4 ; 8 : 13 ; 31 : 3 ; Neh. 10 : 33.

5. Emphasis laid on observance of the sabbath.
   Lev. 19 : 3*b*, 30*a* ; 26 : 2*a* ; Exod. 16 : 22–30 ; 31 : 14–16 ; 35 : 2 ; Numb. 15 : 32–36 ; Neh. 10 : 31 ; 13 : 15–22.

6. Use of the sabbath as a fixed point of time.
   Lev. 23 : 15 f. ; 24 : 8 ; 1 Chron. 9 : 32 ; 2 Chron. 23 : 4, 8.

7. Sabbath *made known* on Sinai.
   Neh. 9 : 14.

8. Law of the sabbatical year.
   Lev. 25 : 1–7 ; 26 : 34, 35.

9. Exile conceived of as a sabbath for the land.
   Lev. 26 : 34 f. ; 2 Chron. 36 : 21.

10. Law of year of jubilee.
    Lev., chap. 25 ; 27 : 17–24 ; Numb. 36 : 4.

[6] References in **bold-face** type are from the Levitical Code.

§ 118. **Questions and Suggestions.**

1. Consider (1) the form of the sabbath observance which must have existed during the exile, viz., the humanitarian and not the ritualistic; the adaptation of this to the possibilities of worship in this period, and the distinctive character which it must have given the Jewish community. (2) What is the meaning of the new phrases *solemn rest, holy convocation, sabbath unto Jehovah?* (3) What is the purpose of the sabbath (*cf.* Ezekiel) ? the penalty for its non-observance ? the connection between sign and perpetual covenant ? (4) The reason assigned for its establishment (*cf.* Exod. 20 : 11) ? (5) Why should the kindling of fire have been prohibited in particular ?

2. Note how the idea of rest now attaches itself to other days, viz., first day of the Passover, first day of the Feast of Trumpets, first and eighth days of the Feast of Booths, the Day of Atonement.

3. Consider the reasons assigned for the sabbath's observance: (1) because God rested on the seventh day; was there any connection between this reason and the fact that the teaching concerning God as Creator is greatly emphasized in the exilic and post-exilic periods ? (2) because it is to serve as a sign between God and Israel ; did this mean that it distinguished Israel from other nations which did not observe it ?

4. Note the details and significance of the special offering made on the sabbath.

5. Consider the rigidity with which the sabbath law was now to be enforced : (1) on the same plane with the honoring of father and mother, and the reverencing of a sanctuary; (2) penalty of death imposed for non-observance ; (3) the story of the man who gathered sticks on the sabbath day and suffered death by stoning ; (4) the gathering of a double amount of manna on the sixth day and the absence of manna on the sabbath ; (5) the agreement to refrain from commercial dealings on the sabbath ; (6) Nehemiah's judicial procedure in the case of those violating the law.

6. Note how the sabbath, having become a fixed date, every seventh day, is used as a point from which to calculate other feasts.

7. Note the tradition preserved by Nehemiah that the sabbath was (first ?) made known on Sinai.

8. Study the details of the law of the sabbatical year : (1) Is all agriculture to be remitted ? (2) What is to be the disposition of the fruit and grain that grows of itself ? (3) Was Palestine a land subject to severe famines ? If so, could such a law have been observed ?

(4) Could it have been observed while the people were mainly agriculturists, *i. e.*, before trade and commerce had come in? How would the people living in rural districts spend their time? (5) Is there any evidence that it was observed before the exile? or that it was not (*cf.* Lev. 26:34, 35)? (6) Did not its observance in later times cause great distress (1 Macc. 6:49, 53)? (7) What connection was there between this sabbatical year, with its fixed time of recurrence, and the year of release for slaves and debt in Deuteronomy (§§ 111, 3; 112, 3)?

9. Consider the idea suggested that the entire period of exile is a period of sabbaths, now enforced because formerly unobserved.

10. Concerning the Year of Jubilee, consider (1) the meaning of the name; (2) the time fixed; was it the fiftieth year following the seventh sabbatical year, that is, was it the second of two successive years of rest? or did it coincide with the forty-ninth year? (3) the procedure; was it, in general, like the sabbatical year? (4) what was the regulation concerning sowing, reaping, gathering? (5) concerning the restoration of real property? (6) the special provision concerning dwelling-houses in walled cities; the houses of the Levites; (7) the regulation concerning Hebrew and non-Hebrew slaves; (8) concerning land dedicated to Jehovah and its redemption; (9) concerning the inheritance of daughters as affected by these laws. (10) How were the people to live during this period of abstinence from work? (11) Is it possible that the law of the jubilee year is an outgrowth of the law of the sabbath? (12) What led to the choice of the fiftieth year? (13) Is there any evidence that this law existed before the time of the exile? (14) Was the Year of Jubilee ever observed? (15) Was it a practical law, or an ideal law? (16) What, in general, is meant by ideal legislation?

§ 119. **Constructive Work.**

Prepare a statement including (*a*) an explanation of the fact that such an exceedingly large place is occupied by the sabbatical system in the legislation and thought of this period; (*b*) an enumeration of the various points of difference between the laws and usages of this period and those of the Deuteronomic period; and (*c*) a brief study of the development of the sabbatical idea in the course of Israel's history.

§ 120. **Literature to be Consulted.**

JENNINGS, *Jewish Antiquities* (1808), pp. 320 f.; EWALD, *History of Israel* (1st ed. 1843–59, transl. 1883), Vol. I, pp. 88 f.; II, pp. 209 f.; V, pp. 166 f., 343, 400, 416; IDEM, *Antiquities of Israel* (1854, transl. 1876), pp. 97–107; KALISCH, *Commentary on Exodus* (1855), *in loc.* 20:8–11; HESSEY, *On the Sabbath* ("Bampton Lecture," 1860, 3d ed. 1866); GILFILLAN, *On the Sabbath* (1862); KURTZ, *Sacrificial Worship of the Old Testament* (1862, transl. 1863), pp. 342 ff.; JOHNSTONE, *Sunday and the*

Sabbath (1863); R. S. Poole, article "Chronology," see section on "Sabbatical and Jubilee Years," Smith's *Dictionary of the Bible* (1st ed. 1863, 2d ed. 1893); Cox, *Literature of the Sabbath Question* (1865); Schultz, *Old Testament Theology* (1st ed. 1869, transl. 1892), see *Index, s. v.* "Sabbath," "Sabbatical Year," "Jubilee;" Kuenen, *The Religion of Israel* (1869 f., transl. 1894), Vol. I, pp. 286 f.; II, pp. 278–84; Sayce, *Records of the Past*, Vol. I (1873), pp. 164 f.; Oehler, *Theology of the Old Testament* (1st ed. 1873, 3d ed. 1891, transl. 1883), pp. 328–45; Sayce, *Records of the Past*, Vol. VII (1876), p. 157; Wellhausen, *Prolegomena to the History of Israel* (1878), pp. 112–20; J. Fenton, *Early Hebrew Life* (1880), pp. 24–6, 29–32, 64–70; W. D. Love, "The Sabbath, etc.," *Bibliotheca Sacra*, 1880, pp. 153–78, 355–89, 419–39, 661–85; 1881, pp. 254–85, 524–52, Schrader, *Cuneiform Inscriptions and the Old Testament* (2d ed. 1882, transl. 1885), Vol. I, pp. 18 ff.; W. R. Smith, *Prophets of Israel* (1st ed. 1882, 2d ed. 1895), pp. 385 f.; Francis Brown, "The Sabbath in the Cuneiform Records," *Presbyterian Review*, 1882, pp. 688–700; Dillmann, *Commentary on Genesis* (5th ed. 1886, transl. 1897 f.), on Gen., chap. 1; Schürer, *History of the Jewish People in the Time of Jesus Christ* (1886, transl. 1891), Div. II, Vol. II, pp. 96–105; W. R. Smith, articles "Jubilee," "Sabbath," *Encyclopædia Britannica* (1887); Sayce, *Religion of the Ancient Babylonians* ("Hibbert Lectures," 1887), pp. 70–77; Doughty, *Travels in Arabia Deserta* (1888), Vol. I, pp. 151, 366; II, pp. 225, 306; McClintock and Strong, *Cyclopædia of Biblical, Theological and Ecclesiastical Literature* (1891), articles "Jubilee," "Sabbath," and "Sabbatical Year;" Jensen, "The Supposed Babylonian Origin of the Week and the Sabbath," *Sunday School Times*, January 16, 1892; Alice M. Earle, *The Sabbath in Puritan New England* (7th ed. 1893); F. Garden, article "Sabbatical Year," Smith's *Dictionary of the Bible* (2d ed. 1893); S. Clark (revised by J. M. Fuller), article "Jubilee," Smith's *Dictionary of the Bible* (2d ed. 1893); W. E. Addis, *Documents of the Hexateuch*, 2 vols. (1893–98), see *Index, s. v.* "Jubilee," "Sabbath," etc.; Sayce, *Higher Criticism and the Verdict of the Monuments* (1893), pp. 74–7; Montefiore, *The Religion of the Ancient Hebrews* ("Hibbert Lectures," 1893), see *Index, s. v.* "Sabbath;" Davis, *Genesis and Semitic Tradition* (1894), pp. 23–35; Driver, *A Critical and Exegetical Commentary on Deuteronomy* (1895), pp. 174–81; Hirschfeld, "Remarks on the Etymology of Šabbath," *Journal of the Royal Asiatic Society*, 1896, pp. 354 f.; Abrahams, *Jewish Life in the Middle Ages* (1897), see *Index, s. v.* "Sabbath;" Morris Jastrow, Jr., "The Original Character of the Hebrew Sabbath," *American Journal of Theology*, Vol. II (1898), pp. 312–52; Cheyne, *Jewish Religious Life after the Exile* (1898), pp. 66 f.; S. R. Driver and H. A. White, *The Book of Leviticus — a New English Translation* (Polychrome Bible, 1898), pp. 97–100; E. A. W. Budge, *Egyptian Magic* (1899), pp. 224–8; Sayce, *Babylonians and Assyrians: Life and Customs* (1899), p. 245; Kent, *A History of the Jewish People During the Babylonian, Persian, and Greek Periods* (1899), see *Index, s. v.* "Sabbath;" Sinker, *Essays and Studies* (1900); J. Estlin-Carpenter and G. Harford Battersby, *The Hexateuch* (1900), Vol. II, p. 112; T. F. Wright, "Sabbath," *New Church Review*, January, 1900; W. R. Smith and I. Benzinger, article "Jubilee," *Encyclopædia Biblica* (1901); McCurdy, *History, Prophecy and the Monuments*, Vol. III (1901), pp. 376 f.; Morris Jastrow, Jr., "Hebrew and Babylonian Accounts of Creation," *Jewish Quarterly Review*, Vol. XIII (1901), pp. 648–50; H. R. Gamble, *Sunday and the Sabbath* (Golden Lectures for 1900–1901); C. F. Kent, *Biblical World*, Vol. XVIII (1901), pp. 344–8.

J. SPENCER, *De legibus Hebraeorum ritualibus* (2d ed. 1686); WAGENSEIL, *De anno iubilaeo Hebraeorum* (1700); J. H. MAI, *Maimonidis tract. de juribus anni septimi et jubilaei* (1708); VAN DER HARDT, *De jubilaeo Mosis* (1728); REINECCIUS, *De origine jubilaeorum* (1730); CARPZOV, *De anno jubilaeo* (1730); HEBENSTREIT, *De sabbato ante leges Mosis existente* (1748); MEYER, *De temporibus et diebus Hebraeorum* (1755), pp. 341–60; MICHAELIS, *Comm. in leg. Mosis* (1775–80), Vol. I, pp. 76–419; FRANKE, *Novum systema chronologiae fundamentalis* (1778); HUG, "Ueber das mosaische Gesetz vom Jubeljahr," *Zeitschrift für das Erzbisthum*, I, 1; DE WETTE, *Lehrbuch der hebräisch-jüdischen Archäologie* (1st ed. 1814, 4th ed. 1864), pp. 211 f.; BAUR, "Der hebräische Sabbath und die Nationalfeste des Mosaischen Kultus," *Tübinger Zeitschrift*, 1832, pp. 125 f.; VATKE, *Die Religion des Alten Testamentes* (1835), Vol. I, pp. 198 f.; KRANOLD, *De anno Hebraeorum jubilaeo* (1835); G. WOLDE, *De anno Hebraeorum jubilaeo* (1837); BÄHR, *Symbolik des mosaischen Cultus* (1839), Vol. I, pp. 572 f.; II, pp. 569 f., 601 f.; WINER's *Biblisches Realwörterbuch* (3d ed. 1847), articles "Sabbath," etc.; EWALD, *Zeitschrift der Deutschen Morgenländischen Gesellschaft*, Vol. I (1847), pp. 410 ff.; BRUGSCH, *ibid.*, Vol. III (1849), pp. 271 ff.; PROUDHON, *De la célébration du Dimanche* (1850); OSCHWALD, *Die christliche Sonntagsfeier* (1850); LIEBETRUT, *Die Sonntagsfeier das Wochenfest des Volkes Gottes* (1851); HERZFELD, *Geschichte des Volkes Israel*, Vol. II (1855), pp. 458–65; SAALSCHÜTZ, *Archäologie der Hebräer*, Vol. II (1856), pp. 224 ff., 308 ff.; ZUCKERMANN, *Sabbathjahrcyclus und Jubelperiode* (1857); HUPFELD, *Commentatio de Hebraeorum festis*, Part III (1858); KEIL, *Handbuch der biblischen Archäologie* (1st ed. 1858 f., 2d ed. 1875), Vol. I, §§ 77 ff.; DOZY, *Die Israeliten zu Mekka* (transl. from Dutch 1864), pp. 34 f.; KÜBEL, "Die sociale und volkswirtschaftliche Gesetzgebung des Alten Testamentes," *Theologische Studien und Kritiken*, 1871, pp. 760 ff.; STEINER, article "Jubeljahr" in SCHENKEL's *Bibel-Lexikon*, Vol. III (1871); SCHRADER, "Der babylonische Ursprung der siebentagigen Woche," *Theologische Studien und Kritiken*, 1874, pp. 343 ff.; MANGOLD, articles "Sabbat" and "Sabbatsjahr" in SCHENKEL's *Bibel-Lexikon*, Vol. V (1875); KÖHLER, *Lehrbuch der biblischen Geschichte*, Vol. I (1875), pp. 431 ff.; KLOSTERMANN, "Über die kalendarische Bedeutung des Jobeljahres," *Theologische Studien und Kritiken*, 1880, pp. 720–48; DILLMANN, *Die Bücher Exodus und Leviticus* (2d ed. 1880), pp. 602 ff.; BUDDE, *Die biblische Urgeschichte* (1883), pp. 493 ff.; LOTZ, *Quaestiones de historia sabbathi* (1883); HOFFMANN, "Versuche zu Amos," *Zeitschrift für die alttestamentliche Wissenschaft*, Vol. III (1883), pp. 120 f.; OEHLER, articles "Sabbath" and "Sabbath- und Jobeljahr," revised by VON ORELLI, in *Realencyklopädie für protestantische Theologie und Kirche* (2d ed. 1884); RIEHM, articles "Jobeljahr," "Sabbath," "Sabbathjahr" in RIEHM's *Handwörterbuch des biblischen Alterthums* (1st ed. 1884, 2d ed. 1893 f.); STADE, *Geschichte des Volkes Israel*, Vol. I (1887), pp. 498 f.; WELLHAUSEN, *Composition des Hexateuchs* (2d ed. 1889), pp. 187 f.; JENSEN, *Zeitschrift für Assyriologie*, Vol. IV (1889), pp. 274 ff.; H. L. STRACK, *Der Mischnatraktat "Sabbath" herausgegeben und erklärt* (1890); BAENTSCH, *Das Bundesbuch—Ex. XX. 22—XXIII. 33* (1892), pp. 115 f.; SMEND, *Lehrbuch der alttestamentlichen Religionsgeschichte* (1st ed. 1893, 2d ed. 1899), see *Index, s. v.* "Sabbath" and "Jubeljahr;" NOWACK, *Lehrbuch der hebräischen Archäologie* (1894), Vol. I, pp. 217, 333; II, pp. 138–44, 159–72; BENZINGER, *Hebräische Archäologie* (1894), pp. 201 f., 464 ff., 473 f.; GUNKEL, *Schöpfung und Chaos* (1895), pp. 13f., 114–17; DILLMANN, *Handbuch der alttestamentlichen Theologie* (1895), see *Index, s. v.* "Jobeljahr" and "Sabbat;" MARTI, *Geschichte der israelitischen Religion* (1897), see *Index, s. v.*

"Sabbat" and "Jobeljahr;" HOLZINGER, *Exodus* (*Kurzer Hand-Commentar zum Alten Testament*), see *Index, s. v.* "Sabbath" (1900); BERTHOLET, *Leviticus* (*Kurzer Hand-Commentar zum Alten Testament*), see *Index, s. v.* "Jobeljahr," "Sabbat," (1901).

See also the Mishnah tracts on "The Sabbath" and "The Book of Jubilees," chap. 50.

§ 121. **Supplementary Topics.**

1. Study the meaning of the word "sabbath," its derivation, its usage.

2. Examine the following texts in which the root שבת occurs, with a view to determining the meaning of the root, viz.: Gen. 2:2 f.; 8:22; Exod. 16:30; 12:15; 23:12; 34:21; Josh. 5:12; Isa. 13:11; 14:5; 30:7; Ps. 8:3; Prov. 20:3.

3. Study the passages in which the word שבתון (ordinarily translated "solemn rest") occurs, viz.: Lev. 23:3, 24, 32, 39; 16:31; 25:4; Exod. 16:23; 35:2; 31:15, with a view to determining its meaning.

4. Examine the words יבל ("jubilee"), דרור ("liberty").

5. From an examination of 1 Macc. 1:39, 43, 45; 2:32–41; 6:49; 9:43 ff.; 10:34; 2 Macc. 5:24–26; 6:6, 11; 12:38; 15:1–5, prepare a statement concerning the sabbath in Maccabean times.

6. Is the sabbath referred to in the Wisdom books, or in the Psalms (*cf.* the title of Ps. 92)? Why not?

7. From a study of the following references from the New Testament discuss the attitude of Jesus and the several New Testament writers toward the sabbath: Matt. 12:1 f., 5, 8, 10 ff.; 24:20; 28:1; Mark 1:21; 2:23 f., 27 f.; 3:2, 4; 6:2; 15:42; 16:1; Luke 4:16, 31; 6:1 ff., 5 ff., 9; 13:10, 14 ff.; 14:1, 3, 5; 23:54, 56; John 5:9 f., 16, 18; 7:22 f.; 9:14, 16; 19:31; Acts 1:12; 13:14, 27, 42, 44; 15:21; 18:4; 21:27; 28:14; Col. 2:16; Heb. 4:4; Rev. 1:10.

8. Compare, in general, the observance of special rest-days among the Egyptians, Greeks, and Romans, and determine whether there is any possible connection between these days and the sabbath.[7]

9. Compare, in general, the observance, on the part of the Assyrians,

[7] *Cf.* MASPERO, *Romans et Poésies au Papyrus Harris, No. 500*, pp. 38 f. 41; CHABAS, *Le calendrier des jours fastes et nefastes de l'année égyptienne;* WIEDEMANN, *Religion of the Egyptians*, pp. 263 f.; JASTROW, "Original Character of the Hebrew Sabbath," *American Journal of Theology*, Vol. II, p. 350, note 116; BUDGE, *Egyptian Magic*, pp. 224–8; IHERING, *Vorgeschichte der Indo-Europäer*, pp. 145, 309–58 ff. (in English translation = *The Evolution of the Aryan*, New York, 1897); H. COHEN, "Der Sabbath in seiner culturgeschichtlichen Bedeutung," *Zeitgeist* (Milwaukee, Wis.), 1881, pp. 4 ff.; DOZY, *Die Israeliten zu Mekka*, pp. 34 f.; KUENEN, *Religion of Israel*,

Arabs, and Canaanites, of special rest-days, and determine whether there is any connection between these days and the sabbath.[8]

10. Consider, in general, the whole sabbatical system, and show (*a*) its origin, (*b*) its various stages of development, (*c*) its social bearings, (*d*) its religious significance, (*e*) its idealism, (*f*) its practical character.

11. Consider the relation of the sabbath to the moon, the new-moon feast, etc. Was the sabbath originally a lunar festival? *Cf.* §§ 97 (9), 104 (4).

12. Consider the origin and significance of the use of the number seven in the Old Testament, as seen, *e. g.*, in the sabbatical system, in the proceedings connected with the capture of Jericho, in the Hebrew verb "to swear, take oath" (literally = "to seven oneself" or "be sevened"), in the seven kine of Pharaoh's dream, etc.

13. What is the relation of the Old Testament sabbath to the "Lord's day" of the New Testament, (*a*) as to the day observed, (*b*) as to the spirit characteristic of the observance?

Vol. I, pp. 262 f.; LEPSIUS, *Chronologie der Aegypter*, Vol. I, pp. 22, 132 ff.; BRUGSCH, *Zeitschrift der Deutschen Morgenländischen Gesellschaft*, Vol. III, p. 271; NOWACK, *Hebräische Archäologie*, Vol. II, pp. 141 f.

[8] *Cf.* MORRIS JASTROW, "Original Character of the Hebrew Sabbath," *American Journal of Theology*, Vol. II, pp. 312–52; SAYCE, *Babylonians and Assyrians: Life and Customs*, p. 245; SCHRADER, *Theologische Studien und Kritiken*, 1874, pp. 343–53; FRANCIS BROWN, "The Sabbath in the Cuneiform Records," *Presbyterian Review*, 1882, pp. 688–700; C. H. W. JOHNS, *Assyrian Deeds and Documents*, Vol, II, pp. 40 f. (See also § 120.)

CHAPTER X.

THE LAWS AND USAGES CONCERNING CLEAN AND UNCLEAN, CONSIDERED COMPARATIVELY.

§ 122. **The Clean and Unclean in the Early Period,** *i. e.*, as described in (*a*) the Covenant Code; (*b*) the historical material of J and E; (*c*) the pre-Deuteronomic portions of Judges, Samuel, and Kings; and (*d*) the pre-Deuteronomic prophetic utterances (see § 59, note 1).[1]

1. Traces of totemism.
   Gen. 43:32; 46:34; Exod. 8:26.
2. Distinction between clean and unclean is ancient.
   Gen. 7:2, 8; 8:20.
3. Sources of uncleanness.
   Gen. 35:2; 2 Sam. 11:4; 2 Kings 5:10–14; Isa. 30:22.
4. Non-Israelitish lands are unclean.
   Amos 7:17; Hos. 9:3.
5. Forbidden food.
   Exod. 23:19*b*; 34:26*b*; 22:31.[2]
6. Cleanness is necessary to participation in religious exercises.
   Gen. 35:2; Exod. 3:5; 19:10; 1 Sam. 20:26; Judg. 13:4, 7, 14; Isa. 6:5; 2 Kings 10:22; 2 Sam. 6:14.
7. Attitude of prophets toward clean and unclean.
   Amos 7:17; Hos. 9:3; Isa. 1:16; 6:5; 30:22.

§ 123. **Questions and Suggestions.**

1. Consider (1) the meaning of "every shepherd is an abomination unto the Egyptians," and what is involved in the statement; (2) the meaning of "sacrifice the abomination of the Egyptians;" (3) whether that which is called an "abomination" may have been something sacred or holy, *i. e.*, something worshiped, for example, an animal; (4) whether, as a matter of fact, there existed in Israel cases of special association between certain kinds of animals and certain tribes or certain towns;[3]

[1] The following references are from J: Gen. 7:2, 8; 8:20; 43:32; 46:34; Exod. 8:26; 34:26*b*. The following are from E: Gen. 35:2; Exod. 22:31*b*; 23:19*b*.

[2] These references are from the Covenant Code.

[3] *Cf.* Nun (Fish), Exod. 33:11; Terah (Ibex), Gen. 11:27; Leah (Wild Cow), Gen. 29:16; and see R. G. MURISON, "Totemism in the Old Testament," *Biblical World*, Vol. XVIII, pp. 170 ff.

(5) whether there are not cases in which animals are regarded as having superhuman power;[4] (6) whether the second commandment does not imply that the Israelites were addicted to animal-worship; (7) whether actual historical proof of this is not found in the story of the worship of the calf (Exod. 32 : 7–24) and of the brazen serpent (Numb. 21 : 8 f.; 2 Kings 18 : 4); (8) the meaning and significance of *totemism*.[5]

2. Note (1) the distinction between clean and unclean animals made in the narrative of the deluge, and consider (2) whether the words *unclean* and *sacred* may not be used synonymously; that is, was not the *unclean thing* (whether animal or person or object) something in connection with which "a superhuman agency of a dangerous kind" was supposed to be acting, and which, therefore, was, from one point of view, sacred, from another, unclean? (3) whether this is not to be closely associated with the usage existing among many nations and called *taboo*.[6]

3. Consider the source of uncleanness in the case of (1) Jacob's household, (2) Bathsheba, (3) Naaman the Syrian, (4) the graven images (Isa. 30 : 22); and formulate a statement which will (*a*) classify these sources and (*b*) explain the idea of uncleanness in each case.

4. Consider the idea that for an Israelite any other land than his own was unclean, and explain the basis on which this idea rests.

5. Note the prohibition of eating (1) a kid boiled in its mother's milk,[7] (2) the flesh torn of beasts; and explain the significance of the usage in each case. Are there in the Covenant Code other prohibitions concerning the eating of food?

6. Explain (1) the "washing of garments" in Exod. 19 : 10; (2) the reason assigned by Saul for Jonathan's absence (1 Sam. 20 : 26); (3) the connection of "eating no unclean thing" with the Nazirite (Judg. 13 : 4); (4) Isaiah's confession of unclean lips (Isa. 6 : 5); (5) the putting off of shoes (Exod. 3 : 5); (6) the use of the vestments (2 Kings 10 : 22); (7) the use of the linen ephod (2 Sam. 6 : 14).

7. How far were the current ideas concerning clean and unclean

[4] *Cf.* Gen. 3 : 1 ff.; Numb. 21 : 8 f.; Ezek. 8 : 10 f.

[5] See especially J. G. FRAZER, *Totemism;* W. R. SMITH, *Religion of the Semites* (2d ed.), pp. 125 ff.; and other literature cited in § 134.

[6] See especially J. G. FRAZER, article "Taboo," *Encyclopædia Britannica;* W. R. SMITH, *Religion of the Semites* (2d ed.), pp. 152 ff., 446 ff.

[7] See KALISCH, *Commentary* on Exod. 23 : 19*b*, and W. R. SMITH, *Religion of the Semites* (2d ed.), p. 221.

accepted by the prophets? Consider, for example, (1) the view held concerning foreign lands; (2) the exhortation to wash and become clean (Isa. 1:6); (3) Isaiah's feeling concerning himself (6:5); (4) the treatment of graven images (Isa. 30:22).

§ 124. **Constructive Work.**—From the material furnished prepare a general statement upon the idea of the clean and unclean in the earliest period.

§ 125. **The Usages and Laws Concerning Clean and Unclean in the Middle Period,** *i. e.*, as described in the laws of Deuteronomy, in the Deuteronomic prophecies, and in the Deuteronomic portions of the books of Samuel and Kings.[8]

1. Traces of totemism.
   Deut. 32:17; 2 Kings 22:12; Jer. 36:10; *cf.* 2 Kings 18:4 and Ezek. 8:7–12.
2. Forbidden food.
   Deut. 12:16, 23 ff.; 14:3–21; 15:23.
3. Sources of uncleanness.
   Deut. 21:22 f.; 23:10 f.; 23:12–14; 7:25 f.; Jer. 16:18; Lam. 4:14 f.
4. Cleanness necessary to participation in religious exercises.
   Deut. 12:15; 15:21 f.; 26:13 f.; Isa. 52:1, 11.
5. Prophetic attitude toward clean and unclean.
   Jer. 2:7, 23; 13:27; 16:18; 33:8; Lam. 4:14 f.; Isa. 52:1, 11.

§ 126. **Questions and Suggestions.**

1. Note that individuals and heads of clans still bear the names of animals, *e. g.*, Shaphan (=Rock Badger), Achbor (=Mouse). What is the significance of this in view of the fact that as recently as the days of Hezekiah the image of a serpent was still being worshiped, and that Ezekiel testifies to the existence of similar worship just prior to the exile?

2. Consider (1) the regulation concerning the eating of blood, and the ground on which it rests; (2) whether in this case the principle of *taboo* is not clearly found; (3) the general command concerning eating anything "abominable:" (4) the animals which might be eaten, and their general characteristics; (5) the animals which might not be eaten, and their general characteristics; (6) the general principles which seem to underlie the selection; (7) the character of a selection arising in this way; (8) the fact that the number of clean quadrupeds is *ten;* (9) whether this distinction was something objective imposed

[8] References in **bold-face** type are from the code of laws contained in Deuteronomy.

upon the people for a purpose (if so, was this purpose (*a*) to train the people in obedience, or (*b*) to provide hygienic dietary laws, or (*c*) to teach important religious truth by an allegorical method, or (*d*) to separate the Israelites from other nations, or (*e*) to prevent the worship of certain animals ?); or, rather, something subjective, of gradual growth, and expressive of certain instinctive feelings (for example, (*a*) that of aversion, or (*b*) appreciation of utility or beauty, or (*c*) experience of the use of this or that kind of flesh); or whether the origin is to be connected with some form or other of totemism; (10) the absence of any list of clean and unclean animals in the Covenant Code, and the significance of so fully developed a list in the Deuteronomic Code.

3. Consider (1) some of the sources of uncleanness as cited, *e. g.*, the body of a man who has been hanged; issues of the body; graven images; "carcasses of detestable things;" contagion; and (2) the method suggested for purification.

4. Note the necessity of cleanness on the part of one who is to engage in a religious exercise, and in this connection (1) the fact that the flesh of certain animals may be eaten alike by those who are clean and by those who are unclean; (2) the prohibition of the lame, the blind, or the blemished in sacrifice; (3) the synonymous use of the words "uncircumcised" and "unclean."[9]

5. Study the prophetic attitude toward infringement of the regulations concerning "clean and unclean," and the punishment which is to follow this infringement. How far do the prophets of this period seem to have shared the ideas of their times on this subject? Does their attitude relate to the minute particulars of the system, or to the general question of loyalty or obedience?

§ 127. **Constructive Work.**—Compare, in general, the minuteness of the regulations of this period in contrast with those of the earlier period; characterize these regulations as a whole; and consider whether they are (1) really new usages which had their origin after the formulation of the book of the covenant, or (2) old usages, for the most part, which are now codified for the first time; (3) in the former case, whence may they be supposed to have come? (4) in the latter case, to what influence are we to ascribe their codification?

§ 128. **The Laws and Usages Concerning Clean and Unclean in Ezekiel.**

1. Traces of totemism.
   Ezek. 8:7–12.

[9] For a further study of the subject of circumcision see §§ 164 f.

2. Forbidden foods.
   Ezek. 4:14.
3. Sources of uncleanness.
   Ezek. 4:14; 22:24; 36:17, 25, 29, 33; 37:23; 39:12, 14, 16, 24; 43:7–9; 44:25.
4. Instruction concerning clean and unclean is an important part of the priestly function.
   Ezek. 22:26; 44:23.
5. Everything connected with religion must be clean.
   Ezek. 22:26; 43:20–26; 44:25; 46:19–24.
6. Methods of purification.
   Ezek. 36:25; 43:18–26; 44:26 f.

§ 129. **Questions and Suggestions.**—Ezekiel's intermediate position and the peculiar situation to which his work is addressed make the material of his sermons especially interesting.

1. Consider the significance of the fact (1) that seventy elders are present, and that the idols (*i. e.*, likenesses of reptiles and abominable beasts) are being worshiped; (2) that the presiding priest was the head of one of the animal clans (viz., the Cony). Does this indicate that even in this late period animal-worship prevails?

2. Note Ezekiel's contention concerning his own cleanness, and the formulation of his idea of uncleanness.

3. Consider the representations made by Ezekiel of uncleanness, including that of the land, and note the various occasions which give rise to uncleanness.

4. Observe the part which the priest is to play in giving instruction upon the subject of cleanness and uncleanness.

5. (1) Note that "clean" now means "holy," "unclean" means "common;" to fail to make the proper distinction is to "profane" Jehovah; and (2) consider how this later and more developed idea has arisen out of the earlier. (3) Observe, also, that every act connected with a religious observance must be ceremonially clean. (4) Consider the bearing on this idea of the establishment of boiling-houses.

6. Consider the methods by which purification from uncleanness might be secured.

§ 130. **Constructive Work.**—Formulate the new phases and details of the idea of "clean and unclean" which appear in Ezekiel, and discuss the relation of all this to Ezekiel's idea of God.

§ 131. **The Laws and Usages Concerning Clean and Unclean in the Later Period,** that is, as described in (*a*) the laws of the Levitical Code, (*b*) by the priestly prophets, and (*c*) in the priestly histories, *e. g.*, Ezra, Nehemiah, Chronicles.[10]

1. Traces of totemism.
   Isa. 65 : 4 f.; 66 : 17 ; **Lev. 19 : 28.**
2. Forbidden food.
   Lev. 17 : 10–16 ; 19 : 26 ; 11 : 1–23, 29 f., 41–47 ; 7 : 16–19 ; 19 : 7 ; 7 : 22–27 ; 3 : 14–17 ; Gen. 9 : 3 f.; Isa. 65 : 4 f.; Dan. 1 : 8.
3. Sources of uncleanness.
   Lev., chaps. 13 and 15 ; 20 : 20 f.; chap. 12 ; 18 : 19 ; 19 : 11–13 ; Numb. 5 : 19, 28 ; 31 : 13 ff.; 35 : 33 f.; 5 : 1–4 ; 2 Chron. 34 : 5 ; Ezra 9 : 11 ; Neh. 13 : 9, 30 ; Josh. 22 : 17 ; Isa. 65 : 4 f.; Dan. 1 : 8.
4. Uncleanness is contagious.
   Lev. 13 : 45 f.; 14 : 46 f.; 15 : 4–12, 19–23, 26 f.; 11 : 8, 24–28, 31–40 ; 22 : 4–6 ; 5 : 2 f.; 7 : 19 ; 6 : 10 f., 27–30 ; 19 : 7–16, 22 ; Hag. 2 : 10–14.
5. Methods of purification.
   Lev., chaps. 14, 15 ; 12 : 6–8 ; 6 : 27 f.; 16 : 19 ; Numb., chap. 19 ; 6 : 10–21 ; 35 : 33 f.; 8 : 1–21 ; 31 : 13–24.
6. Everything connected with religious acts must be clean.
   Lev. 10 : 14 ; 27 : 11, 27 ; chap. 21 ; 22 : 1–25 ; 7 : 19*b*–21 ; 4 : 11 f.; 6 ; 10 f.; 16 : 19 ; Numb. 6 : 6–9 ; 18 : 11, 15 ; 8 : 1–21 ; Exod. 29 : 36 ; 2 Chron. 23 : 19 ; 30 : 17–20 ; 29 : 15 f., 18 f.; Neh. 13 : 9, 22 ; Isa. 66 : 20.
7. Exemption from the requirement of cleanness is made in the case of the Passover.
   2 Chron. 30 : 17–20 ; **Numb. 9 : 6–14.**
8. Non-Israelitish land is unclean, and Israel's land also is unclean.
   Josh. 22 : 19 ; Ezra 9 : 11; **Numb. 35 : 33 f.;** Zech. 13 : 1 f.
9. All foreigners are unclean.
   Isa. 35 : 8 ; Ezra 9 : 11 ; Neh. 13 : 30.
10. Instruction as to clean and unclean is an important part of priestly functions.
    Lev. 10 : 10 f.; 20 : 25 f.
11. Traces of ancestor-worship.
    Lev. 19 : 28, 32.

§ 132. **Questions and Suggestions.**

1. Observe (1) that the old totem-sacrifice still survives in the sacrificial eating of swine, mice, and other abominable animals; did they eat these because they thought that in so doing they were eating the flesh of the deity, and that this meant participation in the virtues

[10] References in **bold-face** type are from the Levitical Code of laws.

of the deity, as well as in the mystic life of the tribe? (2) that the old customs of cutting the flesh and of tattooing exist; were these associated with the old idea of ancestor-worship, and was ancestor-worship connected with totemism?

2. (1) Classify according to the later usage, the various kinds of food forbidden; and (2) compare closely the lists of clean and unclean animals given in Leviticus with that of Deuteronomy (see §§ 125, 2, and 126, 2); (3) note what is implied in the case of Daniel and his companions.

3. Note and classify the sources of uncleanness as they are indicated in the writings of this period.

4. Consider (1) the various cases of uncleanness (*e. g.*, leprosy, plague, bodily issue, unclean food, etc.), and the fact that a person or object, when brought into contact with an unclean thing, itself became unclean. (2) What was the underlying thought of this usage, and its practical working? (3) In what way did a holy thing, when brought into contact with persons or objects, convey its holiness to them?

5. Arrange and classify the various ways adopted in this period for securing purification from uncleanness, and compare them in general with the methods of the middle period.

6. Consider now the extreme emphasis laid upon ceremonial cleanness: (1) the injunctions to this end; (2) the historical facts cited; (3) the practical working out of these commands; (4) the rigidity of the ceremonial as now maintained, in comparison with that of earlier days and other peoples; (5) the explanation of the origin of this rigid ceremonial, viz., the desire to secure the favor of God and the fulfilment of the prophetic promises (which, for the most part, still remained unfulfilled) by bringing the individual Israelite into such a state of piety and obedience as would literally compel God to fulfil his promises; (6) the relation to all this ceremonial of the highly spiritual element found in the Psalter, which was largely the product of this period; (7) the conception of God which was implied in this ceremonial, which, indeed, permeated the ceremonial.

7. Consider (1) the exemption from ceremonial cleanness made in the case of the Passover feast, and (2) the explanation of it; (3) the historical case cited in 2 Chron. 30:17–20.

8. Observe that (1) the idea of the uncleanness of non-Israelitish land still prevails; and also that (2) the land of Israel itself has become unclean; but (3) for what reason?

9. Note that the spirit of exclusivism has become so strong that

all foreigners are regarded as unclean. Consider the part played by this idea in the conflict which later arose between Judaism and Hellenism.

10. Observe (1) that it is now a most important function of the priest to give instruction concerning the clean and unclean, and consider (2) how difficult it must have been to educate all the people in this regard, in view of the great multitude of details involved; and (3) the general effect upon the priesthood of such an occupation of their time and attention.

11. Is there still a survival of the old tendency toward ancestor-worship in (1) the custom of cutting themselves for the dead, which is prohibited, and in (2) the special command to revere the old men?

§ 133. **Constructive Work.**— Prepare a statement which will show the new points which characterize the later period in the development of the idea of the clean and unclean.

§ 134. **Literature to be Consulted.**

HENRY HAYMAN, articles "Unclean Meats" and "Uncleanness," SMITH'S *Dictionary of the Bible* (1st ed. 1863, 2d ed. 1893); EWALD, *Antiquities of Israel* (3d ed. 1866, transl. 1876), pp. 144–60; SCHULTZ, *Old Testament Theology* (1st ed. 1869, transl. 1892), Vol. II, pp. 65–78; J. F. McLENNAN, *Fortnightly Review*, 1869 f.; KUENEN, *Religion of Israel* (1869 f., transl. 1874 f.), Vol. II, pp. 94–7; KALISCH, *Commentary on Leviticus*, Part II (1871), pp. 1–163; OEHLER, *Old Testament Theology* (1st ed. 1873, 3d ed. 1891, transl. 1883), §§ 142 f.; E. B. TYLOR, *Primitive Culture* (1871, 2d ed. 1873), see *Index, s. v.* "Totem Ancestors;" IDEM, *Early History of Mankind* (3d ed. 1878), pp. 284 f.; SPENCER, *Principles of Sociology* (1879), Vol. I, p. 367; W. ROBERTSON SMITH, "Animal Worship and Animal Tribes among the Arabs and in the Old Testament," *Journal of Philology*, Vol. IX (1880), pp. 75 ff.; IDEM, *Old Testament in the Jewish Church* (1st ed. 1881, 2d ed. 1892), p. 366; IDEM, *Kinship and Marriage in Early Arabia* (1885), chap. vii; SCHÜRER, *A History of the Jewish People in the Time of Jesus Christ* (1885, transl. 1890), see *Index, s. v.* "Clean and Unclean;" JOSEPH JACOBS, "Are there Totem-Clans in the Old Testament?" *Proceedings of the Society of Biblical Archæology*, Vol. VIII (1885), pp. 39–41; ANDREW LANG, *Custom and Myth* (2d ed. 1885), pp. 260 ff.; PIEPENBRING, *The Theology of the Old Testament* (1886, transl. 1893), pp. 73–9; ANDREW LANG, *Myth, Ritual and Religion* (1st ed. 1887, 2d ed. 1899), see *Index, s. v.* "Tabu," "Totem," etc.; SAYCE, *Lectures on the Origin and Growth of Religion as Illustrated by the Religion of the Ancient Babylonians* (Hibbert Lectures, 1887), see *Index, s. v.* "Clean and Unclean," "Totemism;" BENNETT, *Diseases of the Bible* (1st ed. 1887, 3d ed. 1896); J. G. FRAZER, *Totemism* (with numerous references to literature; 1887); IDEM, articles "Taboo" and "Totemism," *Encyclopædia Britannica* (1887); W. R. SMITH, article "Sacrifice," *ibid.* (1887), Vol. XXI, p. 135; IDEM, *Religion of the Semites* (1st ed. 1889, 2d ed. 1894), additional notes A, B, C, and I; J. G. FRAZER, *Golden Bough* (1890), see *Index, s. v.* "Taboo," "Totem," etc.; F. W. DAVIES, "Bible Leprosy," *Old and New Testament Student*, Vol. XI (1890), pp. 142–25;

McClintock and Strong's *Cyclopædia of Biblical, Theological and Ecclesiastical Literature*, articles on "Unclean" and "Uncleanness" (1891); J. Lubbock, *Origin of Civilization* (1892), p. 260; Montefiore, *Religion of the Ancient Hebrews* (Hibbert Lectures, 1892), pp. 473 ff.; Menzies, *History of Religion* (1895), pp. 55, 71, 131, 275; Driver, *A Critical and Exegetical Commentary on Deuteronomy* (1895), pp. 70, 164, 291 f.; J. F. McLennan, *Studies in Ancient History* (1896), pp. 492–569; Farnell, *The Cults of the Greek States*, Vol. I (1896) pp. 88–101; Wiedemann, *Religion of the Ancient Egyptians* (1897), see *Index, s. v.* "Animals," etc.; J. Hastings, article "Clean," Hastings' *Dictionary of the Bible*, Vol. I (1898); Morris Jastrow, Jr., *Religion of Babylonia and Assyria* (1898), pp. 397 f., 662 f.; J. G. Frazer, "The Origin of Totemism," *Fortnightly Review*, April and May, 1899; Budge, *Egyptian Magic* (1899), pp. 232 ff.; Paul Haupt, "Medical and Hygienic Features of the Bible," *The Independent*, New York, July 13, 1899, pp. 1906 f.; G. A. Simcox, article "Clean and Unclean," *Encyclopædia Biblica* (1899); F. J. Schamberg, "The Nature of the Leprosy of the Bible," *Biblical World*, Vol. XIII (1899), pp. 162–9; Paul Haupt, "Babylonian Elements in the Levitic Ritual," *Journal of Biblical Literature*, Vol. XIX (1901), p. 60, and note 113; McCurdy, article "Animal-Worship," *Jewish Encyclopædia* (1901); Andrew Lang, *Magic and Religion* (1901), pp. 257–69; R. G. Murison, "Totemism in the Old Testament," *Biblical World*, Vol. XVIII (1901), pp. 176–84; E. Clodd, *Myths and Dreams*, pp. 99 f.

Spencer, *De legibus Hebraeorum ritualibus* (1727); Hebenstreit, *De cura sanit. publ.* (1783), Vol. II, pp. 15 f.; Beyer, *De haemorrh. ex lege Mosis impuris* (1792); Bleek, "Beiträge zu den Forschungen über den Pentateuch," *Theologische Studien und Kritiken*, 1831, pp. 498 f.; Bähr, *Symbolik des mosaischen Kultus* (1839), Vol. II, pp. 159 ff., 462 ff.; Sommer, *Biblische Abhandlungen* (1846), pp. 183–367; Saalschütz, *Das mosaische Recht mit Berücksichtigung des spätern jüdischen* (1st ed. 1846, 1848; 2d ed. 1853), chaps. 22–32; Kurtz, "Ueber die symbolische Dignität des in Num. 19 zur Tilgung der Todesunreinigkeit verordneten Ritus," *Theologische Studien und Kritiken*, 1846, pp. 629 ff.; Danielssen et Boeck, *Traité de la Spedalskhed* [Norwegian = leprosy] *ou Elephantiasis des Grecs* (transl. from the Norwegian, 1847); Chwolsohn, *Die Ssabier und der Ssabismus* (1856), Vol. I, pp. 146 ff.; C. Wolff, "Die Lepra Arabum," in Virchow's *Archiv für path. Anatomie und Physiologie*, Vol. XXVI (1861); S. Finály, "Ueber die wahre Bedeutung des Aussatzes in der Bibel," *Archiv für Dermatologie und Syphilidologie* (1870); Schenkel, article "Reinigkeit," Schenkel's *Bibel-Lexikon*, Vol. V (1875); Köhler, *Lehrbuch der biblischen Geschichte*, Vol. I (1875), pp. 409–19; L. Kotelmann, *Die Geburtshilfe bei den alten Hebräern* (1876); Baudissin, *Studien zur semitischen Religionsgeschichte*, Vol. II (1878), pp. 100 ff.; Franz Delitzsch, "Die Aussatztora des Leviticus," *Zeitschrift für kirchliche Wissenschaft und kirchliches Leben*, Vol. I (1880), pp. 3–10; E. König, article "Reinigungen," *Realencyklopädie für protestantische Theologie und Kirche* (2d ed. 1883); Kamphausen, article "Reinigkeit und Reinigungen," Riehm's *Handwörterbuch des biblischen Alterthums* (1884); Franz Delitzsch, article "Reinigungsopfer," *ibid.*; Nöldeke, "Robertson Smith's Kinship and Marriage in Early Arabia," *Zeitschrift der Deutschen Morgenländischen Gesellschaft*, Vol. XL (1886), pp. 157–69; Stade, *Geschichte des Volkes Israel*, Vol. I (1887), pp. 481 ff.; Wellhausen, *Reste arabischen Heidentums* (= *Skizzen und Vorarbeiten*, III, 1st ed. 1887, 2d ed. 1897), pp. 52, 106, 156, 176 ff.; M. Sandreczky, "Studien über Lepra," *Zeitschrift des Deutschen Palästina-Vereins*, Vol. XVIII (1895), pp. 34–40 (from the English in *The Lancet*, London, August 31, 1889); RIEHM, *Alttestamentliche Theologie* (1889), pp. 124 ff.; SCHWALLY, *Das Leben nach dem Tode* (1892), see *Index, s. v.* "Taboo" and "Unrein;" BAENTSCH, *Das Bundesbuch* (1892), pp. 105 f.; G. N. MÜNCH, *Die Zara'ath der hebräischen Bibel. Einleitung in der Geschichte des Aussatz*, in *Dermatologische Studien*, by G. UNNA (1893); SMEND, *Lehrbuch der alttestamentlichen Religionsgeschichte* (1st ed. 1893, 2d. ed. 1899), see *Index, s. v.* "Reinheit," "Tabu," "Totemismus;" H. SCHURTZ, *Die Speiseverbote* (1893); A. EINSLER, "Beobachtungen über d. Aussatz im heiligen Lande," *Zeitschrift des Deutschen Palästina-Vereins*, Vol. XVI (1893), Heft 4; NOWACK, *Lehrbuch der hebräischen Archäologie* (1894), Vol. I, pp. 116 ff.; II, pp. 275–99; BENZINGER, *Hebräische Archäologie* (1894), pp. 152, 297, 478–89; DILLMANN, *Handbuch der alttestamentlichen Theologie* (1895), see *Index, s. v.* "Reinheit," "Unrein," etc.; ZINSSER, "Bemerkungen über den jetzigen Stand der Lepraforschungen," *Zeitschrift des Deutschen Palästina-Vereins*, Vol. XVIII (1895), pp. 41–4; A. WIENER, *Die jüdischen Speisegesetze* (1895); A. SACK, *Was ist die Zaraath der hebräischen Bibel?* (VIRCHOW'S *Archiv für path. Anatomie und Physiologie*, Band 144, Supplementheft, 1896); STADE, *Theologische Litteratur-Zeitung*, 1896, No. 1, col. 10; BERTHOLET, *Die Stellung der Israeliten und der Juden zu den Fremden* (1896), see *Index, s. v.* "Reinheit," "Reinigung;" MARTI, *Geschichte der israelitischen Religion* (1897), pp. 24 f., 30, 42, 104, 193, 221 f.; FREY, *Tod, Seelenglaube und Seelenkult im alten Israel* (1898), pp. 173–87; N. COHN, *Die Vorschrift betreffs die Zar'ath nach dem Kitab al Kafi* (1898); D. H. MÜLLER, *Südarabische Altertümer im kunsthistorischen Museum zu Wien* (1899); J. PIKLER AND F. SOMLÓ, *Der Ursprung des Totemismus* (1899); J. C. MATTHES, "De begrippen rein en onrein in het Oude Testament," *Theologisch Tijdschrift*, Vol. XXXIII (1899), pp. 293–318; J. HALÉVY, *Revue sémitique*, Vol. VII (1899), pp. 267 ff.; GRÜNEISEN, *Ahnenkultus und Urreligion Israels* (1900); EBSTEIN, *Die Medizin im Alten Testament* (1901).

See also the treatises in the Mishnah entitled *Niddah*, *Parah*, *Tehoroth*, *Zabbim*, *Celim*, *Miscath Arlah;* and the commentaries on Lev., chaps. 11–15, especially those of DILLMANN (1880), BAENTSCH (1900), BERTHOLET (1900), and DRIVER AND WHITE (*Polychrome Bible*, 1898).

§ 135. **Supplementary Topics.**

1. Consider the following references to clean and unclean in the Psalter: 73:1, 13; 19:9, 12; 51:2, 7, 10; 24:4; 18:20; 119:9; and summarize their teachings.

2. Examine the following references in the books of Job and Proverbs: Job 11:4; 33:9; 17:9; 15:14 ff.; 25:4; 9:30; 37:21; 36:14; Prov. 14:4; 16:2; 20:9; and also Eccl. 9:2; and summarize their teachings.

3. Study the allusions to clean and unclean in the books of the Maccabees and formulate a statement covering them: 1 Macc. 1:37, 46 ff., 54, 62 f.; 2:12; 3:51; 4:38, 43 f., 48 f., 54; 13:47 f.; 2 Macc. 1:18, 33, 36; 2:8, 16, 19; 3:12; 4:14; 5:27; 6:2, 5, 7 f., 18 ff.; 7:1 ff.; 10:3, 5; 11:24; 12:40; 13:8; 14:36.

4. What, in general, is the attitude of New Testament writers toward the idea of clean and unclean as gathered from a study

of the principal allusions: Matt. 8:2 f.; 10:1, 8; 11:5; 12:43; 23:25–27; Mark 1:23, 26 f., 40–44; 3:11, 30; 5:2, 8, 13; 6:7; 7:25; Luke 4:27; 5:12 ff.; 6:18; 7:22; 8:29; 4:33, 36; 9:42; 11:24, 39, 41; 17:14, 17; John 15:3; Acts 5:16; 8:7; 10:14 f., 28; 11:8 f.; Rom. 1:24; 6:19; 14:14; 1 Cor. 7:14; 2 Cor. 6:17; 7:1; 12:21; Gal. 5:19; Eph. 4:19; 5:3, 5, 26; Col. 3:5; 1 Thess. 2:3; 4:7; Heb. 9:13; James 4:8; 2 Pet. 2:10; 1 John 1:7, 9?

5. Make a study of the Hebrew words for "clean," viz., קָדוֹשׁ, טָהוֹר, בַּר, זַךְ, and "unclean," viz., טָמֵא; *cf.* תּוֹעֵבָה, שֶׁקֶץ, שִׁקּוּץ, etc.; trace their usage in the cognate languages (especially Assyrian and Arabic), and endeavor to determine their primary meaning and their exact significance in Hebrew literature.

See especially BAUDISSIN, *Studien zur semitischen Religionsgeschichte*, Heft II, pp. 1–40; G. A. SIMCOX, article "Clean and Unclean," *Encyclopædia Biblica;* ZIMMERN, *Beiträge zur Assyriologie*, Vol. I, p. 105; WHITEHOUSE, *Thinker*, 1892, p. 52; and the various lexicons.

6. Compare the similarities between the usages connected with clean and unclean and those connected with the *ban* = חֵרֶם. How may these be most satisfactorily explained?

See § 146, and *cf.* W. H. BENNETT, article "Ban," *Encyclopædia Biblica.*

7. Study the phenomena similar to the Hebrew "clean and unclean" found in other Semitic nations, *e.g.*, the prohibition among the Syrians against eating swine; the putting off of ordinary everyday garments while engaged in sacred acts at Mecca and other ancient Arabic sanctuaries; the Arabian custom and method of removing the impurity of widowhood; the impurity of menstruation, which is recognized by all Semites; and the many parallels found in Egyptian customs and worship. What is the common basis of all these customs?

See especially W. R. SMITH, *Religion of the Semites*, 2d ed., pp. 441–56; W. MAX MÜLLER, article "Egypt," § 19, *Encyclopædia Biblica;* FRAZER, articles "Taboo" and "Totemism," *Encyclopædia Britannica.*

8. Consider the possible bases of classification of the clean and unclean animals, birds, fish, etc. Is the hygienic motive satisfactory? Is the idea that certain things are prohibited because of an instinctive feeling of abhorrence for them applicable to all cases? Does the prohibition of certain things have any connection with their sacrificial or non-sacrificial character? Can certain cases be explained as due to a belief that the animals in question were inhabited by demons? Can

any clearly marked line of demarcation be drawn between clean and unclean beasts, etc.? Is a combination of motives probable?

See especially DRIVER, *Deuteronomy*, p. 164; W. R. SMITH, *Old Testament in the Jewish Church*, pp. 365 f. and note; G. A. SIMCOX, article "Clean and Unclean," *Encyclopædia Biblica;* NOWACK, *Lehrbuch der hebräischen Archäologie*, Vol. I, pp. 116–19.

9. Study the idea of "holiness" carefully in the light of the teaching concerning "clean and unclean." Was it thought of originally as a relation sustained to the deity, or as an inherent quality? What is the history of the conception from this point of view?

10. Consider the close relationship of the idea of "clean and unclean" to the idea of God, and the mutual influence of the two ideas. Note that in the earliest times everything thought to be associated with the deity was regarded as unclean, and that in the later period the exalted idea of God's holiness was expressed concretely by a wide extension of the circle of "uncleanness." Trace the parallel development of these two conceptions through the course of Israel's history.

CHAPTER XI.

THE LAWS AND USAGES CONCERNING PRAYER AND RELATED FORMS OF WORSHIP, CONSIDERED COMPARATIVELY.

§ 136. With *prayer,* offered at times to secure deliverance from trouble or danger, at other times to obtain the presence of the deity and his guidance, there may be associated, for purposes of classification, (1) the vow, which was a promise made to the deity in case of the granting of a request; (2) blessings and curses, which were prayers for good or evil to one's friends or enemies; (3) the ban or sentence to destruction, which was a formal curse or anathema; (4) the oath, which was an invocation of the deity, or a solemn statement in the name of the deity. The following may also be regarded as indirectly connected with prayer, viz.: (5) fasting, a means of making impression upon the deity, and thus securing favor; (6) consultation through oracles, Urim and Thummim, the ephod, and the lot, which were various means of ascertaining the divine will; (7) practice in connection with sorcery, or witchcraft, or magic, or divination, all of which was, likewise, effort to communicate with the spirit or deity and to secure knowledge of the divine will; (8) mourning customs, many of which had their origin in the superstition that the departed spirit had power for evil or good over those who were living, a power to be propitiated or averted by certain acts; (9) circumcision, which was an act of dedication to the deity.

It might be said that every act of worship was really *prayer;* that is, approach to the deity. Sacrifice, for example, was acted prayer.

§ 137. **Prayer.**

1. The early period: readings, questions, and suggestions.[1]

(*a*) Divine mercy and aid are sought through prayer.

Gen. 18:22–33; 19:18–22; 20:7, 17(E); 25:21; 30:6, 17(E), 22; 32:9–12; 35:3(E); Exod. 3:7, 9; 5:22 f.; 8:8, 12, 29 ff.; 9:28 ff.; 10:17 ff.; 14:10, 15(E); 15:25; 17:4, 8–15(E); 32:11–14; 32:30–32 (E); Numb. 11:1–3 (E), 10–15, 18; 12:13(E); 14:13–19(E); 21:7 (E); 23:10(E); Josh. 7:6–9; 10:12–14; 24:7(E); Judg. 10:10, 14 f.; 15:18; 16:28; 1 Sam. 7:8 f.; 15:11; 2 Sam. 15:31; 24:10, 17; 2 Kings 4:33; 6:17–20; 19:1, 4, 14–20.

[1] All the references to the Hexateuch are from J, except those followed by (E).

Study different typical cases of prayer for mercy and aid, and consider (1) the persons who are represented as praying; (2) the nature of the petitions offered, *e. g.*, requests for healing, for children, for relief from frogs, hail, etc., for rescue from Pharaoh, for deliverance of Israel from immediate destruction after sin has been committed; (3) the character of the prayers—simple, informal, naïve; (4) the basis on which request is made; (5) the elements of prayer which seem to be lacking in these cases; (6) the indications of a primitive stage of religious development; (7) the typical and fundamental elements of prayer which are involved.

(*b*) Divine presence and guidance are sought through prayer.

Gen. 24:12–14; Exod. 33:7–11(E); 34:9; Numb. 10:35 f.; 1 Sam. 8:6, 18, 21; 12:17 f.; 2 Sam. 7:18–29; 1 Kings 3:6–9; 18:24–40; 2 Kings 19:2–7, 15–19.

Study, from the same points of view, another class of prayers, in which request is made for the presence of the divine spirit and for its guidance.

2. The middle period: readings, questions, and suggestions.[2]

Deut. 9:18–20, 25–29; **10:10**; **26:15**; 2 Kings 22:19; Jer. 3:21; 10:23–25; 14:7–9, 19–22; 15:15–18; 18:19–23; 20:12; 42:1–6; Judg. 3:9, 15; 4:3; 6:6; 2 Kings 20:3; 1 Kings 8:22–61.

Consider (1) the circumstances attending Moses' prayers for the people, his fear of Jehovah, the ground of intercession, the element of confession, the naïve appeal to the estimate which strangers may make of Jehovah's ability, or of his purpose; (2) the reasons given by the prophetess Huldah for Jehovah's favorable answer to Josiah, viz., humility, supplication; (3) the spirit of dependence seen in Jeremiah's prayer (10:23–25), and its request; (4) Jeremiah's confession and passionate appeal (14:7–9, 19–22); (5) Jeremiah's personal complaints (15:15–18; 18:19–23; 20:12); (6) the request of the people that Jeremiah would pray for them, and his consent (Jer. 42:1–6); (7) the crying of Israel to Jehovah in their distress; (8) the basis of Hezekiah's appeal for preservation from death (2 Kings 20:3); (9) Solomon's prayer (1 Kings 8:20–53) at the dedication of the temple (as expanded and presented by the Deuteronomic editor)—its form, its contents, its spirit, its presuppositions.

[2] References in **bold-face** type are from the code of laws contained in Deuteronomy.

3. The later period: readings, questions, and suggestions.[3]
Gen. 17: 18; Exod. 2:23 f.; 6:5; Numb. 16:20–24; Judg. 20:18, 23; 21:2 f.; Ezra 8:21 ff.; 9:5—10:1; Neh. 1:4–11; 2:4; 4:4 f. 4:9; 5:19; 6:9, 14; 9:5–38; 13:14, 22, 30; Isa. 63: 7—64:12.

Consider (1) that an ejaculation (Gen. 17:18), the cry under oppression, is really prayer; (2) the form and thought of the prayer ascribed to the congregation (Numb. 16:20–24); (3) the various prayers recorded in Ezra and Nehemiah, noting the form, the content, the spirit, the entirely different tone as compared with those of preceding periods; (4) the exact particulars in which this difference of tone consists.

§ 138. **Constructive Work.**—Prepare a brief statement, covering (1) the general content of scriptural prayers; (2) the peculiarities of form; (3) the essential elements which make up such prayers; (4) any differences which appear as characterizing the prayers of different periods; (5) the place of prayer in worship; (6) the usage of prayer (*a*) in the Psalms,[4] (*b*) in the wisdom literature,[5] (*c*) in the apocryphal books,[6] (*d*) in the New Testament,[7] (*e*) among Assyro-Babylonians, Egyptians, etc.[8]

§ 139. **Literature to be Consulted.**

ALFRED BARRY, article "Prayer," SMITH'S *Dictionary of the Bible* (1st ed. 1863, 2d ed. 1893); EWALD, *Antiquities of Israel* (3d ed. 1866, transl. 1876), see *Index, s. v.* "Prayer," etc.; SCHULTZ, *Old Testament Theology* (1st ed. 1869, 5th ed. 1896, transl. 1892), Vol. I, pp. 371 f.; H. FOX TALBOT, "A Prayer and a Vision," *Transactions of the Society of Biblical Archæology*, Vol. I (1872), pp. 346 ff., and *Records of the Past*, Vol. VII (1876), pp. 65 ff.; E. B. TYLOR, *Primitive Culture* (1874), see *Index, s. v.* "Prayer," "Oracles;" H. FOX TALBOT, "Assyrian Sacred Poetry," *Records of the Past*, Vol. III (1874), pp. 131–8; A. H. SAYCE, "Fragment of an Assyrian Prayer after a Bad Dream," *Records of the Past*, Vol. IX (1877), pp. 149–52; B. T. A. EVETTS, "An Assyrian Religious Text," *Proceedings of the Society of Biblical Archæology*, Vol. X (1888), pp. 478 f.; D. G. LYON, "Assyrian and Babylonian Royal Prayers," *Proceedings of the American Oriental Society*, 1888, pp. xciii, xciv; S. A. STRONG, "A Prayer of Assurbanipal," *Records of the Past*, new series, Vol. VI (1892), pp. 102–6; MONTEFIORE, *Religion of the Ancient Hebrews* (1892), pp. 505 f.; J. A. CRAIG, "Prayer of the Assyrian King Ashurbanipal," *Hebraica*, Vol. X (1893), pp. 75–87; MENZIES, *History of Religion* (1895), see *Index, s. v.* "Prayer;" J. L. NEVIUS, *Demon Possession and Allied Themes* (1895), see *Index, s. v.* "Prayer," etc.; JASTROW, *Religion*

[3] All the references to the Hexateuch are from the P document.

[4] See, *e. g.*, Pss. 5; 12; 51; 55; 69.

[5] See, *e. g.*, Job 22:27; 33:26; 41:3; 42:8, 10; Prov. 15:8; 28:9.

[6] See, *e. g.*, 1 Macc. 3:44–54; 4:10, 30–34, 38–40; 5:31–34; 2 Macc. 1:5 f., 8. 23–30; 13:10–12; 14:33–36; 15:21–24; Ecclus. 18:23; chap. 51.

[7] Matt. 6:9 ff.; 17:21; 21:13, 22; 23:14; John, chap. 17.

[8] See literature cited in § 139.

of Babylonia and Assyria (1898), see *Index, s. v.* "Prayers," etc.; T. K. CHEYNE, *Jewish Religious Life after the Exile* (1898), p. 251; DUFF, *Old Testament Theology*, Vol. II (1900), see *Index, s. v.* "Prayer, etc.;" DAY, *The Social Life of the Hebrews* (1901), pp. 215 f.

GASS, article "Gebet," SCHENKEL'S *Bibel-Lexikon*, Vol. II (1869); STADE, *Geschichte des Volkes Israel*, Vol. I (1887), pp. 487 ff.; RIEHM'S *Handwörterbuch des biblischen Alterthums* (2d ed. 1893 f.), Vol. I, pp. 484 ff.; J. A. KNUDTZON, *Assyrische Gebete an den Sonnengott für Staat und königliches Haus aus der Zeit Asarhaddons und Assurbanipals*, 2 vols. (1893); SMEND, *Lehrbuch der alttestamentlichen Religionsgeschichte* (1st ed. 1893, 2d ed. 1899), see *Index, s. v.* "Gebet;" BENZINGER, *Hebräische Archäologie* (1894), pp. 462 ff.; NOWACK, *Lehrbuch der hebräischen Archäologie*, Vol. II (1894), pp. 259 ff.; DILLMANN, *Handbuch der alttestamentlichen Theologie* (1895), pp. 184, 481; MARTI, *Geschichte der israelitischen Religion* (1897), see *Index, s. v.* "Gebet," etc.; F. BUHL, article "Gebet im Alten Testament," *Realencyklopädie für prot. Theologie und Kirche*, Vol. VI (1899).

§ 140. **The Vow.**

1. The early period: readings, questions, and suggestions.

Gen. 14:21 ff.; 28:20 ff. (E); 31:13 (E); Judg. 11:29 ff., 39; 13:4 f., 7, 14; 1 Sam. 1:11, 21; 2 Sam. 15:7 f.; Numb. 21:1–3 (J); Isa. 19:21.

Examine the narratives which record the vows of Abraham, Jacob, Jephthah, the Nazirite, Hannah, Absalom, Israel in connection with Arad, as typical cases of vows, and note in each case (1) the implication of dependence upon and recognition of the power of the deity; (2) the motive actuating the individual to make the vow; (3) the form of expression employed.

2. The middle period: readings, questions, and suggestions.

Deut. 12:6, 11, 17, 26; 23:18, 22 f.; Nah. 1:15; Jer. 44:25.

Examine the references to vows and note (1) the characteristics of each case presented; (2) the close association of the vow with the free-will offering; (3) the prohibition of the use of the harlot's hire; (4) the obligation to pay a vow once made; (5) the making of a vow, wholly voluntary; (6) the prophetic point of view.

3. The late period: readings, questions, and suggestions.[9]

Numb. 6:1–21; 15:3, 8; 29:39; 30:1–16; Mal. 1:14; Jon. 1:16; 2:9; **Lev. 7:16; 27:2, 8; 22:18, 21, 23; 23:38.**

Examine the references cited and note (1) the special cases cited; (2) the increase in complexity of arrangement; (3) the details of the law of the Nazirite; (4) the circumstances under which the vow of a

[9] References in **bold-face** type are from the P document.

woman is obligatory or otherwise; (5) the distinction made between the vow and the free-will offering.

§ 141. **Constructive Work.**—Prepare a statement on the *vow*, which will take up (1) the religious and psychological basis of the usage; (2) the various kinds of motives which are seen to have exerted influence; (3) the words employed and their significance; (4) the relationship of the vow to the free-will offering; (5) the relation to the oath; (6) the modifications in usage which come in later times; (7) the difference in principle between vows of devotion and vows of abstinence; (8) the place of the Nazirite order[10] in Old Testament history; (9) the making of vows among other ancient peoples;[11] (10) the attitude of the prophets; (11) the representations in the Psalms;[12] (12) the representations in wisdom literature;[13] (13) the representations in apocryphal literature;[14] (14) the representations in the New Testament;[15] (15) the relation to prayer and sacrifice.

§ 142. **Literature to be Consulted.**

H. W. PHILLOTT, article "Vows," SMITH'S *Dictionary of the Bible;* SCHULTZ, *op. cit.*, Vol. I, pp. 191 f., 371 f.; W. R. SMITH, articles "Nazarite" and "Vow," *Encyclopædia Britannica* (1875); IDEM, *Rel. of Sem.*, see *Index*, *s. v.* "Vows," "Nazarite," etc.; MENZIES, *op. cit.*, p. 74; G. F. MOORE, *Judges* ("International Critical Commentary," 1895), pp. 232, 279, 380 ff.; DRIVER, *The Books of Joel and Amos* (Camb. Bible, 1897), pp. 152 f.; CHEYNE, *op. cit.*, pp. 189, 254; G. B. GRAY, "The Nazirite," *Journal of Theological Studies*, Vol. I (1900), pp. 201 ff.; D. EATON, article "Nazirite," HASTINGS' *Dictionary*, Vol. III.

VILMAR, "Die symbolische Bedeutung des Naziräergelübdes," *Theologische Studien und Kritiken*, 1864, pp. 438 ff.; SCHRADER, article "Gelübde," SCHENKEL'S *Bibel-Lexikon;* DILLMANN, article "Nasiräer," *ibid.;* OEHLER AND ORELLI, article "Nasiräat," *Realencyklopädie* (2d ed.); GRILL, "Ueber Bedeutung und Ursprung des Nasiräergelübdes," *Jahrbücher für prot. Theologie*, 1880, pp. 645 ff.; MAYBAUM, *Die Entwickelung des israelitischen Prophetenthums* (1883) pp. 147–53; RIEHM, *Handwörterbuch*, articles "Gelübde" and "Nasiräer;" GOLDZIHER, *Muhammedanische Studien*, Vol. I (1888), pp. 23 f.; SMEND, *op. cit.*, see *Index*, *s. v.* "Gelübde;" NOWACK, *op. cit.*, Vol. II, pp. 263 ff.; BENZINGER, *op. cit.*, see *Index*, *s. v.* "Bann," "Gelübde," etc.; DILLMANN, *op. cit.*, p. 141; MARTI, *op. cit.*, pp. 87, 107; BUHL, article "Gelübde im Alten Testament," *Realencyklopädie*, 3d ed., Vol. VI.

[10] See article "Nazirite" in HASTINGS' *Dictionary of the Bible*, Vol. III.

[11] See article "Vow," *Encyc. Brit.;* WELLHAUSEN, *Skizzen und Vorarbeiten*, Vol. III, p. 117; JASTROW, *op. cit.*, pp. 668 f.

[12] See, *e. g.*, Pss. 22:25; 50:14; 56:12; 61:5, 8; 65:1; 66:13; 76:11; 116:14, 18; 132:2.

[13] See, *e. g.*, Eccl. 5:4 f.; Job 22:27; Prov. 7:14; 20:25; 31:2.

[14] See, *e. g.*, 2 Macc. 3:35; 9:13 ff.; Ecclus. 18:22.

[15] See, *e. g.*, Acts 18:18; 21:23 f.

§ 143. **Blessings and Cursings.**

1. The early period: readings, questions, and suggestions.[16]

Gen. 3 : 14, 17; 4 : 11; 9 : 25 f.; 12 : 3; 27 : 27–29, 35 (E), 39 f. (E); 48 : 15 f.; 49 : 1–27; Exod. 12 : 32; 21 : 17 (E);[17] 23 : 21 (E), 25–31 (E); Numb. 22 : 6; 24 : 9; 1 Sam. 2 : 20; 14 : 24, 28; 17 : 43; 2 Sam. 3 : 28 f.; 19 : 39; Deut. 33 : 1–29 (E); Judg. 9 : 57; 21 : 18.

Study and classify the material on blessings and cursings as follows: (1) words used in blessing and cursing; (2) forms of expression used, *e. g.*, Judg. 21 : 18; 1 Sam. 2 : 20; Deut., chap. 33; (3) important cases of blessings or cursings, *e. g.*, (*a*) Jacob's last words (Gen., chap. 49), (*b*) Moses' last words (Deut., chap. 33), (*c*) David's curse on Joab (2 Sam. 3 : 28, 29); (4) the peculiar lack of the moral element in the case of Esau (Gen. 27 : 35); (5) the cursing of a hostile nation, *e. g.*, by Balak (Numb. 22 : 6), by Goliath (1 Sam. 17 : 43); (6) the connection with the oath; (7) the blessing and curse pronounced in connection with the Covenant Code (Exod. 23 : 21, 25–31).

2. The middle period: readings, questions, and suggestions.[18]

Gen. 49 : 25 f., 28; **Deut. 11 : 26–30; 27 : 11–26; 28 : 1–68; 29 : 19–21; 30 : 1, 7, 19**; Josh. 8 : 34; Jer. 29 : 18; Ezek. 34 : 26; 1 Kings 8 : 14 f., 55 f.; *cf.* Ps. 68 : 1–3.

Make a similar classification of the material coming from the middle period, noting as cases of special interest (1) the arrangement for blessings and curses to be announced from Mounts Gerizim and Ebal (Deut. 27 : 11–26); (2) Joshua's reading of the blessings and the curses (Josh. 8 : 34); (3) the old royal *form* of blessing (1 Kings 8 : 14 f., 55 f.); (4) a *form* of national blessing (*cf.* Ps. 68 : 1–3); (5) prophetic use of curse (Jer. 29 : 18) and blessing (Ezek. 34 : 26); (6) the blessings and curses announced in connection with the Deuteronomic Code (Deut. 28 : 3–14, 15–68).

3. The late period: readings, questions, and suggestions.[19]

Gen. 28 : 3 f.; **Lev. 9 : 22; 25 : 21; chap. 26; Numb. 5 : 12–31; 6 : 22–26**; Neh. 10 : 29; 13 : 2; 2 Chron. 34 : 24; Isa. 24 : 6; Zech. 5 : 3; Mal. 2 : 2; 3 : 9; Pss. 109; Prov. 26 : 2; Dan. 9 : 11.

Classify likewise the material of the late period, noting as cases of

[16] All references to the Hexateuch are from J, except those followed by (E).

[17] This reference is from the Covenant Code.

[18] References in **bold-face** type are from the code of laws contained in Deuteronomy.

[19] References in **bold-face** type are from the priestly code of laws.

special interest (1) Isaac's blessing of Jacob (P) (Gen. 28:3 f.); (2) the priestly form of blessing (Numb. 6:22–26); (3) the forms of doxology used in later worship (*cf.* Pss. 134; 150); (4) the blessings and curses announced in connection with the Levitical Code (Lev. 26:3–12, 16–45); (5) the thought even in later times that "it was worth while to curse a bad man" (*cf.* Ps. 109); but (6) the feeling also that only the good might be blessed (*cf.* Ps. 37:26), and that causeless curses were of no avail (*cf.* Prov. 26:2).

§144. **Constructive Work.**—Prepare a statement on *blessings and cursings*, including the following points: (1) the words translated *blessing* and *curse;* (2) the forms of expression used; (3) stereotyped formulas of benediction; (4) the religious idea or superstition underlying the usage—was it really a "spell, pronounced by a holy person"? (5) how was this usage related to magic and sorcery (*cf.* the curse-producing water)? (6) the more important patriarchal blessings—were they cursings as well as blessings? (7) the threefold classification: (*a*) one nation by another, (*b*) one individual by another, (*c*) as attached to laws to secure their better observance; (8) a comparison of the three sets of blessings and cursings connected respectively with the Covenant Code, the Deuteronomic Code, and the Levitical Code; (9) a comparison of the usage as it is found in the three periods, the modifications which are made; (10) a comparison of the New Testament representations on this subject[20]—are blessings and curses found in the speeches of Jesus? if so, how are they to be understood? (11) this usage among the Arabians;[21] (12) this usage among the Assyrians;[22] (13) the relation of this usage to prayer.

§145. **Literature to be Consulted.**

EWALD, *op. cit.*, pp. 76–9; SCHULTZ, *op. cit.*, Vol. II, pp. 335 ff., 346 ff.; BRIGGS, *Messianic Prophecy* (1886), pp. 115–20; W. R. SMITH, *Kinship and Marriage in Early Arabia* (1887), pp. 53, 263; W. R. SMITH, *Rel. of Sem.*, p. 164; L. W. KING, *Babylonian Magic and Sorcery* (1896); J. DENNEY, article "Curse," HASTINGS' *Dictionary*, Vol. I (1898); W. F. ADENEY, article "Blessing," *ibid.;* T. K. CHEYNE, article "Blessings and Cursings," *Encyc. Bib.*, Vol. I (1899); HENRY HAYMAN, "The Blessing of Moses: Its Genesis and Structure," *American Journal of Semitic Languages and Literatures*, Vol. XVII (1901), pp. 96–106.

[20] See, *e. g.*, Matt. 5:44; 14:19; 26:26; Mark 10:16; Luke 2:28, 34; 9:16; 24:50 f.; Acts 3:26; 23:12, 14; Rom. 12:14; Gal. 3:13; Mark 7:10; 11:21; Matt. 15:4; 25:41.

[21] *Cf.* GOLDZIHER, *Muhammedanische Studien.*

[22] *Cf.* KING, *Babylonian Magic and Sorcery, passim.*

MERX, articles "Fluch" and "Fluchwasser," SCHENKEL'S *Bibel-Lexikon*, Vol. II (1869); SCHENKEL, article "Segen," *Bibel-Lexikon*, Vol. V (1875); BURGER, article "Segen, Segnung," *Realencyklopädie*, 2d ed., Vol. XIV (1884); RIEHM, article "Fluch," *Handwörterbuch des bibl. Alterthums* (1884); WELLHAUSEN, *op. cit.*, p. 126; SCHWALLY, "Miscellen," *Zeitschrift für die alttestamentliche Wissenschaft*, Vol. XI (1891), pp. 170 ff.; NOWACK, *op. cit.*, Vol. II, pp. 251 f., 261 f.; BENZINGER, *op. cit.*, p. 146; MARTI, *op. cit.*, pp. 91, 116.

§ 146. **The Ban.**

1. The early period.
   Exod. 22:19; (E);[23] Numb. 21:2 (J); Josh. 8:26 (E); Judg. 1:17; 21:11; 1 Sam. 15:3, 8, 15, 18, 20.
2. The middle period.[24]
   Josh. 2:10; 6:18; 10:28, 35, 40; 11:11 f., 21; Mic. 4:13; Isa. 43:28; Deut. 2:34; 3:6; 7:2, 26; **13:17 f.**; **20:17**; Jer. 25:9; 50:21, 26; 51:3.
3. The late period.[25]
   Isa. 34:2, 5; Mal. 4:6; **Lev. 27:21, 28 f.**; **Numb. 18:14**; Isa. 11:15; Zech. 14:11; 1 Chron. 2:7; 4:41; 2 Chron. 32:14; Ezra 10:8; Dan. 11:44.

Examine the passages cited in the various periods, and classify the material thus gathered as follows: (1) words used to mean *ban* or *destruction*, and their significance; (2) classes of persons or objects subject to ban, *e. g.*, (*a*) idols, (*b*) individuals regarded as enemies of the nation, (*c*) cities or nations regarded as hostile (the Canaanites), (*d*) individuals personally objectionable, (*e*) metals; (3) the regulations at various times relating to the ban; (4) the modifications which are made from period to period, *e. g.*, Josh. 6:24; Numb. 18:14; Ezek. 44:29.

§ 147. **Constructive Work.**—Prepare a statement on the *ban*, taking up (1) the sociological basis; (2) its relationship (*a*) to the vow, (*b*) to the idea of clean and unclean, (*c*) to taboo; (3) a classification of persons or things liable to the *ban*; (4) the changes which came in later times; (5) the attitude of the prophets; (6) the non-appearance of the term in the Psalms and in the wisdom literature; (7) the New Testament development of the idea (*cf.* 1 Cor. 16:22); (8) the place of the idea in other Semitic nations (*cf.* Moab, Arabia, and Assyria).[26]

[23] This reference is from the Covenant Code.

[24] References in **bold-face** type are from the code of laws contained in the book of Deuteronomy.

[25] References in **bold-face** type are from the priestly code of laws.

[26] *Cf.* Mesha Inscription, line 17; VON TORNAUW, *Zeitsch. d. Deutschen Morgenländischen Gesellschaft*, Vol. XXXVI, pp. 297 ff.; W. R. SMITH, *Rel. of Sem.*, *Index*, *s. v.* "Ban;" STADE, *Gesch.*, Vol. I, pp. 490 f.

§ 148. Literature to be Consulted.

EWALD, *Antiquities*, pp. 75–8; SCHULTZ, *op. cit.*, Vol. I, p. 390; II, p. 87; W. R. SMITH, *Rel. of Sem.*, pp. 150, 371, 453; S. R. DRIVER, *Notes on the Hebrew Text of the Books of Samuel* (1890), pp. 100 ff.; MCCURDY, *History, Prophecy and the Monuments* (1895–1901), § 550; J. DENNEY, article "Curse," HASTINGS' *Dictionary*, Vol. I; W. H. BENNETT, article "Ban," *Encyc. Bib.*, Vol. I; DAY, *op. cit.*, pp. 180, 212 f.

MERX, article "Bann," SCHENKEL'S *Bibel-Lexikon*, Vol. I (1869); WEBER, *Die Lehren des Talmud* (1880), pp. 138 ff.; VON TORNAUW, *Zeitschrift der Deutschen Morgenländischen Gesellschaft*, Vol. XXXVI (1882), pp. 297 ff.; STADE, *Geschichte*, Vol. I (1887), p. 490; SMEND, *op. cit.*, pp. 21, 39, 147 f., 288; NOWACK, *op. cit.*, Vol. I, pp. 371 f.; II, pp. 266–9; BENZINGER, *op. cit.*, p. 363; DILLMANN, *op. cit.*, pp. 45, 126, 149; BERTHOLET, *Die Stellung der Israeliten und der Juden zu den Fremden* (1896), pp. 10, 89; MARTI, *op. cit.*, pp. 31, 39, 47 f.; S. MANDL, *Der Bann* (1898).

§ 149. Oaths.

1. The early period: readings, questions, and suggestions.[27]

   Gen. 14:22; 15:8–11, 17 f.; 21:22–24 (E); 22:15 (JE); 24:1–3, 27; 25:33 (E); 26:3 (JE), 26–31; 31:53 (E); 42:15 (E); 47:29; 50:25 (E); Exod. 13:19 (E); Josh. 2:12–14, 20; 6:26; Judg. 21:1; 1 Sam. 14:24–30, 39, 44 f.; 19:6; 24:21; 30:15; 2 Sam. 3:9 f.; 19:23; 21:1 f., 7; 1 Kings 1:13, 17, 30, 51 f.; 2:23 f., 36–46.

Examine and classify the cases of oaths cited, determining, in each case, (1) whether it is an oath sworn by man to man, by God to man, or by man to God; (2) the ritual of the oath, whether, for example, accompanied by sacrifice of certain victims, by taking hold of the thigh, by stretching upward the hand; (3) the penalty expected or prescribed in case of the violation of the oath; (4) any specially interesting uses of or usages in connection with the oath, *e. g.*, Abraham's oath to Melchizedek, the dividing of the animals (Gen. 15:10), the treaty between Jacob and Laban (Gen. 31:44–54), Rahab and the spies (Josh. 2:12–14), Saul's adjuration (1 Sam. 14:24–30, 39, 44 f.), David's oath concerning Solomon (1 Kings 1:13), Shimei and Solomon (1 Kings 2:42); (5) what is prohibited in Exod. 20:7, *thou shalt not take the name of Jehovah thy God in vain* (blasphemy, perjury, profanity, or sorcery and witchcraft)?

2. The middle period: readings, questions, and suggestions.

   Jer. 4:2; 22:5; 31:33; 34:18 f.; 38:16; Ezek. 17:16–19; Deut. 19:19 ff.[28]

Examine and classify as above, noting particularly points of special interest in connection with (1) false swearing (Deut. 19:19 ff.); (2)

[27] All references to the Hexateuch are from J, except those marked otherwise, and Gen. 14:22, which is from an independent source.

[28] This reference is from the code of laws contained in the book of Deuteronomy.

the cutting of the calf (Jer. 34 : 18 f.); (3) the new covenant (Jer. 31 : 33); (4) Zedekiah's oath (Jer. 38 : 16); (5) breaking the covenant (Ezek. 17 : 16–19).

3. The late period : readings, questions, and suggestions.[29]

Numb. 5 : 11–28 ; chap. 30 ; Josh. 9 : 15, 19 f.; Judg. 21 : 5, 7; Zech. 5 : 1 ff.; Ezra 10 : 5 ; Neh. 10 : 29 ; Dan. 12 : 7.

Examine and classify as above, noting points of special interest in connection with (1) the water of bitterness that causeth the curse (Numb. 5 : 11 ff.); (2) vows (Numb., chap. 30); (3) the oath to the Gibeonites (as described in Josh. 9 : 15 f., 19 f.); (4) the oath concerning strange wives (Ezra 10 : 2–5); (5) the flying-roll and false swearing (Zech. 5 : 1–4); (6) the man clothed in linen (Dan. 12 : 7).

§ 150. **Constructive Work.**— Prepare a statement upon the use of the oath among the Hebrews, taking up the following points : (1) the significance of the usual word translated *swear*, viz., " to come under the influence of *seven* things ;" (2) the ritual ; (3) the various forms of the oath ; (4) its irrevocable character and the penalty of its violation ; (5) its sociological basis ; (6) the significance of an oath made by the deity; (7) the meaning of the third commandment ; (8) the changes in usage which may be noted between the three periods ; (9) the attitude of the prophets ;[30] (10) the representations concerning swearing in the wisdom literature ;[31] (11) the representations in the apocryphal literature ;[32] (12) the attitude of the New Testament ;[33] (13) the use of the oath among the Arabs ;[34] (14) its use among the Assyrians and Babylonians ; (15) its relation to prayer.[35]

§ 151. **Literature to be Consulted.**

H. W. PHILLOTT, article "Oath," SMITH'S *Dict. of the Bible* (1st ed. 1863, 2d ed. 1893); EWALD, *op. cit.*, see *Index*, *s. v.* " Oath," etc.; SCHULTZ, *op. cit.*, Vol. II, p. 70 ; E. B. TYLOR, article "Oath," *Encyc. Brit.* (1875); W. R. SMITH, *Rel. of Sem.*, pp. 180 ff., 480 ; F. J. COFFIN, "The Third Commandment," *Journal of Biblical Literature.*

[29] References in **bold-face** type are from the priestly code of laws.

[30] See, *e. g.*, Hos. 4 : 2, 15 ; 10 : 4 ; Amos 4 : 2 ; 6 : 8 ; 8 : 7, 14 ; Isa. 14 : 24 ; 19 : 18 ; 45 : 23 ; 48 : 1 ; 54 : 9 ; 62 : 8 ; 65 : 16 ; Ezek. 21 : 23.

[31] See, *e. g.*, Eccl. 8 : 2 ; 9 : 2.

[32] See, *e. g.*, 1 Macc. 6 : 61 f.; 7 : 18, 35 ; 2 Macc. 14 : 33–36 ; Ecclus. 44 : 21.

[33] See, *e. g.*, Matt. 5 : 33 ff.; 14 : 7–9 ; 23 : 16 ff.; Mark 6 : 23, 26 ; Luke 1 : 73 ; Acts 2 : 30 ; 23 : 21 ; Jas. 5 : 12.

[34] *Cf.* WELLHAUSEN, *Reste arab. Heidenthums*, p. 122 ; W. R. SMITH, *Religion of the Semites*, see *Index*, *s. v.* " Oath."

[35] *Cf.* DRIVER, *Deuteronomy*, pp. 94 f.

Vol. XIX (1900), pp. 166–88; DUFF, *op. cit.*, Vol. II (1900), see *Index, s. v.* "Oath;" G. FERRIES, article "Oath," HASTINGS' *Dict. of the Bible*, Vol. III (1900); DAY, *op. cit.*, p. 184.

SAALSCHÜTZ, *Das mosaische Recht* (1846), pp. 615 ff.; BRUCH, article "Eid," SCHENKEL'S *Bibel-Lexikon*, Vol. II (1869); RIEHM, article "Eid," *Handwörterbuch;* WELLHAUSEN, *op. cit.*, p. 122; SMEND, *op. cit.*, see *Index, s. v.* "Schwur;" NOWACK, *op. cit.*, Vol. II, pp. 262 ff.; BENZINGER, *op. cit.*, see *Index, s. v.* "Eid;" FREY, *Tod, Seelenglaube und Seelenkult* (1898), pp. 108 f.; BENZINGER, article "Eid bei den Hebräern," *Realencyklopädie*, 3d ed., Vol. V (1898).

§ 152. Supplementary Study on Fasting as a Means for Securing the Divine Mercy and Help.

1. The early period.
   Exod. 34 : 28 (J), *cf.* 24 : 18 (E); 1 Sam. 7 : 5 f.; 31 : 13; 2 Sam. 1 : 12; 3 : 35; 12 : 16–23; 1 Kings 21 : 9, 12, 27.
2. The middle period.
   Deut. 8 : 3; 9 : 9, 18–20, 25–29; 10 : 10; Jer. 14 : 12; 36 : 6, 9.
3. The late period.
   Judg. 18 : 17(?); 20 : 26 ff.; Ezra 8 : 21–23; 10 : 6; Neh. 1 : 4–11; 9 : 1, 31; Esther 4 : 1–3, 16; Zech. 7 : 1–7, 18–23; 8 : 19; Isa. 58 : 3 ff.; 1 Chron. 10 : 12; 2 Chron. 20 : 3; Joel 1 : 14; 2 : 12, 15; Jon. 3 : 5; Dan. 9 : 3; Lev. 16 : 29, 31.[36]

§ 153. Questions and Suggestions.

Consider (1) the reason assigned by David in 2 Sam. 12 : 22 for fasting, viz., to secure Jehovah's pity; (2) the fasting of Moses on Sinai (Exod. 34 : 28; Deut. 9 : 9) as a preparation for an important act, the receiving of the law; (3) the fasting of Elijah (1 Kings 19 : 8 ff.) as a preparation for communion with God; (4) the fasting of the men of Jabesh for Saul (1 Sam. 31 : 13), and of David for Saul (2 Sam. 1 : 12), that is, in mourning for the dead (*cf.* 2 Sam. 3 : 35); and determine the original meaning of the act, *i. e.*, an explanation with which these various cases may be connected; is it to raise the pity of the deity? or in preparation for a sacrificial meal?[37]

Consider the various cases of fasting cited and note (1) the motive or purpose in each case, *e. g.*, David, Ahab, Nehemiah, Ezra; (2) whether they were private or public (*cf.*, in earlier and middle periods, 1 Kings 21 : 9 ff.; Isa. 1 : 13*b* (Sept.); Jer. 36 : 6 ff.; and, in later period, Joel 1 : 13 f.; 2 Chron. 20 : 3); (3) the change by which the act becomes spiritualized (*cf.* Ahab's case, 1 Kings 21 : 29); (4) the connection between fasting and penitence (*cf.* 1 Sam. 7 : 6; Neh. 9 : 1); (5) the

[36] This reference is from the Priestly Code.

[37] W. R. SMITH, *Religion of the Semites*, p. 434.

circumstances which led to greater importance being given to fasting, and the changes in frequency of the act and in meaning which came in the later period; (6) the conception which makes it a "meritorious work," and the prophets' attitude toward this (Isa. 58 : 3 ff.; Zech. 7 : 5 f.).

Consider the various occasions on which, in the later period, public fasting was observed and the events thereby commemorated: (1) in the fourth month, the capture of Jerusalem (Jer. 52 : 6, 7); (2) in the fifth month, the destruction of the temple and city (Jer. 52 : 12 f.); (3) in the seventh month, the murder of Gedaliah (Jer. 41 : 1 ff.); (4) in the tenth month, the beginning of the siege (Jer. 52 : 4) (*cf.* Zech. 7 : 1–7, 18–23); (5) the Day of Atonement (Lev., chap. 16), noting (*a*) that this is the only fast required by the laws, (*b*) that there is no allusion to its observance in any of the historical literature of the Old Testament, (*c*) the purpose of the day, (*d*) its relation to the religious thought and spirit of the later times; (6) the thirteenth of Adar, the case of Haman.

Consider the usage of fasting as referred to (1) in the Psalms;[38] (2) in the apocryphal literature;[39] (3) in the New Testament;[40] (4) among other Semitic nations.[41]

§ 154. Literature to be Consulted.

SAMUEL CLARK, article "Atonement, Day of," SMITH'S *Dictionary of the Bible* (1st ed. 1863, 2d ed. 1893); SCHULTZ, *op. cit.*, Vol. I, pp. 367 ff., 372, 402 ff., 431; OEHLER, *Old Testament Theology* (1st ed. 1873, 3d ed. 1891, transl. 1883), §§ 140 f.; EDERSHEIM, *The Temple, its Ministry and Services* (1874), pp. 263–88; WELLHAUSEN, *Prolegomena*, pp. 110–12; J. S. BLACK, article "Fasting," *Encyclopædia Britannica*, Vol. IX (1879); KUENEN, *The Hexateuch* (2d ed. 1885, transl. 1886), pp. 86, 312; W. R. SMITH, *Rel. of Sem.*, pp. 303, 388 ff., 433 f.; MONTEFIORE, *op. cit.*, pp. 509 f.; C. J. BALL, article "Fasting and Fasts," SMITH'S *Dictionary of the Bible* (2d ed. 1893); H. C. TRUMBULL, *Studies in Oriental Social Life* (1894), pp. 186, 286 ff., 383; MCCURDY, *op. cit.*, §§ 1116, 1118, 1346 n.; S. R. DRIVER AND H. A. WHITE, article "Atonement, Day of," HASTINGS' *Dictionary*, Vol. I (1898); E. E. HARDING, article "Feasts and Fasts," *ibid.*, Vol. I (1898), pp. 862 f.; CHEYNE, *op. cit.*, pp. 9–11; M. JASTROW, *op. cit.*, p. 688; BENZINGER AND CHEYNE, article "Atonement, Day of," *Encyclopædia Biblica*, Vol. I (1899); BENZINGER, article "Fasting, Fasts," *Encyclopædia Biblica*, Vol. II (1901); OTTLEY, *A Short History of the Hebrews to the Roman Period* (1901), pp. 305 f.

[38] See, *e. g.*, Pss. 35 : 13; 69 : 10; 109 : 24.

[39] See, *e. g.*, 1 Macc. 3 : 44–54; Ecclus. 34 : 26.

[40] See, *e. g.*, Matt. 4 : 2; 6 : 16 ff.; 9 : 14 f.; 17 : 21; Mark 2 : 18 ff.; 9 : 29; Luke 2 : 37; 5 : 33 ff.; 18 : 12; Acts 10 : 30; 13 : 2 f.; 14 : 23; 27 : 9, 33; 1 Cor. 7 : 5; 2 Cor. 6 : 5; 11 : 27.

[41] See, *e. g.*, the references to the works of W. R. Smith, Wellhausen, Jastrow, and Black cited in § 154.

HOLTZMANN, article "Fasten," SCHENKEL'S *Bibel-Lexikon*, Vol. II (1869); ORELLI, article "Versöhnungsfest," *Realencyklopädie* (2d ed. 1875); H. OORT, "De groote Verzoendag," *Theologisch Tijdschrift*, Vol. X (1876), pp. 142–65; D. HOFFMANN, Berliner's *Magazin*, 1876, pp. 1 ff.; DELITZSCH, *Zeitschrift für kirchliche Wissenschaft und kirchliches Leben*, Vol. I (1880), pp. 173–83; J. DERENBOURG, "Essai de restitution de l'ancienne rédaction de Masséchet Kippourim," *Revue des études juives*, No. 11 (1883), pp. 41–80; ADLER, "Der Versöhnungstag in der Bibel, sein Ursprung und seine Bedeutung," *Zeitschrift für die alttestamentliche Wissenschaft*, Vol. III (1883), pp. 178–84; KUENEN, *Theologisch Tijdschrift*, Vol. XVII (1883), pp. 207–12; RIEHM, article "Fasten," *Handwörterbuch*, Vol. I (1884); DELITZSCH, article "Versöhnungstag," RIEHM'S *Handwörterbuch*, Vol. II (1884); STADE, *Geschichte*, Vol. II (1888), pp. 182, 258 ff.; BENZINGER, "Das Gesetz über den grossen Versöhnungstag, Lev. XVI," *Zeitschrift für die alttestamentliche Wissenschaft*, Vol. IX (1889), pp. 65–88; SCHWALLY, *Das Leben nach dem Tode* (1892), pp. 26 ff.; SMEND, *op. cit.*, pp. 142, 319, 330 ff., 396; NOWACK, *op. cit.*, Vol. II, pp. 270 ff.; BENZINGER, *op. cit.*, pp. 165, 464, 477; DILLMANN, *op. cit.*, p. 184; MARTI, *op. cit.*, pp. 234, 283 f.; BUHL, "Fasten im Alten Testament," *Realencyklopädie*, 3d ed., Vol. V (1898); FREY, *Tod, Seelenglaube und Seelenkult im alten Israel* (1898), pp. 37, 81–5, 117.

§ 155. Supplementary Study on Consultation with the Deity through Oracles, Urim and Thummim, the Ephod, the Lot.

1. The early period.

(*a*) *Oracles.*—Gen. 24:12–14 (J); 25:22 f. (J); Judg. 1:1; 18:5 f.; 1 Sam. 10:22; 14:19, 37; 23:2, 4, 10 ff.; 28:6; 30:7 f.; 2 Sam. 2:1; 5:19, 23 f.; 16:23; 21:1 f.; 2 Kings 8:7 ff.; Numb. 24:3, 15; Isa. 15:1; Amos 2:11, 16.

(*b*) *Urim and Thummim.*—1 Sam. 14:41 f.; 28:4–6; 22:10, 13; 23:2, 4, 6, 9–12; 30:7; 2 Sam. 2:1; 5:19, 23 f.; 21:1; Deut. 33:8 (E).

(*c*) *The ephod.*—Judg. 8:27*a*; 17:5; 18:14, 20; 1 Sam. 14:18; 21:9 f.; 23:6, 9 ff.; 30:7 f.; Hos. 3:4.

(*d*) *The lot.*—Josh. 16:1 (J); 17:14, 17 (J); Judg. 1:3; 20:9; Isa. 17:14; Mic. 2:5.

2. The middle period.

(*a*) *Oracles.*—Mic. 4:6; 5:9; Nah. 2:13; Zeph. 1:2; Ezek. 5:11; 11:8, 21; Jer. 1:8; 2:3.

(*b*) *The ephod.*—Deut. 2:28; Judg. 8:27*b*.

(*c*) *The lot.*—Josh. 18:6, 8, 10 (R^d); Isa. 34:17; Jer. 13:25; Ezek. 24:6; Obad. 11; Nah. 3:10; Deut. 32:9.

3. The late period.[42]

(*a*) *Oracles.*—Joel 2:12; Hag. 1:9; 2:4; Zech. 1:3; 3:9; 10:12; 12:1; Mal. 1:2; Pss. 36:1; 110:1.

(*b*) *Urim and Thummim.*—**Exod. 28:30; Lev. 8:8; Numb. 27:21**; Ezra 2:63; Neh. 7:65.

[42] References in **bold-face** type are from the Priestly Code.

(*c*) *The lot.*—**Lev. 16 : 8–10 ; Numb. 26 : 55 f.; 33 : 54 ; 34 : 13 ; 36 : 2 f.;** Josh. 14 : 2 ; 15 : 1 ; 17 : 1 ; 19 : 1, 10, 17, 24, 32, 40, 51 ; 21 : 4, 5 f., 8, 10, 40 ; 1 Chron. 6 : 54, 61, 63, 65 ; 16 : 18 ; 24 : 5, 7, 31 ; 25 : 8 f.; 26 : 13 f.; Neh. 10 : 34 ; 11 : 1 ; Esther 3 : 7 ; 9 : 24 ; Isa. 57 : 6 ; Joel 3 : 3 ; Jon. 1 : 7 ; Dan. 12 : 13.

§ 156. **Questions and Suggestions.**

Examine the various means of consultation with the deity which seem to have been recognized as *legitimate* and *proper*, viz., oracles, Urim and Thummim, ephod, and lot ; note the instances cited of each, and consider (1) the various circumstances under which such consultation is held ; (2) the underlying motive in each case ; (3) the relative frequency in the different periods ; (4) the differences (if any) between the usages named ; (5) the various senses in which the word *oracle* is used ; (6) the different views as to the method of employing the Urim and Thummim ; (7) the meaning of the ephod and its use ; (8) the place of the lot in connection with religious acts.

Consider whether, with the growth of religious conceptions and the higher ideas entertained of God in later times, the use of these external helps increases or diminishes.

Consider the use of these or similar external helps in consulting the deity, as they may be referred to in (1) the Psalms,[43] (2) the wisdom literature,[44] (3) the apocryphal literature,[45] (4) the New Testament ;[46] and likewise as they were employed among (5) the Egyptians,[47] (6) the Assyrians and Babylonians,[48] (7) the ancient Arabs,[49] (8) the Greeks and Romans.[50]

§ 157. **Literature to be Consulted.**

KALISCH, *Exodus* (1855), pp. 540–45; E. H. PLUMPTRE, article "Urim and Thummim," SMITH'S *Dictionary of the Bible* (1st ed. 1863, 2d ed. 1893); W. L. BEVAN, article "Ephod," *ibid.* (1st ed. 1863), revised by J. M. FULLER (2d ed. 1893); KUENEN, *Religion of Israel*, Vol. I (1869 f., transl. 1874), pp. 96–100 ; W. M. RAMSAY,

[43] See, *e. g.*, Pss. 16 : 5 ; 22 : 18 ; 36 : 1; 110 : 1; 125 : 3.

[44] See, *e. g.*, Prov. 1 : 14 ; 16 : 33 ; 18 : 18 ; 30 : 1; 31 : 1.

[45] *Cf.* Wisdom of Solomon 8 : 8.

[46] See, *e. g.*, Matt. 27 : 35; Mark 15 : 24 ; Luke 1 : 9 ; 23 : 34 ; John 19 : 24 ; Acts 1 : 26 ; 7 : 38 ; 8 : 21; Rom. 3 : 2 ; Heb. 5 : 12 ; 1 Pet. 4 : 11.

[47] See, *e. g.*, WIEDEMANN, *Religion of the Ancient Egyptians*, see *Index*, *s. v.* "Oracle, etc."

[48] See references to Pinches, Strong, and Jastrow cited in § 157.

[49] See references to W. R. Smith and Wellhausen cited in § 157.

[50] See, *e. g.*, WARRE CORNISH, *Concise Dictionary of Greek and Roman Antiquities*, *s. v.* "Sortes."

article "Oracle," *Encyclopædia Britannica* (1875); WELLHAUSEN, *Prolegomena*, p. 130; T. G. PINCHES, "The Oracle of Ishtar of Arbela," *Records of the Past*, Vol. XI (1878), pp. 59–72; see also *ibid.*, Vol. V, new series (1891), pp. 129–40; S. F. HANCOCK, "The Urim and Thummim," *Old Testament Student*, Vol. III (1884), pp. 252–56; KÖNIG, *Religious History of Israel* (1885), pp. 107 ff.; W. R SMITH, *Rel. of Sem.*, see *Index, s. v.* "Oracles, etc.;" KIRKPATRICK, *The First Book of Samuel* (Camb. Bible, 1891), pp. 217 f.; H. E. DOSKER, "The Urim and Thummim," *Presbyterian and Reformed Review*, 1892, pp. 717–30; S. A. STRONG, "On Some Oracles to Esarhaddon and Assurbanipal," *Beiträge zur Assyriologie*, Band II (1894), pp. 627–45; J. F. MCCURDY, *op. cit.*, see *Index, s. v.* "Oracles;" G. F. MOORE, *Judges* (International Critical Commentary, 1895), p. 381; HOMMEL, *Ancient Hebrew Tradition* (1897), pp. 280 ff.; S. R. DRIVER, article "Ephod," HASTINGS' *Dictionary*, Vol. I (1898); JASTROW, *op. cit.*, see *Index, s. v.* "Oracles;" T. C. FOOTE, "The Biblical Ephod," *Johns Hopkins University Circulars*, XIX, No. 145 (1900), p. 40; O. C. WHITEHOUSE, article "Lots," HASTINGS' *Dictionary*, Vol. III (1900); W. MUSS-ARNOLT, "The Urim and Thummim," *American Journal of Semitic Languages and Literatures*, Vol. XVI (1900), pp. 193–224; C. H. PRICHARD, article "Oracle," HASTINGS' *Dictionary*, Vol. III (1900); G. F. MOORE, article "Ephod," *Encyclopædia Biblica*, Vol. II (1901).

BRAUN, *De vestitu sacerdotum* (1698), pp. 462 ff.; BELLERMANN, *Die Urim und Thummim* (1824); BÄHR, *Symbolik des mosaischen Cultus*, Vol. II (1839), pp. 131–41; G. KLAIBER, *Das priesterliche Orakel der Israeliten* (1865); KÖHLER, *Lehrbuch der biblischen Geschichte des Alten Testamentes*, Vol. I (1875), pp. 349 f.; STEINER, article "Urim und Thummim," SCHENKEL'S *Bibel-Lexikon*, Vol. V (1875); RIEHM, *Handwörterbuch* (1st ed. 1884, 2d ed. by Baethgen 1893 f.), articles "Ephod" and "Licht und Recht;" KAUTZSCH, article "Urim," *Realencyklopädie* (2d ed. 1885); STADE, *Geschichte*, Vol. I (1887), pp. 466, 471; WELLHAUSEN, *Reste arab. Heidenthums*, pp. 126 f., 133, 167, etc.; BAUDISSIN, *Geschichte des alttestamentlichen Priesterthums* (1889), pp. 70 f., 205 ff.; LAGARDE, *Mittheilungen*, Vol. IV (1891), p. 17; SELLIN, *Beiträge zur israelitischen und jüdischen Religionsgeschichte*, Heft II (1897), p. 119; WILHELM LOTZ, article "Ephod," *Realencyklopädie*, Vol. V (3d ed., 1898); VAN HOONACKER, *Le sacerdoce lévitique* (1899), pp. 370 ff.

§ 158. Supplementary Study on Consultation with the Deity or Supernatural Powers through Magic, Divination, Sorcery, Witchcraft.

1. The early period.[51]

(*a*) *Magic and divination.*—Gen. 44:5, 15 (J); **Exod. 22:17**; Numb. 22:7 (J); 23:23; 1 Sam. 6:2; 28:8; Mic. 3:6 f., 11; Isa. 2:6.

(*b*) *Sorcery and witchcraft.*—**Exod. 22:18**; 1 Sam. 15:23; 2 Kings 9:22.

2. The middle period.[52]

(*a*) *Magic and divination.*—**Deut. 18:9–14**; Jer. 8:17; 14:14; 27:9; 29:8; Ezek. 12:24; 13:7–9, 23; 21:21 ff., 29; 22:28; 2 Kings 17:17; Isa. 44:25; Mic. 5:12.

[51] References in **bold-face** type are from the Covenant Code.

[52] References in **bold-face** type are from the code of laws contained in Deuteronomy.

(*b*) *Sorcery and witchcraft.*—**Deut. 18:10**; Mic. 5:12; Nah. 3:4; Jer. 27:9; Isa. 47:9, 12; 57:3.

3. The late period.[53]

(*a*) *Magic and divination.*—Josh. 13:22; **Lev. 19:26, 31; 20:6, 27**; Zech. 10:2.

(*b*) *Sorcery and witchcraft.*—Exod. 7:11; Mal. 3:5; 2 Chron. 33:6; Dan. 2:2.

§ 159. **Questions and Suggestions.**

Examine the various means of consultation with higher powers which seem always to have been regarded as improper and illegitimate, viz., *magic*, *divination*, *sorcery*, and *witchcraft*, noting (1) the various circumstances under which such consultation is held; (2) the underlying motive in each case; (3) the relative frequency in different periods; (4) the various methods thus employed; (5) the external sources of these influences; (6) any internal source from which they may have sprung; (7) the prophetic attitude in the different periods; (8) the explanation of this attitude; (9) the relation of all this to idolatry; (10) the essential element of injury which it contributed; (11) the gradual disappearance, and the occasion of this disappearance.

Consider (1) the significance of references in the Psalms;[54] (2) in the wisdom literature;[55] (3) in the apocryphal literature;[56] (4) in the New Testament.[57]

Consider the use of these methods among (1) the Egyptians;[58] (2) the ancient Arabs;[59] (3) the Assyrians and Babylonians;[60] (4) the Greeks and Romans.[61]

§ 160. **Literature to be Consulted.**

F. W. FARRAR, article "Divination," SMITH'S *Dictionary of the Bible* (1st ed. 1863, 2d ed. 1893); SCHULTZ, *op. cit.*, Vol. I, pp. 250 ff., 281 ff., 283 ff.; E. B. TYLOR, article "Divination," *Encyclopædia Britannica*, Vol. VII (1878); IDEM, article

53 References in **bold-face** type are from the Priestly Code.

54 See, *e. g.*, Ps. 58:5.

55 See, *e. g.*, Prov. 16:10.

56 See, *e. g.*, Ecclus. 34:2–7.

57 See, *e. g.*, Acts 8:9, 11; 13:6, 8; 16:16; Gal. 5:20; Rev. 9:21; 18:23; 21:8; 22:15.

58 See, *e. g.*, BUDGE, *Egyptian Magic.*

59 See, *e. g.*, W. R. SMITH, *Rel. of Sem.*, *Index*, *s. v.* "Omens," etc.; WELLHAUSEN, *Reste arab. Heid.*, pp. 135–64.

60 See, *e. g.*, LENORMANT, *Chaldæan Magic;* L. W. KING, *Babylonian Magic and Sorcery.*

61 See, *e. g.*, E. B. TYLOR, article "Magic," *Encyc. Brit.*

"Magic," *ibid.*, Vol. XV (1883); W. R. SMITH, *Rel. of Sem.*, see *Index*, *s. v.* "Charms," "Omens," "Magic," "Witches;" SCHÜRER, *A History of the Jewish People in the Time of Jesus Christ*, Div. II, Vol. III, pp. 151–5; ERMAN, *Life in Ancient Egypt* (transl. 1894), see *Index*, *s. v.* "Magic Art," etc.; MENZIES, *op. cit.*, pp. 72, 91, 153; MCCURDY, *op. cit.* (1895–1901), §§ 644, 851 n., 858; L. W. KING, *Babylonian Magic and Sorcery, Being "The Prayers of the Lifting of the Hand"* (1896); T. W. DAVIES, *Magic, Divination and Demonology* (1898); JASTROW, *op. cit.*, see *Index*, *s. v.* "Magical Texts," "Sorcer, etc.," "Witchcraft;" F. B. JEVONS, article "Divination," HASTINGS' *Dictionary*, Vol. I (1898); O. C. WHITEHOUSE, article "Exorcism," *ibid.;* T. W. DAVIES, article "Divination," *Encyc. Bib.*, Vol. I (1899); E. A. W. BUDGE, *Egyptian Magic* (1899); RAMSAY, *The Expositor*, July, 1899, p. 22; O. C. WHITEHOUSE, article "Magic," HASTINGS' *Dictionary*, Vol. III (1900); DUFF, *op. cit.*, Vol. II, see *Index*, *s. v.* "Divination;" CHEYNE, article "Exorcists," *Encyc. Bib.*, Vol. II (1901); DAY, *op. cit.*, pp. 185 f., 220, 222; ANDREW LANG, *Magic and Religion* (1901).

BRECHER, *Das Transcendentale, Magie, und magische Heilarten im Talmud* (1850); P. SCHOLZ, *Götzendienst und Zauberwesen bei den alten Hebräern und den benachbarten Völkern* (1877); MAYBAUM, *Die Entwickelung des israelitischen Prophetenthums* (1883), pp. 7–29; STADE, *Geschichte*, Vol. I, pp. 503 ff.; WELLHAUSEN, *Reste arabischen Heidenthums* ("Skizzen und Vorarbeiten," III), pp. 126, 135–64, 215; SMEND, *op. cit.*, see *Index*, *s. v.* "Wahrsagung," "Zauberei;" TALLQVIST, *Assyrische Beschwörungsserie Maqlu* (1894); DILLMANN, *op. cit.*, see *Index*, *s. v.* "Wahrsager;" ZIMMERN, *Beiträge zur Kenntnis der babylonischen Religion* (1896, 1899); MARTI, *op. cit.*, p. 45; FREY, *Tod, Seelenglaube und Seelenkult* (1898), pp. 180, 202; LEHMANN, *Aberglaube und Zauberei;* BLAU, *Das alt-jüdische Zauberwesen.*

§ 161. Supplementary Study on Mourning Customs.

1. The early period.

   Amos 5:16; 8:10; Mic. 1:8, 16; Isa. 3:24; 15:2; 22:12; 2 Sam. 3:31; 21:10; 1 Kings 21:27; 2 Kings 19:1 f.; Gen. 37:34 (E), 35 (J); *cf.* 1 Kings 20:31 f.

2. The middle period.

   Deut. 14:1 f.; Jer. 16:6–8; 41:5; 47:5; 49:3; 48:37; 4:8; 6:26; Ezek. 24:16–17; 29:18; 27:31; 7:18.

3. The late period.

   Lev. 19:27 f.; 21:5; Joel 1:8; Jon. 3:5 ff.; Ezra 9:3; Dan. 9:3.

§ 162. Questions and Suggestions.

Study the references given to mourning customs, and note (1) the custom of *weeping* and its significance, in contrast with the modern conception; (2) the more intense expression of grief, termed *wailing;* (3) the beating of the breast, tearing of the hair, rending of clothes, putting on sackcloth, and mutilation of the body, as expressions of mourning; (4) the putting away of food to (or for) the dead (Deut. 26:14); (5) fasting (*cf.* 1 Sam. 31:13).

Consider, in connection with these customs, (1) to what extent they are survivals from the age in which ancestor-worship prevailed; (2) to what extent, therefore, they had their origin in the effort to propitiate the spirit of the dead, which was supposed to have power for good or evil, rather than in the desire to express grief for the loss that had been incurred; (3) the reasons for forbidding certain of these customs (*cf.* Deut. 14:1; 26:14; Lev. 19:28); (4) changes which seem to have come about in the progress of history.

Consider the representations made concerning mourning customs in the Psalms,[62] (2) in the wisdom literature,[63] (3) in the apocryphal literature,[64] (4) in the New Testament,[65] (5) among other ancient nations.[66]

§163. **Literature to be Consulted.**

THOMSON, *The Land and the Book* (1859), see *Index, s. v.* "Manners and Customs;" H. W. PHILLOTT, article "Mourning," SMITH'S *Dictionary of the Bible*, (1st ed. 1863, 2d ed. 1893); MASPERO, *Egyptian Archæology* (transl. 1887), pp. 108–63; W. R. SMITH, *Rel. of Sem.*, pp. 322 f., 336, 370, 430; A. P. BENDER, "Beliefs, Rites, and Customs of the Jews, Connected with Death, Burial, and Resurrection," *Jewish Quarterly Review*, Vol. VI (1893–94), pp. 317–47, 664–71; Vol. VII (1894–95), 101–18, 259–69; ERMAN, *Life in Ancient Egypt* (transl. 1894), pp. 306–27; E. A. WALLIS BUDGE, *The Mummy* (2d. ed. 1894); H. C. TRUMBULL, *Studies in Oriental Social Life* (1894), pp. 143–208; MENZIES, *op. cit.* (1895), see *Index, s. v.* "Funeral Practices;" JASTROW, *op. cit.*, see *Index, s. v.* "Dead," etc.; PERITZ, "Woman in the Ancient Hebrew Cult," *Journal of Biblical Literature*, Vol. XVII (1898), pp 137 f.; T. NICOL, article "Mourning," HASTINGS' *Dictionary*, Vol. III (1900); DUFF *op. cit.*, Vol. II, see *Index, s. v.* "Mourning and Bewailing;" DAY, *op. cit.*, pp. 204 ff.; WIEDEMANN, *The Realm of the Egyptian Dead.*

PERLES, "Die Leichenfeierlichkeiten des nachbiblischen Judenthums," *Monatsschrift für Geschichte und Wissenschaft des Judenthums*, Vol. X (1861), pp. 345–55, 376–94; M. GEIER, *De Ebraeorum luctu lugentiumque ritibus* (3d ed. 1868); ROSKOFF, article "Klage," SCHENKEL'S *Bibel-Lexikon*, Vol. III (1871); OORT, "De doodenvereering bij de Israeliten," *Theologisch Tijdschrift*, Vol. XV (1881), pp. 350 ff.; KAMPHAUSEN, article "Trauer," RIEHM'S *Handwörterbuch*, Vol. II (1884); LEHRER, article "Trauer bei den Hebräern," *Realencyklopädie*, Vol. XV (2d ed. 1885); STADE, *Geschichte*, Vol. I, pp. 387 ff.; G. A. WILKEN, *Ueber das Haaropfer* (1886 f.); WELLHAUSEN, *Reste arab. Heidenthums* (1887), pp. 159 ff., 178 f.; GOLDZIHER, *Muhammedanische Studien* (1888), Vol. I, pp. 229–63; SCHWALLY, *Das Leben nach dem Tode* (1892); SMEND, *op. cit.*, pp. 153 f.; WELLHAUSEN, *Israelitische und jüdische Geschichte* (1st ed.

[62] See, *e. g.*, Pss. 35:14; 38:6; 42:9; 43:2; 88:9.

[63] See, *e. g.*, Prov. 29:2; Job 2:11; 5:11; 30:28; Eccles. 3:4.

[64] See, *e. g.*, Ecclus. 7:34; 22:11 f.; 38:16 ff.; 41:1 ff.

[65] See, *e. g.*, Matt. 2:18; 5:4; 9:15; 11:17; 24:30; Mark 16:10; Luke 6:25; 7:32; 1 Cor. 5:2; 2 Cor. 7:7; Jas. 4:9; Rev. 18:8, 11.

[66] See especially the references to the works of W. R. Smith, Wellhausen, Menzies, Jastrow, and Trumbull cited in §163.

1894), p. 143; NOWACK, *op. cit.*, Vol. I, pp. 187–98; BENZINGER, *op. cit.*, pp. 102, 165 ff., 428; MARTI, *op. cit.*, pp. 37, 40 ff., 116; FREY, *Tod, Seelenglaube und Seelenkult im alten Israel* (1898); BERTHOLET, *Die israelitischen Vorstellungen vom Zustand nach dem Tode* (1899); KREHL, *Religion der Araber;* F. J. GRUNDT, *Die Trauergebräuche der Hebräer.*

§ 164. **Supplementary Study on Circumcision.**

1. The early period.

   Exod. 4:24 ff. (J); Josh. 5:2 f., 9 (J); Judg. 14:3; 15:18; 1 Sam. 14:6; 17:26, 36; 18:25 ff.; 31:4; 2 Sam. 1:20; 3:14.

2. The middle period.

   Deut. 10:16; 30:6; Hab. 2:16; Jer. 4:6; 6:10; 9:24 f.; Josh. 5:4–8; Ezek. 28:10; 31:18; 32:19, 21, 24–32; 44:7, 9; Isa. 52:1.

3. The late period.[67]

   Lev. 12:3; 19:23 ff.; 26:41; Gen. 17:10–14, 23–27; 21:4; 34:14 f., 17, 22, 24; Exod. 6:12, 30; 12:44, 48; 1 Chron. 10:4.

§ 165. **Questions and Suggestions.**

Study the references to *circumcision*, considering (1) the more interesting narratives concerning instances of circumcision, *e. g.*, (*a*) Moses' son and Zipporah, (*b*) the circumcision at Gilgal, (*c*) the circumcision of Abraham's family, of Shechem and his family; (2) the characterization of other nations as uncircumcised; (3) the early origin, how shown.

Consider (1) the explanation of the origin which makes it sanitary, *i. e.*, instituted as a preventive of certain diseases; (2) the explanation which connects it with marriage, as thereby promoting fruitfulness; (3) the explanation that makes it a tribal badge, *i. e.*, a mark of initiation into full membership in the tribe (which included religious privileges), and therefore an act of sacramental communion, an act of sacrifice, a dedication.

Consider (1) the place of circumcision in the early period, viz., of young men (*e. g.*, Gen., chap. 34; Josh. 5:2 f.; Exod. 4:25), and as a tribal distinction (*cf.* Gen., chap. 34; Ezek. 31:8); (2) its place in the middle period: (*a*) not mentioned in history or in the older laws, not regarded as important; (*b*) circumcision of heart called for (Jer. 9:24, 25), while the circumcision of Israelites is placed on the same plane with that of Edomites, Ammonites, and other nations; (*c*) the spiritualization by the prophets furnishing the basis for more extended use in the next period;

[67] References in **bold-face** type are from the Priestly Code.

(3) its place in the later period: (*a*) the representations of its origin; (*b*) the regulations for the performance of the rite; (*c*) its position as one of the two distinctive ordinances of Judaism, the other being the sabbath; (*d*) its significance as a rite of purification.

Consider representations concerning circumcision (1) in the apocryphal literature;[68] (2) in the New Testament,[69] and the lack of allusion to it in the Psalms and in the wisdom literature. (3) Consider the practice of circumcision among the Egyptians, Arabs, and other nations.[70]

§ 166. Literature to be Consulted.

T. T. PEROWNE, article "Circumcision," SMITH'S *Dict. of the Bible* (1st ed. 1863, 2d ed. 1893); EWALD, *op. cit.*, pp. 89–97; SCHULTZ, *op. cit.*, Vol. I, pp. 192 ff.; II, pp. 7–70; KUENEN, *Religion of Israel* (1869 f., transl. 1874), Vol. I, pp. 238, 290; ASHER, *The Jewish Rite of Circumcision* (1873); E. B. TYLOR, *Primitive Culture*, Vol. II (1874), pp. 363 ff.; T. K. CHEYNE, article "Circumcision," *Encyclopædia Britannica*, Vol. V (1877); E. B. TYLOR, *Early History of Mankind* (3d ed. 1878), pp. 214–19; KALISCH, *Bible Studies*, Part II (1878), pp. 4–11; WELLHAUSEN, *Prolegomena*, p. 340; RENAN, *History of the People of Israel*, Vol. I (1887, transl. 1894), pp. 104–9; W. R. SMITH, *Rel. of Sem.*, p. 328; BANCROFT, *Native Races* (1890), Vol. III, see *Index;* P. C. REMONDINO, *History of Circumcision from the Earliest Times to the Present* (1891); H. C. TRUMBULL, *The Blood Covenant* (1893), pp. 79, 215–24, 351 f.; ERMAN, *Life in Ancient Egypt* (transl. 1894), pp. 32 f., 539; SCHECHTER, *Studies in Judaism* (1896), p. 343; A. H. SAYCE, *Expository Times*, November, 1897; I. J. PERITZ, "Woman in the Ancient Hebrew Cult," *Journal of Biblical Literature*, Vol. XVII (1898), p. 136; MACALISTER, article "Circumcision," HASTINGS' *Dictionary*, Vol. I (1898); BENZINGER, article "Circumcision," *Encyc. Bib.*, Vol. I (1899).

BORHECK, *Ist die Beschneidung ursprünglich hebräisch?* (1793); COHEN, *Dissertation sur la circoncision* (1816); AUTENRIETH, *Ueber den Ursprung der Beschneidung* (1829); LÜBKERT, "Der jüdische ἐπισπασμός," *Theologische Studien und Kritiken*, 1835, pp. 657–64; COLLIN, *Die Beschneidung* (1842); S. HOLDHEIM, *Ueber die Beschneidung in religiös. Beziehungen;* BERGSON, *Die Beschneidung* (1844); SALOMON, *Die Beschneidung histor. und medizin. dargestellt* (1844); BRECHER, *Die Beschneidung* (1845); STEINSCHNEIDER, *Ueber die Beschneidung der Araber* (1845); G. EBERS, *Aegypten und die Bücher Moses*, Vol. I (1868), pp. 278–84; STEINER, article "Beschneidung," SCHENKEL'S *Bibel-Lexikon*, Vol. I (1869); AUERBACH, *Berith Abraham, oder, der Beschneidungsfeier* (2d ed. 1880); WEBER, *Die Lehren des Talmud* (1880), p. 373; PLOSS, *Das Kind in Brauch und Sitte der Völker* (2d ed. 1882), pp. 360 ff.; RIEHM, article "Beschneidung," *Handwörterbuch* (1884); STADE, *Zeitschrift für die alttestamentliche Wissenschaft*, Vol. VI (1886), pp. 132–43; WELLHAUSEN, *Reste arab. Heidenthums* (1st ed. 1887), pp. 154, 168, 215; HOLZINGER,

[68] See, *e. g.*, 1 Macc. 1:14, 48, 60 f.; 2 Macc. 6:10.

[69] See, *e. g.*, Luke 1:59; John 7:22 f.; Acts 15:5; 16:3; 21:21; Rom. 2:25 ff.; 1 Cor. 7:18 f.; Gal. 5:2 f.; 6:13; Col. 3:11; Phil. 3:5.

[70] See especially the references to the works of Tylor, Bancroft, W. R. Smith, Wellhausen, Ploss, Ebers, Erman, and Reitzenstein, cited in § 166.

Einleitung in den Hexateuch (1893), pp. 133, 365, 437; SMEND, *op. cit.*, pp. 37 f., 116; NOWACK, *op. cit.*, pp. 167–71; BENZINGER, *op. cit.*, pp. 153 ff.; BUDDE, *Zeitschrift für die alttestamentliche Wissenschaft*, Vol. XIV (1894), p. 250; GLASSBERG, *Die Beschneidung* (1896); KRAETZSCHMAR, *Die Bundesvorstellung im Alten Testament* (1896), pp. 165, 174; BERTHOLET, *Die Stellung der Israeliten und der Juden zu den Fremden* (1896), see *Index, s. v.* "Beschneidung;" MARTI, *op. cit.*, pp. 43, 163 f.; J. JAEGER, "Ueber die Beschneidung," *Neue kirchliche Zeitschrift*, July, 1898, pp. 479–91; ZEYDNER, "Kainszeichen, Keniter und Beschneidung," *Zeitschrift für die alttestamentliche Wissenschaft*, Vol. XVIII (1898), pp. 120–25; REITZENSTEIN, *Zwei religionsgeschichtliche Fragen* (1901).

Part Fourth

THE LITERATURE OF WORSHIP — THE LEGAL LITERATURE

CHAPTER XII.

THE LEGAL LITERATURE—THE DEUTERONOMIC CODE OF LAWS.

§ 167. **The Literature of Worship** includes that portion of the Old Testament literature which concerns itself with the subject of worship in any of its forms, or was written by men imbued with the priestly spirit. Here belong:

1. The legal literature (*cf.* § 9), or codes of laws and regulations dealing with the various elements in worship; these codes include more than can properly be classified under the head of worship, but everything in them may be said to be priestly in its character.

2. The historical literature (§ 10), viz., Chronicles, Ezra, Nehemiah, and the priestly history in the Hexateuch (=P).

3. The hymnal literature (§ 8), as found in the book of Psalms.

A marked spirit of unity characterizes all this literature, and distinguishes it from the prophetic and the wisdom literature (§ 2).

§ 168. **The Legal Literature** of the Old Testament is found in four groups or codes of legislation, viz.:

1. The covenant code (§ 20), the earliest form of legislation, ordinarily called the prophetic code, because it is incorporated in literature of a prophetic character. **Exod. 20:23—23:19; 34:10-26.**

2. The Deuteronomic code (§§ 25–28), so called because it forms the principal part of the book of Deuteronomy. **Deut. 12:1—26:19; chap. 28.**

3. Ezekiel's system of worship (§ 31), which is, strictly speaking, priestly and legalistic, although the work of a prophet. **Ezek., chaps. 40-48.**

4. The Levitical code (§§ 41–44), so called because it is found in the book of Leviticus (with portions of Exodus and Numbers).

§ 169. **The Covenant Code** (§ 20), or prophetic code, is the codification of law and usage in Israel down to about 650 B. C. Concerning this code there may be noted:

Judg. 17:7 ff. 1. Its prevalence is synchronous with the period in which the order of priests does not occupy the place of power in Israelitish thought. When the priests take a more influential place in the affairs of the nation, another code appears (the Deuteronomic), in which this higher position is recognized.

2. Its form, contents, and character are rather pro-
Exod. 20:24 ff. phetic than priestly, since, although (1) the act of wor-
Exod. 23:14–17. ship is recognized (§ 73, 1), (2) provision is made for
Exod. 22:18. feasts and offerings (§ 96), (3) reference is made to magic and sacrifice to other gods (§ 158, 1), all this is of the simplest character, and no tendency exists toward the development of a priestly system, there being no mention even of a priest or a priestly order (§ 59, 1).

3. It furnishes a formulation under prophetic influence of the old Semitic usage, and, at the same time, the basis on which the later codes are developed.

4. Its relation to these later codes has been shown in the comparative examination of various usages (§§ 59–166).

2 Kings 22:3—23:25. § 170. **The Story of the Discovery of Deuteronomy** (§ 25).[1]

2 Kings 21:1–26. 1. Consider the conditions of the times in which this event occurred, viz., the preceding reigns of Manasseh and Amon, their character, the forms of worship encouraged, the prophetic attitude (2 Kings 21:10–15), the particular royal acts regarded with disfavor (§ 24).

See KITTEL, *History of the Hebrews*, Vol. II, pp. 370–79; BUDDE, *Religion of Israel to the Exile*, pp. 161–9; KENT, *A History of the Hebrew People*, Vol. II, pp. 159–64; WELLHAUSEN, *Prolegomena to the History of Israel*, pp. 485 ff.

[1] It is generally acknowledged by interpreters that the original story of the discovery of Deuteronomy has been edited from the point of view of later times. The account, as it now stands, comes from three sources: (1) the early narrative, (2) the pre-exilic redaction, (3) the post-exilic redaction. The parts that show the clearest evidence of the work of the post-exilic editor are 2 Kings 22:14–20; 23:8 ff., 16–18, 21–23, 25*b*–27; the work of the earlier editor appears in 23:3, 13, 24 f.; while 22:5*b*, 6, 8 ("the high-priest"); 23:4*b*, 5, 7*b*, 14, 16–20, seem to be minor glosses. The purpose of these additions and modifications was to furnish an explanation, from the later point of view, of the disaster that fell upon Judah so soon after this reform.

2. Study the principal details of the discovery, *e. g.*, (1) the chief agent, the priest; (2) the phrase "the book of the law;" (3) the strange effect of the reading upon the king; (4) the consultation with Huldah—her oracle, its original form and meaning; (5) the convocation of the nation and the public reading; (6) the covenant entered into; (7) the phrase "his commandments, and his testimonies, and his statutes;" (8) the phrase "with all his heart and all his soul;" (9) one by one, the various acts of reformation instituted by Josiah; (10) the observance of the passover; (11) the purpose of these acts, viz., to confirm "the words of this covenant which were written in this book," etc.

2 Kings 22:4, 8, 14; 23:4. 2 Kings 22:8. 2 Kings 22:11. 2 Kings 22:14-20. 2 Kings 23:1 f. 2 Kings 23:3. 2 Kings 23:4-20. 2 Kings 23:21-23. 2 Kings 22:8; 23:3, 21, 24.

3. Consider (§26) the immediate results of the finding of this book, and compare these results with the actual provisions of the book of Deuteronomy, and determine: (1) whether Deuteronomy commands any essential thing which Josiah did not try to do; (2) whether Josiah undertook any act of reformation for which Deuteronomy does not make provision.

2 Kings 23:4-24.

4. Take up now three important questions: (1) Is there any reasonable doubt as to the identity of the book found by Hilkiah with the book of Deuteronomy, or, at least, a portion of it? (2) Does the story in Kings of the finding of the book definitely indicate a belief, on the part of its writer, that the book discovered was one written by Moses, or of Mosaic origin? (3) If such Mosaic origin is implied in the narrative, what explanation of the narrative is possible from the point of view of those who deny the Mosaic origin of the book?

2 Kings 23:8-13.

5. Take up, still further, these questions: (1) Do the facts of the reformation furnish evidence that the book which authorizes them is of ancient date, that is, Mosaic? (2) Could these facts be accounted for just as easily and naturally on the other supposition, that is, that the book of Deuteronomy was prepared during Manasseh's reign, lost, and found in Josiah's reign? (3) In this latter case, what motive, worthy of the situation, could be ascribed to those who took part in the transaction? Would it be sufficient to say that it was done to recommend certain

2 Kings 23:4-24.

reforms and to establish more firmly the national religion?

§171. **Representations in Deuteronomy Concerning its Authorship.**

1:1–5;[2] 4:1 f., 44 ff.; 5:1; 27:1, 9, 11; 29:1 f.; 31:1 f., 9 f., 24 f., 30; 32:44 ff.; 33:1 f.

1. Read and interpret the passages in Deuteronomy which make reference to its authorship, noting the particular portions of the book which contain these references, and noting, further, that the strictly legal portion, 12:1—26:19, contains nothing of this kind.

Prov. 10:1; 25:1.

Pss. 103; 122; 124; etc.

Isa., chaps. 40–66.

2. Consider whether it was customary in ancient times to ascribe to great men writings whose authorship was unknown, and whether instances of this custom are found (in sacred writings) in the case of (1) Solomon,[3] to whom are ascribed proverbs and psalms and books which are of a manifestly later age; (2) David,[4] to whom psalms are ascribed which certainly date from a post-exilic time; (3) Isaiah,[5] to whom prophetic discourses are ascribed which are now almost universally recognized as belonging to the exilic and post-exilic periods; and (in secular writings) (4) the letters and many of the dialogues assigned to Plato;[6] (5) the "Shield of Hercules" and many other works ascribed to Hesiod.[7]

Eccles. 1:1, 12.

Song of Solomon 1:1.

Dan. 8:1; 9:2; 10:2; etc.

3. Consider also the ancient custom in accordance with which writers, for certain reasons, ascribed their own writings to great men, as in the case of (1) the writer of Ecclesiastes;[8] (2) the writer of the Song of Solomon;[9] (3) the authors of the "Wisdom of Solomon" and of the "Psalms of Solomon;"[10] (4) the author of the

[2] All Scripture references in this chapter which are cited without the name of the book are from Deuteronomy.

[3] See, *e. g.*, DRIVER, *Introduction to the Literature of the Old Testament* (6th ed.), pp. 406 ff.

[4] See, *e. g.*, DRIVER, *op. cit.*, pp. 373 ff.

[5] See, *e. g.*, CHEYNE, *Introduction to the Book of Isaiah.*

[6] See JEVONS, *History of Greek Literature*, pp. 482 f.

[7] See JEVONS, *op. cit.*, p. 86.

[8] See articles on "Ecclesiastes" in HASTINGS'S *Dictionary of the Bible* and in *Encyclopædia Biblica.*

[9] See DRIVER, *op. cit.*, pp. 437 ff.

[10] See articles on "Apocrypha" in *Encyclopædia Biblica* and in HASTINGS'S *Dictionary of the Bible..*

book of Daniel;[11] (5) Plato putting his words into the mouth of Socrates;[12] (6) the alleged correspondence between St. Paul and Seneca, consisting of fourteen letters.[13]

4. Consider the Egyptian custom of placing in con- *Cf.* 31:26.
nection with religious works the statement "found in the temple," this being understood to be, not a statement that a book had been lost and found, but a conventional fiction of the priestly class to affirm its sacred and authoritative character.[14]

5. Consider, however, whether, after all, it is not quite certain that the leaders of the time, as well as the people, supposed the "found" book to have been (1) lost for many years, (2) actually discovered, and (3) of Mosaic origin.

§ 172. **The Point of View and Coloring of the Book.**

1. Consider, as bearing upon the Mosaic origin, (1)
the situation — border of the wilderness — outside the 1:1f.
Holy Land; (2) the lack of any reference to Jerusalem
or the temple; (3) the frequent representation that the 1:8; 4:1; 6:10f.; 7:1.
land is not yet occupied; (4) the constant reference to 7:1-5, 17-24; 9:1 ff.
the Canaanites as Israel's enemies; (5) the references to 6:21; 7:8, 18; 11:3.
Egypt as a recent place of dwelling; (6) the references 4:3, 4.
to events which those addressed had themselves seen;
(7) the many Egyptian reminiscences, *e. g.*, of methods 11:10; 25:2, 3; 27:3; 6:8; 11:18; 11:10; 7:15; 28:60; 28:27, 35; 5:15; 15:15; 16:12.
of irrigation, bastinado, writing of law on plastered stones, wearing of law as amulet, deliverance from Egypt, Egyptian diseases, motives of kindness to servants.

2. Consider, on the other hand, whether all these points are not capable of other explanation. (1) Is it inconceivable that the writer planned to give his book a Mosaic setting — in other words, that all this material is merely to be regarded as a part of the dramatic representation? Is the book not thoroughly dramatic in its

[11] See DRIVER, *The Book of Daniel* (Cambridge Bible), pp. xlvii–lxxvi.

[12] See the "Charmides," "Lysis," "Protagoras," etc.; and compare JOWETT, *Dialogues of Plato* (Macmillan Co., New York, 5 vols.).

[13] See LIGHTFOOT, *St. Paul's Epistle to the Philippians*, p. 260.

[14] See CHEYNE, *Jeremiah, His Life and Times*, p. 85; MASPERO, *Histoire ancienne de l'Orient* (1st ed.), pp. 57, 73; BRUGSCH, *Geschichte Aegyptens* (1st ed.), pp. 60, 84.

5:6-21; *cf.* Exod. 20:2-17. whole presentation?[15] (2) Is it not to be expected
14:21*b*; *cf.* Exod 23:19*b*. that the writer, if a late one, would include material of
16:4*b*; *cf.* Exod. 23:18*b*. the earlier times? Is there anywhere a claim that he
23:7, 8; *cf.* 23:3. includes only late material? (3) Is the author of the book really as hostile to the Egyptians as a writer would be expected to be, if he lived in the generation following the exodus? If so, how explain the permission to admit an Egyptian to religious privileges in the third generation, when this privilege is denied other nations
17:14-17. until the tenth generation? (4) Is not the writer living in a time when the upper classes have an attachment to Egypt, which he must oppose, for how otherwise explain
Isa., chaps. 30, 31; 36:6; 2 Kings 18:21; *cf.* 25:26. Deut. 17:14-17? (5) Is it not true that there was constant communication with Egypt between 750 B. C. and 600 B. C., and may not these Egyptian references be explained on the ground of this intimacy?

3. Are there not allusions which furnish direct evidence that the writer is living at a distance from the
2:34; 3:4, 8, etc.; 3:14. period of which he treats; *e. g.*, (1) are the phrases "at that time," "unto this day," appropriate in the mouth of Moses, when the events described occurred during the preceding six months (*cf.* 1:3 with Numb. 33:38, thus fixing the date of Numb. 20:22-28)? (2) How
24:9; 25:17; 23:5; *cf.* 4:45*b*, 46*b*. explain 2:12 as Mosaic? (3) Could Moses have used appropriately the phrase "when ye came forth out of
1:1, 5; 3:8; etc. Egypt"? (4) Must the writer not have lived in western Palestine in view of his use of the phrase *beyond the Jordan* of eastern Palestine?

§ 173. **The Language and Style of the Book.**

1. Examine a list of special words and phrases[16] frequently occurring in the book of Deuteronomy, and consider (1) the bearing of the fact of such a list upon the question of authorship; does it argue for or against identity of authorship with the other books of the Pentateuch? (2) the general character of these expressions as indicating early or later authorship.

[15] *Cf.* the same element in the book of Job, viz., a dramatic representation of antiquity in connection with the presentation of a (comparatively) modern thought.

[16] See, *e. g.*, DRIVER, *A Critical and Exegetical Commentary on Deuteronomy*, pp. lxxvii-lxxxiv.

2. Examine a list of the linguistic peculiarities appearing in the book,[17] *i. e.*, the peculiar forms, idioms, etc., and consider whether these exhibit evidence (1) of antiquity of date, or (2) of late date. With what writer in the Old Testament does the book of Deuteronomy show the largest number of similarities? *Cf.* Jer. 7:1–26; 11:1–8; 16:1–13; 21:3–10.

3. Consider (1) the general style of Deuteronomy, viz., classical, pure, broad, copious, idiomatic; (2) the striking points of style which distinguish this book from the other Pentateuchal books, and, indeed, from other Old Testament books, viz., (*a*) individual, affecting even quotations; (*b*) the hortatory element, based upon (*c*) the oratorical. *Cf.* 2:28 with Numb. 20:19; 1:28 with Numb. 13:28; 1:35, 36, 39, 41 with Numb. 14:23, 24, 31, 40*b*.

§ 174. **The Material of the Book.**—Make an examination of the material of the book with a view to finding evidence for and against the Mosaic authorship, as follows:

1. Note (1) the prohibition of intercourse with the Canaanites; 7:1. (2) references to Israel's condition in the wilderness; 4:3, 4; 7:1; 8:1; 9:1. (3) the directions for appointing a king; 17:14. (4) the law for the cities of refuge, possible only at the time of the entrance; 19:1–10. (5) the order to recall what Amalek did to them; 25:17–19. (6) directions for the blessing and cursing on Mount Ebal; 27:11–16. and consider whether material of this kind could possibly have had its origin at any other than a very early time, viz., the time of Moses.

2. Consider, on the other hand, (1) whether the presence of this material has not already been accounted for in the statement (see § 172, 2) that the book is conceded to contain much very old material which has been handed down and incorporated side by side with the newer material; and (2) whether the presence of the newer material can possibly be explained in a book of Mosaic origin, *e. g.*, (*a*) the prohibition of star-worship, which is late; 4:19; 17:3. (*b*) warnings against lower forms of prophecy, which cannot have antedated Amos and Hosea; 18:10–12.

[17] See, *e. g.*, DRIVER, *op. cit.*, p. lxxxiv; HOLZINGER, *Einleitung in den Hexateuch*, pp. 282–91; STEUERNAGEL, *Deuteronomium* ("Handkommentar zum Alten Testament"), pp. xxxii–xli.

12:1-7. (*c*) the law centralizing worship at one place; (*d*) laws
Chaps. 15; 21; 23; 24. like those concerning contracts and inheritance, which mark an advanced state of social development.

3. Consider from the point of view of the material the truth or falsity of the following statements: "The Israel of Deuteronomy is separated from the Israel of the exodus by a complete social revolution;" "The nomadic tribes have grown into a settled and wealthy community whose organization no longer needs to be constituted, but only to be reformed."

4. Consider in their bearing on this question the
31:9; 33:1, 4; 4:44-49; chap. 34. following: (1) certain passages which manifestly cannot be ascribed to Moses, *e. g.*, the account of his death;
Mal. 4:4. (2) the fact that the first reference in the prophets to a Mosaic code occurs in post-exilic times; (3) the lack of consistency which appears in so many cases in com-
1:9-13; *cf.* Exod. 18:13-26. parison with the other parts of the Pentateuch, *e. g.*, the difference in the representations concerning the appoint-
1:22 f.; *cf.* Numb. 13:1-3. ment of assistants to Moses in his work as judge; the different accounts of the sending out of the twelve spies;
1:37 f.; *cf.* Numb. 20:12. the different causes assigned for Jehovah's anger against
19:1-13; *cf.* Numb. 35:9-34. Moses; the many differences between the last chapters of Numbers and the book of Deuteronomy, though both
14:21; *cf.* Exod. 23:19; 34:26. are assigned to the same year; (4) the repetitions of laws
Chap. 16; *cf.* Exod. 23:14; Lev., chap. 23. which occur also in other books, *e. g.*, the law against seething a kid in its mother's milk; the law concerning
Chap. 5; *cf.* Exod., chap. 20; chap. 14; *cf.* Lev., chap. 11. feasts; the decalogue; the law of clean and unclean.

5. Consider the cases in which Israel's leaders in the
1 Sam. 9:12-14; 16:2; 10:3, 5, 8; 1 Kings 18:30 ff.; 2 Sam. 6:13, 17 f. early period show utter disregard of Deuteronomic laws, without any indication that what they do is regarded as illegal; *e. g.*, Samuel sacrifices at other places than Jerusalem; Elijah sacrifices on Mount Carmel; David also offers sacrifice.

6. Consider the bearing upon this question of the more important teachings (see § 178).

§ 175. The Book of Deuteronomy as Related to Other Old Testament Literature.

Josh. 1:22, 23; 2:10, 11; 3:7; 10:28-43; 11:10-15; Judg. 2:11-23; 1. Examine the strongly Deuteronomic character of certain passages in Joshua, Judges, and Kings, and consider whether these are to be explained (1) as themselves early, and indicating the existence of the book of Deuteronomy at an early date; or (2) as later interpolations and expansions by Deuteronomic editors after the publication of Deuteronomy in 621 B. C. (see § 180). 3:4–6; 4:1–3; 6:1; 10:6–16; 1 Kings 2:3, 4; 3:2, 3; 9:1–9; 11:1–13; 2 Kings 9:7–10*a*; 17:7–23; etc.

2. Examine the remarkable cases of similarity (in thought and form) between Jeremiah and Deuteronomy[18] (*cf.* the sixty-six passages from Deuteronomy of which there are echoes in not less than eighty-six of Jeremiah); and consider whether this is to be explained by supposing (1) that Jeremiah was particularly fond of, and familiar with, the ancient Deuteronomy; or (2) that Deuteronomy and Jeremiah are the product of nearly the same times, the latter being strongly influenced by the former; or (3) that Jeremiah was himself the author of Deuteronomy.[19] 4:20; *cf.* Jer. 11:4; 6:3; *cf.* Jer. 7:23. 8:19; *cf.* Jer. 25:6. 18:20; *cf.* Jer. 29:23. 28:26; *cf.* Jer. 7:33. 28:36; *cf.* Jer. 16:13. 28:49, *cf.* Jer. 5:15. 29:23; *cf.* Jer. 22:8. 12:31; *cf.* Jer. 7:31. 13:18; *cf.* Jer. 42:12.

3. Consider the significance of the fact that in the genuine portions of Amos, Hosea, and Isaiah none of these Deuteronomic phrases are to be found.

4. Consider, still further, the cases in later literature in which the Deuteronomic phrases still maintain themselves, *e. g.*, Nehemiah, Chronicles, and Daniel. Neh. 1:5–11; 9:6 ff.; Dan. 9:4–19; 1 Chron. 29:19; 22:13; 28:8, 20; 2 Chron. 32:7.

§ 176. **The Book of Deuteronomy and the New Testament.**

1. Examine the allusions in the New Testament to the "law of Moses," and consider the bearing of these statements on the authorship of the Pentateuch in general. Mark 1:44; 12:26; Matt. 8:4; Luke 5:14; 16:29, 31; 24:27, 44; John 5:46 f.; 8:5; 1:17; 7:19; Acts 15:21; 28:23; 2 Cor. 3:15.

2. Examine the quotations in the New Testament taken from the book of Deuteronomy, and consider the bearing of the statements made in connection with them on the authorship of Deuteronomy in particular. Matt. 19:7 f.; 22:24; Mark 10:3 f.; 12:19; Luke 20:28; Acts 3:22; 7:37; Rom. 10:19.

3. Consider the three interpretations which have been made of these and similar passages: (1) that the statements are literally true and are to be accepted as final;[20]

[18] ZUNZ, *Zeitschrift der deutschen morgenländischen Gesellschaft*, 1873, pp. 671–3; DRIVER, *Deuteronomy*, pp. xciii ff.

[19] But see DRIVER, *Deuteronomy*, pp. xciii f.; CHEYNE, *Jeremiah, His Life and Times*, pp. 81 f.; J. L. KÖNIG, *Alttestamentliche Studien*, II; KLEINERT, *Das Deuteronomium und der Deuteronomiker*, pp. 185–90, 235.

[20] See ALVAH HOVEY, "The New Testament as a Guide to the Interpretation of the Old Testament," *Old Testament Student*, Vol. VIII, pp. 207–13.

(2) that Jesus and the New Testament writers, though knowing the real facts, accommodated themselves to the point of view of their times and accepted the traditional interpretation, not wishing to arouse opposition over a matter of comparatively slight importance and thereby detract attention from the great truths they wished to teach;[21] (3) that Jesus and the New Testament writers were not sent to teach historical and biblical criticism, hence were not given any more knowledge concerning such questions than was possessed by their contemporaries.[22]

§ 177. Is Not the Book a Forgery and a Fraud, if Not Written by Moses?

1. Consider (1) whether, in view of its own assertions and the general belief, this book is not a fraudulent imposture, if Moses did not write it; (2) whether, if a forgery, it could under any circumstances be counted among the sacred writings; (3) how, if a forgery, it could possibly have gained acceptance in the Jewish nation; (4) whether the writer, whoever he was, did not secure its acceptance on the pretense that it was the work of Moses.

2. Consider, on the other hand, (1) whether, in those days, there was anything in existence like the literary usages and laws of the modern world, *e. g.*, any literary proprietorship, any literary copyright; and, if these were not in existence, can the modern conception of forgery or plagiarism have existed? (2) the suggestions made above (§ 171, 2, 3) concerning ancient customs in connection with writings; (3) whether there are not books of excellent morality which are, nevertheless, literary forgeries;[23] (4) whether there have not been cases in which a modern lawbook has been palmed off as ancient;[24] (5) whether the proposition of forgery is possible in view of the fact that
Chap. 18. the supposed forgers, the priests of Zadok, include laws

[21] See G. B. Stevens, "The Bearing of New Testament Statements upon the Authorship of Old Testament Books," *Old Testament Student*, Vol. VIII, pp. 164–70.

[22] See C. H. Toy, "The New Testament as Interpreter of the Old Testament," *Old Testament Student*, Vol. VIII, pp. 124–33.

[23] *E. g.*, the Sibylline oracles.

[24] *Cf.* Sir Henry Maine, in *Ancient Law*, p. 82

touching the interests of the country-Levites which are in direct conflict with the interests of the Zadokites;[25]
(6) whether the mass of the people who heard the read- 5:1; 31:1, 9.
ing of the law was in any proper position to consider critically the question of authorship; (7) whether Hilkiah in permitting the belief in the Mosaic authorship was really guilty of *delusion;* was it not rather *illusion?* (8) whether the principle of illusion is not (*a*) necessary in all educational work;[26] (*b*) practiced in the Old and New Testaments;[27] (*c*) one of the greatest elements in the teaching of Jesus himself;[28] (9) whether, after all, the writer of this book was not properly using the word *Moses*, inasmuch as (*a*) this work was only a continuation of the work of Moses, along the same lines and for the same ends; (*b*) this work was but the fuller growth of the seed planted by Moses; (*c*) even where the older usage is changed, as in the case of the place of worship, the principle underlying the change is one enunciated by Moses; (*d*) the writer is doing only what Moses himself under the changed circumstances would have done; (*e*) the writer has done just what modern writers do, as in the case of the name of Webster's *Dictionary*, the original author having long been dead, and the dictionary, although greatly modified and enlarged, still bearing his name; or the name of Gesenius's *Hebrew Grammar*, many editions having appeared since the death of the author, with very significant changes in system and matter.

§ 178. **The Religious Teachings of the Book.**— Consider (1) the general religious teachings and their significance (see § 28); (2) the teachings of Deuteronomy upon the special subjects compared in §§ 52–166.

§ 179. **The Structure and General Character of the Book of Deuteronomy.**

1. Consider the various sections which constitute the

[25] *Cf.* CHEYNE, *Jeremiah, His Life and Times*, pp. 76 f.

[26] *Cf. ibid.*, pp. 77 f.

[27] *Cf.* Jer. 20:7, in which the prophet utters his disappointment in his discovery that he had been illuded (not deluded); also Heb. 4:8, 9.

[28] *Cf.* John 16:12.

book of Deuteronomy as it now stands, and note their specific contents:

1:1–5. (1) Introduction.
1:6—4:40. (2) The *first* discourse of Moses, introductory.
4:41–43. (3) Appointment of three cities of refuge.
4:44–49. (4) Superscription to the second discourse of Moses.
5:1—26:19; chap. 28. (5) The *second* discourse—the law.
Chaps. 5–11. (*a*) Hortatory introduction.
Chaps. 12–26, 28. (*b*) Code of laws.
Chap. 27. (6) The acceptance of the code.
29:1—30:20. (7) The *third* discourse, supplementary.
31:1–8. (8) Moses's last words of encouragement.
31:9–13. (9) Delivery of the law to the priests.
31:14, 15, 23. (10) Commission of Joshua.
31:16–22, 24–30; 32:1–43, 44. (11) Song of Moses.
32:45–47. (12) Final commendation of the law to Israel.
32:48—34:12. (13) Moses's blessing and death.

2. Consider the literary structure of this material upon the modern hypothesis:[29] (1) To P are assigned the few touches found in 1:3; 32:48–52; 34:1*a*, 5*b*, 7–9; consider these passages in connection with the commonly accepted idea of P, and note that by means of them, at a late date, Deuteronomy was brought into the Hexateuch. (2) To JE are assigned the earlier parts of the book, viz., the incorporation of the blessing (chap. 33, this being taken from JE in its original form); 27:5–7*a*; 31:14, 15; 31:23; 34:1*a*, 1*b*–5*a*, 6, 10. (3) To D, the first Deuteronomic writer, and to D^2, a second Deuteronomic writer, is assigned the remainder, divided as follows (D^2 being in black type): 1:1 f.; 1:4—3:13; **3:14–17**; 3:18—4:28; **4:29–31**; 4:32–40; **4:41–49**; 5:1—26:19; **27:1–4**; **27:7*b*–8**; 27:9 f.; **27:11–26**; 28:1—29:8; **29:9–28**; **30:1–10**; 30:11–20; 31:1–13; **31:16–22**; 31:24–27; **31:28–30**; 32:45–47; **34:11 f.** D^2 followed some time after D, and, besides making the additions, incorporated the JE portion and the song 32:1–43.

[29] So DRIVER, *Deuteronomy;* for variations consult BERTHOLET, *Deuteronomium* ("Kurzer Hand-Commentar"); STEUERNAGEL, *Deuteronomium* ("Hand-Kommentar"); G. F. MOORE, "Deuteronomy," *Encyclopædia Biblica;* STAERK, *Das Deuteronomium, sein Inhalt und seine literarische Form.*

3. Consider the general character of the material in Deuteronomy, consisting as it does of (1) historical, (2) legal, (3) hortatory elements. Which of these elements is the controlling one? Is the history narrated simply for the sake of imparting a knowledge of historical events, or is it used rather for the purpose of illustrating and enforcing great truths? Notice also that the laws are imbedded in a didactic setting, and that their general tone is not imperative, but argumentative and persuasive; reasons are assigned for yielding obedience to them and rewards are promised to the obedient. Consider also the way in which the prophetic and priestly elements are combined in Deuteronomy, how the great ideas of the book are of a prophetic character, and how the priestly laws are calculated to give concrete expression to these prophetic ideas and secure their lodgment in the life and thought of the people.

§ 180. **Other Work of the Deuteronomic Writers.**— After the book of Deuteronomy was accepted as the law-book of Israel, there seems to have arisen a school of writers controlled by the spirit of Deuteronomy whose activity may be clearly traced in the Old Testament literature during the years immediately preceding the exile and onward for a century or more. Their work may be seen most clearly in the books of Judges and Kings, which they edited from the Deuteronomic point of view, inserting interpretations of the history of Israel based wholly on the teachings of Deuteronomy. Much of their work is found also in Joshua, and some traces of it appear in Samuel and in the preceding books of the Hexateuch (§ 175).[30]

Josh. 1:3-9, 12-18; 4:21—5:1; 5:4-8; 10:28-43; etc.

1 Kings 2:10-12; 3:2 f., 14 f.; 8:14-66; 9:1-9; 15:1-5; etc.

Judg. 2:7, 11-23; 3:4-15*a*; 4:1-3; 6:1, 7-10; etc.

1 Sam. 1:7 f., 12.

Gen. 26:1-5; Exod. 15:26.

§ 181. **Literature to be Consulted.**

HÄVERNICK, *Introduction to the Pentateuch* (1836, transl. 1850), pp. 410 f.; HENGSTENBERG, *Genuineness of the Pentateuch* (1839, transl. 1847); KEIL, *Introduction to the Old Testament* (1853, 3d ed. 1873, transl. 1869); KUENEN, *The Hexateuch* (1861, 2d ed. 1885, transl. 1886); KEIL, *Deuteronomy* (1862, 2d ed. 1870, transl. 1867); SCHROEDER, *Deuteronomy* (LANGE'S "Commentary," 1866, transl. 1879); ESPIN, *Deuteronomy* ("Speaker's Commentary," 1871); KUENEN, *Religion of Israel*, Vol. II, pp. 7–44 (1869 f., transl. 1874 f.); WELLHAUSEN, *Prolegomena to the History of Israel*, pp. 402 ff. (1st ed. 1878, 2d ed. 1883, 4th ed. 1895, transl. 1885); W. R. SMITH,

30 *Cf.* ADDIS, *Documents of the Hexateuch*, Vol. II, pp. 29 ff.

Old Testament in the Jewish Church (1st ed. 1881, 2d ed. 1892); BISSELL, *The Pentateuch, Its Origin and Structure* (1885); G. VOS, *The Mosaic Origin of the Pentateuchal Codes* (1886); CHEYNE, *Jeremiah, His Life and Times* (1888, chaps. v–vii); DRIVER, *Introduction to the Literature of the Old Testament* (1891, 6th ed. 1897), pp. 69–103; KITTEL, *History of the Hebrews*, Vol. II, pp. 7–44 (1892, transl. 1896); H. E. RYLE, *Canon of the Old Testament* (1892, 2d ed. 1895), see *Index;* MONTEFIORE, *Religion of the Ancient Hebrews* ("Hibbert Lectures," 1892), pp. 161–221; S. R. DRIVER, article "Deuteronomy," SMITH'S *Dictionary of the Bible* (2d ed. 1893); B. W. BACON, *The Triple Tradition of the Exodus* (1894); CORNILL, *The Prophets of Israel* (1895), pp. 80–92; W. H. GREEN, *The Higher Criticism of the Pentateuch* (1895), see *Index;* DRIVER, *A Critical and Exegetical Commentary on Deuteronomy* (1895), pp. i–xcv; A. HARPER, *Deuteronomy* (*Expositor's Bible*, 1895); C. J. BALL, "The Blessing of Moses," *Proceedings of the Society of Biblical Archæology*, 1896, pp. 118–37; L. W. BATTEN, "The Origin and Character of Deuteronomy," *Biblical World*, April, 1898, pp. 246–54; ED. KÖNIG, "The Unity of Deuteronomy," *Expository Times*, Oct. and Dec., 1898, pp. 16–19, 124–7; Feb., 1899, pp. 227–30; G. L. ROBINSON, "The Genesis of Deuteronomy," *Expositor*, Oct. and Nov., 1898, pp. 241–61, 351–69; Feb., Apr., and May, 1899, pp. 151–60, 271–95, 356–71; H. E. RYLE, article "Deuteronomy," HASTINGS'S *Dictionary of the Bible*, Vol. I (1898); TH. TYLER, "Notes on Deut. 32 : 42," *Jewish Quarterly Review*, 1898, pp. 379 f.; ADDIS, *The Documents of the Hexateuch*, Vol. II (1898), pp. 2–30; W. P. McKEE, "Transient and Permanent Elements in Deuteronomy," *Biblical World* April, 1899, pp. 249 ff.; H. G. MITCHELL, "The Use of the Second Person in Deuteronomy," *Journal of Biblical Literature*, 1899, pp. 61–109; BUDDE, *Religion of Israel to the Exile* (1899), pp. 170–80; F. H. WOODS, article "Hexateuch," HASTINGS'S *Dictionary of the Bible*, Vol. I, (1899); G. F. MOORE, article "Deuteronomy," *Encyclopædia Biblica*, Vol. I (1899); MARTIN, *The Tora of Moses* (1900); STIBITZ, "The Centralization of Jehovah Worship in Israel," *Reformed Church Review*, Jan., 1900; DUFF, *Old Testament Theology*, Vol. II (1900); J. E. CARPENTER AND G. HARFORD-BATTERSBY, *The Hexateuch*, Vol. I (1900); HAYMAN, "The Blessing of Moses," *American Journal of Semitic Languages and Literatures*, Vol. XVII (1901), pp. 96–106; WELLHAUSEN AND CHEYNE, article "Hexateuch," *Encyclopædia Biblica*, Vol. II (1901); WARREN, "The Origin of the Pentateuch," *Biblical World*, Vol. XVIII (1901), pp. 194 ff.

KUEPER, *Jeremias librorum sacrorum interpres et vindex* (1838), pp. 4–45; J. L. KÖNIG, "Das Deuteronomium und der Prophet Jeremiah," *Alttestamentliche Studien*, Vol. II (1839); RIEHM, *Die Gesetzgebung Mosis im Lande Moab* (1854); K. H. GRAF, *Der Segen Mose's* (1857); F. W. SCHULTZ, *Das Deuteronomium* (1859); KNOBEL, *Das Deuteronomium* ("Exegetisches Handbuch zum Alten Testament," 1861); KAMPHAUSEN, *Das Lied Moses* (1862); KOSTERS, *De Historie-Beschouwing van den Deuteronomist met de Berichten in Gen.—Num. vergeleken* (1868); KLOSTERMANN, "Das Lied Mose's und das Deuteronomium," *Studien und Kritiken*, 1871 f.; KLEINERT, *Das Deuteronomium und der Deuteronomiker* (1872); REINKE, "Ueber das unter dem Könige Josia aufgefundene Gesetzbuch," *Beiträge zur Erklärung des Alten Testaments*, 8 (1872), pp. 131–80; RIEHM, *Studien und Kritiken*, 1873, pp. 165–200; ZUNZ, *Zeitschrift der deutschen morgenländischen Gesellschaft*, Vol. XXVIII (1873), pp. 669–76; KAYSER, *Das vorexilische Buch der Urgeschichte Israel und seine Erweiterungen* (1874); HOLLENBERG, "Die deuteronomischen Bestandtheile des Buches Josua," *Studien und Kritiken*, 1874, pp. 462–506; HAVET, *Le Christianisme et ses origines*,

Vol. III (1878), pp. 32 ff.; REUSS, *L'histoire sainte et la loi*, Vol. I (1879), pp. 154 ff.; J. J. P. VALETON, "Deuteronomium," *Theologische Studiën*, Vol. V (1879), pp. 169–206, 291–313; VI (1880), pp. 133–74, 303–20; VII (1881), pp. 39–56, 205–28; STEINTHAL, "Das fünfte Buch Mose," *Zeitschrift für Völkerpsychologie und Sprachwissenschaft*, 1879, pp. 1–28; IDEM, "Die erzählenden Stücke im fünften Buche Mose," *ibid.*, 1880, pp. 253–89; DELITZSCH, "Pentateuch-kritische Studien," *Zeitschrift für kirchliche Wissenschaft und kirchliches Leben*, Vol. I (1880), pp. 445 ff., 503 ff., 559 ff.; STADE, *Zeitschrift für die alttestamentliche Wissenschaft*, Vol. V (1885), pp. 292–300; D'EICHTHAL, *Mélanges de critique biblique* (1886); STADE, *Geschichte des Volkes Israel*, Vol. I (1887), pp. 148–73, 649–71; MARTIN, *Introduction à la critique générale de l'Ancien Testament*, Vol. I (1887), pp. 295 ff.; VERNES, *Une nouvelle hypothèse sur la composition du Deut.; examen des vues de M. d'Eichthal* (1887); KUENEN, "De Jongste Phasen der Critiek van den Hexateuch," *Theologisch Tijdschrift*, 1888, pp. 35 ff.; HORST, "Études sur le Deut.," *Revue de l'histoire des religions*, Vol. XVI (1888), pp. 28–65; XVII (1889), pp. 1–22; XVIII (1890), pp. 320–34; XXIII (1895), 184–200; XXVII (1899), pp. 119–76; WELLHAUSEN, *Die Composition des Hexateuch und der historischen Bücher des Alten Testaments* (1889, 3d ed. 1899); BAUDISSIN, *Geschichte des alttestamentlichen Priesterthums* (1889); VAN HOONACKER, *L'origine des 4 premiers chapitres du Deut.* (1889); A. ZAHN, *Das Deuteronomium* (1890); KLOSTERMANN, "Beiträge zur Entstehungsgeschichte des Pentateuch," *Neue kirchliche Zeitschrift*, 1890–92; MONTET, *Le Deutéronome* (1891); CORNILL, *Einleitung in das Alte Testament* (1891, 2d ed. 1892), pp. 29–45; WESTPHAL, *Les sources du Pentateuch*, Vol. II (1892), pp. 32 ff.; OETTLI, *Das Deuteronomium* (1893); H. PREISS, *Zum Deuteronomium — ein Beitrag zur Kritik des Pentateuchs* (1892); MARTI, "Das erste officielle Bekenntnis," *Zeitschrift für Theologie und Kirche*, 1892, pp. 29–73; REUSS, *Die heilige Geschichte und das Gesetz* (1893), pp. 106 ff.; SMEND, *Lehrbuch der alttestamentlichen Religionsgeschichte* (1st ed. 1893, 2d. ed. 1899), § 16; KÖNIG, *Einleitung in das Alte Testament* (1893), pp. 209–25; WILDEBOER, *Die Litteratur des Alten Testament* (1893, tr. 1894), § 11; HOLZINGER, *Einleitung in den Hexateuch* (1893), pp. 255–331; STEUERNAGEL, *Der Rahmen des Deuteronomium* (1894); WILLY STAERK, *Das Deuteronomium, sein Inhalt und seine literarische Form* (1894); PIEPENBRING, "La réforme et le code de Josias," *Revue de l'histoire des religions*, Vol. XXIX (1894), pp. 123 ff.; STEUERNAGEL, *Die Entstehung des deuteronomischen Gesetzes* (1896); NAUMANN, *Das Deuteronomium* (1897); D. CASTELLI, "Una congettura sopra Deuteronomio 32 : 5," *Zeitschrift für die alttestamentliche Wissenschaft*, Vol. XVII (1897), pp. 337 f.; M. LAMBERT, "Le cantique de Moïse, Deut. XXXII," *Revue des études juives*, Vol. XXXVI (1898), pp. 47–52; VON GALL, "Deuteronomium und Deuteronomius," *Zeitschrift für die alttestamentliche Wissenschaft*, Vol. XIX (1899), pp. 173–7; J. HALÉVY, "Le Deutéronome," *Revue sémitique*, Vol. VII (1899), pp. 313–32; BERTHOLET, *Deuteronomium erklärt* ("Kurzer Hand-Commentar zum Alten Testament," 1899), pp. ix–xxix; FINKE, *Wer hat die 5 Bücher Moses verfasst?* (1900); KLOSTERMANN, *Deuteronomium und Grâgâs* (1900); STEUERNAGEL, *Uebersetzung und Erklärung der Bücher Deuteronomium und Josua, und allgemeine Einleitung in den Hexateuch* ("Hand-Kommentar zum Alten Testament," 1900); BAUDISSIN, *Einleitung in die Bücher des Alten Testamentes* (1901), pp. 103–22; HERNER, *Ist der zweite Dekalog älter als das Bundesbuch?* (1901); HUMMELAUER, *Commentarius in Deuteronomium* (1901).

CHAPTER XIII.

THE LEGAL LITERATURE—EZEKIEL'S CONTRIBUTION.

§ 182. **The Historical Situation** of which Ezekiel and his work formed a part deserves careful study (§§ 30 ff.).[1]

Kings 24:1-7. 1. Gather together the principal facts (1) of the *first* deportation as narrated in Kings, viz., the reign of Jehoiakim, its character; the reign of Jehoiachin, the invasion of Nebuchadnezzar, the carrying away of the princes, etc. (vs. 14); the date of this being 597 B. C.;
2 Kings 25:1-21; Jer., chap. 52. (2) of the *second* deportation, including the reign of Zedekiah, the siege of Jerusalem, its destruction, the carrying away of the residue (vs. 11).

2 Kings 25:22-26. 2. Note (1) the situation after the destruction of the city under Gedaliah, and the story of Gedaliah's murder;
Jer., chap. 24; 29:15-20. (2) the prophet's estimate of those taken away captive and those allowed to remain (the good and the bad figs), and consider (*a*) whether it was the captives or those left behind who were adjudged the more important;
Ezek. 11:14-21; Jer., chaps. 42-44. also (*b*) which of these two classes was supposed to be suffering the more keenly;
Ezek. 33:24 f. still further (*c*), how the lower classes left behind regarded these matters.

Jer., chap. 29. 3. Study Jeremiah's letter[2] to the captives in Babylon and formulate the policy therein advocated in respect to business, marriage, etc.

[1] See McCurdy, *History, Prophecy and the Monuments*, Vol. III, pp. 227–431; Wellhausen, *Prolegomena to the History of Israel*, pp. 488–98; Stade, *Geschichte des Volkes Israel*, Vol. I, pp. 675–703; II, 1–67; Guthe, art. "Israel," §§ 40–47, *Encyclopædia Biblica*, Vol. II.

[2] It is very probable that Jer., chap. 29, at least in its present form, is from a later writer, for: (1) Jeremiah is spoken of in the third person and described "as the prophet;" (2) the nature of the advice given suggests that it comes from one looking back upon the conditions he is dealing with, rather than one living in the midst of movements the outcome of which was still uncertain; (3) parts of it seem to be dependent upon the Books of Kings; (4) the booklet, chaps. 26–29, bears marks of late workmanship, linguistic and otherwise. See, *e. g.*, Cornill, *The Book of Jeremiah* (SBOT); Schmidt, art. "Jeremiah," *Encyclopædia Biblica;* Duhm, *Das Buch Jeremia* ("Kurzer Hand-Commentar zum A. T.").

4. Consider the general effect which the news of the fall of Jerusalem must have had when it reached the ears of those who were already in captivity, among whom was Ezekiel. Ezek. 33:21 f.

See GUTHE, *Geschichte des Volkes Israel*, pp. 239 ff.

5. Note (1) that the period was one of transition, or, perhaps more truly, of revolution; one in which monolatry was to be supplanted by monotheism, idolatry by the sole worship of Jehovah; (2) that the principal scene of action was no longer Palestine, but Babylon; (3) that Israel was now scattered, the nationality broken; (4) that the work of the prophetic order was giving place to that of the priestly order; for Jeremiah and Ezekiel were priests, and the books of Haggai, Zechariah, Jer. 1:1; Ezek. 1:3.
and Malachi, which follow, are far more priestly than prophetic (*cf.* § 34).

§ 183. **The Preparation of Ezekiel.**

1. Consider (1) the significance of the fact that he was 1:3.[3]
a priest, and the great influence, at this time, of the priestly position, second only to that of the king; (2) the character of the training which he would receive; 22:25, 26; 4:14.
(3) the influence which must have been exercised over him by the book of Deuteronomy and by Jeremiah's sermons (see § 184).

2. Note (1) the fact that Ezekiel had been in captivity already eleven years[4] when news of the fall of 33:21; *cf.* 26:1 f.
Jerusalem was received; (2) the fact that the call came to 1:2.
him after five years' experience in captivity (592 B. C.); (3) the latest date in the book (570 B. C.). 29:17.

3. Study (1) the strange and wonderful character of

[3] All Scripture references in this chapter cited without the name of the book are from Ezekiel.

[4] 33:21 states that the tidings came in the twelfth year of the captivity; but we learn from 26:1 f. that Ezekiel already knew of the fall of Jerusalem in the eleventh year of the captivity. The Syriac version has *eleventh* year in 33:21 also, and this is probably correct. Jerusalem fell on the ninth day of the fourth month of the eleventh year of Zedekiah's reign (2 Kings 25:2 f.; Jer. 39:2), which was also the eleventh year of the captivity, since Zedekiah was placed on the throne when Jehoiachin was removed to Babylon (2 Kings 24:15 ff.); and it is not reasonable to suppose that the captives in Babylon did not hear of the fall of their city until a year and a half after the event.

the visions which constituted the call, including (*a*) the
1:4-28. vision of God — what conceptions of God are implied
in the four living creatures (vss. 5–14), the four wheels
2:1 ff. (vss. 15–21), the throne and glory (vss. 22–28)? (*b*) the
2:3-7. prophet's introduction to his work by the God seen in
2:8—3:3. the vision — the people a rebellious one, the inspira-
3:4-9. tion accorded him, the special strength given him, his
3:10-15. particular mission to the captives of Tel-abib, the pre-
3:16-21. cise character of his function, viz., to be a watchman ; (2)
33:1-9. his later feeling of responsibility as a watchman.

4. Examine, for the purpose of gaining a better point of view for an appreciation of his work, certain refer-
3:4-11, 26; 14:1-5. ences to his life and activity in exile : (1) the character
11:25. of the people with whom he was called to work; (2) his
20:1; 8:1; 14:1-5. own character as Jehovah's spokesman ; (3) the fact that
he was frequently consulted in his own house by the
24:15-18, 19-27. elders of Israel ; (4) his use of the death of his wife as
an occasion for a public message; (5) the threatening
character of his early sermons; (6) the consolatory
33:30-33. character of his later sermons ; (7) his place and stand-
ing among the exiles.

§ 184. **Ezekiel's Prophetic Work.** — For the better understanding of Ezekiel's work as a priest, and the priestly structure of which he was the author, it is important that his work as prophet should be appreciated. This is perhaps most easily considered in connection with that of Jeremiah.

1. Consider the degree of dependence which Ezekiel exhibits in relation to Jeremiah as seen in the following passages: 3 : 3, *cf.* Jer. 15 : 16; 3 : 17, *cf.* Jer. 6 : 17; 7 : 14, 27, *cf.* Jer. 4 : 5–9; chap. 13, *cf.* Jer. 14 : 13–16; 13 : 10, *cf.* Jer. 6 : 14; 16 : 51, *cf.* Jer. 3 : 11; chap. 18, *cf.* Jer. 31 : 29 f.; chap. 20, *cf.* Jer. 11 : 3–8; 24 : 16–23, *cf.* Jer. 16 : 3–9; chaps. 29–31, *cf.* Jer., chap. 46; chap. 34, *cf.* Jer. 23 : 1–4; 36 : 26, *cf.* Jer. 24 : 7; 37 : 24, *cf.* Jer. 30 : 9; 38 : 15, *cf.* Jer. 6 : 22.

See especially SMEND, *Der Prophet Ezechiel* ("Kurzgefasstes exegetisches Handbuch," 1880), pp. xxiv f.; C. H. TOY, art. "Ezekiel," *Encyclopædia Biblica*, Vol. II, col. 1462 ; DAVIDSON, *The Book of the Prophet Ezekiel* (*Camb. Bible*, 1892), pp. xix f, xlvi ff.

2. Study (1) the place occupied in his preaching by the teaching of *individual responsibility* — does he elaborate the teaching of Jeremiah on this subject? does he give it any special application to the exiles? (2) his counsels concerning submission to Babylon and his predictions concerning Jerusalem's fall, as compared with those of Jeremiah. **Chap. 18; *cf.* Deut. 24: 16; Jer. 31: 29 f. 33: 1–17. 17: 11–21; *cf.* Jer. 28: 12–17; 38: 14–23.**

3. Consider (1) his ethical and social teachings as enunciated, *e. g.*, in chaps. 18 and 22, and note their high character so far as concerns relations between Israelites; (2) his attitude toward the outside nations, to which no obligations are due, there being as yet no international code. **Chaps. 18, 22. Chaps. 25–32.**

4. Consider, also, if possible, Ezekiel's conceptions concerning (1) *God* — how far does he sympathize with the older ideas, how far with the new? Is he a monotheist? or does he accept the existence of other deities? Is the conception of Jehovah as a universal God associated with the older idea of the tribal God? (2) *Man* — his inward life, his outward life, reward and punishment, the hereafter — *sheol*, transformation of the heart (regeneration); *cf.* Jer. 31: 33. **1: 26, 28; 10: 19; 34: 30; 37: 26 f.; 43: 7. 18: 28; 18: 5–8. 26: 20; 31: 14–17; 32: 17–32. 36: 26 f.**

See TOY, art. "Ezekiel," *Encyclopædia Biblica*, Vol. II, cols. 1467 ff; DAVIDSON, *op. cit.*, pp. xxxi–xliii.

§ 185. **Ezekiel's Own Representations Concerning Chaps. 40–48.** — Frequent references are made by the prophet to the origin of the material contained in these chapters. Consider the various statements: (1) the man with an appearance like brass and a line of flax in his hand, and a measuring reed — what or whom did this man symbolize? what was his function? what the purpose of his work? (2) the various steps in his guidance of the prophet; (3) the messages delivered from time to time in the progress of the journey; (4) the visions of divine glory revealed; (5) the use of the phrase, "thus saith the Lord God." **40: 1–4. 40: 17, 24, 28, 32, 48, etc.; 47: 1–5. 42: 13; 43: 6–12. 44: 5–8; 47: 6 ff. 43: 1–5; 44: 4. 42: 18; 44: 9; 45: 9; 46: 1, 16; 47: 13.**

Formulate, upon the basis of this material, a statement covering the author's point of view on this question.

§ 186. The Structure and General Character of Ezek., Chaps. 40–48.

40:1—43:12. 1. Note the contents of the section: (1) plans and
43:13–27. specifications for the future temple; (2) the ordinances
44:4–31. for the erection and dedication of the altar; (3) the law
45:1–5. concerning the priesthood; (4) the sacred territory
5:6–25. located and defined; (5) regulations in reference to
44:1–3; 46:1–18. sacrifices; (6) the function of "the prince," with special
46:19–24. reference to his religious obligations; (7) the law providing special places for the cooking of the sacrifices
47:1–12. offered by the people; (8) description of the living
47:13—48:29. waters issuing from the temple; (9) a statement of the boundaries of the land and its allotment among the tribes, with especial provision for proselytes (47:22 f.);
48:30–35. (10) the dimensions of the Holy City and the location of its twelve gates.

40:1. 2. Consider (1) that this material comes from a date twelve years later than any portion of the book[5] except 29:17, 18; (2) that there is in this section no "teaching" on any subject; (3) that there is given here a *picture* in which a people is represented as living in an ideal condition; (4) "that it does not describe how salvation is to be attained, for the salvation is realized and enjoyed; it describes the people and their condition and their life now that redemption has come;"[6] (5) that, with the temple occupying the central place, there are taken up questions relating to the priests, the sacrifices, the land including the Dead Sea, the division of territory, the laying out of the city; (6) that, in addition, there are the regulations regarding the functions of the "prince;" (7) that, in other words, it is an ideal state

[5] Attention may be called here to the fact that the genuineness of the book or of certain parts of it has been called in question by some scholars; *e. g.*, ZUNZ, *Gottesdienstliche Vorträge der Juden* (2d ed.), pp. 165 ff., and in *ZDMG.*, Vol. XXVII, pp. 676 ff., and GEIGER, *Urschrift und übersetzungen der Bibel*, p. 23, place the whole book in the Persian period; SEINECKE, *Geschichte des Volkes Israel*, Vol. II (1884), pp. 1 ff., assigns it to the Maccabæan period; VOLZ, *Die vorexilische Jahweprophetie und der Messias* (1897), p. 84, note, regards the last nine chapters as the work of a disciple of Ezekiel. These views, however, have not met with any general acceptance.

[6] A. B. DAVIDSON, *op. cit.*, p. 288.

which is thus presented, a conception which constitutes the germ of the doctrine of the *kingdom of God.*

3. Consider, still further, (1) its form, namely *vision*, 40:2; 43:3.
in contrast with the form of Deuteronomy, which was the *sermonic;* (2) how, not infrequently, it lapses into 45:1 ff.; 46:1 ff.; 47:21.
the form of sermon or address to the people; (3) whether in *spirit* it more nearly resembles Deuteronomy or Leviticus; (4) the strange and confusing mingling of the natural and supernatural elements, and show the origin of this in the prophetic conception of life; (5) the relation of this picture to the preceding context, in 39:25–29.
which Israel is represented as having now received the outpouring of the divine spirit—is it not the climax of the book?

§ 187. **The Principal Ideas** of the section deserve classification and formulation:

1. Note the statement, made above, to the effect that there were no "teachings" in the section; this does not mean, however, that the picture does not rest upon certain conceptions, or *imply* the truth of certain great ideas.

2. For a general statement of the ideas of Ezekiel in this section, see § 31. For the material on the priest, see §§ 65, 66; on the place of worship, §§ 77, 78; on sacrifice, §§ 89, 90; on feasts, § 102; on the sabbath, §§ 114, 115; on clean and unclean, §§ 128, 129.

3. Consider some of the more important of the great ideas that underlie the form of presentation employed in these closing chapters, keeping in mind constantly the necessity in many cases of basing our conclusions largely upon the general tone and character of the material rather than upon specific statements and texts. (1) The idea of God—what is the bearing upon this idea of (*a*) the fact that the temple, Jehovah's house, is placed in the 45:1–8.
middle of the Holy Land and surrounded on all sides by the land of the priests, Jehovah's ministers, thus being kept from contact with everything profane and polluting? (*b*) the stringent regulations concerning those who 44:4–28.
may approach Jehovah to offer sacrifice, and concerning their apparel, etc.? (*c*) the exclusion of foreigners from

the temple and of the laity from the inner court of the temple? Does not the whole representation in chaps. 40–48 give the impression of the great exaltation and
43:1–5. holiness of Jehovah in comparison with everything
43:6–9; 48:35. human? (2) Jehovah's relation to Israel—note that Jehovah is represented as having restored his people to favor, and as requiring of them holiness in order that
44:7, 9. they may enjoy his favor forever. Note also the feeling of superiority over all foreigners that appears in the restrictions placed upon the latter, though provision is made for proselytes. Does not the spirit of particularism appear here very clearly? (3) The subordination of political to *religious* ideals—note (*a*) the fact that the "prince's" functions are almost wholly religious; (*b*) the
45:8–12; 46:16 ff. exceedingly few non-religious matters that are dealt with; (*c*) the complete silence on all matters relating to national ambition or development; (*d*) the fact that the nation is represented rather as a community existing only for religious purposes; (*e*) the emphasis laid on the *ceremonial* as compared with the ethical side of the reli-
43:21 ff.; 44:27; 45:17. gious life. (4) The great emphasis laid upon the idea of atonement as an evidence of an increasing sense of the exceeding sinfulness of sin. Is this not a correlative of the exalted idea of Jehovah's holiness?

§ 188. **The General Relation of Ezek., Chaps. 40–48, to Deuteronomy.**

44:10–15; *cf.* Deut. 18:1–8. 1. Consider the place of the priests in both sections, noting that Deuteronomy makes no distinction between priests and Levites, while Ezekiel degrades the Levites, gives the reasons for so doing, and restricts the priesthood to the sons of Zadok.

44:17–27; *cf.* Deut. 17:9. 2. Consider the comparative fulness in the treatment
44:29 f.; chaps. 45, 48; *cf.* Deut 18:1–4. of (1) the duties of priests, (2) the provision made for the priests; does not this indicate a great advance in the conception of the place and dignity of the priesthood?

3. Consider the absence in Ezek., chaps. 40–48, as compared with Deuteronomy, of warnings against idolatry.

Deut., chap. 16. 4. Consider the feasts as enumerated in Deuteronomy, the sacrificial details being absent; while in

Ezekiel[7] the details of the material are given, and a special ceremony of purification of the sanctuary on the first day of the first and seventh months. Ezek. 45:21-25. 45:18-20 (LXX).

5. Consider the apparent failure of the Deuteronomic scheme in the catastrophe of the exile; for was not this scheme intended for a "holy" people, and to serve as the expression of a people closely united with a "holy" God? Was it not intended to bring the people into a life which should be worthy of Jehovah, their Lord, and was not the destruction of Jerusalem understood to separate them from him? Deut. 7:6.

6. Is not Ezekiel's scheme clearly prepared for a people restored from captivity, and not only restored, but actually purified and regenerated? "It opens with an elaborate account of a new temple set on the sacred hill. The 'law of the house' is expounded with much detail, and the prophet then announces the ordinances of the altar. These are followed in turn by regulations for the priesthood and the appropriate sacrifices, and a scheme of cultus is thus displayed by which the people, once more consecrated, shall be preserved from further temptation to unfaithfulness, and shall secure the presence of Jehovah in their midst forever."[8] 36:24-28. 40:1—43:12.

The relationship of Ezekiel's cultus to that of P will be considered in the next chapter.

§ 189. **Literature to be Consulted.**

P. FAIRBAIRN, *Exposition of the Book of Ezekiel* (1851); HENDERSON, *The Book of the Prophet Ezekiel Translated, etc.* (1855); H. SMITH WARLEIGH, *Ezekiel's Temple* (1856); COLENSO, *The Pentateuch and Book of Joshua Critically Examined* (1862–79), Vol. VI, pp. 3–23; KUENEN, *Religion of Israel* (1869–70, transl. 1882), Vol. II, pp. 190 ff.; CURRIE, *Ezekiel* ("Speaker's Commentary," 1876); KUENEN, *The Prophets and Prophecy in Israel* (1877), pp. 238–42; WELLHAUSEN, *Prolegomena to the History of Israel* (1878, transl. 1885), pp. 378 ff.; W. R. SMITH, *The Old Testament in the Jewish Church* (1st ed. 1881, 2d ed. 1892), pp. 442 f.; PLUMPTRE, "Ezekiel: An Ideal Biography," *Expositor*, 1884; KUENEN, *Modern Review*, Oct., 1884, pp. 617–40; KUENEN, *The Hexateuch* (transl. from the Dutch, 1886), § 15, 10; H. SULLEY, *The Temple of Ezekiel's Prophecy* (1888); KITTEL, *History of the Hebrews*, Vol. I (1888–92, transl. 1895), pp. 125 ff.; F. W. FARRAR, "The Last Nine Chapters of Ezekiel," *Expositor*, 1889, pp. 1 ff.; DRIVER, *Introduction to the Literature of the Old Testament* (1891, 6th ed. 1897), pp. 145 ff., 278–98; KIRKPATRICK, *Doctrine of the Prophets* (1892),

[7] Probably from oversight the Feast of Weeks is omitted.

[8] J. E. CARPENTER AND G. HARFORD-BATTERSBY, *The Hexateuch*, Vol. I, p. 127.

pp. 320–45; MONTEFIORE, *Religion of the Ancient Hebrews* ("Hibbert Lectures," 1892), see *Index;* A. B. DAVIDSON, *The Book of the Prophet Ezekiel* ("Camb. Bible," 1892); SKINNER, *Ezekiel* ("Expositor's Bible," 1895); CORNILL, *The Prophets of Israel* (1895) pp. 115–30; L. B. PATON, *Presbyterian and Reformed Review*, Jan., 1896, pp. 98 ff.; BRIGGS, *Higher Criticism of the Hexateuch* (2d ed. 1897), pp. 126 ff.; DOUGLAS, "Ezekiel's Temple," *Expository Times*, Vol. IX (1898), pp. 515 ff.; SKINNER, article "Ezekiel," HASTINGS'S *Dictionary of the Bible*, Vol. I (1898); WOOD, article "Hexateuch," HASTINGS'S *Dictionary of the Bible*, Vol. II (1899), p. 374; C. H. TOY, *The Book of the Prophet Ezekiel—A New English Translation* ("Sacred Books of the Old and New Testaments," Part XII, 1899); J. E. CARPENTER AND G. HARFORD-BATTERSBY, *The Hexateuch*, Vol. I (1900), pp. 126 ff.; C. H. TOY, article "Ezekiel," *Encyclopædia Biblica*, Vol. II (1901); WELLHAUSEN AND CHEYNE, article "Hexateuch," *Encyclopædia Biblica*, Vol. II (1901), coll. 2051 f.; KÖNIG, "The Priests and the Levites in Ezek. 44:7–15," *Expository Times*, April, 1901; COBERN, *Ezekiel and Daniel* (1901).

HAFENREFFER, *Templum Ezekiel* (1613); E. F. ROSENMÜLLER, *Scholia in Vetus Testamentum*, Pars VI (2d ed. 1826), pp. 575 ff.; ZUNZ, *Die gottesdienstlichen Vorträge der Juden* (1832, 2d ed. 1892), pp. 165–70; J. F. BÖTTCHER, *Proben alttestamentlicher Schrifterklärung* (1833), pp. 218–365; HÄVERNICK, *Commentar über den Prophet Ezechiel* (1843); HITZIG, *Der Prophet Ezechiel erklärt* (1847); BALMER-RINCK, *Des Propheten Ezechiel Gesicht vom Tempel* (1856); TH. KLIEFOTH, *Das Buch Ezechiels übersetzt und erklärt* (1864 f.); GRAF, *Geschichte der Bücher des alten Bundes* (1866), pp. 81–3; HENGSTENBERG, *Der Prophet Ezechiel* (1867); KEIL, *Der Prophet Ezechiel* (1868, 2d ed. 1882); SCHRADER, article "Ezechiel," Schenkel's *Bibel-Lexikon*, Vol. II (1869); ZUNZ, "Bibelkritisches. II: Ezechiel," *Zeitschrift der Deutschen Morgenländischen Gesellschaft*, Vol. XXVII (1873), pp. 676–81; SCHRÖDER, *Das Buch Ezechiel* ("Langes Bibelwerk," 1873); G. C. STEYNIS, *De Verhouding van de Wetgeving bij Ezekiel tot die in den Pentateuch* (1873); GRAETZ, "Die Echtheit des Buches des Propheten Ezechiel," *Monatsschrift für Geschichte und Wissenschaft des Judenthums*, Vol. XXIII (1874), pp. 433–46, 515–25; KAYSER, *Das vorexilische Buch der Urgeschichte Israels und seine Erweiterungen* (1874), pp. 176 ff.; DUHM, *Theologie der Propheten* (1875), pp. 208–11, 216 f., 252–63; NÖLDEKE, *Jahrbücher für protestantische Theologie*, 1875, pp. 355 ff.; KLOSTERMANN, "Ezechiel, ein Beitrag zur bessern Würdigung seiner Person und seiner Schrift," *Theologische Studien und Kritiken*, 1877, pp. 391–439; KLOSTERMANN, "Hat Ezechiel die in Lev. 18–26 am deutlichsten erkennbare Gesetzessammlung verfasst?" *Zeitschrift für Lutherische Theologie*, 1877, pp. 406–45 (reprinted in *Der Pentateuch*, 1893, pp. 368 ff.); SMEND, *Der Prophet Ezechiel* ("Kurzgefasstes exegetisches Handbuch zum A. T.," 1880); HORST, *Lev. 17–26 und Hezekiel* (1881); E. KÜHN, "Ezechiel's Gesicht vom Tempel der Vollendungszeit," *Theologische Studien und Kritiken*, Vol. LV (1882), pp. 601–88; CORNILL, *Der Prophet Ezechiel geschildert* (1882); MAYBAUM, *Die Entwickelung des altisraelitischen Prophetenthums* (1883), pp. 38–60; P. WURSTER, "Zur Charakteristik und Geschichte des Priestercodex und Heiligkeitsgesetzes," *Zeitschrift für die alttestamentliche Wissenschaft*, Vol. IV (1884), pp. 122 f.; SEINECKE, *Geschichte des Volkes Israel*, Vol. II (1884), pp. 1–20; DILLMANN, *Die Bücher Numeri Deuteronomium und Joshua* (2d ed. 1886), pp. 644 ff.; CORNILL, *Das Buch des Prophet Ezechiel* (1886); ARNDT, *Die Stellung Ezechiels in der alttestamentlichen Prophetie* (1886); VALETON, *Viertal Voorlez. over Prophet. des Ouden Verbonds* (1886); STADE, *Geschichte des Volkes Israel*, Vol. II (1888), pp. 1–63; ORELLI, *Ezekiel* ("Kurzgefasster Commentar," 1888, 2d ed. 1896); H. MEULENBELT, *De Prediking van den Profeet Ezechiël* (1888); PERROT ET CHIPIEZ, *Le temple de Jérusalem et la maison du Bois-Liban restitués d'après Ezékiel et le livre des Rois* (1889); RIEHM, *Einleitung in das alte Testament* (1889–90), Vol. II, pp. 111–26; KNABENBAUER, *Commentarius in Ezek.* (1890); L. GAUTIER, *La mission du prophète Ezékiel* (1891); BAENTZSCH, *Das Heiligkeitsgesetz* (1893), pp. 121 ff.; DIESTEL, article "Hesekiel," RIEHM'S *Handwörterbuch des biblischen Alterthums*, Vol. I (2d ed., 1893); GAUPP, "Die Eigentümlichkeit des Ezekiel," *Neue kirchliche Zeitschrift*, Vol. V (1894), pp. 613 ff.; KAMRATH, "Der messianische Theil des ezech. Proph., besonders in seinen Verhältnissen zum Hexateuch," *Jahrbücher für protestantische Theologie*, Vol. XVII (1891), pp. 585 ff.; CORNILL, *Einleitung in das Alte Testament* (1891), pp. 77 f., 168–70; WILDEBOER, *Die Litteratur des Alten Testaments* (1893, transl. 1895), pp. 245–57; KÖNIG, *Einleitung in das Alte Testament* (1893), pp. 354–60; D. H. MÜLLER, *Ezechiel-Studien* (1895); BERTHOLET, *Die Verfassungsentwurf des Hesechiel* (1896); BERTHOLET, *Das Buch Hesekiel erklärt* ("Kurzer Hand-Commentar zum Alten Testament," 1897); DUSSAUD, "Les visions d'Ezékiel," *Revue de l'histoire des religions*, Vol. XIX (1898), pp. 301 ff.; ORELLI, article "Ezechiel," *Realencyklopädie für Protestantische Theologie und Kirche*, Vol. V (3d ed., 1898); KRAETZSCHMAR, *Das Buch Ezechiel übersetzt und erklärt* ("Hand-Kommentar zum Alten Testament," 1900); BAUDISSIN, *Einleitung in die Bücher des Alten Testamentes* (1901), pp. 190 ff., 453–71; SCHMALZL, *Ezechiel erklärt* ("Kurzgefasster wissenschaftl. Commentar," 1901).

CHAPTER XIV.

THE LEGAL LITERATURE — THE PRIESTLY CODE.

§ 190. **The Story of the Adoption of the Law in Ezra's Times** (§§ 40–44).[1]

1. Consider the conditions of the times in which this
Ezra 7:1, 7-9; 8:31. event occurred: (1) the date of the event;[2] (2) the char-
Neh. 7:73; 9:1. acter of Ezra and his constituency; (3) the duration of
Ezra 7:1-9; 8:21 ff.; 9:5 ff. Ezra's journey, March to August; (4) the gifts and let-
Ezra 7:11-26; 8:24-30. ters; (5) the work of Nehemiah (§ 40); (6) the work of
Ezra (§ 41).

Neh., chaps. 8-10. 2. Study the account of the formal adoption, includ-
ing (1) the place of the assembly; (2) the duration of the
Neh. 8:3. reading; (3) the circumstances attending the reading;
Neh. 8:8. (4) the reception given the law by the people; (5) the
Neh. 8:9. method of interpretation; (6) the occasion of their
Neh. 8:13 ff. weeping; (7) the reading on the second day in refer-
ence to the Feast of Booths, and the compliance of the
Neh. 9:39; 10:29-39. people; (8) the various things which they covenanted to
Neh. 10:37-39. do (§ 43); (9) the fact that the priests are clearly distin-
guished from the Levites (§§ 43, 68).

2 Kings 22:1—22:25. 3. Compare the general circumstances of the accept-
ance of the book of Deuteronomy (§ 25) with those of
the acceptance of this book, noting points of similarity
and difference, *e. g.*, (1) the national assembly; (2) the
celebration of a feast, in one case the Passover, in the other

[1] Ezra's work is probably to be placed *after* that of Nehemiah; for the arguments in support of this position see KOSTERS, *Het Herstel van Israël* (1894; transl. into German, 1895); KENT, *A History of the Jewish People during the Babylonian, Persian, and Greek Periods*, pp. 196 ff.; CHEYNE, *Jewish Religious Life after the Exile*, pp. 36–81; C. C. TORREY, *The Composition and Historical Value of Ezra-Nehemiah*, pp. 51–65; GUTHE, art. "Israel" (§§ 55 ff.), *Encyc. Biblica;* A. VAN HOONACKER, *Nouvelles études sur la restauration juive après l'exile de Babylone* (1896).

[2] The arrival of Ezra at Jerusalem is placed shortly after 433 B. C. by KOSTERS and CHEYNE, *Encyc. Biblica*, Vol. II, col. 1487, and others. PROFESSOR VAN HOONACKER, however, places it in the seventh year of Artaxerxes II., viz., 398–7; while KUENEN, *Gesammelte Abhandlungen zur biblischen Wissenschaft* (1894), ED. MEYER, *Die Entstehung des Judenthums* (1896), and others retain the date 458 B. C.

the Feast of Booths, in a manner different from that in which they had previously been observed in Canaan.

4. Consider, now, whether the law adopted thus by the people in Ezra's time was (1) the entire Hexateuch as we now possess it; or (2) the so-called Holiness Code, that is, Lev., chaps. 17–26; or (3) the whole Levitical code known as P (§ 43).[3]

5. Consider why, if Ezra brought the law with him in 458 B. C., he took no steps to make it known to the people until twelve years later, after Nehemiah had come (446 or 445 B. C.). Is it enough to answer that this was delayed by (1) the troublous character of the times which followed the expulsion of the foreign wives; (2) the necessity of Ezra's taking time to acquaint himself with the conditions of the country and the adjustment of the details of the law to those conditions; (3) the need of such a character as Nehemiah to arouse the enthusiasm of the people? Ezra 7:14. Ezra 10:7.

§ 191. **Representations in P Concerning its Authorship** (*cf.* closely § 171).

1. Read and compare some of the various passages in P which refer to its authorship, noting particularly the phraseology employed, *e. g.*, (1) "And Jehovah spake unto Moses, saying;" (2) "And he gave unto Moses the two tables of the testimony, tables of stone, written with the finger of God;" (3) "And Moses assembled all the congregation of the children of Israel, and said unto them;" (4) "And it came to pass on the eighth day, that Moses called Aaron and his sons, and the elders of Israel; and he said unto Aaron;" (5) "And Jehovah spake unto Aaron, saying;" (6) "And Jehovah spake unto Moses and to Aaron, saying;" (7) "These are the statutes and ordinances and laws, which Jehovah made between him and the children of Israel in Mount Sinai by Moses." Exod. 25:1. Exod. 31:18. Exod. 35:1, 4. Lev. 9:1. Lev. 10:8, 12. Lev. 11:1; 14:33; 15:1. Lev. 26:46; *cf.* 27:34.

[3] This point may well be omitted, except by those who desire to go into the critical questions involved; see J. E. CARPENTER AND G. HARFORD-BATTERSBY, *The Hexateuch*, Vol. I, pp. 138 ff.; HOLZINGER, *Einleitung in den Hexateuch*, § 57; STEUERNAGEL, *Deuteronomium und Josua* ("Handkommentar z. A. T."), pp. 277 ff.; WELLHAUSEN, *Prolegomena to the History of Israel*, pp. 405 ff.; the articles on the Hexateuch in the various Bible dictionaries; and the discussions in the many introductions to the Old Testament.

Numb. 33:2. 2. Read the interesting passage in which *writing* is ascribed to Moses, and consider whether the contents are consistent with an assignment to the times of Moses.

3. Take up now, one by one, the suggestions which have been offered in explanation of a non-Mosaic authorship, as indicated in § 171 under 2, 3, 4, 5.

§ 192. **Point of View and Coloring of the Priestly Code** (*cf.* § 172).

1. Consider, as bearing upon the Mosaic origin, (1)
Numb. 35:1; 36:13. the representation concerning the plains of Moab as the
Numb. 1:1; 3:14; 9:5; Exod. 24:18—25:1. scene of certain legislation concerning Levitical cities; (2) the situation at Sinai as the scene of certain events
Exod. 12:1. and legislation; (3) the situation in Egypt as the place
Numb. 10:11. of the initiation of the Passover; (4) the exact statement
Exod. 29:46. Exod., chaps. 25 ff., 35–40. Exod. 40:17–38. of the date of departure from Sinai; (5) the date of the ordinances of the tabernacle and of its erection, together with the statement that it accompanied Israel through
Lev. 14:34; 18:3; 19:23; Numb. 15:2, 18; 33:51; 34:2. all the wanderings; (6) the fact that it looks forward to entrance into Canaan, and introduces legislation appli-
Lev. 18:3, 27 f.; 20:22 ff. cable only to settled life in Canaan; (7) the warnings uttered against practices of Egypt which they had known and practices of Canaan which they are to know;
Lev. 19:34, 36; 25:2, 54; Numb. 8:17; 14:2. (8) the allusions to Egypt and Jehovah's deliverance of Israel from bondage there; (9) the absence of any mention of Jerusalem and the temple.

Lev. 20:1–5. 2. Consider, as bearing further upon this question,
Lev., chap. 23; Numb., chaps. 28, 29. (1) the regulations against Molech worship; (2) the agricultural character of the feasts; (3) the experiences
Numb. 34:15; 35:14. of the exile as depicted in Lev., chap. 26; (4) the phrase "beyond the Jordan," used of the east side of Jordan;
Lev. 7:28; 8:1; 9:1, 5 f.; 23:1. (5) the constant reference to Moses in the third person; (6) the apparent distance of Moses and Aaron in the
Exod. 16:55. narrative Exod. 6:26 f., and of the eating of manna in the
Lev. 18:24 ff.; 20:23. description of the same; (7) passages in which Israel seems to be represented as in possession of the land of Canaan; (8) the significance of the great periods passed over in silence (is it not against the supposition that the author was a contemporary?), *e. g.*, (*a*) between Exod. 1:5–7 and 1:13, a period of two or four hundred years;[4] (*b*) between

[4] For an analysis of the text here see J. E. CARPENTER AND G. HARFORD-BATTERSBY, *The Hexateuch*, Vol. II, pp. 80 f., or the commentaries of Dillmann and Baentsch. On the historical events see the histories of Kittel, Stade, Wellhausen, Kent.

Numb. 20:1 and 20:22*b*, a period of thirty-eight years (*cf.* 10:11 and 33:37);[5] (*c*) the representation that Dan's descendants in the fourth generation numbered 62,700. **Numb. 1:38; 2:26.**

§ 193. **The Language and Style of the Priestly Code.**

1. Examine a list of special words and phrases frequently occurring in this code,[6] and consider (1) the bearing of the fact of such a list upon the question of authorship; does it argue for or against identity of authorship with the other books of the Hexateuch? (2) the general character of these expressions as indicating early or late authorship. Note especially that the months are numbered rather than named, and that the New Year comes in the spring, not in the autumn. When did this method of enumeration prevail? **Exod. 40:2, 17; Lev. 16:29; chap. 23.**

2. Examine a list of the linguistic peculiarities appearing in the book, *i. e.*, peculiar forms, idioms, etc., and consider whether these exhibit evidence of antiquity of date, or of late date. With what writer in the Old Testament does the Priestly Code show the largest number of similarities? ***Cf.*, *e. g.*, Lev. 18:2*b* with Ezek. 20:5, 7, 19; Lev. 18:25 with Ezek. 42:20.**

3. Consider (1) the general style of the Priestly Code, viz., stereotyped, repetitious, statistical, rigid, prosaic, precise, systematic; (2) the striking points of style which distinguish this code from other portions of the Hexateuch and, indeed, from other Old Testament writings, viz., (*a*) legal, (*b*) imperative, (*c*) idealistic.[7]

§ 194. **The Material of the Priestly Code as Bearing on the Date and Authorship.**

1. Examine the great number of *repetitions* of laws found in other portions of the Pentateuch and within P itself (*e. g.*, Exod., chaps. 25–28 and 35–40; Lev. 3:5–

[5] See CARPENTER AND HARFORD-BATTERSBY, *The Hexateuch*, Vol. I, p. 28.

[6] Extensive lists of the various linguistic phenomena of the Priestly Code are to be found in J. E. CARPENTER AND G. HARFORD-BATTERSBY, *The Hexateuch*, Vol. I, pp. 208–21; HOLZINGER, *Einleitung in den Hexateuch*, §§43, 44, 51, 58; ADDIS, *Documents of the Hexateuch*, Vol. II, pp. 170–73; BRIGGS, *Higher Criticism of the Hexateuch*, pp. 172–80; RYSSEL, *De Elohistae Pentateuchi Sermone* (1878); GIESEBRECHT, "Der Sprachgebrauch des hexateuchischen Elohisten," *Zeitschrift für die alttestamentliche Wissenchaft*, Vol. I (1881), pp. 177–276; DRIVER, *Journal of Philology*, Vol. XI, pp. 201–36.

[7] On literary style of P see the articles by W. R. HARPER in *Hebraica*, Vols. V, VI.

4:35 and chap. 18; 19:3*b*, 30 and 26:2; 19:9 and 23:22; 19:26*a* and 17:10–14; 24:21 and 24:17; 18:6–23 and 20:10–21; Lev., chap. 8; Exod. 30:1—31:11, and Numb., chap. 8), and consider (1) how these repetitions may be accounted for upon the supposition that all portions of the Hexateuch had their origin within one man's lifetime and as one man's work; (2) how these repetitions may be explained upon the supposition of three or more distinct codes of law, which originated as codifications of teachings and usages that had grown up through many centuries.

2. Examine passages which seem to furnish instances of *discrepancy and variation* between P and other legislation (*e. g.*, the differences in the lists of "clean and unclean" as given in Lev., chap. 11, and Deut., chap. 14; the variations in the details of the structure of the ark of the covenant as described in Exod. 25:10; 37:1; 40:20, and Deut., chap. 9; 10:1, 3, 5; the representation of the tabernacle as located *within* the camp in Exod., chaps. 25–29, but *without* the camp in Exod. 33:7; Numb. 11:24–30; 12:4; 10:33—all E passages; the law of the altar as given in Exod. 20:24 (E) and the totally different altar provided for in Exod., chaps. 25–29; the law of slaves, Lev. 25:39–42, *cf.* Exod. 21:1–6 (E) and Deut. 15:12; the regulations concerning the priest as found in Deuteronomy and in the Priestly Code—see §§ 62, 63, and 68, 69), and consider (1) how these discrepancies may be accounted for upon the supposition that all portions of the Hexateuch had their origin within one man's lifetime and as one man's work; (2) how they may be explained upon the supposition of three or more distinct codes of law, which originated as codifications of teachings and usages that had grown up through many centuries.

3. Examine the narratives relating to the tabernacle,
Exod., chaps. 25–29. viz., (*a*) the directions for its erection and decoration;
Exod., chaps. 35–40. (*b*) the record of its erection and decoration; and in the study of these narratives consider the following questions: (1) are the representations concerning the tabernacle in the wilderness consistent with each other?[8]

[8] See CARPENTER AND HARFORD-BATTERSBY, *The Hexateuch*, Vol. I, pp. 52, 129.

(2) What is the significance of the fact that the first statement made represents the tent as in actual use before it was constructed?[9] (3) What are the various names by which the tent is designated in the several documents?[10] (4) To what extent do the various codes describe a different service in connection with it?[11] (5) Is it possible to understand this representation as an ideal one, and as corresponding to the prophetic pictures of the future? **Exod. 33:7.**

§ 195. **Structure and Contents of the Priestly Code.**

1. Consider the extent to which the P history and legislation constitute the basis on which the entire Hexateuch rests, or the framework into which the rest of the material is fitted.

2. Compare the relation of the P legislation to the P history with that of the Deuteronomic legislation to the Deuteronomic historical setting.

3. Consider (1) whether there are not to be found formulæ which mark the end of small codes and, consequently, (2) whether the P legislation is not made up of several separate collections of laws, *e. g.:* (*a*) Lev., chaps. 17–26; (*b*) Lev., chaps. 1–7; (*c*) Exod., chaps. 25–28; (*d*) Exod., chaps. 35–40; (*e*) Lev., chap. 11; (*f*) Lev., chaps. 13, 14; (*g*) Lev., chap. 15; (*h*) Numb., chaps. 28–36. **Lev. 7:37 f.; 11:46 f.; 13:59; 16:34; etc.**

4. Examine the contents and character of P^g, so called because it forms the historical groundwork of the entire P legislation, considering (1) its central theme, viz., Jehovah's purpose from the creation of the world to develop and train Israel as his peculiar people, and the means and institutions employed by him to accomplish this purpose; (2) the extent of the ground covered, viz., from the creation to the establishment of the nation; **Gen. 1:1; Josh., chaps. 14 ff.**

[9] The account of the construction of the tabernacle is given by P (= Exod., chaps. 35–40) as having taken place after the arrival at Sinai; while E in Exod. 33:7 speaks of "the tent of meeting" as a familiar institution of the camp.

[10] See Exod. 33:7 (E); Exod. 25:8 (P); Exod. 25:9 (P); Numb. 11:24*b* (E); 9:15 (P); Exod. 39:32 (P); 35:11 (P); the name does not occur in J or Deuteronomy.

[11] See CARPENTER AND HARFORD-BATTERSBY, *op. cit.*, Vol. I, p. 55.

Gen. 2:4; 5:1; 10:1; 25:19; etc. Exod. 6:2. Gen., chap. 17. Josh., chaps. 14 ff.

(3) the logical presentation, viz., (*a*) the *toledhoth* sections leading up to the Sinaitic revelation; (*b*) the work of Moses in the deliverance from Egypt; (*c*) the special covenant between Jehovah and Israel; (*d*) the settlement of Abraham's descendants in Palestine; (4) the character of all this as compared with the similar narrative of J, especially the differences which characterize it, such as the emphasis placed upon religious institutions, the lack of the personal element.[12]

Lev. 26:3-45; 18:2-5, 24-30; 19:2-4, 10, 12, 14, 16, 18, 36; 20:22-26; 22:31-33.

5. Consider now the great passage which stands apart and constitutes P^h, that is, the Holiness Code, taking up (1) certain peculiar exhortations, which are intended to emphasize the idea of *holiness*, and the deity of Jehovah who led Israel out of Egypt; (2) certain laws which do not seem to be consistent with other parts of P; (3) other peculiarities of the form and contents;[13] (4) the probability of the independence of this section, and in this connection (*a*) the question as to the origin of this material, (*b*) its self-consistency, (*c*) the amount of editorial work which has been connected with it; (5) other passages which seem to show the same peculiarities;[14] (6) the question of date, distinguishing (*a*) the regulations of which it is composed, (*b*) the hortatory framework, and examining in detail the forms of the various laws with reference to their sociological setting.

Numb. 5:5—6:21; etc.

6. Consider in the same general manner the portions assigned to P^t, that is, priestly teaching (*torah*), which treat especially of sacrifice, clean and unclean, and similar topics.[15]

Exod. 35:4—40:38; etc.

7. Consider, likewise, the portions assigned to P^s, that

[12] For further consideration of P^g see chap. XV.

[13] *E. g.*, a different style and phraseology (see DRIVER, *Introduction*, pp. 49 ff.); a parenetic framework unknown to other parts of P; repetitions of laws found elsewhere in P; commands addressed to the people, not to the priest as in P.

[14] Scholars differ somewhat as to the limits of the Holiness Code; *e. g.*, DRIVER (*Introduction*, p. 151) assigns to P^h: Lev., chaps. 17–26; Exod. 6:6–8; 12:12; 31:13–14*a*; Lev. 10:9*a*, 10; 11:44; Numb. 15:37–41; ADDIS (*Documents of the Hexateuch*, Vol. II, p. 178): Lev., chaps. 17–26; 11:43–45; Numb. 15:37–41; CARPENTER AND HARFORD-BATTERSBY (*op. cit.*, Vol. I, p. 145): Lev., chaps. 17–26; Exod. 31:13, 14*a*; Numb. 10:9; 15:38*b*–41.

[15] For a statement of the limits and character of P^t see CARPENTER AND HARFORD-BATTERSBY, *op. cit.*, Vol. I, pp. 152 f.; and for a similar statement concerning P^s see the same work, Vol. I, pp. 153–5.

is, certain secondary expansions along many lines, tending toward "the heightening of ritual and the elaboration of detail."

§ 196. **The Relation of Ezek., Chaps. 40–48, to the Priestly Code.**—The question as to the relation of the scheme of legislation contained in Ezek., chaps. 40–48, to that of the Priestly Code, and especially the Holiness Code, is one of especial interest, and has been the occasion of much discussion. Nothing more can be attempted here than to indicate the nature of the problem and the various lines of investigation.

1. Examine lists[16] of the phraseological and linguistic affinities existing between P and Ezek., chaps. 40–48, and consider whether they are to be accounted for on the supposition (1) that Ezekiel was especially fond of, and thoroughly familiar with, the P legislation, and drew up his scheme on the basis of it; or (2) that Ezek., chaps. 40–48, served as a model for the authors of P and was largely drawn upon by them; or (3) that Ezekiel was the author of the Holiness Code; or (4) that Ezek., chaps. 40–48, and the earlier parts of P originated at about the same time, were both influenced largely by the earlier existing legislation, and were both actuated by a similar spirit and motive.

2. Consider from the same point of view the similar regulations found in Ezek., chaps. 40–48, and in P; *e. g.*, (1) the distinction between priests and Levites; (2) the emphasis laid upon the necessity of ceremonial "cleanness;" (3) the close similarity of the laws concerning the priests; (4) the large ritualistic element common to both; (5) the special sanctity of the sabbath; (6) the predominance in both of the *religious* element, almost to the exclusion of secular matters; (7) the great emphasis laid by both upon the sanctuary.

Ezek. 44:10–15; *cf.* Numb., chaps. 1–4.
Ezek. 43:7–9; *cf.* Lev., chaps. 15, 21, etc.
Ezek. 44:17–27; *cf.* Lev. 21:1—22:16.
Lev. 19:30; *cf.* Ezek. 20:12.
Ezek. 40:5—43:12; *cf.* Exod., chaps. 25–29 and 35–40.

3. Consider, further, the points of difference between the two schemes of legislation, *e. g.*, (1) in P the priests are sons of Aaron, in Ezekiel sons of Zadok; (2) the high-priest occupies a large place in P, but is not mentioned in Ezekiel; (3) the function of "the prince" is

Ezek. 44:15; *cf.* Lev. 21:1.
Lev. 21:10.
Ezek. 46:2 ff.

[16] See, *e. g.*, DRIVER, *Introduction*, pp. 130–35, 145–9; SMEND, *Der Prophet Ezechiel* (1880), pp. xxv–xxviii.

Lev., chap. 16; *cf.* Ezek. 45:18 ff. Ezek., chaps. 45, 48; *cf.* Numb. 35:1-8; Josh. 21:4. Ezek. 45:21-25; *cf.* Lev., chap. 23; Numb., chaps. 28, 29. Lev., chap. 25; 26:34 f.; 27:17-24; *cf.* Ezek. 46:17.

peculiar to Ezekiel; (4) the legislation for the Day of Atonement is unknown to Ezekiel; (5) the assignment of property to the priests is radically different, the scheme of Ezekiel having no parallel in this respect; (6) the legislation concerning feasts differs in many details; (7) Ezekiel knows nothing of a sabbatical year, or Year of Jubilee, upon which P lays great emphasis; (8) in general, the legislation of P is much more detailed and elaborate than that of Ezekiel. What is the bearing of these and other differences upon the answer to the questions suggested above?

§ 197. **The Principal Ideas of the Priestly Code.**

1. Consider that, for the most part, the Priestly Code is not *didactic*, as is Deuteronomy, but is rather a manual of religious customs and practices. To what extent, however, does it give concrete expression to certain great conceptions which lay at the basis of all its regulations, and were deeply impressed upon the minds and hearts of the worshipers as they participated in the ceremonies prescribed by it?

2. For a general statement concerning the ideas of P, see § 49. For the P material on the priest, see §§ 68, 69; on the place of worship, see §§ 79, 80; on sacrifice, see §§ 91, 92; on feasts, see §§ 103, 104; on the sabbath, see §§ 117, 118; on clean and unclean, see §§ 131, 132.

3. In an effort to discover the chief ideas of the Priestly Code consideration must be paid, not only to specific statements that may be found in the text, but also to the general tone and character of the material as a whole and to the amount of attention given to the various features of the system of worship: (1) The idea of God here reaches the highest plane attained in the Old Testament. He is a Being so great, so holy, so awful, that access to him is permitted only under the most stringent conditions and always through the mediation of a specially consecrated priest; into his inmost presence only one man in the entire nation, viz., the holiest man—the high-priest—may come, and that but once a year. (2) In the light of this unapproachable holiness, the blackness of sin is immeasurably intensified;

Lev., chap. 16; Exod. 25:16 f. Lev., chaps. 21, 22.

Lev. 4:1—6:7; 6:24—7:10.

he cannot look upon sin with the least degree of allowance; his holiness, pervading everything, is in constant danger of violation; hence the possibilities of sin are
greatly multiplied. Sin was the cause of all of Israel's **Lev. 26:3–45.**
calamities in the past; hence, in order to insure Jehovah's favor and blessing for the future, every precaution must be taken to avoid sin, and to make propitiation to him when sin is unavoidable or for any reason has been com-
mitted. (3) The holy God demands a correspondingly **Lev. 11:44 f.; 19:2; 20:7, 26; 21:7 f.; 22:32.**
holy people who shall honor him with a holy worship. It is the purpose of the P legislation to secure this end.
This explains the great emphasis laid upon (4) ritual **Lev., chaps. 8, 12, 13, etc.**
and ceremony. Everything is carefully prescribed and intrusted to the execution of the priests whose especial function it is to guide and lead the people in the presentation of an acceptable worship unto Jehovah. (5) Religion has become the great business of life; it has stepped in and occupied the place formerly held by national politics and ambitions. (6) The exalted con-
ception of Jehovah and the necessity of constant propi- **Lev., chap. 23.**
tiatory rites have completely done away with the joyous abandon of the worship of early days, and the spirit of confidence and fellowship has been largely replaced by that of reverence and godly fear.

§ 198. Literature to be Consulted.

COLENSO, *The Pentateuch and the Book of Joshua Critically Examined* (7 parts; 1862–69); WELLHAUSEN, *Prolegomena to the History of Israel* (1878, 5th ed. 1897; transl. from German 1885), pp. 374–91, 404–10; DRIVER, *Journal of Philology*, Vol. XI (1882), pp. 201–36; KUENEN, *An Historico-Critical Enquiry into the Origin of the Hexateuch* (1885, transl. 1886); BISSELL, *The Pentateuch, Its Origin and Structure: An Examination of Recent Theories* (1885); KITTEL, *History of the Hebrews* (1888, transl. 1895), Vol. I, pp. 96–132; W. R. HARPER and W. H. GREEN, *Hebraica*, Vols. V–VIII (1888–91); W. R. SMITH, *The Old Testament in the Jewish Church* (1889, 2d ed. 1892); DRIVER, *Introduction to the Literature of the Old Testament* (1891, 6th ed. 1897), pp. 42–59, 126–59; BRIGGS, *The Higher Criticism of the Hexateuch* (1892, 2d ed. 1897), pp. 108 f., 172–80, 233 ff.; PATON, "The Relation of Lev. XX to Lev. XVII–XIX," *Hebraica*, Vol. X (1893), pp. 111–21; B. W. BACON, *The Triple Tradition of the Exodus* (1894); DRIVER AND WHITE, *Leviticus* ("Sacred Books of the Old and New Testaments;" Hebrew text 1894, English transl. 1898); W. H. GREEN, *The Higher Criticism of the Pentateuch* (1895); PATON, "The Holiness Code and Ezekiel," *Presbyterian and Reformed Review*, 1896, pp. 98–115; KÖNIG, *Expositor*, August, 1896, p. 97; PATON, "The Original Form of Lev. 17–19," *Journal of Biblical*

Literature, 1897, pp. 31–7; ADDIS, *Documents of the Hexateuch*, Vol. II (1898), pp. 170–91; F. H. WOODS, art. "Hexateuch," HASTINGS'S *Dictionary of the Bible*, Vol. II (1899), pp. 368–71; PATON, "The Original Form of Leviticus, Chaps. 21 and 22," *Journal of Biblical Literature*, Vol. XVII (1899), pp. 149–75; IDEM, "The Original Form of Leviticus, Chaps. 23, 25," *ibid.*, Vol. XVIII (1899), pp. 35–60; J. E. CARPENTER AND G. HARFORD-BATTERSBY, *The Hexateuch* (1900), Vol. I, pp. 121–57; WELLHAUSEN, art. "Hexateuch," §§ 29 f., *Encyclopædia Biblica*, Vol. II (1901); H. G. MITCHELL, *The World before Abraham* (1901), pp. 17 ff., 29 ff., 58 ff.; KENT AND SANDERS, "The Growth of Israelitish Law," in *Biblical and Semitic Studies* by the Members of the Semitic and Biblical Faculty of Yale University (1901), pp. 41–90; G. F. MOORE, art. "Leviticus," *Encyclopædia Biblica*, Vol. III (1902); G. B. GRAY, art. "Law Literature," *ibid.*

E. BERTHEAU, *Die sieben Gruppen mosaischer Gesetze in den drei mittleren Büchern des Pentateuchs* (1840); J. POPPER, *Der biblische Bericht über die Stiftshütte* (1862); MERX, "Kritische Untersuchungen über die Opfergesetze, Lev. I–VII," *Zeitschrift für wissenschaftliche Theologie*, Vol. VI (1863), pp. 41–84, 164–81; GRAF, *Die geschichtlichen Bücher des Alten Testaments* (1866); STADE, *Geschichte des Volkes Israel*, Vol. I (1887), pp. 62 ff.; NÖLDEKE, *Die alttestamentliche Literatur* (1868); NÖLDEKE, *Untersuchungen zur Kritik des Alten Testaments* (1869), pp. 1–144; KUENEN, "De priesterlike Bestanddeelen van Pentateuch en Josua," *Theologisch Tijdschrift*, Vol. IV (1870), pp. 391–426, 492–500; KAYSER, *Das vorexilische Buch der Urgeschichte Israels und seine Erweiterungen* (1874); HOFMANN, "Einheit und Integrität der Opfergesetze Lev. 1–7," *Magazin für Wissenschaft des Judenthums*, 1877; KLOSTERMANN, "Ezechiel und das Heiligkeits-Gesetz," *Zeitschrift für luth. Theologie und Kirche*, 1877, pp. 406–44 (republished in *Der Pentateuch*, 1893, pp. 368–418); BLEEK-WELLHAUSEN, *Einleitung in das Alte Testament* (1878); VON RYSSEL, *De Elohistae Pentateuchi Sermone* (1878); MAYBAUM, *Die Entwickelung des altisraelitischen Priesterthums* (1880), pp. 74 ff.; FRANZ DELITZSCH, *Zeitschrift für kirchliche Wissenschaft und kirchliches Leben*, Vol. I (1881), pp. 617–26; HORST, *Leviticus XVII–XXVI und Hezekiel* (1881); GIESEBRECHT, "Der Sprachgebrauch des hexateuchischen Elohisten," *Zeitschrift für die alttestamentliche Wissenschaft*, Vol. I (1881), pp. 177–276; P. WURSTER, "Zur Charakteristik und Geschichte des Priestercodex und Heiligkeitsgesetz," *ibid.*, Vol. IV (1884), pp. 112–33; DILLMANN, *Die Bücher Numeri, Deuteronomium und Josua* ("Kurzgefasstes exegetisches Handbuch zum Alten Testament," 2d ed. 1886), pp. 593–690; WELLHAUSEN, *Die Composition des Hexateuchs und der historischen Bücher des Alten Testaments* (1889, 3d ed. 1899); WESTPHAL, *Les sources du Pentateuque* (1888, 1892); RIEHM, *Einleitung in das Alte Testament* (1889); STEINTHAL, *Zeitschrift für Völker-Psychologie*, Vol. XX (1890), pp. 54 ff.; CORNILL, *Einleitung in das Alte Testament* (1891, 3d ed. 1896), pp. 56–86; KÖNIG, *Theologische Studien und Kritiken*, 1893, pp. 464–8, 478; WILDEBOER, *De Letterkunde des Ouden Verbonds naar de Tijdsorde van haar Ontstaan* (1893, German transl. 1895), § 20; HOLZINGER, *Einleitung in den Hexateuch* (1893), pp. 332–475; KÖNIG, *Einleitung in das Alte Testament* (1893), § 48; BAENTSCH, *Das Heiligkeits-Gesetz* (1893); MEYER, *Die Entstehung des Judenthums* (1896), pp. 208–15; WELLHAUSEN, *Die Composition des Hexateuchs und der historischen Bücher des Alten Testaments* (3d ed. 1899); GUTHE, *Geschichte des Volkes Israel* (1899), pp. 259 f.; STEUERNAGEL, *Uebersetzung und Erklärung der Bücher Deuteronomium und Josua und allgemeine Einleitung in den Hexateuch* ("Handkommentar zum Alten Testament," 1900), pp. 271–8; HALÉVY,

"Influence du code sacerdotal sur les prophètes," *Revue sémitique*, January, 1901; BAUDISSIN, *Einleitung in die Bücher des Alten Testamentes* (1901), §§ 31, 41–4, 50–55.

See also the commentaries on Exodus by DILLMANN (1897), HOLZINGER (1900), BAENTSCH (1900), and KENNEDY ("The Temple Bible," 1901); and on Leviticus by KALISCH (1867), KEIL (2d ed. 1870), LANGE (1874), STRACK (1894), DILLMANN-RYSSEL (1897), BAENTSCH (1900), BERTHOLET (1901), and PATERSON ("The Temple Bible," 1901).

Part Fifth

THE LITERATURE OF WORSHIP – THE HISTORICAL LITERATURE

CHAPTER XV.

HISTORICAL LITERATURE — PRIESTLY NARRATIVE IN THE HEXATEUCH.

§ 199. **The New Tendency Encouraged in the Exile.**— Consider (1) the effect of the exile upon the ambition of Israel to be a *nation* among other nations of the earth; (2) the actual condition, in the exile, of all political institutions and political machinery; (3) the certainty that under these conditions the minds of the leaders and the energies of the people would be turned in some other direction; (4) the naturalness and, indeed, the inevitableness of a turning in the direction of a more definitely religious, as distinguished from a political, régime; (5) the foundation for this movement already prepared in the two great doctrines of *individualism*, as preached by the priest Jeremiah, and *solidarity*, as preached by the priest Ezekiel—doctrines preached in view of and in connection with the fall of the nation.

Isa. 57:17-20. 2 Chron. 35:17-21. Isa. 41:17-20. Ezek., chaps. 40-48. Isa. 44:24-28. Jer. 31:29 f. Ezek., chaps. 18, 33.

See J. R. SLATER, "Individualism and Solidarity as Developed by Jeremiah and Ezekiel," BIBLICAL WORLD, Vol. XIV (1899), pp. 172-83; MONTEFIORE, *Lectures on the Origin and Growth of Religion as Illustrated by the Religion of the Ancient Hebrews*, pp. 216-19, 251-3; DUFF, *Old Testament Theology*, Vol. II, pp. 488 f.

§ 200. **The Basis of This Tendency toward Priestly Influence.**— Observe now three things: (1) that the priestly influence had long been in existence, and that only a century or so before the fall of Jerusalem it had been greatly strengthened by the union of effort in which prophet and priest joined, and of which the promulgation of Deuteronomy was the result (*cf.* §§ 25-8, 170); (2) that the prophetic work in these last days had in large measure fallen to priests, *e. g.*, Jeremiah and Ezekiel; (3) that, inasmuch as the will of God had now been presented so clearly in the prophetic word (for prophecy had practically completed its work, having reached its highest development in Jeremiah) and in the written law (the law as found in Deuteronomy having been canonized in

2 Kings 22:3—23:52. Jer. 1:1; Ezek. 1:3. 2 Kings 22:3; 23:3.

621 B. C.), the task that remained was not so much the revelation of new truth as the interpretation, organization, and application of the great body of truth already known. Such ministration was the work of the priest.

Deut. 10:8.

§201. **The Origin of the Idea of the Church or Community.**—Consider now to what extent the idea and practice of the *community* or *church* (1) were the further development of the priestly conception and ritual which existed before the exile and were formulated during the exile by Ezekiel in his visions; (2) were the direct outcome of the prophetic teaching of individualism and solidarity (see §199); and still further (3) were the necessary result of the historical forces which combined to destroy the nation and put an end to prophetic work and leadership.

Exod. 20:23—23:33; Deut., chaps. 16-26.

Ezek., chaps. 40-48.

§202. **The Purpose of the Church.**—(1) Study, as widely as possible (*e. g.*, in Ezekiel's code, the Levitical code, and the priestly prophets), the purpose of the church as it now began to take the place of the nation, as that purpose exhibited itself (*a*) in the emphasis placed on worship, (*b*) in the multiplication of ordinances seeking to preserve, organize, and develop the ritual of the temple; and (2) consider how greatly such interest (already existing in the exile) would be strengthened when the return had taken place, the temple had been rebuilt, and worship had actually been established in the new environment.

Mal. 1:6-14; Zech. 14:16 ff. Leviticus.

Hag. 1:7-14; 2:1-9; Zech. 6:9-14.

§203. **The Desire to Prepare Histories of Worship.**—Consider how, under these circumstances, there would come into existence the desire (1) to trace the beginnings of these ordinances to the earliest times, and to show the place assigned them under the great leaders of the past; (2) to write a narrative which would present their history through the long centuries from David's time down to the last days—a story parallel with that other narrative (prepared by the prophets who had now passed away) which, in representing prophetic truth, had almost entirely ignored the priest-side of the national history; and (3) to show just how these institutions were finally

Cf. P (below).

Cf. Chronicles.

reinstated or re-established after the return by the great leaders Ezra and Nehemiah. This desire found its realization in what we may call the histories of the priestly school. *Cf.* Ezra and Nehemiah.

§ 204. **The Histories of the Prophetic School.** — Recall (1) the history of J, the work of a Judean prophet, probably the oldest of the prophetic histories, which gathers up the stories and traditions of the earliest times down to the settlement of Israel in Canaan and uses all this material for the purpose of illustrating and enforcing the truths of prophecy;[1] (2) the history of E, which covers practically the same ground as J, but is written from the point of view of northern Israel, and is somewhat less naïve in its conception of God and in respect to other theological ideas;[2] (3) the histories found in Judges, Samuel, and Kings, which trace the progress of the nation from the conquest to the exile; and note the principal characteristics, common to them all, viz.: (*a*) that they are in large part compilations of older material; (*b*) the emphasis laid by them upon the thought of sin as the cause of all of Israel's troubles; (*c*) the purpose of their work as evidently didactic, rather than historical in the modern sense of the word;

Gen. 2:4*b*—4:26; etc.

Gen. 15:1, 5, 16; chap. 20; etc.

2 Sam. 1:18; 1 Kings 11:41; 14:29; 2 Kings 15:26; etc. 2 Kings, chap. 24.

[1] The J-material in Gen., chaps. 1–40, is: 2:4*b*—4:26; 5:29; 6:1–8; 7:1–5, 7–10, 12, 17*b*, 22 f.; 8:2*b*, 3*a*, 6–12, 13*b*, 20–22; 9:18–27; 10:1*b*, 8–19, 21, 24–30; 11:1–9, 28–30; 12:1–4*a*, 6–20; 13:1–5, 6*b*–11*a*, 13–18; 15:3 f., 6–11, 17 f.; 16:1*b*, 2, 4–14; 18:1—19:28, 30–38; 21:1*a*, 2*a*, 7, 28–30, 33; 22:20–24; 24:1—25:6, 18, 21–26*a*, 28; 26:1–3*a*, 6–14, 16 f., 19–33; 27:1*a*, 2, 3, 4*b*, 5*b*, 6, 7*a*, 15, 18*b*–20, 24–29*a*, 29*c*, 30*a*, 30*c*, 31*b*–34, 41*b*–42, 43*b*, 45*a*; 28:10, 13–16, 19; 29:2–14, 31–35; 30:3*b*–16, 22*c*, 23*a*, 24 f., 27, 29–31*a*, 34–38*a*, 39–40*a*, 40*c*–43; 31:1, 17, 18*a*, 25, 27, 31, 43 f., 46, 48–50; 32:3–7*a*, 13*b*–22*a*, 23*b*–29, 31 f.; 33:1–18*a*; 34:2*b*, 3*a*, 3*c*, 5, 7, 11, 19, 26, 29*b*–31; 35:14, 16–22*a*; 36:31–39; 37:2*b*, 2*d*–4, 12, 13*a*, 14*b*, 18*b*, 21, 25*b*–27, 28*b*, 32*a*, 35; 38:1—39:6*b*, 7*b*–23. The remainder of the document may be found in J. E. CARPENTER AND G. HARFORD-BATTERSBY, *The Hexateuch*, Vol. II; or in ADDIS, *Documents of the Hexateuch*, Vol. I; or in DRIVER, *Introduction to the Literature of the Old Testament.*

[2] The E-material in Gen., chaps. 1–40, is: 15:1, 2, 5, 16; 20:1–18; 21:6, 8–27, 31 f., 34; 22:1–13, 19; 25:25*b*, 27, 29–34; 27:1*b*, 4*a*, 7*b*–14, 16–18*a*, 21–23, 30*b*, 31*a*, 35–41*a*, 44, 45*b*; 28:11 f., 17 f., 20, 21*a*, 22; 29:1, 15–23, 25–28*a*, 30; 30:1–3*a*, 17–20, 26, 31*b*–33, 38*b*, 40*b*; 31:2–16, 19–24, 26, 28–30, 32–42, 47, 51—32:2, 23*a*, 30; 33:18*c*–20; 35:1–5, 6*b*–8; 37:5–11, 13*b*, 14*a*, 17*b*, 19 f., 22–25*a*, 28*a*, 28*c*–31, 32*b*, 33*a*, 34, 36; 39:6*c*, 7*a*; 40:1–23. For the remainder of the document see literature cited in the foregoing footnote.

(*d*) the selection and arrangement of material, which is such as to enforce the great lessons of prophecy.

§ 205. **The Priestly Histories.**— Under this head may be classified (1) the priestly narrative in the Hexateuch; (2) the books of Chronicles, which furnish a parallel history, as understood by the priest, for the entire period covered by the prophetic history found in
See § 204.
Judges, Samuel, and Kings; and (3) the books of Ezra and Nehemiah, which describe the restoration from exile and the re-establishment of the temple and its elaborate system of worship. These all possess the same general characteristics of style, are controlled by the same theological ideas, are interested in the same general subject, and are written from the same priestly point of view.

§ 206. **The Historical Character of the Priestly Histories.**— Keep in mind (1) the purpose of these so-called histories, viz., to represent the *priest-side*, that is, the element of worship; (2) the consequent necessity of making *selections* from the large body of material in existence; (3) the fragmentary and disconnected character of the material which comes by selection; (4) the only method that, under these circumstances, can be employed — that of compilation; (5) the danger of confusion and disorder; (6) the certainty that material having its origin centuries after the event described will not be intended to serve as a chronicle of the event, but rather to meet some definite and practical end in view; (7) the difference between *actual history* and *idealized story;* (8) the meaning of the word "pragmatic" as applied to history.

See, *e. g.*, my article in *Sunday School Times*, July, 1889; GEO. F. MOORE, art. "Historical Literature," *Encyclopædia Biblica*, Vol. II; W. E. BARNES, "The Religious Standpoint of the Chronicler," *American Journal of Semitic Languages and Literatures*, Vol. XIII (1896–97), pp. 14–20; T. G. SOARES, "The Import of the Chronicles as a Piece of Religio-Historical Literature," *American Journal of Theology*, Vol. III (1899), pp. 251–74; C. C. TORREY, *The Composition and Historical Value of Ezra-Nehemia* ("Beiheft zur *Zeitschrift für die alttestamentliche Wissenschaft*," II, 1896); L. DIESTEL, "Die hebräische Geschichtesschreibung," *Jahrbücher für deutsche Theologie*, Vol. XVIII (1873), pp. 365 ff.; FRANZ DELITZSCH, "Die

Formenreichtum der israelitischen Geschichtsliteratur," *Zeitschrift für lutherische Theologie und Kirche*, Vol. XXXVI (1870), pp. 31 ff.; J. E. McFadyen, *The Messages of the Prophetic and Priestly Historians* (1901), pp. 241 ff., 271 ff.

§ 207. **The Scope of the Priestly Narrative.**— This document is found alongside of the prophetical histories J and E in the Hexateuch.[3] Like them it goes back to the time of creation and sketches the course of events up to the settlement of Israel in Canaan. This leads it in many cases to duplicate the narratives of the prophetic historians; but, although the same events are often narrated in both accounts, the point of view is widely different, since the purposes of the two schools of writers are of a different character. The priestly narrative is primarily concerned with questions like (*a*) the divine choice of Israel as the peculiar people of God; (*b*) the divine origin of her system of worship; (*c*) the growth of the accompanying institutions and customs.

Gen. 1:1—2:4*a*; Josh., chaps. 14, 15, 17, etc.

Gen. 34:1, 2*a*, 3*b*, 4, 6, 8–10, 12–18, 20–25, 27–29*a*; *cf.* 34:2*b*, 3*a*, 3*c*, 5, 7, 11, 19, etc.

§ 208. **The Gradual Growth of the Priestly Narrative.**— A careful examination of this priestly narrative reveals that it is not all the work of one hand or one time, but, like the prophetic histories, is a compilation of older materials, which have gradually been brought together and wrought into a homogeneous narrative. This appears (*a*) from the fact that there are many repetitions

[3] The material belonging to the priestly narrative, as indicated in *The Hexateuch*, by J. E. Carpenter and G. Harford-Battersby, is as follows: Gen. 1:1—2:4*a*; 5:1–28, 30–32; 6:9–22; 7:6, 11, 13–17*a*, 18–21, 24; 8:1, 2*a*, 3*b*–5, 13*a*, 14–19; 9:1–17, 28, 29; 10:1*a*, 2–7, 20, 22, 23, 31, 32; 11:10–27, 31, 32; 12:4*b*, 5; 13:6*a*, 11*b*, 12; 16:1*a*, 3, 15, 16; 17:1–27; 19:29; 21:1*b*, 2*b*–5; 23:1–20; 25:7–17, 19, 20, 26*b*; 26:34, 35; 27:46—28:9; 29:24, 28*b*, 29; 30:21, 22*a*; 31:18*b*; 33:18*b*; 34:1–2*a*, 3*b*, 4, 6, 8–10, 12–18, 20–25, 27–29*a*; 35:6*a*, 9–13, 15, 22*b*—36:30, 40–43; 37:1, 2*a*, 2*c*; 41:45*b*, 46*a*; 46:6–27; 47:5, 6*a*, 7–11, 27*b*, 28; 48:3–7; 49:1*a*, 28–33*a*, 33*c*; 50:12, 13; Exod. 1:1–5, 7, 13, 14*b*; 2:23*b*–25; 6:2—7:13, 19, 20*a*, 21*b*, 22; 8:5–7, 15*b*–19; 9:8–12; 11:9—12:20, 24, 28, 40—13:2, 20; 14:1–4, 8, 9*b*, 15*b*, 16*b*–18, 21*a*, 21*c*–23, 26, 27*a*, 28*a*, 29; 16:1–3, 5–35; 17:1*a*; 19:1, 2*a*, 24:15*b*–18*a*; 25:1—31:18*a*; 34:29—40:38; Lev. 1:1—27:34; Numb. 1:1—10:28, 34; 13:1–17*a*, 21*b*, 25, 26*a*, 32; 14:1*a*, 2, 5–7, 9*a*, 10, 26–30, 32–39*a*, 15:1–41; 16:1*a*, 1*b*, 2*b*, 3–11, 16–24, 26*a*, 27*a*, 32*b*, 33*c*, 35—20:1*a*, 2, 3*b*, 4, 6–8*a*, 8*c*–13, 22*b*–29; 21:4*a*, 10, 11*a*; 22:1; 25:6—32:38; 33:1—36:13; Deut. 32:48–52; 34:1*a*, 1*c*, 5*d*, 7–9; Josh. 3:4*a*, 8, 15, 16; 4:7*b*, 8*a*, 13, 15–17, 19; 5:10–12; 9:15*c*, 17–21; 13:15—14:5; 15:1–12, 20–61; 16:4–9; 17:1–10; 18:1, 11—19:46, 48—21:42; 22:9–34.

Exod., chaps. 25–30, *cf.* 35–40; Numb., chaps. 1–3, *cf.* 26; Lev., chap. 23, *cf.* Numb., chaps. 28, 29.

within the priestly narrative itself, *e. g.*, the repetition of the account of the structure of the tabernacle, the double account of the census of Israel, the two recensions of the laws concerning feasts, etc.; and (*b*) from the different tone and character of various parts of the narrative. It is now generally granted that there are at least four different strata in this work. These are (1) a continuous narrative from the creation to the settlement in Canaan, which forms the groundwork of the priestly narrative (=P^g); (2) the Holiness Code (=P^h); (3) a collection of priestly teachings on subjects connected with the various institutions (=P^t); (4) "a miscellaneous set of secondary enlargements, ranging over a wide variety of topics—genealogical expansions, legislative elaborations, illustrative narratives, etc." (=P^s).

Lev., chaps. 17–26. Numb. 15:1–31; etc.

Exod. 30:22—31:11; etc.

See, *e. g.*, J. E. CARPENTER AND G. HARFORD-BATTERSBY, *The Hexateuch*, Vol. I, pp. 142 ff.; ADDIS, *Documents of the Hexateuch*, Vol. II, pp. 186 ff.; HOLZINGER, *Einleitung in den Hexateuch*, pp. 332 ff.; STEUERNAGEL, *Deuteronomium und Josua, und allgemeine Einleitung in den Hexateuch*, p. 272; BAUDISSIN, *Einleitung in die Bücher des Alten Testamentes*, pp. 154 ff.; WELLHAUSEN, *Prolegomena to the History of Israel*, p. 385.

§ 209. **The Sources of the Priestly Narrative.**—(1) Examine carefully some of the narratives contained in both the prophetic history and in the priestly narrative, *e. g.*, the accounts of the deluge, the story of Dinah,[4] the bringing of water from the rock in the wilderness,[5] etc., and consider whether the prophetic and priestly writers are to be regarded (*a*) as having used the same sources, or (*b*) as having used different sources, or (*c*) as being dependent one upon the other; if the latter, which is the original?

Gen. 6:5–8; 7:1–5, 7–10, etc.; *cf.* 6:9–22; 7:6, 11, etc.

(2) Consider, further, whether it is probable that any sources other than popular traditions were ever in existence for the study of the earliest prehistoric times. In cases where the priestly and prophetic accounts of the

[4] In the Dinah narrative the following material is from P: Gen. 34:1, 2*a*, 3*b*, 4, 6, 8–10, 12–18, 20–25, 27–29*a*; and the remainder of chap. 34 belongs to J.

[5] In Numb., chap. 20, the following material is assigned to P: 20:1*a*, 2, 3*b*–4, 6–8*a*, 8*c*–13, 22*b*–29; the following to J: 20:1*b*, 3*a*, 5, 8*b*, 19 f.; and the remainder to E.

same event differ widely, *e.g.*, in the accounts of the events at Sinai,[6] what explanation may be given?[7] Is the difference to be explained as due to the use of varying sources or as a result of the different purpose and point of view of these writers?

(3) Compare the creation accounts of J and P with each other, and still further with the creation stories as found on Babylonian tablets. Note carefully the points of resemblance and difference, and try to determine (*a*) which of the two shows the clearer traces of Babylonian influence; (*b*) whether they both resemble the same Babylonian tradition; or (*c*) whether each reflects a different Babylonian tradition; or (*d*) whether the Hebrew and Babylonian accounts are to be considered as parallel, but independent, narratives. (*e*) If the Babylonian accounts are considered as sources of the Hebrew narratives, note how thoroughly the Hebrew writers have edited their sources and the different style of editing done by P as compared with J. **Gen. 1:1—2:4*a*; *cf.* Gen. 2:4*b*–24.**

For English translations of these Babylonian stories see W. MUSS-ARNOLT'S rendering in R. F. HARPER'S *Assyrian and Babylonian Literature* ("The World's Great Books," Aldine edition, New York, 1901), pp. 282–300. On the relations of the Hebrew and Babylonian accounts, see LENORMANT, *The Beginnings of History*, pp. 47–66; GUNKEL, *The Legends of Genesis;* JOHN D. DAVIS, *Genesis and Semitic Tradition*, pp. 1–22; H. ZIMMERN, *Biblische und babylonische Urgeschichte* (1901); J. BARTH, *Babel und israelitisches Religionswesen* (1902), pp. 21–31.

§ 210. **The Legislation Embodied in the Priestly Narrative.** — Note that, just as the prophetic histories included some elements of legislation, viz., the smaller Book of the Covenant in J, and the greater Book of the Covenant, with the Decalogue (Exod. 20:1–17), in E, so the priestly narrative contains its proportion of laws. **Exod. 34:17–28. Exod. 20:23—23:3; 20:1–17.**

[6] For the distribution of material among the various sources in Exod., chaps. 19–40, in the book of Leviticus, and in Numb., chaps. 1–10, see the literature cited in note 1.

[7] Other stories which are thought to be duplicates are: (1) the account of the birth of Hagar, etc., in Gen., chap. 16 (P = 16:1*a*, 3, 15, 16; the remainder belongs to J); (2) the birth of Isaac (P = Gen. 21:1*b*, 2*b*, 3–5; the remainder belongs to J and E): the revelation of God to Jacob at Bethel (P = Gen. 35:6*a*, 9–13, 15; the remainder belongs to J and E).

Exod. 12:1-20, 25 f., 43-49; 13:1; 25:1—31:17; chaps. 35-40; Numb. 5:1—9:10; chaps. 15, 18, 19, 28-31, and 35.

This legal element is found in portions of Exodus and Numbers and in the entire book of Leviticus. (1) Notice the relatively large amount of space and consideration given to legal matters in P, as compared with J and E. Is it not true that in J and E the legal material is incidental, while in P it is the essential and all-important thing? (2) How may this increase of legal material be accounted for? Is it perhaps due to the greater interest of the priestly writers in such matters?

§ 211. **Orderly, Systematic Treatment of Material.**—

Gen. 1:1—2:4*a*.

Read the priestly narrative of the creation, and (1) notice that the order of events is carefully distributed throughout six days, corresponding to the working days of the week, and that God is represented as resting upon the

Gen. 2:4*a*-25.

seventh day. (2) Is not the whole account much more systematic than the prophetic account of the same sub-

Gen. 2:4*a*; 5:1; 6:9; 10:1; 11:10; 11:27; 25:12; 25:19; 36:1; 37:2.

ject in the following chapter? (3) Consider also the division of the patriarchal period into ten "generations," beginning with the "generations of the heaven and of the earth,"[8] and ending with the generations of Jacob.

Gen. 1:1; 8:1; etc.

(4) Notice that prior to the time of Abraham the gen-

Gen. 17:1.

eral name *elôhîm* is used; between Abraham and Moses

Exod. 6:2 f.

the name *el shaddai* appears; after the times of Moses the name is Jehovah. (5) Observe the similar system which appears in the presentation of the covenant idea; the first covenant being represented as having been made

Gen. 9:8-17.

with Noah, its sign—the rainbow; the second covenant

Gen., chap. 17.

being with Abraham, its sign—circumcision; while still

Exod. 31:16 f.

later the sabbath is spoken of as a covenant, and as the sign of a covenant.

See DRIVER, *Introduction to the Literature of the Old Testament* (6th ed.), pp. 129 ff.; HOLZINGER, *Einleitung in den Hexateuch*, pp. 353 ff.; J. E. MCFADYEN, *The Messages of the Prophetic and Priestly Historians*, pp. 245 f.; STEUERNAGEL, *Deuteronomium und Josua u. s. w.*, pp. 271 f.

§ 212. **The Fondness of the Priestly Narrative for Genea-**

Gen. 1:1—2:4*a*; 5:1; 10:1; etc.

logical Statements.—(1) Recall the fact, previously mentioned, that the creation account and the patriarchal

[8] Gen. 2:4*a* belongs to P's preceding narrative and should probably be transposed to the beginning of chap. 1.

history are presented in the form of genealogies. (2) Notice further the large amount of genealogical material in the priestly narratives, and that long periods of time are frequently represented by nothing more than a genealogical list. (3) Does it seem that the writer uses these lists in large part as connecting links for his narrative, hastening over by their means long periods of time in which he has no especial interest, in order to give more attention to matters in which he is vitally concerned?

Exod. 6:14-27; Numb. 1:5-16, 20, 47; 3:14-39; 26:1—27:11.

§ 213. **Prevalence of Statistics and Dates in the Priestly Narrative.**—In illustration of this characteristic of P, recall the fact that it gives the ages of the antediluvians; the dimensions of the ark; the date of the flood; the depth of the waters of the flood and its duration; the age of Abraham at various junctures in his life; the price paid for the field of Ephron; the number of people that entered Egypt; the duration of the sojourn in Egypt; the date of the arrival in the wilderness of Sin and of that at Sinai; the dimensions and specifications of the ark of testimony, the table of shewbread, and the golden candlestick; most minute specifications for the tabernacle with all its furnishings; the exact dates of all feasts; a census of Israel at Sinai; the exact value of the offerings made in connection with the dedication of the altar; a careful demarkation of the boundaries of the various tribes; etc. Does not the presence of so much material of this sort render the general style stiff and precise as compared with the free, flowing narratives of J and E?

Gen., chap. 5; 6:15f.; 7:6, 11, 13, 20, 24; 8:3ff., 13, 14; 12:4; 16:3, 16; 17:1, 24ff.; 21:5; 23:16; 46:27; Exod. 12:40f.; 16:1; 19:1; 25:10ff., 23, 25, 31ff.; chaps. 26-30 and 35-40; Lev., chap. 23; Numb., chaps. 28, 29; chaps. 1-3, and 26; chap. 7; 34:1-15.

§ 214. **The Style of the Priestly Narrative is Repetitious.**—(1) Observe that the account of the structure of the tabernacle is given in full twice; also that the census of Israel at Sinai is twice narrated. (2) Read Numb., chap. 7, and notice that six verses are used twelve times in this chapter. (3) Consider, further, the large extent to which certain formulas and stereotyped phrases are repeated, and the fact that many sentences are cast in the same mold. (4) Are some of these repetitions due to the fact that the priestly narrative is a compilation? But can the tendency to the repeated use of the same phraseology

Exod., chaps. 26-30 and 35-40; Numb., chaps. 1-3 and 26; 7:13-17; Gen. 1:5, 8*b*, 13, etc.; 10:5, 20, 31f.; 25:16; 36:40, 43, etc.; Gen. 5:6-8, 9-11, 12-14, etc.; 11:10-11, 12-13, etc.; 12:4*b*; 16:16; 17:24f.; 21:5; 25:26*b*; 41:46*a*; Exod. 7:7; Numb. 33:39; 1:20f., 22f., etc.; 2:3-9, 10-16, etc.

be so explained? Is it not a marked characteristic of the priestly style?

On the style of the priestly narrative in general see: DRIVER, *Introduction to the Literature of the Old Testament* (6th ed.), pp. 126–35; J. E. CARPENTER AND G. HARFORD-BATTERSBY, *The Hexateuch*, Vol. I, pp. 125 f.; GUNKEL, *The Legends of Genesis*, pp. 145 f., 148; HOLZINGER, *Einleitung in den Hexateuch*, pp. 349–54; BAUDISSIN, *Einleitung in die Bücher des Alten Testamentes*, pp. 96–102; and the articles by W. R. HARPER and W. H. GREEN in *Hebraica*, Vols. V and VI.

§215. **The Selection of Material in the Priestly Narrative.**—(1) Consider whether, if it is not the purpose of the priestly writers to write a history in the modern sense of the word, but rather to teach certain truths with reference to God and the proper methods of worship, it may not be reasonable to suppose that they selected and arranged their material with a view to its appropriateness to the end they had in view. (2) Notice, for example, (*a*) that, while in J the narrative of the creation is merely introductory to the account of man's first sin, in P the creation narrative is treated in a manner to emphasize strongly the sanctity of the sabbath; (*b*) that between the creation and Abraham the centuries are bridged over by means of genealogies, with the single exception of the deluge and the account of the covenant with Noah; (*c*) that the only incidents in Abraham's life to which P gives any consideration are the account of the institution of circumcision with the accompanying covenant, and the purchase of the field of Ephron; (*d*) that the only incident treated in the life of Isaac is the care taken to provide for his son's marriage to a woman of his own race; and in Jacob's life the failure of the proposed alliance between the sons of Jacob and the men of Shechem, the appearance of God to him at Bethel with the promise to bless his descendants, and his entrance into Egypt with his sons; (*e*) that in the account of the exodus the only incidents receiving any considerable attention are the institution of the Passover, the giving of manna on six days and its withholding on the seventh, and the legislation at Sinai which constitutes the bulk of the priestly narrative. (3) Consider in

Gen. 1:1—2:4*a*.

Gen., chap. 17.

Gen., chap. 23.

Gen. 28:1–9.

Gen. 34:1 f., 3*b*, 4, 6, 8–10, 12–18, etc.; 35:9–13, 15; 46:6–27.

Exod. 12:1–20, 40–51.

Exod., chaps. 25–40; Lev., chaps. 1–27; etc.

each of the above cases why the incident was chosen for treatment to the exclusion of other material, much of which would have been of more interest and value as pure history.

See, *e. g.*, GUNKEL, *The Legends of Genesis*, pp. 146 f.; HOLZINGER, *Einleitung in den Hexateuch*, pp. 359 f.

§216. **The Theological Point of View of the Priestly Narrative.**—(1) Is not the conception of God that appears in the priestly narrative in many respects the highest attained in the Old Testament? Note that in the creation account of P, as compared with that of J, all anthropomorphic features are lacking; it is sufficient for God to speak and the thing is done. He is most holy, so that none but members of the holiest class may come near his altar or perform the highest functions of his worship; and these ministers are set apart by a most solemn service of consecration. The usual manifestation of his presence is by means of a cloud resting upon the tent of meeting and the appearance of his "glory." In the presence of such a holy Being the sinfulness of man is greatly intensified; constant sacrifices are necessary to make atonement; and there is an obligation resting upon all Israel to be holy, because God is holy. This exalted conception of God can be traced everywhere in the narrative and in the legislation. (2) To what extent is it due to this conception of God and of Israel's relation to him that the accounts of Israel's ancestors given by P differ so widely in spirit from the corresponding narratives of J and E? (3) Consider the significance of the fact that none of the sins and shortcomings of the patriarchs, so freely mentioned by the prophetic writers, are alluded to in the priestly narrative; it being taken for granted that the patriarchs, who were the founders of the holy nation, as such must themselves have been holy. (4) Note also that no sacrifices are offered nor altars built by the patriarchs according to the priestly narrative, in contrast with the prophetic account, because sacrifice was not legal until the Mosaic legislation had been given and the proper means for the right conduct of sacrifice provided.

Gen. 1:1–2:4*a*.

Numb., chap. 18; Lev., chap. 8.

Exod. 40:34 ff.; Numb. 16:19.

Lev. 19:2.

Gen. 35:6, 9 ff.; *cf.* 35:7.

See, *e. g.*, DRIVER, *Introduction to the Literature of the Old Testament* (6th ed.), pp. 128 f.; J. E. CARPENTER AND G. HARFORD-BATTERSBY, *The Hexateuch*, Vol. II, pp, 132 f.; HOLZINGER, *Einleitung in den Hexateuch*, pp. 376–90; KÖNIG, *Einleitung in das Alte Testament*, pp. 231 ff.

§ 217. Literature to be Consulted.

KUENEN, *An Historico-Critical Inquiry into the Origin and Composition of the Hexateuch* (1861, 2d ed. 1885; transl. 1886), pp. 65–107, 272–313; J. W. COLENSO, *The Pentateuch and Book of Joshua, Critically Examined*, Parts I–VII (1862–79); WELLHAUSEN, *Prolegomena to the History of Israel* (1878, 4th ed. 1895; transl. from German 1885), pp. 385–91; W. R. SMITH, *The Old Testament in the Jewish Church* (1881, 2d ed. 1892), Lecture XII; DRIVER, *Journal of Philology*, Vol. XI (1882), pp. 201–36; E. C. BISSELL, *The Pentateuch, Its Origin and Structure* (1885), pp. 318–61; DILLMANN, *Genesis Critically and Exegetically Expounded* (5th ed. 1886; transl. 1897), Vol. I, pp. 1–26; FRANZ DELITZSCH, *A New Commentary on Genesis* (5th ed. 1887; transl. 1889), Vol. I, pp. 1–59; B. W. BACON, "Pentateuchal Analysis," *Hebraica*, Vol. IV (1888), pp. 219–26; KITTEL, *History of the Hebrews* (1888; transl. 1895), Vol. I, pp. 96–134; W. H. GREEN, *Hebraica*, Vol. V (1888–89), pp. 149 ff., 162 f., 174 ff.; Vol. VI, pp. 127, 133, 167, 180 f., 196, 210; Vol. VII, pp. 16, 27, 33, 36 f., 113 ff., 137 f., 141; Vol. VIII, 37 f., 63, 201 f., 228, 243; W. R. HARPER, *Hebraica*, Vol. V (1888–89), pp. 22 f., 25 f., 33 f., 45, 52 ff., 63 ff., 244 f., 253, 266 f., 275, 286; Vol. VI, pp. 2, 11 f., 19, 26 f., 36 ff., 242 f., 252, 265 f., 276 f., 288 f.; DRIVER, *An Introduction to the Literature of the Old Testament* (1891, 6th ed. 1897), pp. 126–35; E. J. FRIPP, *The Composition of the Book of Genesis* (1892); C. A. BRIGGS, *The Higher Criticism of the Hexateuch* (1892, 2d ed. 1897), pp. 69–75; B. W. BACON, *The Genesis of Genesis* (1893), pp. 54–9, 66–94; W. H. GREEN, *The Higher Criticism of the Pentateuch* (1895), pp. 59–133; IDEM, *The Unity of the Book of Genesis* (1895), *passim;* ADDIS, *Documents of the Hexateuch*, Vol. II (1898), pp. 170–88; H. E. RYLE, article "Genesis" (§ iv (*a*)) in HASTINGS'S *Dictionary of the Bible*, Vol. II (1899); C. A. BRIGGS, *General Introduction to the Study of Holy Scripture* (1899), pp., 329 f.; F. H. WOODS, article "Hexateuch" (§ iii, 2 and 4 *D*) in HASTINGS'S *Dictionary of the Bible*, Vol. II (1899); L. W. BATTEN, *The Old Testament from the Modern Point of View* (1899, 2d ed. 1901), pp. 79–119; J. E. CARPENTER AND G. HARFORD-BATTERSBY, *The Hexateuch*, Vol. I (1900), pp. 121–56; G. F. MOORE, articles "Genesis" (§§ 2 f.) and "Historical Literature" (§§ 9 f.) in *Encyclopædia Biblica*, Vol. II (1901); GUNKEL, *The Legends of Genesis* (1901), pp. 144–60; WELLHAUSEN, article "Hexateuch" (§§ 19, 23, 24, 29, 30) in *Encyclopædia Biblica*, Vol. II (1901); J. E. MCFADYEN, *The Messages of the Prophetic and Priestly Historians* (1901), pp. 239–47.

H. HUPFELD, *Die Quellen der Genesis* (1853); K. H. GRAF, *Die geschichtlichen Bücher des Alten Testaments* (1866); NÖLDEKE, *Untersuchungen zur Kritik des Alten Testamentes* (1869); ED. RIEHM, "Ueber die Grundschrift des Pentateuchs," *Theologische Studien und Kritiken*, 1872, pp. 283–307; BLEEK-WELLHAUSEN, *Einleitung in das Alte Testament* (4th ed. 1878), §§ 81 ff.; RYSSEL, *De Elohistae sermone* (1878); GIESEBRECHT, "Der Sprachgebrauch des hexateuchischen Elohisten," *Zeitschrift für die alttestamentliche Wissenschaft*, Vol. I (1881), pp. 177–276; WURSTER, "Zur Charakteristik und Geschichte des Priestercodex," *ibid.*, Vol. IV (1884), pp. 111 ff.; DILLMANN, *Die Bücher Numeri, Deuteronomium und Josua* ("Kurzgefasstes exegetisches

Handbuch zum Alten Testament," 1886), pp. 648 f., 663; KAUTZSCH UND SOCIN, *Die Genesis mit äusserer Unterscheidung der Quellen* (1888, 2d ed. 1891); WELLHAUSEN, *Die Composition des Hexateuchs und der historischen Bücher des Alten Testaments* (1889); RIEHM, *Einleitung in das Alte Testament*, Vol. I (1889), pp. 253–80; C. H. CORNILL, *Einleitung in das Alte Testament* (1891, 3d ed. 1896), pp. 56–68; WESTPHAL, *Les sources du Pentateuque*, Tome 2 (1892), pp. 21–32; WILDEBOER, *Die Litteratur des Alten Testaments* (Dutch, 1893; transl. into German, 1895), pp. 306–33; ED. KÖNIG, *Einleitung in das Alte Testament* (1893), pp. 225–31; HOLZINGER, *Einleitung in den Hexateuch* (1893), pp. 332–425; STEUERNAGEL, *Uebersetzung und Erklärung der Bücher Deuteronomium und Josua, und allgemeine Einleitung in den Hexateuch* ("Handkommentar zum Alten Testament," 1900), pp. 271–8; BAUDISSIN, *Einleitung in die Bücher des Alten Testamentes* (1901), pp. 96–102.

§ 218. **Constructive Work.**

1. Prepare a brief survey of early Israelitish history from the passages ordinarily assigned to P (see p. 199, note 3), noting especially (*a*) the gaps which are found to exist, that is, the periods left untouched, or passed over in the genealogical method (see § 212); (*b*) the portions on which large emphasis is laid.

2. Make a list of all the so-called duplicates (*cf.* § 209), that is, those events which are described by some other writer (*e. g.*, J or E) as well as by P, and observe particularly the characteristics which distinguish the account of P from other accounts.

3. Prepare a statement which (*a*) will present in logical order the various elements of style that characterize P, (*b*) will show the relationship existing between these characteristics of style and the contents, and (*c*) will exhibit the contrast between the style of P and that of the prophetic narrators (J and E).

4. Trace the growth of P in its various stages, viz., P^h, P^g, P^t, P^s, and indicate (*a*) the chronological order of these various elements of P; (*b*) the ideas and laws peculiarly characteristic of each stage of the P legislation.

5. Formulate P's conception of God, and trace the influence of this conception in (*a*) the contents, that is, as explaining why certain things are included or omitted; (*b*) the style, that is, as explaining why the style is in such marked contrast, *e. g.*, with the prophetic style; (*c*) the conception, that is, as explaining the thought of the writer on various subjects, *e. g.*, man, angels, worship, etc., etc.

CHAPTER XVI.

HISTORICAL LITERATURE — THE BOOKS OF CHRONICLES.

§ 219. **The Scope of the History in Chronicles.**—Observe that the narrative in Chronicles (1) begins, like that in P, with the very beginning of the human race; (2) runs rapidly over the early history of mankind in general; (3) takes up that of the Hebrew people, beginning with Abraham and hastening on to the death of Saul; while (4) with the accession of David it treats the history more elaborately, and covers the period from David to the exile in the remainder of the work. Observe further that, as compared with the prophetic history in Judges, Samuel, and Kings, (1) while beginning at an earlier point in history, it gives very much less consideration to the pre-Davidic period; (2) it leaves the history of the Northern Kingdom almost entirely out of account; and (3) both stop with the exile, the end of Israel's national life.

1 Chron 1:1; *cf.* Gen. 1:1. 1 Chron. 1:1–27. 1 Chron. 1:28–10:14. 2 Chron. 36:22 f.; *cf.* 2 Kings 25:27 ff.

Consider, now, the purpose of the compiler (1) as gathered from the scope of his work; (2) as gathered from a comparison with Judges, Samuel, and Kings; (3) as gathered from the comparative fulness of treatment of different parts.

§ 220. **The Date of the Books of Chronicles.**— Considering the relationship and significance of old materials in the book, side by side with materials which indicate a comparatively late date for the origin of the book as a whole, note (1) that the history extends to the "first year of Cyrus, king of Persia;" (2) that the common titles of Cyrus and all the Persian kings were "the King," the "Great King," the "King of Kings," the "King of the Lands;" they are never called kings of Persia in contemporaneous literature; does not this fact point to a period considerably later than that of the Persian empire? (3) that the daric, a Persian coin introduced in the time of Darius I. (521–486 B. C.) and named

2 Chron. 36:22. 2 Chron. 36:20, 22 f.; Ezra 4:8; 5:6 f.; 7:27 f.; 8:1; Neh. 1:11; 2:1 ff.; Hag. 1:1, 15; Zech. 7:1. 1 Chron. 29:7.

after him, is spoken of as in use in the time of David; does not this suggest that the coin had been so long in use when Chronicles was prepared that the time and place of its origin had been forgotten? (4) that the language of the book has a very strong Aramaic coloring, is full of words and phrases characteristic of post-exilic literature, and that the syntax is of a decidedly late character;[1] (5) that in the list of Zerubbabel's descendants six generations are enumerated according to the Hebrew text, while the Septuagint gives eleven. Since Zerubbabel lived about 520 B. C., and a generation may be reckoned at about twenty years, this genealogy, according to the Hebrew text, gives us a date about 400 B. C.; or, if the Septuagint be accepted, about 300 B. C. (6) If Chronicles, Ezra, and Nehemiah are the work of the same editor (see § 226), may we not use data furnished by Ezra and Nehemiah to determine the date of Chronicles? In Nehemiah, the high-priest Jaddua is mentioned, and the phrase "the days of Jaddua" is employed to indicate a date *in the past*. Does not this suggest that the writer lived some time after Jaddua? But, according to the narrative of Josephus,[2] Jaddua was the high-priest who met Alexander the Great as he marched through Syria (333 B. C.) and rendered him favorable to the Jews. Hence we get a date about 300 B. C. for the compilation of Chronicles.

1 Chron. 3:19–24.

Hag. 1:1.

Neh. 12:11, 22.

See, *e. g.*, BARNES, *The Books of Chronicles* ("Cambridge Bible," 1899), pp. xi f.; W. R. SMITH AND S. R. DRIVER, article "Chronicles," *Encyclopædia Biblica*, Vol. I, col. 764; FRANCIS BROWN, article "Chronicles I and II," HASTINGS'S *Dictionary of the Bible*, Vol. I, p. 392; DRIVER, *Introduction to the Literature of the Old Testament* (6th ed.), pp. 518 ff.

§ 221. **The Sources of the Books of Chronicles.**—Since the chronicler was one of the latest contributors to the collection of writings known as the Old Testament, consider the probability of his having used many sources

[1] For the linguistic data and their bearing on the date of Chronicles see especially FR. BROWN'S article "Chronicles," in HASTINGS'S *Dictionary of the Bible*, Vol. I, pp. 389–92; DRIVER, *Introduction to the Literature of the Old Testament* (6th ed.), pp. 504 ff.; and article "Chronicles, Books of," in *Encyclopædia Biblica* (§ 11).

[2] *Antiquities*, XI, viii, 4, 5.

2 Chron. 9: 29; 12: 15; 13: 22; 20: 34; 26: 22; 32: 34; 33: 19; 1 Chron. 29: 29.

1 Chron. 9: 1; 16: 11; 20: 34; 25: 26; 27: 7; 28: 26; 32: 32; 33: 18; 35: 27; 36: 8.
1 Chron. 23: 27; 27: 24.
2 Chron. 35: 25.
2 Chron. 24: 27.
2 Chron. 30: 22 ff., *cf.* 1 Kings 22: 43; 24: 2, *cf.* 2 Kings 12: 3; 25: 1–4, *cf.* 2 Kings 14: 2 f., 5 f.; 1 Chron. 14: 3–7, *cf.* 2 Sam. 15: 13–16; 20: 1, *cf.* 2 Sam. 11: 1.
1 Chron. 5: 17.
1 Chron. 16: 8–36, *cf.* Pss. 105: 1–15; 96: 1–13; 106: 1, 47 f.

already in existence both within and outside of the Old Testament writings, and notice his frequent references to such sources, viz.: (1) a series of prophetic narratives,[3] (*a*) the "words of Nathan, the prophet;" (*b*) the "prophecy of Ahijah, the Shilonite;" (*c*) the "visions of Iddo, the seer;" (*d*) the "words of Iddo, the seer;" (*e*) the "midrash of the prophet Iddo;" (*f*) the "words of Shemaiah, the prophet;" (*g*) the "words of Jehu, the son of Hanani;" (*h*) "the rest of the acts of Uzziah, first and last, did Isaiah the prophet, the son of Amoz, write;" (*i*) the "vision of Isaiah, the prophet, the son of Amoz;" (*j*) the "words of Hozai;" (*k*) the "words of Samuel, the seer, and of Gad, the seer;" (2) a set of court records, variously cited as (*a*) "the book of the kings of Israel;" (*b*) "the book of the kings of Judah and Israel;" (*c*) "the book of the kings of Israel and Judah;" (*d*) "the affairs of the kings of Israel;" (3) a similar record of the reign of David; (4) a collection of lamentations; (5) "the midrash of the book of the kings," which is perhaps identical with the "book of the kings" cited under (2); (6) the canonical books of Samuel and Kings must have been known to the chronicler, and many passages indicate a close relationship between the two; (7) ancient genealogical lists; (8) collections of psalms.

In connection with an investigation of the sources, the following general questions are to be considered: Did the chronicler use any sources other than those used by the compiler of Samuel and Kings? Is the relationship between Chronicles, on the one hand, and Samuel and Kings, on the other, to be explained as due to (*a*) direct borrowing of the former from the latter, or to (*b*) the use of the same sources by both, or to (*c*) the use by the chronicler of a work based upon the canonical books of Samuel and Kings? What is the significance of the name "midrash" applied to two of the above-mentioned sources? How much material, if any, did the chronicler himself contribute?

[3] It is probable, however, that these existed only as a part of the more comprehensive work cited under (2).

On the sources of Chronicles see, *e. g.*, BARNES, *op. cit.*, pp. xviii–xxi; FR. BROWN, *op. cit.*, pp. 394 f.; DRIVER, *Introduction, etc.*, pp 519 ff.; W. R. SMITH AND DRIVER, *Encyclopædia Biblica*, Vol. I, coll. 766 ff.; BENZINGER, *Die Bücher der Chronik*, pp. x ff.; KUENEN, *Einleitung u. s. w.*, §§ 28–32; KITTEL, *History of the Hebrews*, Vol. II, pp. 244–30.

§ 222. **The Chronicler's Treatment of His Sources.**—This is most easily seen by means of a comparison between Chronicles on the one hand and Samuel and Kings on the other. (1) Note that some material appears in both works in almost exactly the same form. Consider the character of this material, (*a*) with reference to its fitness for the chronicler's purpose, (*b*) as conveying ideas that were in keeping with those represented by the chronicler (*cf.* § 227). (2) Note the presence of some material not found in Samuel and Kings. Consider (*a*) the reason for its incorporation by the chronicler, (*b*) the source whence it was derived, (*c*) the question of its historical credibility. (3) Note the absence from Chronicles of some material found in Samuel and Kings. Consider the reason for its rejection by the chronicler as bearing on the question of the purpose of the latter. (4) Note that there are many cases in which the chronicler modifies the material in Samuel and Kings in some degree, sometimes condensing a narrative greatly, sometimes expanding; at other times changing the significance of an event, or magnifying the size of an army, or disregarding historical fact. Consider, with reference to such cases, whether the divergence is to be explained (*a*) as due to the greater faithfulness of one or the other compiler to the source whence the material was taken; or (*b*) as demanded by the chronicler's more advanced conception of God; or (*c*) as an outgrowth of the chronicler's idea of the temple and the cultus; or (*d*) as a result of the different historical circumstances and influences amid which the chronicler lived, as compared with the times in which Samuel and Kings were edited; or (*e*) as due to other historical or theological influences.

1 Chron. 10: 1–12 (*cf.* 1 Sam. 31: 1–13); 11: 1–9 (*cf.* 2 Sam. 5: 1–3, 6–10); 14: 1–16 (*cf.* 2 Sam. 5: 11–25); chap. 17 (*cf.* 2 Sam., chap. 7); 2 Chron. 1: 14–17 (*cf.* 1 Kings 10: 26–29); 9: 29—10: 19 (*cf.* 1 Kings 11: 41—12: 19); etc.

1 Chron. 10: 13 f.; 14: 17; chaps. 22–29; 2 Chron. 14: 9–15; 24: 20–22; 33: 10–13; etc.

2 Sam. 5: 4 f.; 11: 2—12: 23; 13: 1—14: 33; 1 Kings. chaps. 17, 18, 19; 2 Kings 3: 1—8: 15; chap. 10; etc.

1 Chron. 13: 15 f. (*cf.* 2 Sam., chap. 6); 2 Chron. 5: 4 (*cf.* 1 Kings 8: 3); chap. 23 (*cf.* 2 Kings, chap. 11); chap. 20 (*cf.* 2 Kings, chap. 3); 12: 2*b*–8 (*cf.* 1 Kings 14: 25 f.), 14: 5 and 17: 6 (*cf.* 1 Kings 15: 14; 22: 43); 3: 1–13 (*cf.* 1 Kings 6: 1–3, 15–35); 8: 12–16 (*cf.* 1 Kings 9: 25); 14: 3–5 (*cf.* 1 Kings 15: 12); 16: 12–14 (*cf.* 1 Kings 15: 23*b*–24*a*); 28: 5–15 (*cf.* 2 Kings 16: 5); 29: 3—31: 21 (*cf.* 2 Kings 18: 4–7*a*); 32: 24–33 (*cf.* 2 Kings, chap. 20); 36: 9 f. (*cf* 2 Kings 24: 8–17).

§ 223. **The Chronicler's Use of Genealogies.**—Chronicles resembles P in its abundant use of genealogical

1 Chron., chaps. 1–9. lists. Note (1) that the period from Adam to the death of Saul is merely outlined by a series of genealogies; 1 Chron., chaps. 23–27. (2) the genealogical character of much of the material in the narrative of David's preparations for the building 2 Chron. 29:12–14; 31:11–19. and care of the temple; (3) the emphasis placed upon genealogies of the priests and Levites. How is this use of genealogies to be explained? Why is so much care taken in tracing the descent of priests and Levites? Was there any connection between this and the later Hebrew law, which was very stringent in prohibiting the participation of foreigners and non-Levites in the conduct of the temple worship? Whence may we suppose that the chronicler secured these long lists of names? May they be depended upon as historically accurate?

§ 224. **The Chronological and Statistical Character of** 1 Chron. 12:23–37; 29:1–9; 2 Chron. 2:17 f.; 15:11; 17:11, 14–19; 25:5 f.; 26:11 ff.; 27:6; 29:17, 21, 32 f.; 30:24; 34:3. **Chronicles.**—Note that, in addition to statistics given in the narrative of Samuel and Kings, Chronicles states the number of the Israelites who came to make David king in Hebron; the value of the offerings made in David's last days for the building of the temple; the number of "strangers" pressed into the work of building the temple; the number of oxen and sheep sacrificed in one day in the third month of the fifteenth year of Asa; the number of sheep and goats brought to Jehoshaphat as tribute by the Arabians; the number of soldiers in Jehoshaphat's standing army; the number of the warriors of Judah led forth by Amaziah to battle against Edom in the valley of Salt; the size of Uzziah's standing army; the number of Judah's warriors slain by Pekah of Israel; the exact date of the cleansing of the temple in Hezekiah's reign; the number of sheep, oxen, and goats sacrificed in connection with this occasion; the dates of Josiah's first steps toward religious reform; and other similar data. (1) Can any principle, or principles, be discovered which will account for part or all of this statistical information? or (2) is it merely a characteristic of the chronicler's literary style? (3) What is the bearing on this question of the fact that there are divergencies between Chronicles and Kings in many cases where they give figures for the same event? (*Cf.* § 222, (4).)

§ 225. **The Literary Style of Chronicles.**—Consisting, as it does, in large part of excerpts from earlier sources which have been edited and supplemented by the editor of Chronicles, may we expect to find the unity of style that is manifest in a work that comes from one hand? Examine lists of the peculiarities of vocabulary and syntax in Chronicles[4] and read large portions of the book with a view to determining (*a*) the style of the chronicler as distinguished from that of the sources he uses; (*b*) the style of the chronicler as compared with that of the prophetic narratives in J, E, Judges, Samuel, and Kings, on the one hand, and with that of P, on the other. Is the style seen to be involved, stiff, prosaic, repetitious?

§ 226. **The Chronicler's Selection of Material.**—If it was not the aim of the chronicler to write a history, but to use history in such a way as to illustrate and enforce great ideas which he wished to present, should we not expect to find that he selects and arranges his material with a view to his purpose? Note that (1) he passes over the history of northern Israel in silence, except in a few places where the intimate relation of the two kingdoms compels him to mention Israel; why? (2) that he fails to mention the sins of David, Solomon, Hezekiah, and others who were interested in supporting the temple and its worship; why? (3) that he emphasizes the activities of these kings in behalf of the temple and priesthood to such an extent as to make them appear more like priests than kings; why? (4) that he assigns the priests an essential part in the battle-array; why? (5) that the religious institutions are given an exceedingly large place as compared with the books of Samuel and Kings. What light do these and other similar facts shed upon the nature of the purpose of Chronicles? Is it not a *church* history rather than a history of the nation?

2 Chron., chap. 10; 11:1-4; chap. 13; 16:1-6; chap. 18; 20:35-37; 22:5-9; 25:6-10, 17-24; 28:5-15; etc.

1 Chron., chaps. 15-17; 21:18—29:22; 2 Chron. chaps. 1-7; 17:1-9; 19:4-11; 24:4-16; chaps 29-31; 34:1—35:19; etc.

1 Chron. 13:12.

1 Chron. 6:1-81; 9:10-34; chaps. 23-26; 2 Chron 35:1-19 (*cf.* 2 Kings 23:21 ff.); chaps. 29-31 (*cf.* 2 Kings 18:4).

§ 227. **The Religion of the Chronicler.**— Note (1) that the Priestly Code serves as the standard in all

2 Chron. 13:10; 15:2-15; 8:12 f.; 13:9-11; 26:16-21; 29:12-36; etc.

[4] See, *e. g.*, DRIVER, *Introduction, etc.*, pp. 535-40; FR. BROWN, HASTINGS'S *Dictionary of the Bible*, Vol. I, pp. 389 ff.

1 Chron. 21:5; 2 Chron. 17:14–19; 25:5; 26:11 ff.; 11:1.
2 Chron. 27:6; 33:11–13; 31:21; 13:11; 17:4 f.; 26:5.
1 Chron. 10:13 f.; 2 Chron. 25:20; 24:24 f.; 28:5 ff., 19; 26:16 ff.; 21:12 ff.
2 Chron. 13:15, 18; 26:5; 16:7, 12.
1 Chron. 28:9; 2 Chron. 14:11; 5:22, 26; 16:9.
2 Chron. 30:9, 18 f.
2 Chron. 30:19.

matters of ritual and worship; (2) that the most religious kings are represented as the mightiest, David having more than a million and a half of soldiers, Jehoshaphat over a million, Asa more than half a million, Amaziah and Uzziah only 300,000, Rehoboam only 180,000; (3) that prosperity is declared to be due to faithfulness to Jehovah and his worship as conducted at the temple; (4) that disaster is declared to be due to sin in abandoning Jehovah or his worship; (5) that Jehovah is the only and all-sufficient source of help and deliverance; (6) that Jehovah is omnipotent and omniscient; (7) that Jehovah is merciful and good, ever ready to pardon the penitent; (8) that, though great emphasis is laid upon ritual, the spirit of an act is recognized as more important than the form.

2 Chron., chaps. 23–28; 2 Chron., chaps. 3, 4.
1 Chron. 14:17; 2 Chron. 1:14–17; 17:10–19; 32:23, 27–31.
See, *e.g.*, 1 Chron., chaps. 13, 15, 16, 17; 21:18–29:22.
2 Chron. 7:5; 13:3; 17:10–19; 25:11–13; 27:6, 8; etc.
2 Chron. 8:2; 21:12 (*cf.* 2 Kings 3:11; 8:16).

§ 228. **The Idealistic Character of Chronicles.**— Recall (1) that there is silence as to the great sins of David and other religious leaders (see § 222 (3)); (2) that the Mosaic system as it existed in the chronicler's day is represented as in full operation in the times of David and Solomon; (3) that the splendor and power of the kingdom in the days of David, Solomon, Jehoshaphat, Hezekiah, and others are rather a reflection of the greatness of the Persian empire, with which the chronicler was familiar, than a representation of the actual state of affairs; (4) that a disproportionate prominence is given to matters of temple and ritual in the early days of the kingdom; (5) that there is a tendency to use extraordinarily large numbers in calculations and estimates; (6) that occasionally he changes the natural course of historical events, *e. g.*, representing Hiram of Tyre as giving cities to Solomon, though the book of Kings states that the cities were given to Hiram by Solomon in payment for assistance rendered by Hiram in the work of building the temple; and Elijah as writing a message to King Jehoram, although Elijah had been dead for some time. How may these things be most satisfactorily explained? Are they due merely to a lack of historical perspective? Can they be accounted for as necessary to the accomplishment of the chronicler's purpose? Is there a sense in which they represent a larger truth than could be imparted by a statement of bare fact? In other words, can these representations be regarded as ideally true, if not literally?

§ 229. **Literature to be Consulted.**

EWALD, *History of Israel* (1843, 3d ed. 1864, transl. 1883), Vol. I, pp. 169 ff.; C. F. KEIL, *The Books of Chronicles* (1870, transl. 1872); ZÖCKLER-MURPHY, *The Books of Chronicles* (LANGE'S "Commentary," 1874); W. R. SMITH, art. "Chronicles,' *Encyclopædia Britannica* (1876); WELLHAUSEN, *Prolegomena to the History of Israel* (1878, 5th ed. 1899, transl. 1885), pp. 171–227; W. R. SMITH, *Old Testament in the Jewish Church* (1881, 2d ed. 1892), pp. 140 ff., 182 ff.; BALL, *Chronicles* (ELLICOTT'S "Commentary for English Readers," 1883); WILDEBOER, *Origin of the Canon of the Old Testament* (1891, transl. 1895), see *Index;* S. R. DRIVER, *Introduction to the Literature of the Old Testament* (1891, 6th ed. 1897), pp. 516–40; KITTEL, *History of the Hebrews*, Vol. II (1892, transl. 1896), pp. 224–9; J. ROBERTSON, *Book by Book* (1892), pp. 111–19; JENNINGS, "Chronicles," *The Thinker*, July, Sept., Nov., 1892; RYLE, *Canon of the Old Testament* (1892), pp. 138 f., 145, 151, 162; MONTEFIORE, *The Religion of the Ancient Hebrews* ("Hibbert Lectures," 1892), pp. 447 ff., 454, 483; RENAN, *History of the People of Israel, from the Rule of the Persians to That of the Greeks* (1893, transl. 1895), pp. 151 ff.; W. H. BENNETT, *The Books of Chronicles* ("Expositor's Bible," 1894); GIRDLESTONE, *Deuterographs* (1894), *passim;* DRIVER, "The Speeches in Chronicles," *Expositor*, Apr. and Oct., 1895; G. B. GRAY, *Studies in Hebrew Proper Names* (1896), chap. iii; KAUTZSCH, *An Outline of the History of the Literature of the Old Testament* (1896, transl. 1899), pp. 121–8; W. E. BARNES, "The Religious Standpoint of the Chronicler," *American Journal of Semitic Languages and Literatures*, Vol. XIII (1896–97), pp. 14–20; IDEM, *An Apparatus Criticus to Chronicles in the Peshitta Version* (1897); IDEM, "Chronicles a Targum," *Expository Times*, Vol. VIII (1897), pp. 316 f.; CROCKETT, *A Harmony of Samuel, Kings, and Chronicles* (1897); FR. BROWN, art. "Chronicles," HASTINGS'S *Dictionary of the Bible*, Vol. I (1898); T. K. CHEYNE, *Jewish Religious Life after the Exile* (1898), see *Index;* T. G. SOARES, "The Import of the Chronicles as a Piece of Religio-Historical Literature," *American Journal of Theology*, Vol. III (1899), pp. 251–74; W. R. SMITH AND S. R. DRIVER, art. "Books of Chronicles," *Encyclopædia Biblica*, Vol. I (1899); C. F. KENT, *History of the Jewish People during the Babylonian, Persian, and Greek Periods* (1899), pp. 101 ff.; BARNES, *The Books of Chronicles* ("Cambridge Bible," 1899); BEECHER, "Is the Chronicler a Veracious Historian for the Post-Exilian Period?" *Bible Student*, Oct., 1899, Jan. and Feb., 1900; HOWLETT, "Wellhausen and the Chronicler," *Dublin Review*, Apr., 1900; MACMILLAN, "The Date of Chronicles," *Presbyterian and Reformed Review*, July, 1900; J. E. MCFADYEN, *The Messages of the Prophetic and Priestly Historians* (1901), pp. 270–85; R. SOMERVELL, "The Historical Character of the Old Testament Narratives," *Expository Times*, April, 1902, pp. 298–302.

DE WETTE, *Kritischer Versuch über die Glaubwürdigkeit d. Chron.* ("Beiträge," Vol. I (1806)); C. P. W. GRAMBERG, *Die Chronik nach ihrem geschichtlichen Charakter und ihrer Glaubwürdigkeit geprüft* (1823); C. F. KEIL, *Apologetischer Versuch über die Bücher der Chronik* (1833); MOVERS, *Kritische Untersuchungen über die bibl. Chron.* (1834); E. BERTHEAU, *Die Bücher der Chronik* ("Kurzgefasstes exegetisches Handbuch zum Alten Testament," 1854, 2d ed. 1873; 3d ed. by Ryssel, 1887);

KUENEN, *Historisch-kritisch Onderzoek* (1861, 2d ed. 1887), §§ 28–32; GRAF, *Die geschichtlichen Bücher des Alten Testaments* (1866), pp. 114–247; DE WETTE-SCHRADER, *Einleitung in das Alte Testament* (1869), §§ 224–33; WELLHAUSEN, *De gentibus et familiis Judaeis quae 1 Ch. 2—4 enumerantur* (1870); FRANZ DELITZSCH, "Die Formenreichtum der israelitischen Geschichtsliteratur," *Zeitschrift für lutherische Theologie und Kirche*, Vol. XXXVI (1870), pp. 31 ff.; L. DIESTEL, "Die hebräische Geschichtsschreibung," *Jahrbücher für deutsche Theologie*, Vol. XVIII (1873), pp. 365 ff.; OETTLI, *Die Bücher der Chronik* ("Kurzgefasster exegetischer Kommentar zum Alten Testament," 1889); RIEHM, *Einleitung in das Alte Testament*, Vol. II (1890), pp. 316–28; CORNILL, *Einleitung in das Alte Testament* (1891, 2d ed. 1896), § 46; BUDDE, "Vermutungen zum 'Midrasch' des Buches der Könige," *Zeitschrift für die alttest. Wissenschaft*, Vol. XII (1892), pp. 37 ff.; H. WINCKLER, *Alttestamentliche Untersuchungen* (1892), pp. 157–67 (= "Bemerkungen zur Chronik als Geschichtsquelle"); KÖNIG, *Einleitung in das Alte Testament* (1893), pp. 269–76; WILDEBOER, *De Letterkunde des Ouden Verbonds naar de Tijdsorde van haar Ontstaan* (1893; German transl. 1895), pp. 404–20; KLOSTERMANN, art. "Chronik," *Realencyklopädie für prot. Theologie und Kirche*, Vol. IV (3d ed. 1898); BENZINGER, *Die Bücher der Chronik* ("Kurzer Hand-Commentar zum Alten Testament" (1901); BAUDISSIN, *Einleitung in die Bücher des Alten Testamentes* (1901), pp. 266–78; ROTHSTEIN, *Die Genealogie des Königs Jojachim und seiner Nachkommen (1 Chron. 3:17–24) in geschichtlicher Beleuchtung* (1902).

§ 230. **Constructive Work.**

1. Make a minute comparison of 2 Chron. 2:1—9:31 with 1 Kings 5:1—11:43, and (1) classify the variations which are found; (2) explain the motive which may have led to the making of the change.

2. Make a similar comparison of the psalms found in 1 Chron. 16:8–36 with the form of these same psalms as they occur in the Psalter, viz., Pss. 105:1–15; 96:1–13; 106:1, 47 f.

3. Study the classification of the sources of Chronicles as presented by Driver, viz.: (1) the canonical books from Genesis to Kings; (2) the "book of the kings of Israel and Judah," which included the prophetic writings referred to in 2 Chron. 20:34; 32:32; 33:19, and possibly those mentioned in 1 Chron. 29:29; 2 Chron. 9:29; 12:15; (3) the "acts of Uzziah," 2 Chron. 26:22; (4) the "midrash of the prophet Iddo," 2 Chron. 13:22; and (5) the "midrash of the book of the kings" (2 Chron. 24:27), unless this be identical with (2).

4. Study the classification of sources as given by Kautzsch, viz.: (1) excerpts from canonical books of Samuel and Kings: 1 Chron., chaps. 1–9; 10:1–12; 11:1–9; 14:1–17; 16:43—17:27; 2 Chron. 1:13—3:1; 5:2–10; 5:13*b*—6:12; 6:14–39; 7:4, 5, 7, 8; 7:17—8:1; 8:6–11*a*; 9:1–28; 9:30—11:4; 12:2*a*, 9*b*–11, 13*b*; 12:15*b*—13:2; 13:23*a*; 15:16–18; 18:3–34; 21:1; 24:1–2*a*; 24:27*b*—25:4; 25:17–20*a*, 21–26; 25:27*b*—26:4; 27:1–2*a*, 3*a*; 28:1–2*a*, 3, 4; 29:1, 2; 32:33*d*—33:9; 34:1, 2; (2) similar excerpts which were edited by the

chronicler: 1 Chron. 13:1–14; 15:25–29; 18:1—21:27; 2 Chron. 1:7–12; 3:2—5:1; 7:11–16; 8:17 f.; 16:1*b*–6; 20:31–33*a*; 21:5–10*a*; 24:4–14; 26:21–23; 27:7–9; 32:9–21; 32:24; 33:20–25; 34:8–32*a*; 35:18 f., 20*b*; 35:26—36:6*a*; 36:8*b*–12*a*; (3) contributions of the chronicler himself and older sources which were thoroughly worked over by him into conformity with his own point of view: 1 Chron. 10:13 f.; 11:10—12:40; 15:1–24; 16:1–42; 21:28—29:30; 2 Chron. 1:1–6; 5:11–13*a*; 6:13; 6:40—7:3; 7:6, 9 f.; 8:2–5, 11*b*–16; 9:29; 11:5—12:1; 12:2*b*–9*a*, 12, 13*a*, 14, 15*a*; 13:3–22; 13:23*b*—15:15; 15:19—16:1*a*; 16:7—18:2; 19:1—20:30; 20:33*b*–37; 21:2–4; 21:10*b*—23:21; 24:2*b*, 3, 15–27*a*; 25:5–16, 20*b*, 27*a*; 26:5–20; 27:2*b*, 3*b*–6; 28:2*b*, 5–25; 29:3—32:8; 32:22 f., 25–33*c*; 33:10–19; 34:3–7; 34:32*b*—35:17; 35:20*a*, 21–25; 36:6*b*–8*a*, 12*b*–23.

5. Prepare an outline statement in which you will embody the principal propositions (perhaps six or eight) which seem to hold good concerning the contents, style, date, and character of the books of Chronicles.

§ 231. **Supplementary Topics.**

1. Take up the question of *genealogies in the Old Testament*, and consider (1) the extent to which they appear; (2) the form in which they are given; (3) the purpose, in each case, of the insertion; (4) the accuracy of the representation; (5) similar usage in other Semitic literatures, especially Arabic.

See, *e. g.*, E. L. CURTIS, article "Genealogy," HASTINGS'S *Dictionary of the Bible;* W. R. SMITH, *Kinship and Marriage in Early Arabia*, chap. i; S. A. COOK, article "Genealogies," *Encyc. Biblica;* GUTHE, *Geschichte des Volkes Israel*, pp. 2–6; WELLHAUSEN, *De gentibus et familiis Judaeis quae 1 Ch. 2–4 enumerantur;* M. BERLIN, "Gershonite and Merarite Genealogies," *Jewish Quarterly Review*, Vol. XII (1900), pp. 291 ff.; MCLENNAN, *Studies in Ancient History*, 2d series, chap. 9 (= "Examples of Fabricated Genealogies"); G. B. GRAY, *Studies in Hebrew Proper Names*, chap. iii; SMEND, *Die Listen der Bücher Esra und Nehemia.*

2. Consider the question of *numbers in Chronicles*, including (1) the variations between Chronicles and the prophetic histories of Samuel and Kings; (2) the motive for insertion; (3) the method of representation; (4) the general accuracy.

See, *e. g.*, FRANCIS BROWN, article "Chronicles," HASTINGS'S *Dictionary of the Bible*, Vol. I, p. 394; T. G. SOARES, *American Journal of Theology*, Vol. III, pp. 264 f.; BENZINGER, *Chronik*, p. ix.

3. Take up for study the *lost books* of Scripture which are cited in Chronicles, and in connection with these (1) other lost books cited elsewhere in Scripture, *e. g.*, the book of Jashar; (2) the character, in general, of these books; (3) the relation of these books to the canonical books.

CHAPTER XVII.

HISTORICAL LITERATURE—THE BOOKS OF EZRA AND NEHEMIAH.

§232. **The Scope of the History in Ezra-Nehemiah.**—
Ezra 1:1-4. Note that the narrative in these books (1) begins with the decree of Cyrus permitting the exiled Jews to return
Neh. 13:6-30. from Babylon; (2) closes with an account of the activities of Nehemiah during his second visit to Jerusalem; (3) covers a period, therefore, of about one hundred years; and (4) that comparatively few of the events and movements belonging to this period are treated in the history, much being passed over in silence.

Ezra 1:5-11; 2:1-70. Observe the order of presentation: (1) The account of the return gives the decree of Cyrus, a statement about the gifts sent to the temple, and a long list of the names of the returning exiles; nothing being said of the journey
Ezra 3:1—4:24. itself. Then follows (2) the account of the building of an altar to Jehovah and of the attempt to rebuild the temple; with (3) the story of the successful opposition
Ezra 5:1—6:22. of the enemies of the Jews. (4) The next section describes (*a*) the renewed effort to build the temple, under the leadership of Haggai and Zechariah; (*b*) the renewed opposition on the part of the enemy and the resulting correspondence with Darius; (*c*) the completion of the work, and the festivities connected with the
Ezra 7:1—8:36. dedication of the restored temple. Then (5), passing over in silence a period of about sixty years, the historian gives the story of Ezra's visit to Jerusalem, including the letter of authority given to him by Artaxerxes, a list of the names of all who accompanied Ezra, and a list of the presents sent up from Babylon for the temple. (6)
Ezra 9:1—10:44. The last section of the book of Ezra deals with Ezra's efforts to put a stop to the marriages of Jews with foreigners, and gives much space to Ezra's prayer in reference to this subject, and to a list of the names of those who had married foreign wives.

Notice that the book of Nehemiah (1) opens with **Neh. 1:1—2:8.**
the account of Nehemiah's purpose to visit Jerusalem,
and his success in securing the sanction and the support
of Artaxerxes the king. Then follows (2) the narrative of **Neh. 2:9-20.**
Nehemiah's arrival at Jerusalem, his tour of inspection
made under cover of darkness, and his success in arousing
the citizens to repair the walls of the city. (3) At this point **Neh. 3:1-32.**
is inserted a list of those who engaged in the work, with
careful indication of the special portion performed by each
family or group; together with a description of the efforts
of the Samaritans to hinder the work and the measures **Neh. 4:1-23.**
taken by Nehemiah to bring the plans of the Samaritans
to nought. Thereupon (4) comes a digression con- **Neh. 5:1-19.**
cerning Nehemiah's championship of the cause of the
oppressed debtors among the Jews, and his own policy of
refraining from levying upon the people for his support
as former governors had done. (5) The story of the **Neh. 6:1—7:4.**
building of the walls is then continued by a recital of
various conspiracies made by the Samaritans against the
life and the influence of Nehemiah until the work of
building was completed and the city was properly
guarded. (6) A list of those who had returned from **Neh. 7:5-73; *cf.* Ezra 2:1-70.**
exile is next included, this list being a duplicate of one
given in Ezra. Upon this list follows (7) the account of **Neh. 8:1—9:38.**
Ezra's introduction of the law and of its adoption by
the people in public assembly. Then comes (8) a list **Neh. 10:1-27; 10:28-39.**
of those who signed the new covenant and an account of
the terms of the covenant itself, with still other lists of **Neh. 11:1—12:26.**
names. (9) A description of the ceremonies in connec- **Neh. 12:27-43.**
tion with the dedication of the wall is then given. (10)
To this are subjoined brief statements concerning the **Neh. 12:44—13:3.**
provision made by Nehemiah for the support of the tem-
ple ministry and concerning the expulsion of foreigners.
The narrative closes (11) with the reforms in the inter- **Neh. 13:4-31.**
ests of the temple and its ministry, sabbath observance,
and the prohibition of mixed marriages, carried through
by Nehemiah after his return from a visit to Babylon.

§ 233. **Constructive Work.**— Prepare a statement, based upon a study of the foregoing outline of the books of Ezra and Nehemiah, concerning the purpose of these narratives, as it appears (*a*) in the kind of matter selected for treatment; (*b*) in the relative amount of prominence given to the various subjects; (*c*) in the places assigned respectively to Ezra and to Nehemiah.

§ 234. **The Unity of the Books of Ezra-Nehemiah.**—Consider the following facts: (1) Some most ancient Jewish and early Christian writers speak of the book of Ezra in such a way as to indicate that they include with it the present book of Nehemiah.[1] (2) The old Jewish commentators, *e. g.*, Rashi and Aben Ezra, pass from Ezra 10:44 to Neh. 1:1 without any break such as is customary in passing from one book to another. (3) The Massoretic notes attached to each book in the Hebrew Bible are not found at the close of Ezra, but do appear at the end of Nehemiah, and there give facts showing that the Massoretes regarded Ezra-Nehemiah as one book; *e. g.*, they declare Neh. 3:12 to be the middle verse of this book. (4) The sections into which the Hebrew text was divided by the Massoretes for use in the synagogue service show that they thought of Ezra-Nehemiah as a single book, one section being Ezra 8:35—Neh. 2:1. (5) The two books are united in the Septuagint translation.

§ 235. **Constructive Work.**—In the light of these facts, and the additional fact that the two books treat the same period, are concerned with the same general problems, and furnish much evidence pointing to their having been edited by the same hand, formulate an extended answer to the question: Shall we consider the books of Ezra and Nehemiah, now treated separately, as a single literary production?

See especially RYLE, *Ezra and Nehemiah* ("Cambridge Bible"), pp. i–xiii.

§ 236. **The Unity of Chronicles and Ezra-Nehemiah.**—

2 Chron. 36:22 f.; *cf.* Ezra 1:1–3. What is the significance of the following facts? (1) The closing verses of Chronicles are repeated at the opening of the book of Ezra. (2) Both works are compilations from various sources (see §§ 221, 228). (3) Both give especial prominence to genealogical lists (see §§ 223; 230, (1)). (4) The two works greatly resemble each other in general literary style and in their vocabulary (see §§ 225; 230, (4)). (5) The two exhibit the same absorbing interest in matters relating to the temple and

[1] So, *e. g.*, Talmud, *Baba bathra*, folio 14, c. 2; Melito, bishop of Sardis (*ca.* 180 A. D.), cited in EUSEBIUS, *Hist. Eccles.*, IV, 26.

its service; *e. g.*, (*a*) great prominence is given to the Levites, who are mentioned more than sixty times in Ezra-Nehemiah and about one hundred times in Chronicles; (*b*) in both the musical service is emphasized; (*c*) in both prayer is highly esteemed, and hence is frequently placed in the mouths of Israel's great leaders; (*d*) religious festivals and ceremonies are described in detail by both; (*e*) the porters are mentioned as a part of the temple staff nowhere except in Ezra-Nehemiah and Chronicles, in which books they are often so spoken of; (*f*) the Nethinim, mentioned frequently in Ezra-Nehemiah, are mentioned in no other book except Chronicles; (6) Ezra-Nehemiah and Chronicles come from the same period (see §§ 220, 227); (7) Ezra-Nehemiah takes up the history at the point where it stops in Chronicles and continues it until the building of the second temple is narrated, the two books, Chronicles and Ezra-Nehemiah, thus constituting a history of the temple and its worship from the time of the building of Solomon's temple until the restoration of worship in the days of Ezra and Nehemiah.

Ezra 3:8–12; Neh. 8:7–13; *cf.* Chron.

Ezra 3:10 f.; Neh. 12:27, 36, 46; *cf.* Chron.

Ezra 9:6–15; Neh. 1:4; 4:9; *cf.* Chron.

Ezra 6:19–22, Neh. 12:27–43, *cf.* 2 Chron., 5:1—7:10.

Ezra 2:42; Neh. 12:25, 45, 47; *cf.* Chron.

Ezra 7:7; 8:17; Neh. 3:26; 10:28; *cf.* 1 Chron. 9:2.

See, *e. g.*, RYLE, *Ezra and Nehemiah*, pp. xxvi ff.; REUSS, *Das Alte Testament*, pp. 8 ff.; KÖNIG, *Einleitung in das Alte Testament*, p. 285; DRIVER, *Introduction, etc.*, pp. 516 f.; SAYCE, *Introduction to Ezra, Nehemiah and Esther*, pp. 29 f.; *cf. Higher Criticism and the Verdict of the Monuments*, pp. 537 f., 548.

§ 237. **Constructive Work.**—Prepare a statement discussing the explanation of these facts, whether (1) by the supposition that the two editors, working in the same period and upon the same subjects and with the same interests, used the same methods and arrived at similar results; or (2) by the supposition that the two books are really one, being the product of the same editor's labors.

§ 238. **The Date of Ezra-Nehemiah** (*cf.* § 220).—Note (1) the use of the expression "the days of Nehemiah;" does the writer not seem to regard these days as long past? (2) the use of the title "king of Persia," in view of the fact that contemporary sources when speaking of Persian monarchs use simply "the king;" does not this suggest that the Persian dominion was a thing of the past in the writer's time? the words "of Persia" would be superfluous while the Persian empire was supreme,

Neh. 12:26, 47.

Ezra 1:1 f., 8; 3:7; 4:3, 5, 7, 24; 6:14; 7:1.

Hag. 1:1, 15; Zech. 7:1; Ezra 7:27 f.; 8:1, 22, 25, 36; Neh. 1:11; 2:1 ff.; 5:4, 14; 6:7; 13:6.

Neh. 12:10 f., 22; *cf.* 13:4, 28; Josephus, *Antiquities*, XI, vii, 8. but entirely appropriate after its overthrow; (3) the reference to Jaddua, the high-priest, who lived three generations later than Eliashib, the contemporary of Nehemiah; this points to a time as late as the days of Alexander the Great for Jaddua, and the phrase "the days of Jaddua," would seem to indicate that the
Neh. 12:22. priesthood of Jaddua was now long past; (4) the reference to "the reign of Darius, the Persian," as a period some time past; it is generally agreed that the king referred to is Darius Codomannus, 336–332 B. C.; (5)
Neh. 12:23. the reference to "the book of the chronicles" which is said to have contained the register of the Levites as far down as the high-priesthood of Johanan, the son of
Ezra 4:6–23; 7:1–10; etc. Eliashib; (6) the treatment of the sources, which is such as no contemporary historian would have ventured (*cf.* § 229).

§ 239. **Constructive Work.**—Discuss the significance of the preceding facts; and determine whether they point (1) to the work of a later editor, who inserted all these allusions to late history in a book that had been written at an earlier period, or (2) to the probability that the book as a whole was not compiled and edited until a time somewhere about 300 B. C.

See, *e. g.*, RYLE, *Ezra and Nehemiah*, pp. xxiii ff.; DRIVER, *Introduction, etc.*, p. 545; BAUDISSIN, *Einleitung in die Bücher des Alten Testamentes*, pp. 266 ff.

§ 240. **The Sources of Ezra-Nehemiah.**—In support of the position that Ezra-Nehemiah is the work of an editor who compiled largely from existing sources, consider (1)
Ezra 2:1; 5:1; 7:1; 9:1; Neh. 1:1; 7:73*b*; 12:27; 13:4. the many cases of abrupt transition from one topic or incident to another, an abruptness which is natural in a work made up of extracts from older works placed side by side, but hard to account for in a work all of which originated from the same hand; (2) the frequent change from the third to the first person, and *vice versa*, in closely related sections of the work, without any indication of
Ezra 4:8—6:18; 7:12–26. reason for the change; (3) the presence of two large sections written in Aramaic, without any apparent reason for
Neh. 7:6–73; 11:3–36; 12:1–26. the change of speech; (4) the presence of lists of names which have no close connection with the context to
Ezra 2:2; 3:2; 4:5, 6; 6:15; Neh. 12:22, 32. which they belong; (5) the use of important names in such a way as to imply that they had occurred in some

previous context from which they are now severed; (6) the marked differences in style and language appearing in various parts of the narrative; (7) the fact that all the other historical books of the Old Testament are compilations; for the book of Chronicles especially see § 221; (8) the allusion to the "books of the chronicles," apparently a temple-register from which the editor obtained some materials. **Neh. 12:23.**

As materials which the editor seems to have derived from earlier sources may be noted (1) the decree of Cyrus permitting the exiles to return home; (2) the Aramaic sections containing (*a*) the letter sent by the Jews' enemies to Artaxerxes; (*b*) the king's reply; (*c*) the account of the building of the temple in the days of Haggai and Zechariah, with certain letters that passed between Jerusalem and Babylon with reference to it; (*d*) the firman of Artaxerxes endowing Ezra with such authority as he desired; (3) various lists, including (*a*) the vessels of the temple; (*b*) the Jews who came back from exile with Zerubbabel; (*c*) the men who married foreign wives; (*d*) the builders of the wall; (*e*) the signers of the covenant; (*f*) the dwellers in Jerusalem and in other cities; (*g*) the priests and Levites; (4) the account of the adoption of the law and the new covenant in the time of Nehemiah; (5) certain portions of the narrative which use the first person and seem to have belonged to the memoirs of Ezra; (6) similar sections which seem to have been taken from the memoirs of Nehemiah. **Ezra 1:1-4. Ezra 4:7-16; 4:17-24; 5:1—6:18; 7:12-26. Ezra 1:9-11; Ezra 2:1-70 and Neh. 7:6-73; Ezra 10:20-44; Neh., chap. 3; 10:1-27; 11:3-36; 12:1-26. Neh. 7:73*b*—10:39. Ezra 7:27—8:34; 9:1-15. Neh., chaps. 1-6; 7:1-73*a*; 12:27-43; 13:4-31.**

§ 241. **The Treatment of the Sources in Ezra-Nehemiah.**—Consider (1) the form of the decree of Cyrus with reference to the return of the exiles as it is given in two different places in Ezra, and note the differences in phraseology and contents; is it probable that there were two copies of the decree in existence differing so much as these, or is it more natural to ascribe the variations to the hand of the editor? (2) the fact that a large section of Nehemiah appears to belong to the memoirs of Ezra, being closely connected with them in the period with which they deal, in tone, and in phraseology; (3) the fact that the opposition of the Samaritans to the Jewish **Ezra 1:2 ff.; *cf.* 6:3 ff. Neh., chaps. 8-10; *cf.* Ezra, chaps. 7-10. Ezra, chaps. 4-6; Neh., chaps. 4, 6.**

Ezra 2:1—3:1*a*; *cf.* Neh. 7:6–73.

community is all crowded together at the beginning of the narrative, though, as a matter of fact, the dates given show that this opposition extended over a period of about eighty years and grew more and more bitter; (4) the fact that there are more than one hundred variations in two copies of the same genealogical list, and, in particular, that the numbers differ oftener than they agree.

Neh. 13:25; *cf.* Ezra, chap. 10.

Ezra 9:9.

Consider further (5) the evidence pointing to the conclusion that Ezra's expedition really *followed* that of Nehemiah instead of preceding it, as the editor's narrative reads; *e. g.*, (*a*) Nehemiah's memoirs make no allusion to any previous work of Ezra; (*b*) those who came back with Ezra seem to have taken no part in the rebuilding of the walls, as they certainly would have done had they been present; (*c*) Ezra's measures, especially with reference to intermarriage, all seem more decisive than those of Nehemiah, which have the appearance of being tentative; (*d*) the fact that, according to the editor's narrative, Ezra's law was not promulgated until after the arrival of Nehemiah, and that no explanation of this long delay is offered by the editor; (*e*) the fact that Ezra gives thanks to Jehovah that the walls have been rebuilt at a time when Nehemiah, the builder of the walls, had not yet appeared on the scene, according to the editor's narrative. What motive could have led to such a rearrangement of the documentary sources? Is it sufficient to say that it was for the purpose of giving Ezra, the priest, precedence over Nehemiah, the layman?

Ezra, chap. 2; 8:1–20; 10:18–44; Neh. 3:1–32; 7:8–65; 10:1–27; 11:3—12:26.

Ezra 1:10 f.; 2:64–69; 6:16–18; 7:22; 8:26 ff., 35; Neh. 5:17, 18; 7:66–72.

Ezra 1:1; 3:1, 6, 8; 4:6 f., 24; 6:15; 7:1, 7–9; 8:31 ff.; 10:9, 16 f.; Neh. 1:1; 2:1, 11; 5:14; 6:15; 7:73; 8:2 f., 13, 17 f.; 9:1; 13:6.

§ 242. **The Style of Ezra-Nehemiah.**—As indicative of the editor's tastes and interests note (1) the large amount of *genealogical* material he incorporates into his narrative, giving lists of those who took part in the first return from exile, of those who helped build the wall, of those who dwelt in Jerusalem, etc., etc.; (2) the similar fondness for *statistical* statements, as evidenced in connection with the above lists and on every other possible occasion; (3) the numerous *chronological* data with which his work abounds. In connection with these characteristics, recall the similar features seen to have been characteristic of the books of Chronicles (see §§ 223, 224). Consider (4) the style of the editor's own contributions to the work as distinguished from the style of the sources used by him.

§ 243. **Constructive Work.**—Examine lists of phrases and words peculiar to the various sources, and read each source separately, as far as possible, in order that its literary style may impress itself upon your mind. Then treat the editor's own contribution in the same way, and compare its style with that of the editorial contributions to the books of Chronicles, with a view to the light that may be thrown by such a comparison upon the question of the unity of Chronicles, Ezra, and Nehemiah.

See, *e. g.*, RYLE, *Ezra and Nehemiah*, pp. xviii f., xxviii f.; DRIVER, *Introduction, etc.*, pp. 546 ff., 553; GEISSLER, *Die literarische Beziehungen der Esramemoiren, insbesondere zur Chronik und den hexateuchischen Quellenschriften* (1899).

§ 244. **The Religion of Ezra-Nehemiah.**—If Ezra-Nehemiah is the result of a compiler's work, the religious interests of the compiler must be looked for in three directions: (1) the nature of the subjects he selects for treatment; (2) the relative prominence given by him to various matters; (3) the religious tone of the material contributed by himself. In reference to (1) it may be noted that the subjects treated are all of a religious character, such matters as are not in themselves distinctively religious being given a religious interpretation, *e. g.*, the building of the walls and the movement against intermarriages with foreigners. As to (2) we may note the great prominence given to the temple and its affairs, the important place in the community assigned to priests and Levites, and the large amount of attention bestowed upon matters of ritual, descriptions of religious ceremonies, and the like. Concerning (3) we observe the priestly interest dominant in the editor's work, and that the Priestly Code serves as the standard in all matters of ritual and worship.

Neh. 12:27–43; Ezra, chaps. 9, 10.

Ezra 1:2–11; 2:68 ff.; chap. 3; Neh. 3:4–14; Ezra 6:16–22; Neh. 12:27–47; Ezra 2:40–63; 3:8–10, 12; 7:7, 11–13, 24; 8:15–20; 10:18 ff.; Neh. 12:1–26. Ezra 6:16–22; 7:1–10; 8:35 f.; Neh. 12:44–47; 13:1–3.

In general, is there any appreciable difference between the religious ideals and feelings of the editor of Ezra-Nehemiah and those of the Chronicler (*cf.* § 227)? If not, is not this a strong indication of the unity of Ezra-Nehemiah and Chronicles?

§ 245. **Literature to be Consulted.**

F. W. SCHULZ, *Ezra, Nehemiah and Esther* (LANGE'S "Commentary on the Holy Scriptures," 1876, transl. 1877); EWALD, *History of Israel*, Vol. I (1843, 3d ed.

1864, transl. 1883), pp. 169–96; KEIL, *Commentary on the Books of Ezra, Nehemiah and Esther* (1870, transl. 1879); D. H. HAIGH, "Coincidence of the History of Ezra with the First Part of the History of Nehemiah," *Transactions of the Society of Biblical Archæology*, Vol. II (1873), pp. 110–13; J. S. BLACK, articles on "Ezra" and "Books of Ezra and Nehemiah," *Encyclopædia Britannica*, Vol. VIII (1878); W. R. SMITH, *The Old Testament in the Jewish Church* (1881, 2d ed. 1892), pp. 42 f.; GEO. RAWLINSON, *Ezra and Nehemiah* ("Pulpit Commentary," 1881); KUENEN, *National Religions and Universal Religion* (Hibbert Lectures, 1882), pp. 323–7 (on "Ezra and the Establishment of Judaism"); A. H. SAYCE, *An Introduction to the Books of Ezra, Nehemiah and Esther* (1885, 3d ed. 1893); MARCUS DODS, "Ezra" and "Nehemiah," *Expositor*, 3d series, Vol. VI (1887), pp. 53–64, 287–97; P. H. HUNTER, *After the Exile*, Vol. II (1890); G. RAWLINSON, *Ezra and Nehemiah, Their Lives and Times* ("Men of the Bible" series, 1890); DRIVER, *Introduction to the Literature of the Old Testament* (1st ed. 1891, 6th ed. 1897), pp. 540–54; W. F. ADENEY, *Ezra, Nehemiah and Esther* (1893); SAYCE, *Higher Criticism and the Verdict of the Monuments* (1893), pp. 537–53; A. C. HERVEY, "The Chronology of Ezra II and IV, 6–23," *Expositor*, June, 1893, pp. 431–43; July, 1893, pp. 50–63; H. E. RYLE, *The Books of Ezra and Nehemiah* ("Cambridge Bible," 1893); G. S. GOODSPEED, "Ezra and Nehemiah," *Biblical World*, Vol. I (1893), pp. 40–48, 208–19; H. HOWORTH, *The Academy*, 1893, Jan. 7, pp. 13 f.; Jan. 21, p. 60; Feb. 4, p. 106; Feb. 25, pp. 174 f.; April 15, pp. 326 f.; June 17, p. 524; July 22, pp. 73 f.; Sept. 16, pp. 233 f.; IDEM, "A Criticism of the Sources and Relative Importance and Value of the Canonical Book of Ezra and the Apocryphal Book Known as Esdras I," *Transactions of the Ninth International Congress of Orientalists*, Vol. II (1893), pp. 68–85; C. C. TORREY, *The Composition and Historical Value of Ezra–Nehemiah* ("Beihefte zur Zeitschrift für die alttestamentliche Wissenschaft," II, 1896); KAUTZSCH, *The Literature of the Old Testament* (1896, transl. 1899), pp. 121–8; J. A. SELBIE, "Van Hoonacker on Israel's Return from Exile," *Expository Times*, Vol. VII (1897), pp. 71–3; IDEM, "Israel's Return from Exile," *ibid.*, pp. 320–22; IDEM, "Ezra-Nehemiah," *ibid.*, pp. 509–11; IDEM, "Kosters on Israel's Return from Exile," *ibid.*, Vol. IX, pp. 66–8; A. R. S. KENNEDY, "Did the Jews Return under Cyrus?" *ibid.*, Vol. VIII (1897), pp. 268–71; VAN HOONACKER, "The Return of the Jews under Cyrus," *ibid.*, Vol. VIII (1897), pp. 351–4; CHEYNE, *Jewish Religious Life after the Exile* (1898), pp. 36–81; IDEM, "The Times of Ezra and Nehemiah," *Biblical World*, Vol. XIV (1899), pp. 238–50; N. SCHMIDT, "Nehemiah and His Work," *ibid.*, Vol. XIV (1899), pp. 329–43; L. W. BATTEN, art. "Ezra and Nehemiah," HASTINGS's *Dictionary of the Bible*, Vol. II (1899); C. F. KENT, *A History of the Jewish People during the Babylonian, Persian and Greek Periods* (1899), pp. 126–36, 167–214; J. O. BOYD, "The Documents of the Book of Ezra," *Presbyterian and Reformed Review*, 1900, pp. 414–37; J. E. MCFADYEN, *The Messages of the Prophetic and Priestly Historians* (1901), pp. 314–34; CHEYNE, "From Isaiah to Ezra," *American Journal of Theology*, 1901, pp. 433–41; KOSTERS AND CHEYNE, art. "Ezra-Nehemiah," *Encyclopædia Biblica*, Vol. II (1901); GUTHE AND BATTEN, *The Books of Ezra and Nehemiah — Critical Edition of the Hebrew Text, etc.* ("Polychrome Bible," 1901); J. W. HARPER, *The Books of Ezra, Nehemiah and Esther* ("The Temple Bible," 1902).

KLEINERT, in *Beiträge zu den theologischen Wissenschaften von den Professoren zu Dorpat*, Band I (1832), pp. 1–304 (on origin, structure, and date of Ezra-Nehemiah); KEIL, *Apologetischer Versuch über die Bücher der Chronik und über die*

Integrität des Buches Ezra (1833); KUENEN, *Historisch-kritisch Onderzoek naar het Ontstaan en de Verzameling van de Boeken des Ouden Verbonds*, Vol. II (1861, 2d ed. 1887, German transl. 1892), pp. 103–83; SCHRADER, "Die Dauer des zweiten Tempelbaues. Zugleich ein Kritik des Buches Ezra," *Theologische Studien und Kritiken*, 1867, pp. 460–504; MARGRAF, "Zur Aufhellung der nachexilischen Chronologie," *Theolog. Quartalschrift*, 1870, pp. 567 ff.; DE SAULCY, *Étude chronologique des livres d'Esdras et de Néhémie* (1868); BÖHME, *Nehemia 1–6* (1871); FRANZ DELITZSCH, "Der Esra der Überlieferung und der Esra der neuesten Pentateuch-Kritik," *Zeitschrift für die gesamte lutherische Theologie u. Kirche*, Vol. XXXVIII (1877); J. HALÉVY, "Esdras et le code sacerdotal," *Revue de l'histoire des religions*, Vol. IV (1877); EB. NESTLE, "Zum Frage nach der ursprüngliche Einheit der Bücher Chronik, Esra und Nehemia," *Theologische Studien und Kritiken*, 1879, pp. 155–21; SMEND, *Die Listen der Bücher Ezra und Nehemia* (1881); A. ROSENZWEIG, *Das Jahrhundert nach dem babylonischen Exil mit besonderer Rücksicht auf die religiöse Entwicklung des Judentums* (1885); J. HALÉVY, "Esdras a-t-il promulgué une loi nouvelle?" *Revue de l'histoire des religions*, Vol. XII (1885); KUENEN, "L'œuvre d'Esdras," *ibid.*, Vol. XIII (1886), pp. 334–58 (German transl. by K. BUDDE in *Gesammelte Abhandlungen zur biblischen Wissenschaft von Dr. Abraham Kuenen* (1894), pp. 370–91); BLEEK-WELLHAUSEN, *Einleitung in das Alte Testament* (5th ed. 1886), pp. 205–22; BERTHEAU-RYSSEL, *Die Bücher Esra-Nehemia und Esther erklärt* ("Kurzgefasstes exegetisches Handbuch zum Alten Testament," 1887); RYSSEL, "Die Anfänge der jüdischen Schriftgelehrsamkeit," *Theologische Studien und Kritiken*, 1887, pp. 149–82; STADE, *Geschichte des Volkes Israel*, Vol. II (1888), pp. 95–193; OETTLI, *Ezra und Nehemia* (STRACK UND ZÖCKLER'S "Kurzgefasste Kommentar," 1889); RIEHM, *Einleitung in das Alte Testament*, Vol. II (1890), pp. 329–38; VAN HOONACKER, *Néhémie et Esdras. Une nouvelle hypothèse sur la chronologie de l'époque de la restauration* (1890); KUENEN, "De Chronologie van het Perzische Tijdvak der Joodsche Geschiedenis," *Verslagen en Mededeelingen der Koninklijke Akademie van Wetenschappen*, Afdeeling Letterkunde, Amsterdam, 1890, pp. 273–322 (German transl. by K. BUDDE, in *Gesammelte Abhandlungen u. s. w.* (1894), pp. 212–51); CORNILL, *Einleitung in das Alte Testament* (1891, 3d ed. 1896), §45; VAN HOONACKER, *Zorobabel et le second temple: étude sur la chronologie des six premiers chapitres du livre d'Esdras* (1892); IDEM, *Néhémie en l'an 20 d'Artaxerxès I, Esdras en l'an 7 d'Artaxerxès II* (1892); ZUNZ, *Die gottesdienstlichen Vorträge der Juden* (1892), pp. 20–31; KÖNIG, *Einleitung in das Alte Testament* (1893), pp. 276–85; CH. HUYGHE, "La chronologie des livres d'Esdras et de Néhémie," *Revue des questions historiques*, 1893; WILDEBOER, *De Letterkunde des Ouden Verbonds naar de Tijdsorde van haar Ontstaan* (1893, German transl. 1895), pp. 404–20; KOSTERS, *Het Herstel van Israël in het Perzische Tijdvak* (1894, German transl. 1895); LAGRANGE, "Néhémie et Esdras," *Revue biblique*, Oct. 1894; WELLHAUSEN, "Die Rückkehr der Juden aus dem babylonischen Exil," *Nachrichten der königlichen Gesellschaft der Wissenschaft zu Göttingen*, 1895, pp. 166–86; KOSTERS, "Het Tijdvak van Israëls Herstel," *Theologisch Tijdschrift*, 1895, pp. 549–57; 1896, pp. 489–504; 1897, pp. 518–54; FL. DE MOOR, "L'époque de la restauration juive d'après les livres d'Esdras et de Néhémie," *Science catholique*, 1895; VAN HOONACKER, *Nouvelles études sur la restauration juive après l'exil de Babylone* (1896); ED. MEYER, *Die Entstehung des Judenthums* (1896); WELLHAUSEN, *Göttingischer gelehrter Anzeiger*, 1897, No. 2, pp. 89 ff. (review of MEYER'S *Entstehung des Judenthums*); ED. MEYER, *J. Wellhausen und meine Schrift, "Die*

Entstehung des Judenthums" (1897); J. MARQUART, *Fundamente israelitischer und jüdischer Geschichte* (1897), pp. 28–68; SELLIN, *Serubbabel—ein Beitrag zur Geschichte der messianischen Erwartung und der Entstehung des Judenthums* (1898), pp. 48–61; KLOSTERMANN, art. "Esra und Nehemia," *Realencyklopœdie für prot. Theol. u. Kirche*, Vol. V (3d ed. 1898); GUTHE, *Geschichte des Volkes Israel* (1899), pp. 245–60; J. GEISSLER, *Die literarische Beziehungen der Esramemoiren insbesondere zur Chronik und den hexateuchischen Quellenschriften* (1899); MOULTON, "Über die Überlieferung und den textkritischen Werth des dritten Esrabuches," *Zeitschrift für die alttestamentliche Wissenschaft*, Vol. XIX (1899), pp. 209–58; Vol. XX (1900), pp. 1–35; WINCKLER, "Die Zeit der Herstellung Judas," *Altorientalische Forschungen*, zweite Reihe, Band II (1899), pp. 210–27; IDEM, "Die Zeit von Ezras Ankunft in Jerusalem," *ibid.*, pp. 241–4; IDEM, "Die doppelte Darstellung in Ezra-Nehemia," *ibid.*, Band III (1901), pp. 458–89; NIKEL, *Die Wiederherstellung des jüdischen Gemeinwesens nach dem babylonischen Exil* (1900); C. SIEGFRIED, *Esra, Nehemia und Esther übersetzt und erklärt* ("Handkommentar zum Alten Testament," 1901); SELLIN, *Studien zur Entstehungsgeschichte der jüdischen Gemeinde*, Band II (1901); BAUDISSIN, *Einleitung in die Bücher des Alten Testamentes* (1901), pp. 264–6, 279–300; BERTHOLET, *Die Bücher Esra und Nehemia erklärt* ("Kurzer Hand-Commentar zum Alten Testament," 1902); CARL HOLZHEY, *Die Bücher Ezra und Nehemia. Untersuchung ihres litterarischen und geschichtlichen Charakters* (1902).

§ 246. **Supplementary Topics.**

1. Make a careful comparison of the parallel passages, Ezra 2:1—3:1*a* and Neh. 7:6–23, noting and classifying the variations in the two lists.

2. Analyze Ezra-Nehemiah carefully, with a view to determining for yourself the sources of the various materials of which it is composed and the historical value of the narrative as it has been presented by the editor.

Cf. especially TORREY, *The Composition and Historical Value of Ezra-Nehemiah;* GUTHE, *Ezra and Nehemiah* ("Polychrome Bible," 1901); SIEGFRIED, *Esra, Nehemia und Esther* ("Handkommentar z. A. T."), pp. 7–14; KOSTERS, *Het Herstel van Israel in het Perzische Tijdvak* (1894, Germ. transl. 1895); CARL HOLZHEY, *Die Bücher Ezra und Nehemia; Untersuchung ihres litterarischen und geschichtlichen Charakters* (1902); MEYER, *Die Entstehung des Judenthums;* SCHRADER, *Theologische Studien und Kritiken*, 1867, pp. 460–504; VAN HOONACKER, *Néhémie et Esdras;* J. O. BOYD, "The Documents of the Book of Ezra," *Presbyterian and Reformed Review*, 1900, pp. 414–37.

3. Compare the canonical book of Ezra with the apocryphal book, Esdras I, noting (1) the materials common to both, (2) the materials peculiar to each; and consider the relative value of each as historical sources.

See, *e. g.*, H. HOWORTH, "A Criticism of the Sources and Relative Importance and Value of the Canonical Book of Ezra and the Apocryphal Book Known as Esdras I," *Transactions of the Ninth International Congress of Orientalists*, Vol. II (1893), pp. 68–85; MOULTON, "Über die Überlieferung und den text-kritischen Werth des dritten Esrabuches," *Zeitschrift für die alttestamentliche Wissenschaft*, Vol. XIX, pp. 209–58;

XX, 1-35; BERTHOLET, *Esra und Nehemia*, p. xvi: SIEGFRIED, *Esra, Nehemia und Esther*, pp. 14 f.

4. Study the contents of the numerous genealogical lists in Ezra-Nehemiah from the point of view of (1) their origin, (2) their historical value, (3) their purpose.

See SMEND, *Die Listen der Bücher Ezra und Nehemia* (1881).

5. Study the descriptions of priestly ceremonies, and customs, the provision made for the support of the temple and its ministry, and all other references to laws and usages of worship, and note the points of contact with the codes of worship, with a view to determining which stratum of laws is reflected by the narrative of Ezra-Nehemiah.

6. Consider the fact that certain portions of Ezra-Nehemiah are written in Aramaic, and the best explanation of this fact. In this connection study the significance of the presence of an Aramaic section in the book of Daniel.

See, *e. g.*, BERTHOLET, *op. cit.*, p. xv; SIEGFRIED, *op. cit.*, p. 7; RYLE, *op. cit.*, p. xx; BAUDISSIN, *Einleitung*, p. 283. On Daniel see the commentaries by Driver, Marti, Behrmann, Bevan, and Prince.

Part Sixth

THE LITERATURE OF WORSHIP—THE HYMNAL LITERATURE

XVIII. The Priestly Element in the Psalter.

CHAPTER XVIII.

THE HYMNAL LITERATURE—THE PRIESTLY ELEMENT IN THE PSALTER.

§ 247. **The Scope of the Priestly Element in the Psalter.**—The Psalter was used in the ritual of worship. But more than this; a considerable portion of it had its origin in connection with such ritual. It was, therefore, very largely a result, directly or indirectly, of the priestly activity. Its outward form (§ 259) shows many peculiarities which are distinctly priestly. It abounds in allusions (§§ 261 ff.) to the priest, the place of worship, feasts, etc. Its principal contents consist of prayers and songs of praise (§§ 265 f.), that is, material intended for use in worship. Much of the composition, although by no means all, may, indeed, be attributed to priests, or guilds of priests.

§ 248. **Other Elements than the Priestly** occupy a large place in the Psalter. This is due to the fact that at the late period in Hebrew history in which the Psalter finally took on its present form the work of the prophets for the most part had been concluded; the work also of the sage had taken strong hold upon the people, and consequently much of the teaching of both these classes had been absorbed into the general thought and opinion of the times. Accordingly, we may be prepared to find in this collection a very large prophetic element, and a smaller amount of the wisdom material. At the same time, it may fairly be claimed that the priestly element dominates; for in fact, the Psalter has shown itself to be the greatest help to worship that history has known.

Pss. 15, 19, 32, 46, 73, 90.

§ 249. **Constructive Study.**—Take up Pss. 72–99, and distinguish each as predominantly prophetic, priestly, or philosophic (that is, as exhibiting the wisdom element).

Pss. 72–99.

§ 250. **Many Important Problems** present themselves to the student of the Psalter; most of these require at least a tentative solution before the more general questions can be satisfactorily considered. Among such problems are the following:

1. Are the superscriptions, of which so many are found in the Psalter, a part of the psalm in each case, and consequently authorita-

tive? Or are they from a much later date, and consequently to be treated only as editorial and unauthoritative suggestions?

2. May we expect to find, in connection with each of the psalms, a historical background, similar to that which, in recent years, has been emphasized so strongly in connection with the sermons of prophets, and the different codes of legislation?

3. Did David really write all the psalms attributed to him, or any considerable portion of them? Is it reasonable any longer to suppose that any of the psalms in this collection come from so early a period as the reign of David?

4. Is the "I" which plays so important a part in the psalms an individual, or is it a personification of the Israelitish community?

5. Are there psalms in the Psalter which come from as late a date as the times of the Maccabees, *i. e.*, 168 to 161 B. C.?

6. To what extent may it be supposed that editorial work has been done on the collection as a whole, and in connection with individual psalms?

§ 251. **Of What Authority Are the Superscriptions?**— In answering this question, consider—

Pss. 11, 13, 14, 15, 16, 17, 19, 20, 21, 23, 24, 25, 35, 37, 42, 50, 72, 87, 90. 1. *The form and content,* and note that they are complete sentences, or detached phrases which give
Pss. 3, 7, 18, 30, 34, 51, 52, 54, 56, 57, 60, 63, 92, 100, 120-134, 142. information, more or less definite, concerning the *authorship,* or the *circumstances* out of which a psalm
Pss. 4, 6, 8, 9, 12, 22, 45, 61, 62, 84, 88. grew, or matters of a *musical* or *liturgical* character; and that such superscriptions are rarely found outside of the
Isa. 38:9; Hab. 3:1. Psalter.

2. *Their origin,* and determine whether they are to be regarded as coming from the *author* of the psalm in each case; or from *contemporaries* of the author; or from *editors* or *collectors* living long after the original production of the psalm.

3. *Their authority,* and note:

(*a*) The considerations which may be urged in favor of this authority, viz., the fact that they evidently are
1 Chron. 15:20, 21. very old—so old, indeed, that to the writer of 1 Chron. 15:20, 21, the Hebrew words had lost their meaning; the fact that in the Hebrew they form an organic part of
Pss. 51, 54, 59. the psalm itself; the fact that, in some cases at least, the substance of the superscription seems to be entirely consistent with the content of the psalm; the fact, also, that

they are not distributed indiscriminately, but evidently were intended to subserve a particular purpose.

(*b*) The considerations which are urged as opposing their authority, viz., the fact that very frequently the manuscripts and versions differ, while the Septuagint and the Peshitto present many deviations and additions,[1] thus indicating that even in the most ancient days there were many differences of opinion; the fact that the superscription in many cases is plainly inconsistent with the content of the psalm; the fact that so few authors are named, when probably there were many; the fact, also, that statements referring to historical circumstances are limited to psalms ascribed to David.

Pss. 27, 74, 79.

4. *The tests to which they must be subjected*, viz.: (*a*) that of linguistic and rhetorical consistency when examined with reference to the content of the psalm; (*b*) that of historical and logical consistency with the content of the psalm.

In all this each superscription should be taken up for separate consideration.

§ 252. **Constructive Study.**—Examine a series of superscriptions and tabulate the questions suggested by each case, with the results which may fairly be accepted in each instance.

E. g., **Pss. 18, 72, 90, 3, 7, 19, 22, 23, 34, 45, 51, 60, 110.**

§ 253. **Is there an Historical Element** in the Psalter, like that which has been found to form the background of Old Testament prophecy and Old Testament legislation? That is, can we find any connection between these psalms and the history of the people in the midst of which they were first uttered? Did Israel's history, or did the experiences of Israel's leaders, find expression in the Psalms?

1. Consider, now, the various kinds of psalms which may be thought of as in one way or another historical:

[1] See W. T. DAVISON, art. "Psalms," in HASTINGS'S *Dictionary of the Bible*, Vol. IV, p. 150; KIRKPATRICK, *The Book of Psalms*, Books IV and V (1901), pp. xxxi f.; DRIVER, *Introduction to the Literature of the Old Testament* (6th ed., 1897), pp. 370 f.; BAETHGEN, *Die Psalmen* ("Handkommentar zum Alten Testament," 2d ed., 1897), p. v; DUHM, *Die Psalmen* ("Kurzer Hand-Commentar zum Alten Testament," 1899), p. xvii.

Pss. 106, 78.

(*a*) Certain psalms describe in a concrete way certain historical events, either individual or national; may these, and others like them, be called *objectively* historical?

Pss. 24:7-10; 46, 76, 60, 65, 122.

(*b*) Certain psalms, although not descriptive of historical events, may be regarded as the outgrowth, and in themselves the expression, of an historical event—*subjectively* historical.

Pss. 22, 51, 69, 84, 86, 130, 139.

(*c*) Certain psalms may be regarded as the expression, although not the description, of individual experience.

2. Note some points of general interest in respect to the historical element in the Psalms:

(*a*) The absence, in general, of distinct allusion to specific historical events. How far may this be explained (1) on the ground of the lyric character of the Psalms? (2) On the ground of the divine purpose as to the use of the Psalter as a hymn-book for all ages? (3) On the supposition that changes and omissions have been introduced throughout the centuries, as editors have transmitted the collection from hand to hand?

(*b*) The great importance of discovering this historical element wherever possible (1) for the sake of the freshness and vividness which is thereby added to the material; (2) for the sake of the new historical data thus brought to light; (3) for the sake of the evidence thus gained respecting the growth and development of psalmody.

3. Still further, make a study of three closely related points, viz.:

(*a*) The sources from which help may be obtained for reaching a decision on these questions, *e. g.*, (1) biblical history; (2) the style and language of the Psalms; (3) the present position and arrangement in the Psalter; and (4) the superscriptions.

(*b*) The character of the knowledge thus obtained: is it definite? is it trustworthy? is it abundant?

(*c*) The analogy furnished by a study of the modern hymn-book.

Pss. 78, 81, 105, 106, 114, 44, 74, 79, 126, 137.

§254. **Constructive Study.**—Examine certain psalms; and (1) classify each under one of the heads (1. (*a*) (*b*) and (*c*)) indicated above; (2) point out in detail and discuss the historical element which you find.

§ 255. **What Is David's Place in Connection with the Psalter?**—Perhaps no problem more important than this may be found in Old Testament literature. It is well worth while to examine into the scope and the significance of this problem. Consider, therefore—

1. The psalms assigned to David by tradition—in all seventy-three, and ordinarily classified by periods as follows: (*a*) psalms reflecting his early life; (*b*) psalms connected with Saul's persecution; (*c*) psalms connected with the removal of the ark; (*d*) psalms connected with David's wars; (*e*) psalms connected with David's fall; (*f*) psalms connected with his flight from Absalom; (*g*) others not definitely connected with any period.

Pss. 8, 19, 29.

Pss. 59, 54, 56, 34 (?), 57, 142, 52, 63 (?) 7, 6 (?), 11, 55.

Pss. 101, 15, 24, 68, 132, 30.

Pss. 20, 21, 110, 2, 60, 18.

Pss. 51, 32.

Pss. 63, 3, 4, 23, 26, 62, 27, 28, 41, 55, 69, 109.

Pss. 5, 9, 11–14, 16, 17, 22, 25, 31, 36–40, 53, 58, 61, 64, 65, 70, 86, 103, 108, 109, 122, 124, 131, 133, 138–141, 143–145.

2. The reasons urged for the probability of so large a number of Davidic psalms, *e. g.*:

(*a*) The period preceding David was just what would have been expected to produce such a result, since it included, *e. g.*, (1) the religious revival under Samuel; (2) a wonderful activity on the part of the prophets, like Samuel, Gad, Nathan; (3) the founding of the prophetic schools; (4) a marked degree of development in the way of spiritual activity.

(*b*) The times of David furnished an excellent basis for these psalms, since they were times of national struggle, of multiform experience, of high aspiration.

(*c*) The several historical references to David as a musician and a poet substantiate this claim.

1 Sam. 16:17, 18; 18:10: 2 **Sam.** 1:19-27; **Amos** 6:5.

(*d*) The many-sidedness of David's character as it is revealed in his private life, as shepherd, soldier, statesman; priest, prophet, king; friend, father, leader.

(*e*) The overwhelming evidence furnished by the superscriptions, which, at all events, show that from very early times David was regarded as the author.

(*f*) The ease with which the events of David's life may be fitted into connection with the content of the Psalms.[2]

[2] On this point the following statements present the opposing views: "References to the more remarkable passages in David's life occur in places without number. There are psalms, not a few, which it is impossible for anyone to read without being reminded that they are his."—BINNIE, *The Psalms.*

The view that these psalms come from David "implies absolute incapacity to

3. The reasons urged against the probability of so large a number of Davidic psalms:

(*a*) The uniform tendency of tradition to magnify the work of a particular man; as seen in the parallel cases of Moses, to whom all Hebrew legislation is ascribed; Isaiah, to whom the work of four or more prophets is ascribed; and Solomon, to whom so large a portion of the wisdom literature is assigned.

E. g., Lev. 1:1; 4:1; Deut. 27:1; Prov. 1:1; Eccl. 1:1; Cant. 1:1.

(*b*) The fact that only in the case of psalms assigned to David are the circumstances of occasion or origin indicated.

E. g., Pss. 3, 18, 34, 51.

(*c*) The certainty that in many cases the assignment to David is unquestionably wrong; and, with this, the unreliable character in general of the superscriptions.

E. g., Pss. 122, 124, 139, 142.

(*d*) The difficulty involved in the proposition that the composition of psalms was thus restricted to so few periods. Were there not many historical situations in which conditions existed favorable to psalmody?

(*e*) The difficulties involved in the proposition that psalms which represent the highest and latest stage of Israelitish spiritual development should have had their origin (1) before the work and utterances of a single prophet of those who have written; (2) before there was any considerable acceptance on the part of the Israelitish nation of the doctrine of one God; (3) during a period when Israel was steeped in superstition and continually relapsing into idolatry of the foulest character; (4) in connection with the life of a king characterized by a spirit at once fierce and warlike, and by a life abounding in the most heinous crimes, among which were adultery and murder.

Cf. Pss. 90, 97.

Cf. Pss. 91, 96.

Cf. Pss. 86, 39.

4. The views presented in some of the more important contributions to the subject, *e. g.*: König (1893) maintains the historical probability of the Davidic authorship of certain psalms and finds no objection to assigning 3, 4, 6, 7, 8, 11, 15, 18, 23, 29, 30, and 32 to David. Driver (*Introduction*, 6th ed., 1897) grants that a majority

understand the difference between old Israel and later Judaism, and makes almost anything possible in the way of ascription of comparatively modern pieces to ancient authors."—W. R. SMITH, *Encyclopædia Biblica*, col. 3931.

of the "Davidic" psalms are not David's, but insists upon the possibility of Davidic psalms, and declares that if there are any such, they may safely be looked for among those on Ewald's list, which is possibly too large. Baethgen (1897) says, "of the seventy-three psalms ascribed to David, in the case of only a few at the most can Davidic authorship be defended with any plausibility, *e. g.*, 3, 4, 18; and that even for these the supposition of a later redaction is hardly to be avoided." Wellhausen (1898) says: "It is not a question whether there be any post-exilic psalms, but rather whether the psalms contain any poems written before the exile." Duhm (1899) denies the existence of any Davidic psalms, and is doubtful whether any psalms come from a time earlier than the Greek period. Kirkpatrick (1901) argues for the Davidic authorship of Ps. 18, and adds: "If this be acknowledged, important consequences follow. For depth of devotion, simplicity of trust, joyousness of gratitude, and confidence of hope, not less than for its natural force and poetic beauty, that psalm has few rivals. It has all the freshness of creative genius. It can hardly have been the solitary production of its author. If such a psalm could have been written by David, so might many others." Cheyne (*Encyclopædia Biblica*) denies the historical possibility of Davidic psalms in our Psalter, and explains the superscription *of David* as a corruption of an original *of Jedithun*.[3]

5. The various tests to which each psalm, thought to be Davidic, must be subjected, viz.:

(*a*) The historical test; that is: Is the background of the psalm in harmony with the conditions of David's time? Are the historical and social presuppositions of the psalm met by the facts of the Davidic period?

(*b*) The theological test; that is: Are the ideas concerning God, man, and sin which the psalm reflects in keeping with the stage of theological thought to which David and his contemporaries may fairly be said to have belonged?

(*c*) The rhetorical test; that is: Are the poetical

[3] See also pp. 23 f.

form and the general literary style such as were characteristic of the earlier days of Hebrew poetry?

(*d*) The grammatical test; that is: Are the syntax, the order of words, the structure of sentences, and the grammatical forms such as are found in the earlier stages of the language of the Old Testament?

(*e*) The vocabulary test; that is: Is the language of the psalm the pure Hebrew of the Davidic age, or does it contain Aramaic, Persian, and Greek words, so many of which crowded into the Hebrew speech in the course of the later history?

§ 256. **Constructive Study.**— Select from each of the following groups of psalms one or more, and apply the tests suggested above:

Pss. 122, 124, 131, 133, 138–145. 1. Psalms which, although assigned by tradition to David, are almost universally believed to be wrongly so assigned.

Pss. 3, 4, 7, 11, 18, 29. 2. Psalms which are certainly to be regarded as Davidic, if there are any Davidic psalms.

Pss. 8, 19, 22, 23, 24, 25, 32, 37. 3. Psalms which, while assigned to David by some eminent authorities, are, to say the least, uncertain.

§ 257. **Constructive Study.**—Formulate a statement which will present briefly what is involved in a decision to assign no psalms to David, in contrast with the traditional view ascribing to him seventy-three, or even a more liberal position ascribing ten or twelve.

§ 258. **Does the "I" of the Psalter** represent an individual, or the entire Israelitish community? Consider, in connection with this problem, the following points:

1. The use of the rhetorical figure, termed *personification* in general literature.[4]

2. The use of personification by the Arabs in the effort to find concrete expression for the origin of a tribe or community.[5]

[4] On the general subject of personification see especially FREYTAG, *Technique of the Drama*, trans. by E. J. MACEWAN (3d ed., 1900), pp. 246 ff.

[5] W. R. SMITH, *Kinship and Marriage in Early Arabia* (1885, 2d ed., 1903), pp. 20 f.

3. Some specific examples: *me*= Egyptians (Exod. 14:15); and the frequent interchange of singular and plural. *E. g.*, Numb. 20: 18, 19; Isa. 12: 1, 2; 25:1; 26: 9; Jer. 10:19; Mic. 7:7-10; Lam. 1:11*b*-16, 18-22; Isa. 61: 10 f.

4. Some important examples of personification in the Old Testament:

(*a*) *The servant of Jehovah*, under which figure is set forth the mission of the community of pious Jews as the representative of Jehovah in a wicked world. Isa., chaps. 40-55.

(*b*) *The character of Job* in the Book of Job; under the guise of a person, the sufferings of the Jewish community at the hands of heathen oppressors are portrayed and discussed, the poet setting forth the doubts and questions which arose in the minds of pious Jews, the various theories proposed in explanation of the sufferings, and his own point of view.

(*c*) *The common practice of the prophets*, *e. g.*, Amos's dirge over the approaching destruction of northern Israel; Hosea's representation of Israel as the bride of Jehovah; the representation of Jerusalem as a person in Isaiah; Ezekiel's characterization of Samaria and Jerusalem as two harlots; and the use of the title "virgin daughter of Israel." Am. 5:1 ff. Hos., chap. 2. Isa., chap. 60. Ezek., chap. 23.

5. Some of the points involved in interpreting the "I" as of the community:

(*a*) If the "I" be the community of Israel, and the statements made represent the thought of the community as a whole, will it be necessary to find a date for these psalms in which there was a fair degree of unanimity of opinion in the community?

(*b*) If these psalms are the expression of the heart of the community at large, could they have been written at a time when the prophets and priests were in definite conflict with each other, *i. e.*, down until 621 B. C.?

(*c*) When, as a matter of fact, did there first come to be a community feeling in Israel?

(*d*) Is a difference to be found between national feeling and community feeling? If so, in what does this consist? Is the idea of a church-nation evident?

(*e*) Is it, in general, true that the community interpretation requires a later date for the psalms than the individual interpretation?

(*f*) Would the following description of the "I" meet the demands of the case, viz.: "the company of faithful Israelites and diligent frequenters of the temple who formed the *kernel* of the post-exilic Judean community"?

(*g*) Would one expect to find, at this age of religious development, in a hymn-book intended for a community and for public worship, psalms of so strongly marked an individual character?

(*h*) Is it not true, on the other hand, that the lyric poet always generalizes, and that, while describing his own experiences, he really includes all whose situation is like his own?

(*i*) Are not these psalms, when interpreted of the community, much more significant?

(*j*) Is it also true that a writer may as a representative include with himself a few others, perhaps an entire party, who have the same feelings with himself?

§ 259. **Constructive Study.**— Take up, now, the special study of certain passages, and determine whether, on the whole, the individual, or the community interpretation seems more fitting, *e. g.:*

Pss. 44:4, 6, 15; 51; 60:9; 66:13 ff.; 71; 74:12; 89:50; 102; 118.

1. A group which most modern writers would regard as representing the community.

Pss. 7; 9; 10; 28; 37; 92; 119.

2. A group thought by some to have as subject the godly portion of the community.

Pss. 44; 56; 57; 60; 65; 74; 102; 145.

3. A group thought by some to have as subject the nation as a whole.

§ 260. **Did Any Psalms Have Their Origin in the Maccabean Period** (*i. e.*, 168–161 B. C.)?— Consider, in this connection:

1. The question of the close of the Old Testament canon. When may this be supposed to have happened, and under what circumstances? What bearing on this question does the book of Ecclesiasticus (see Prologue) have? And, further, in what relation with this event does the persecution of Antiochus Epiphanes stand?

2. The question of the age of the Book of Daniel; *e. g.:* (*a*) What considerations may be urged against the older view which placed the book in the days of the exile, and in favor of the modern view which assigns it to the age of the Maccabees? (*b*) What important difference in the interpretation of chap. 11 turns on this decision?

3. The question of the origin and date of the Septuagint; *e. g.:* (*a*) Could books have found their place in the canon as late as 161 B. C., and yet have secured a place in the Greek version? (*b*) At what periods were the various divisions of the Old Testament translated into Greek? (*c*) The significance of the fact that the Septuagint includes a psalm not found in the Hebrew.

4. The special circumstances of the Maccabean times which cannot be found in connection with any earlier period of Israelitish history; *e. g.:* (*a*) a time when protestation of *national innocence* was possible (*cf.* Ps. 44); (*b*) a time when synagogues were in existence (*cf.* Ps. 74:8); (*c*) a time when Israel and the opposing nations constitute the *two classes* mentioned.

§ 261. **Constructive Study.**—Take up certain psalms, and determine for yourself whether they seem to fit into the Maccabean times; *e. g.:*

1. Certain psalms, generally acknowledged to be **Pss. 44, 74, 79, 83.**
Maccabean.

2. Certain psalms concerning which there is con- **Pss. 80, 60, 113–118.**
siderable doubt.

3. Certain psalms concerning which there is still a **Pss. 20, 21, 33, 101.**
greater degree of doubt.

§ 262. **In What Ways Did the Editorial Factor Enter into the Psalter?**—This question can only be touched upon. Consider—

1. The editorial element which appears in connection with the superscriptions (see above, § 251); a work involving selection, arrangement, interpretation, and designation as to use. Is there evidence of difference of opinion in this work?

2. The editorial work suggested by the fact that the
Greek text (Septuagint) has a psalm not contained in the **Ps. 151.**
Hebrew Psalter, concerning David as a shepherd.

3. The editorial work to be inferred from (*a*) the
fact that Pss. 42, 43, now *two*, were quite certainly *one* **Pss. 42, 43, 113, 114.**
at an earlier time; *cf.* also Pss. 113, 114; and (*b*) the fact
that Ps. 24, now *one*, was perhaps originally two, vss. **Pss. 24, 27, 32.**
1–6 and vss. 7–10 being separate pieces; *cf.* also Ps. 27:1–6 and 7–14; Ps. 32:1–7 and 8–11.

4. The editorial work implied in the two editions of
the same psalm which are to be found, in which one **Ps. 18 and 2 Sam., chap. 22.**

word in every four shows a variation, the more common of which may be classified as (*a*) the incorporation of glosses, (*b*) correction of harsh and unusual terms, (*c*) alterations for the purpose of securing greater harmony, or of removing words which were objectionable from the dogmatic point of view.[6]

5. Editorial work which went so far as to add new
Ps. 51:18, 19. verses to an old psalm.

6. Who these editors were; *e. g.*, those connected with the song service of the temple? prophets? priests? scribes?

§ 263. **Constructive Study.**— Select from any part of
E. g., Pss. 72–76. the Psalter half a dozen psalms, and, taking them up one by one, tabulate carefully anything that looks like editorial work.

§ 264. **The Priestly Factor in the Psalter** is plainly discernible in certain external elements affecting its outward form and use:

Ps. 41:13. 1. Read the doxology which closes Book I; compare
Pss. 72:18, 19; 89:52; 106:48; 150. the similar doxologies in other psalms, and note that by means of these doxologies the Psalter is divided into *five* books. Was this suggested by the division of the *law* into five books? May both arrangements be ascribed to the priests?

E. g., Pss. 51:7, 16, 17, 19; 27:1–6; 65:1–3; 74:1–8; 119. 2. Examine the phraseology, tone, and style of several passages, and observe how definitely all this points to the *priest*.

Ps. 24. 3. Note, (*a*) in Ps. 24, the question asked in vs. 3, with the answer given in vss. 4–6; likewise, (*b*) the similar interchange of general statement, answer, and ques-
Pss. 42, 43. tion in vss. 7–10; (*c*) the thrice-recurring refrain in Pss. 42, 43 (vss. 5, 11, and vs. 5); (*d*) the monotonous refrain
Ps. 136. in Ps. 136; and consider whether these examples do not seem to show that, in some cases at least, there was antiphonal singing by divisions of the temple choir, as well as that the psalms were used in public song. Consider also (*e*) the many musical terms employed.

Pss. 122, 124, 134. 4. Examine Pss. 122, 124, 134, and consider their

[6] *Cf.* W. H. BENNETT, "Notes on a Comparison of Psalm XVIII with 2 Sam. XXII," *Hebraica*, Vol. III, pp. 65–86.

adaptation to the purpose which seems to be suggested in their title, "Songs of Ascents," viz., songs sung by companies of pilgrims on their way to the temple at Jerusalem. With what spirit is the temple itself regarded?

5. Read carefully the group of psalms numbered 146–150, and note that the entire content is an invitation or call to worship—exhortations to the whole congregation of worshipers to sing praises to Jehovah. Pss. 146–150.

6. Consider the use of certain psalms in connection with special occasions of worship; *e. g.:* (*a*) with *feasts;* (*b*) with the temple-worship; (*c*) with the dedication of the wall at Jerusalem; (*d*) with the bringing up of the ark to Jerusalem. Pss. 81:1–5; 33:1–3; 98:4–6. 1 Chron. 15:16–28. Neh. 12:27, 29, 35 f., 38, 40–43. *Cf.* 1 Chron. 16:8–36 with Pss. 105:1–15; 96:1–13; 106:47 f.

§ 265. **Constructive Study.**—Summarize the material suggested in § 264, and formulate a statement on the priestly element in the Psalter as seen in the external use.

§ 266. **References to the Priest** are found in the Psalter. What, briefly, is the evidence furnished by these passages concerning the priest, his position, and his influence? Pss. 58:64; 99:6; 105:26; 106:16, 30 f.; 110:4; 115:10, 12; 118:3; 132:9, 16; 134:1–3; 135:19 f.

§ 267. **References to the Place of Worship** are found in the Psalter. What may be inferred from this material concerning the attitude of the psalmists toward the temple and its worship? Pss. 5:7; 11:4; 20:2; 22:25; 24:3; 26:6–8, 12; 27:4–6; 28:2; 29:9; 36:8; 40:9; 42:4; 43:3 f.; 46:4; 48:1 f., 8 f.; 51:18 f.; 52:8; 55:14; 61:4; 63:2; 65:1, 4; 66:13; 68:15–17, 24, 29; 69:9; 73:17; 74:2 ff.; 76:2; 77:13; 78:54, 58, 60, 68 f.; etc.

§ 268. **References to Sacrifice** are found in the Psalter. What light do these references throw upon the subject of the priestly tone and spirit of the Psalter? What is the attitude of the psalmists toward sacrifice?

§ 269. **References to Feasts** are found in the Psalter. Consider also the significance of the Psalms of Ascents in this connection.[7] Do the psalms furnish any evidence as to the ideas concerning feasts at the time of their composition? Pss. 4:5; 20:3; 40:6; 50:5, 8–14, 23; 51:16 f., 19; 54:6; 56:12; 66:13, 15; 96:8; 106:28, 37 f.; 107:22; 116:17; 118:27. Pss. 4:7; 81:3.

§ 270. **The Very Essence of the Psalter is Priestly,** since in its purpose and contents it may be explained

[7] On these psalms see the literature cited on p. 106, note 10; also BAETHGEN, *Die Psalmen übersetzt und erklärt* ("Handkommentar," u. s. w.; 2d ed., 1897), pp. xvii f.; W. T. DAVISON, in HASTINGS'S *Dictionary of the Bible*, Vol. IV, pp. 153 f.; and the commentaries of EWALD and DELITZSCH, *in loc.*

See, *e. g.*, Pss. 69, 88, 17, 26, 143.
See, *e. g.*, Pss. 29, 95, 113, 135, 9, 103.
See, *e. g.*, Pss. 42, 91, 23, 73.
Pss. 69, 88.

only as a *Book of Worship*. In this regard it may be considered from three points of view, according as it served the purpose of (1) *Book of Prayer*, for the Israelitish church; (2) *Book of Praise;* (3) *Manual of Personal Communion with God.*

§ 271. **The Psalter as a Book of Prayer.**—Note that—

Cf. Ps. 21:1-21 with Ps. 22:22-31.

1. Sometimes throughout an entire psalm the tone is that of supplication or penitence, or both; while at other times the tone of supplication with which the psalm begins passes over into one of triumphant praise.

Pss. 80, 85, 90, 123.

2. Sometimes the prayer is unquestionably the formal prayer spoken by the congregation as such; while at other times the prayer is clearly that of an individual soul "in converse with God, disclosing to him its manifold emotions, desires, aspirations, or fears."

3. The Psalter is as definitely a prayer-book as it is a hymn-book, and to be interpreted as such.

§ 272. **Constructive Studies.**—Take up, in turn, the following assignments of work:

Pss. 69, 88, 79, 74, 38, 43.

1*a*. Examine carefully certain prayers offered for *deliverance*, and analyze the thought which they contain, in order to determine, *e. g.*, (*a*) the nature of the calumny or trouble from which deliverance is sought; (*b*) the outward circumstances of the suffering described; (*c*) the grounds on which petition for relief is based; (*d*) the extent to which faith exists that deliverance will ultimately be secured; (*e*) the stage of religious thought marked by these utterances.

2 Kings 19:15-19; 20:3; Amos 7:5; Jon. 2:1-9; Hab., chap. 3.

1*b*. Study in the same way similar utterances found outside of the Psalter, and note the points of difference.

Pss. 17, 26, 55, 57, 69, 70.

2*a*. Examine certain prayers which demand from God *vindication of character;* and analyze the thought presented, in order to formulate, *e. g.*, (*a*) the nature of the accusation which seems to have been preferred against the defendant; (*b*) the injury which he is represented as having suffered in consequence; (*c*) the grounds on which the demand for vindication is made; (*d*) the measure of the suppliant's consciousness of rectitude; (*e*) the stage of religious development suggested by these utterances.

2*b*. Study in the same way similar pieces found outside of the Psalter, and note any points of difference. Isa. 57:1 f.; Job, chaps. 22, 30.

3*a*. Examine passages containing petition for *guidance* in the midst of danger and difficulty; and analyze the same in order to determine, *e. g.*, (*a*) the nature of the trouble or difficulty in which the suppliant finds himself; (*b*) the historical background which is implied; (*c*) the tone of the supplication put forth for guidance; (*d*) the degree of expectation which is exhibited as to the answer to be vouchsafed; (*e*) the stage of religious development indicated. Pss. 143, 61, 86, 42, 25.

3*b*. Study in the same way similar utterances found outside the Psalter, and note the points of difference. Numb. 11:10-15; Jos. 7:6-9; 1 Sam. 23:2, 7-12; 30:7 f.

4. Examine certain prayers which exhibit more of the element of *contemplation;* and analyze the thought expressed, adopting as the basis of analysis your own form of logical development. *E. g.*, Pss. 77, 73.

§ 273. **The Psalter as a Book of Praise.**—Observe—

1. That the very name of the Hebrew Psalter (*t^e hillîm*) means "praise-songs;" and that still other words expressing various phases of the idea of *song* are employed. *E. g.*, Pss. 66, 112, 113.

2. That in many cases the tone of prayer passes into that of praise, and in still others, the tone of praise passes into that of prayer. *E. g.*, Pss. 13, 22, 27, 28, 106, 138.

3. That everything of a musical character points to the use of the psalms as media of *praise.*

§ 274. **Constructive Studies.**—Take up, in turn, the following assignments of work:

1*a*. Examine carefully certain praise-songs, in which the author seeks to find expression for the praise of God because of the manifestation of his power; and analyze the thought according as it is related to (*a*) the writer's situation; (*b*) the form of manifestation of the divine power; (*c*) the way in which the writer's situation has been affected by this particular manifestation; (*d*) the stage of religious thought marked by these utterances. *E. g.*, Pss. 65, 107, 114, 124, 136.

1*b*. Study in the same way similar utterances found outside the Psalter and note points of similarity and difference. *E. g.*, Isa., chap. 12; Exod., chap. 15.

Pss. 104, 103, 48, 46, 146, 147.

2*a*. Examine certain praise songs, in which the writer seeks to find expression for praise of God, on the ground of what he *is*, perhaps, in history or in nature; in other words, his attributes, analyzing the thought with reference to (*a*) the writer's situation; (*b*) the particular attributes referred to; (*c*) the bearing upon the writer's position; (*d*) the stage of religious thought marked by these utterances.

E.g., Job, chaps. 36, 37, 38, 39; Isa. 40: 27–31; 44: 24–28; 45: 18 f.; 63: 7–19.

2*b*. Take up, in the same way, similar utterances outside the Psalter, and note points of similarity and difference.

§275. **The Psalter as a Manual of Personal Communion with God.**—Observe—

1. "The surprising variety of mood and subject and occasion in the Psalms which gives them their catholicity, and, combined with their deep spirituality, adapts them to be" a manual of meditation and communion.

2. The strange and significant expression of the community-feeling in the personified "I"—a fact which adds greatly to the use of the book for practical and devotional purposes.

3. The incomparable freedom with which the soul is represented as in converse with the Deity, laying bare its inmost feelings.

§276. **Constructive Studies.**—Take up the following lines of work:

Pss. 46, 64, 102.

1*a*. An examination of certain psalms with a view to (*a*) the position of the author; (*b*) his relation of trust and dependence on God; (*c*) the analysis of this feeling; (*d*) the conception of God which underlies it.

Jer. 20: 7–13; Isa., chap. 26.

1*b*. A similar examination of certain passages outside of the Psalter.

Pss. 51, 38, 39.

2*a*. An examination of certain psalms, with a view to (*a*) the position of the author; (*b*) the consciousness before God of the "exceeding sinfulness of sin," and an intense longing for forgiveness; (*c*) the analysis of this feeling; (*d*) the conception of God which underlies it.

Ezra, chap. 9; Lev., chap. 16; Isa., chap. 1, 6: 5; Am. 5: 10–15.

2*b*. A similar examination of certain passages outside of the Psalter.

Pss. 42, 22, 13.

3*a*. An examination of certain psalms with a view to (*a*) the psalmist's position; (*b*) his longing for communion with God; (*c*) the analysis of this feeling; (*d*) the conception of God which underlies it; (*e*) the custom referred to in this psalm of praising God in public worship.

3*b*. A similar examination of certain passages outside of the Psalter. Lam., chap. 5; Isa., 63:15–64:12.

4*a*. An examination of certain psalms with a view to (*a*) the psalmist's position; (*b*) the confidence, security, joy, and comfort resulting from fellowship with God; (*c*) the analysis of this feeling; (*d*) the underlying conception of God. Pss. 91, 23, 73.

4*b*. A similar examination of certain passages outside of the Psalter. Deut. 33:26–29; Am. 7:10–17; Jer. 20:7–13; Josh. 1:1–11.

§277. **The Significance of the Psalter as Related to the Priestly System.**—Consider, now—

1. The various elements of worship that have found tangible expression in the Psalter, *e. g.*, prayer, praise, penitence, gratitude, thanksgiving, trust, fellowship with God; and discover, if possible, any fundamental religious emotion which does not find full expression in it.

2. The full and definite evidence cited that the Psalter (*a*) had its origin in connection with the temple-worship; (*b*) was largely the creative work of the priests; (*c*) exercised great influence upon the priests; (*d*) was employed as a manual of temple-worship; (*e*) served also as a manual of private individual devotion. And, in view of all this, ask yourself the following questions:

(*a*) If all this is a part of the priestly system of the Old Testament, what is the conception of this priestly work which we must hold?

(*b*) Could a priestly system, including as its climax a hymnal, breathing a devotion so rich, be wholly formal and mechanical, devoid of life and of spiritual power?

(*c*) Could such a hymnal have owed its origin to a body of priests who were strangers to the spiritual and altogether slaves of the formal?

(*d*) Is there any higher type of spirituality in the Old Testament than that which is thus represented by the Psalter?

(*e*) Is it, then, true or untrue that the highest type of spiritual life known in the Old Testament is of *priestly* origin, *priestly* environment, and on a *priestly* basis?

§278. **Literature to be Consulted.**[8]

H. EWALD, *Commentary on the Psalms* (1835, 3d ed. 1866, transl. 1880); ISAAC TAYLOR, *The Spirit of the Hebrew Poetry* (1861); PEROWNE, *The Book of Psalms*,

[8]Of the extensive literature on the Psalter only the more recent and important works of an exegetical and critical character are cited here.

with Introductions and Notes, explanatory and critical (1864, 8th ed. 1892); FRANZ DELITZSCH, *Biblical Commentary on the Psalms* (1867, 4th ed. 1883 [transl. 1887–89], 5th ed. 1894); *The Psalms Chronologically Arranged* by FOUR FRIENDS (1867, 2d ed. 1891); W. KAY, *The Psalms, with Notes* (1871, 2d ed. 1874); A. C. JENNINGS AND W. H. LOWE, *The Psalms, with Introductions and Critical Notes* (1875–77); T. C. MURRAY, *Lectures on the Origin and Growth of the Psalms* (1880); W. R. SMITH, *The Old Testament in the Jewish Church*, Lecture VII (1881, 2d ed. 1892); C. H. TOY, "Date of the Korah Psalms," *Journal of Biblical Literature*, Vol. IV (1884), pp. 80–92; IDEM, "On the Asaph-Psalms," *ibid.*, Vol. VI (1886), pp. 73–85; BINNIE, *The Psalms, Their Origin, Teachings and Use* (1886); C. H. TOY, "Rise of Hebrew Psalm-Writing," *Journal of Biblical Literature*, Vol. VII, pp. 47–60; T. K. CHEYNE, *The Book of Psalms: A New Translation, with Commentary* (1888); C. G. MONTEFIORE, "Mystic Passages in the Psalms," *Jewish Quarterly Review*, Vol. I (1889), pp. 143 ff.; A. NEUBAUER, "On the Titles of the Psalms According to Early Jewish Authorities," *Studia Biblica*, Vol. II (1890), pp. 1–58; S. R. DRIVER, *Introduction to the Literature of the Old Testament* (1891, 6th ed. 1897), pp. 359–91; A. F. KIRKPATRICK, *The Book of Psalms, with Introduction and Notes*, 3 vols. ("The Cambridge Bible," 1891–1901); T. K. CHEYNE, *Aids to the Devout Study of Criticism* (1892), pp. 129 ff.; W. T. DAVISON, *The Praises of Israel* (1893, 2d ed. 1898); J. P. PETERS, "The Development of the Psalter," *The New World*, 1893, pp. 203 ff.; A. MACLAREN, *The Psalms* ("Expositor's Bible," 1893–94); J. SHARPE, *The Student's Handbook to the Psalms* (1894); T. K. ABBOT, "On the Alphabetical Arrangement of Ps. IX and X, with Some Other Emendations," *Zeitschrift f. d. alttest. Wissenschaft*, Vol. XVI (1896), pp. 292–94; J. W. BEARDSLEE, "The Imprecatory Psalms," *Presbyterian and Reformed Review*, 1897, pp. 490–505; T. K. CHEYNE, "The Book of Psalms; Its Origin and its Relation to Zoroastrianism," *Semitic Studies in Memory of Alexander Kohut* (1897), pp. 111–19; F. BUHL, "The Aid of Criticism in the Interpretation of the Psalms," *American Journal of Theology*, Vol. II (1898), pp. 763–75; E. G. KING, *The Psalms in Three Collections: Translated with Notes* (1898); J. WELLHAUSEN, *The Book of Psalms; A New Translation* (HAUPT'S "Sacred Books of the Old and New Testaments," 1898); S. R. DRIVER, *The Parallel Psalter: Being the Prayerbook Version of the Psalms and a New Version . . . . with an Introduction and Glossaries* (1898); J. ROBERTSON, *The Poetry and Religion of the Psalms* (1898); T. K. CHEYNE, *The Christian Use of the Psalms* (1899); IDEM, "Studies in the Criticism of the Psalms," *Expositor*, 1899, pp. 252–63, 334–44; G. A. BARTON, "The Bearing of the Composition of the Psalter on the Date of the 44th Psalm," *American Journal of Theology*, Vol. III (1899), pp. 740–46; EMILIE G. BRIGGS, "סלה," *American Journal of Semitic Languages and Literatures*, Vol. XVI (1899), pp. 1–29; C. A. BRIGGS, *General Introduction to the Study of Holy Scripture* (1899), pp. 355–426; T. K. CHEYNE, *The Origin and Religious Contents of the Psalter in the Light of Old Testament Criticism and the History of Religions* ("Bampton Lectures" for 1899); A. S. CARRIER, "Notes on the Psalms" *American Journal of Semitic Languages and Literatures*, Vol. XVII (1900), pp. 54–59; WRIGHT, *The Psalms of David and the Higher Criticism* (1900); W. S. PRATT, "A Comparative Study of Ps. 45," *Journal of Biblical Literature*, Vol. XIX (1900), pp. 189–218; D. SMITH, "Songs of the Ascents," *Expository Times*, Vol. XII (1901), pp. 62–65, 161–64, 414–16; Vol. XIII, pp. 118–20, 500–503; Vol. XV, pp. 39–42; W. T. DAVISON, art. "Psalms," HASTINGS'S *Dictionary of the Bible*, Vol. IV (1902); BUDDE, art. "Hebrew

Poetry," *ibid.*, Vol. IV (1902); W. R. SMITH AND T. K. CHEYNE, art. "Psalms," *Encyclopædia Biblica*, Vol. III (1902); DUHM, art. "Poetical Literature," *ibid.*, Vol. III (1902); E. G. HIRSCH, "Note on Psalms 34 and 25," *American Journal of Semitic Languages and Literatures*, XVIII (1902), pp. 167–73; W. W. MARTIN, "A Psalmist's Epithalamion," *ibid.*, Vol. XIX (1902), pp. 49–51; P. HAUPT, "The Poetic Form of the First Psalm," *ibid.*, Vol. XIX (1903), pp. 129–42; C. MARTIN, "The Imprecations in the Psalms," *Princeton Theological Review*, Vol. I (1903), pp. 535–53; J. W. THIRTLE, *The Titles of the Psalms: Their Nature and Meaning Explained* (1904); T. K. CHEYNE, *The Book of Psalms, Translated from a Revised Text with Notes and Introduction* (1904); J. E. MCFADYEN, *The Messages of the Psalmists: The Psalms of the Old Testament Arranged in Their Natural Grouping and Freely Rendered in Paraphrase* (1904).

J. G. VON HERDER, *Vom Geist der ebräischen Poesie* (1782–83); HITZIG, *Die Psalmen* (1835, 2d ed., 1863–65); J. OLSHAUSEN, *Die Psalmen erklärt* ("Kurzgefasstes exegetisches Handbuch zum Alten Testament," 1853); T. NÖLDEKE, *Die alttestamentliche Literatur* (1868), pp. 117–42; C. EHRT, *Abfassungszeit und Abschluss des Psalters zur Prüfung der Frage nach Makkabäerpsalmen historisch-kritisch untersucht* (1869); E. REUSS, *Le Psautier, ou le livre de cantiques de la synagogue* (1879); LAGARDE, *Orientalia*, Vol. II (1880), pp. 13–27; M. KOPFSTEIN, *Die Asaph-Psalmen untersucht* (1881); F. GIESEBRECHT, "Über die Abfassungszeit des Psalters," *Zeitschrift für die alttestamentliche Wissenschaft*, Vol. I (1881), pp. 276–332; H. GRAETZ, *Kritischer Commentar zu den Psalmen nebst Text und Uebersetzung* (1882); F. BAETHGEN, "Der textkritische Wert der alten Uebersetzungen zu den Psalmen," *Jahrbücher der prot. Theologie*, Vol. VIII (1882), pp. 405–59, 593–667; BLEEK-WELLHAUSEN, *Einleitung in das Alte Testament* (5th ed. 1886), pp. 443–75; HUPFELD-NOWACK, *Die Psalmen übersetzt und ausgelegt* (1888); R. SMEND, "Ueber das Ich der Psalmen," *Zeitschrift für die alttestamentliche Wissenschaft*, Vol. VIII (1888), pp. 49–147; KESSLER, *Die asaphitische Psalmengruppe untersucht* (1889); RIEHM, *Einleitung in das Alte Testament*, Vol. II (1890), pp. 171–205; W. CAMPE, *Das Verhältniss Jeremias zu den Psalmen* (1891); J. MÜHLMANN, *Zur Frage nach den makkabäischen Psalmen* (1891); C. H. CORNILL, *Einleitung in das Alte Testament* (1891), pp. 205–20; E. SELLIN, *Disputatio de origine carminum quae primus psalterii liber continet* (1892); F. BAETHGEN, *Die Psalmen übersetzt und erklärt* ("Handkommentar z. Alten Testament," 1892, 2d ed. 1897); W. STAERK, "Zur Kritik der Psalmenüberschriften," *Zeitschrift für die alttestamentliche Wissenschaft*, Vol. XII (1892), pp. 91–151; A. RAHLFS, עָנִי *and* עָנָו *in den Psalmen* (1892); J. BACHMANN, *Praeparation und Kommentar zu den Psalmen, mit genauen Analysen und getreuer Uebersetzung für Gymnasiasten, Studirende und Candidaten* (1892); B. STADE, "Die messianische Hoffnung im Psalter," *Zeitschrift für Theologie und Kirche*, Vol. II (1892), pp. 369–413 (reprinted in *Akademische Reden und Abhandlungen* [1899], pp. 37–76); KUENEN-MATTHES, *Historisch-kritische Einleitung in die Bücher des Alten Testaments*, Vol. III (1893, German transl. 1894), pp. 1–57; E. KÖNIG, *Einleitung in das Alte Testament* (1893), pp. 393–406; WILDEBOER, *Die Litteratur des Alten Testaments* (1894), pp. 388–403; W. DIEHL, *Erklärung von Ps. 47* (1894); G. BEER, *Individual- und Gemeinde-Psalmen* (1894); B. JACOB, "Beiträge zu einer Einleitung in die Psalmen," *Zeitschrift f. d. alttest. Wissenschaft*, Vol. XVI (1896), pp. 129–81, 265–91; Vol. XVII, pp. 48–80, 263–79; Vol. XVIII, pp. 99–120; Vol. XX, pp. 49–80; J. K. ZENNER, *Die Chorgesänge im Buche der Psalmen*

(1896); F. COBLENZ, *Ueber das betende Ich in den Psalmen* (1897); W. STAERK, "Die Gottlosen in den Psalmen," *Theologische Studien und Kritiken*, 1897, pp. 449–88; C. H. CORNILL, *Die Psalmen in der Weltlitteratur* (1898); D. LEIMDÖRFER, *Das Psalter-Ego in den Ich-Psalmen: Beitrag zur wissenschaftlichen Psalmenforschung* (1898); BÜCHLER, "Zur Geschichte der Tempelmusik und der Tempelpsalmen," *Zeitschrift f. d. alttest. Wissenschaft*, Vol. XIX (1899), pp. 96 ff.; W. RIEDEL, "Zur Redaktion des Psalters," *ibid.*, Vol. XIX (1899), pp. 169–72; A. MERX, *Ps. IX und X und andres Maccabaeische* (1899); H. KESSLER, *Die Psalmen* ("Kurzgefasster Kommentar zu den heiligen Schriften," 1899); J. WELLHAUSEN, "Bemerkungen zu den Psalmen," *Skizzen und Vorarbeiten*, Vol. VI (1899), pp. 163–87; B. DUHM, *Die Psalmen erklärt* ("Kurzer Hand-Commentar zum Alten Testament, 1899); IDEM, *Die Psalmen übersetzt* (1899); J. KÖBERLE, *Die Tempelsänger im Alten Testament* (1899); ROTHSTEIN, "Ps. 78, ein Zeuge für d. Jahwistische Gestalt der Exodus-Tradition," *Zeitschrift für wissenschaftliche Theologie*, 1900, No. 4; GRIMME, "Was bedeutet שִׁיר הַמַּעֲלוֹת?" *Orientalistische Literatur-Zeitung*, Vol. IV (1901), pp. 180–82; COUARD, "Behandlung und Lösung des Problems der Theodicée in den Ps. 37, 39 und 73," *Theologische Studien und Kritiken*, Vol. XLVII (1901), pp. 110–24; BAUDISSIN, *Einleitung in die Bücher des Alten Testamentes* (1901), pp. 635–72; E. KAUTZSCH, *Die Poesie und die poetischen Bücher des Alten Testaments* (1902); MATTHES, "Die Psalmen und d. Tempeldienst," *Zeitschrift für die alttestamentliche Wissenschaft*, Vol. XXII (1902), pp. 65–82; GRIMME, *Psalmenprobleme: Untersuchungen über Metrik, Strophik und Paseq des Psalmenbuches* (1902).

§ 279. **Supplementary Topics.**

1. Is the Psalter rightly classified as a *priestly* product? Consider the significance of the fact that it contains a large amount of prophetic and wisdom material as well as priestly. Can it be said to belong to any one of these three classes of Old Testament literature, or does it belong, rather, to all of them? Might it not properly be a class by itself, viz., *devotional literature?*

2. Consider the various possible methods of classifying the Psalms; *e. g.*, as to (*a*) their subject-matter (see Driver, *Introduction*, pp. 368 f.), (*b*) their spirit and tone, (*c*) the time of their origin.

3. Of what value is the Psalter as a source of information concerning Israel's history? What knowledge of Israel's past history does it reveal? What can be legitimately inferred from a study of the individual psalms as to the historical conditions amid which they were composed? What light does the fact of the existence and use of the Psalter throw upon the life and spirit of the post-exilic Jews?

4. In a study of the origin of the Psalter what is the significance of (*a*) the presence within it of such groups as the Korahite psalms, the Asaphite psalms, the Pilgrim psalms; (*b*) the groups of Yahwistic and Elohistic psalms; (*c*) the division into five books; (*d*) the grouping of the "Davidic" psalms? On the basis of these and other similar

phenomena, can any history of the growth of the Psalter through the grouping of various earlier collections be satisfactorily traced?

5. Take up the so-called "Imprecatory Psalms" and study them in the light of the following considerations: (*a*) the times to which they belong, when moral and spiritual conceptions were still in a more or less primitive stage and the spirit of the gospel was not yet shed abroad; (*b*) the great provocation which called forth these utterances, the feeling of injury, oppression, and insult revealed in them; (*c*) the tendency of human nature to seek revenge; (*d*) the deep sense of justice out of which they spring, the feeling that such sins must not and cannot go unpunished, that the vindication of Jehovah's character demands the infliction of drastic penalties upon the notoriously wicked; (*e*) the necessity that this infliction of punishment should take place here and now, since the thought of a future life and a future judgment had not yet developed; (*f*) the doctrine that prosperity was a sign of the divine favor, while misfortune and suffering was manifest evidence of and chastisement for sin.

6. Make a comparison of the Psalms of Solomon with the Old Testament Psalter, and note the points of similarity and difference in the two collections.

On the Psalms of Solomon see especially R. H. CHARLES, art. "Apocalyptic Literature," §77–85, *Encyclopædia Biblica;* RYLE AND JAMES, *The Psalms of the Pharisees* (1901); W. FRANKENBERG, *Die Datierung der Psalmen Salomos: ein Beitrag zur jüdischen Geschichte* ("Beihefte zur Zeitschrift für die alttestamentliche Wissenschaft," 1896).

7. Compare the old Babylonian penitential psalms with corresponding psalms of the Old Testament, with reference to such matters as (*a*) their idea of God, (*b*) their conception of sin, (*c*) their longing for forgiveness, (*d*) their idea of atonement.

On the Babylonian psalms see especially: H. ZIMMERN, *Babylonische Busspsalmen, umschrieben, übersetzt und erklärt* (1885); R. BRÜNNOW, "Assyrian Hymns," *Zeitschrift für Assyriologie*, Vol. IV, pp. 1–40, 225–58; Vol. V, pp. 55–80; T. G. PINCHES, "An Erechite's Lament," *Records of the Past* (New Series), Vol. I, pp. 84 f.; R. F. HARPER, *Assyrian and Babylonian Literature* (1901), pp. 429–44; J. BAHR, *Die babylonischen Busspsalmen und das Alte Testament* (1903); W. CASPARI, "Die Religion in den assyrisch-babylonischen Busspsalmen," *Beiträge zur Förderung Christlicher Theologie*, Vol. VII, No. 4 (1903).

Part Seventh

THE PERMANENT VALUE OF THE PRIESTLY ELEMENT

CHAPTER XIX.

THE ESSENTIAL SIGNIFICANCE OF THE PRIESTLY ELEMENT.

§ 280. **The Priestly Element Had Serious Limitations.** —The agencies, through which the Spirit of God worked upon Israel during long centuries of guidance were human, and therefore imperfect. The prophet, with all his enthusiasm and enlarged vision, suffered serious limitations. The sage, in spite of his careful, methodical and, at times, scientific observation and study, fell far short of reaching even his own ideals. In what way were the priests limited? Consider the following:

1. There were granted to the priests, as such, no great and uplifting visions of the nation's future glory. In later days, to be sure, priests like Ezekiel and Zechariah were given such inspiration; but they and others like them were no longer simply priests: they were prophets. The lack of the presence of the Spirit in their souls placed the ordinary priests in a class essentially different from that of the prophets.

Ezek. 1:1-3:15; 8:1-11:25; chaps. 40-48; Zech. 1:7-6:8.

2. The priest was by the very nature of his profession a *literalist*, and consequently he was forever denied the strength and freshness which those may have who rise higher than the letter and see what is above and beyond it. This fact will account for much that is distinctly disappointing in the priestly element.

Cf. **Exod., chaps. 35-40; Lev., chaps. 1-3, 7, 14; Numb., chaps. 3, 4.**

3. Since the priestly element represented worship, and for that reason (*a*) came out of an early paganism, and (*b*) was constantly being drawn backward into that same paganism, or into other forms of heathen thought with which the sacrificial system was always in more or less close contact, it was forced to carry a heavy burden made up of corrupt and injurious notions and practices, which even long culture would not and could not shake off. From all this prophetism was practically free.

1 Kings 3:3; 12:25-33; 16:31 ff.; 2 Kings 16:11-16; 21:3-7; Ezek. 8:7-13; Jer. 44:17-19.

Exod. 32:1-6, 22-24; Numb. 16:1-3, 12-14; Hos. 4:4, 9; 5-1; 6:9; Isa. 28:7 f.

4. All the ignorance and superstition of the masses were borne by the priestly class, rather than by the prophets. The priest, if he remained a priest, was compelled to live and work with the masses in the midst of all that was degrading.

Lev. 8:1-9:24; chap. 16.

5. The priest had to do chiefly with the outer form of truth, the symbol; and while this was supposed to represent the inner and essential thought, it not infrequently failed to maintain any real connection with that thought.

Zech. 7:4, 5; Isa. 58:3ff., 13 f.

Zech. 6:11; Lev. 16:29-34; 2 Kings 11:4-20.

6. The priest was intensely ambitious of power and wealth, and the fact that, in time, the order gained control of state and church is evidence of success which in itself was detrimental to true and sincere effort.

Numb., chap. 19; Lev., chaps. 1-3.

7. The teachings of the priest were more subjective and less direct than those of the prophet, in that the teaching of the latter was given to the people directly through the spoken or written word, while much of the priest's teaching was dependent upon the worshiper's own interpretation of the symbol employed in the ritual.

2 Kings 22:3-23:25; Neh. 8:1-10:39; Mal. 1:6-2:9.

A strong spirit of conservatism was always in control; progress was secured most frequently by revolution from the outside, in which the prophets took leading part. Under the circumstances the priestly teaching was always slow to penetrate the nation's heart.

§ 281. **The Characteristics of the Priestly System,** regarded as a whole, may be briefly studied:

1. *Its spirit not peculiar.*—What is to be said of the *spirit* of this system when compared with that of other priestly systems? Wherein, if at all, is a distinction to

Lev. 17:6; 20:26; chap. 16; 26:11 f.

be found? Is not the spirit, in this case, just what the true spirit of worship always proves to be, viz., the simplest and most common effort to come into close touch with the higher powers?

2. *Its form not peculiar.*—But what may be said of the *outer form* of this priestly system? Does it not have

Cf. §§ 72:4, 6; 95:6, 7; 107:5, 6, 7; 121:8, 9; 135:7.

much in common likewise with other systems? What is peculiar to it so far as *form* is concerned? Altar? temple? sacrifice? feast? music and prayer? priest and holy order? Are not the Urim and Thummim of foreign origin? How about sacrifices of salt and meal? the clean and unclean? Can you find among the institutions of the Israelitish priestly system *one* which does not have an analogue in other religions?

3. *Its relation to other priestly systems.*—Consider, now, whether or not it is true that in its priestly system the Hebrew religion touches other ancient religions most closely. Have other religions prophetism and prophecy? Or is it not rather soothsaying and divination? Is the Hebrew priestly system as different from other priestly systems as Hebrew prophecy is different from other systems of prophecy?

4. *The system and the people.*—Is it true that at first the people were more in sympathy with their priestly system than with the prophetic ideas which were proposed in opposition? Did the nation ever struggle against the priest as it struggled against the prophet? Does this mean that the priestly conception and expression were something less alien to the hearts of the people?

Amos 2:6 ff., 11 ff.; 3:14; 4:4 f.; 5:4 ff., 21-27; 7:10 ff.; Hos. 2:11; 3:4; 4:11-14; 8:11 ff.

5. *The period of its dominance.*—To what extent were priest and prophet in conflict with each other? And why? Is it the priest whom the prophet always holds responsible for the people's sins? Which of the two orders represented the old? which the new? Which represented form? which spirit? Which held back? which pushed forward? How important in the history of the nation was this struggle between prophet and priest? which conquered? when? why?

Jer. 29:25 ff.; 20:1 ff.; Am. 7:10 ff; Hos. 6:4-10; 5:1; Isa. 1:10-17; 28:7; Mic. 6:6-8.

6. *Its chronological relation to prophecy.*—When in the history of the priestly system was its progress most pronounced? How explain the fact that in the later periods of prophecy the prophets were all priests? But what became of the great teachings of the prophets when prophetism as a movement had died out and the priestly order was in power? Was this teaching lost? or was it appropriated by the priests and incorporated into their system? Of what importance was the legacy left by prophecy at its death? Are priest and prophet now *one*, the priest being the spokesman? But why did

Jer. 1:1; Ezek. 1:3; 4:14; chaps. 40-48; Hag. 1:2; 2:10 ff.; Zech. 6:9 ff; Mal. 1:6 ff; 2:1-9.

Deut., chaps. 6-11; Lev. 23:22; 25:39 ff; 26:14-46.

prophecy die? And how did it happen that the priest, who had always opposed the prophet and his work, took up that work when there were no longer prophets to conduct it?

Exod. 20:24; Deut. 12:2-4. Deut. 18:1-8; Numb. 18:1-7; Lev. 21:10-15.

7. *Its variations and contradictions.*— Does not this priestly element seem to be full of contradictions? But what is the nature of these contradictions? Is it that of change from time to time? Is it the result of adjustment to great changes in national life? What, for example, led to the change from the system in which worship was distributed throughout the nation to that of centralization at one place? Why was worship in Babylon during the exile impossible? Explain the recentralization later in the second temple; and still later its redistribution in the synagogues. All this points to what characteristics besides those of flexibility and capability of adjustment?

Cf. §§ 76; 80; 82:4.

Cf. §§ 60, 62, 66, 69.

8. *Its autocratic and democratic character.*— Consider the change in character that has taken place between the early days when every man might be his own priest, and the last days which witnessed the firm establishment of the hierarchy. How is this to be accounted for?

Cf. chaps. ii, iii, iv, and §§ 84, 92, 97, 104.

9. *Its purity, impurity, and artificiality.*— Compare this priestly system (*a*) when it was mingled with all the impurities of Canaanitish worship, and (*b*) when it has been purged and purified of its dross by the fire of captivity; and still again (*c*) when it has become one of the most artificial rituals ever accepted by a nation. What is to be said of these different stages?

10. *Its narrowness and breadth.*— Compare, again, the character of this system in its later days when, from one point of view, it was most narrow and artificial; while, from another, it was most broad and spiritual; since, at a time when animals were being slain by tens of thousands, and the body was being worn out with worship and purifications, *then*, and not till then, did this religious system give birth to the Psalter, which contains the greatest examples of higher spiritual contemplation and communion with God that religion has ever produced.

Lev., chaps. 4, 5, 6, 7, 12, 14, 15, 21; Numb., chaps. 6, 8

Cf. §§ 270-77.

§ 282. **The Purpose or Function of the Priestly System.** —Which of these words is to be employed, "purpose" or "function"? What is the point of view involved in each?

1. *Its purpose or function in general.*—What may be said as to the purpose or function of the priestly system in any religion? What other elements, aside from the priestly element, are required to make up religion, or to constitute the religious spirit? What is the relation sustained by the priestly element to the others? *Cf.* § 1.

2. *Its purpose or function for the individual.*—(*a*) Was there a meaning in the various acts of worship for each and every person who participated in the worship? Did oil and salt, blood and fat, meal and incense, represent ideas? What, in the case of each of these? Did these ideas, thus symbolically represented, come from men's hearts and express various phases of their feelings? (*b*) In what sense was the temple a laboratory in which men were required to go through a certain process, doing the detail of the work, every detail representing an experience of one or another kind in the religious life? Would the doing of these things impress upon the doer the meaning which they were supposed to represent? What was the answer to the oft-recurring questions: "Why do I wash? Why do I touch no unclean thing? Why do I observe the sabbath?" Was it not in each case a great truth? Was the act, therefore, a lesson repeated every time the act was performed? But would many, perhaps the great majority, perform the act without asking the question, and so without being conscious of any lesson involved in it? Is it just so in acts of worship today? Does this fact, in itself, affect essentially the point in question? *Cf.* §§ 84:2; 87:2; 90:2.

3. *Its purpose or function for the nation.*—(*a*) Did the *national* idea precede or follow that of the *individual?* When did the first conception of the individual as distinguished from the nation begin to appear? Did the idea of individualism have large development in Old Testament times? or even in the first centuries of Christianity? Was the priestly system, on the whole, **Am. 2:6; 5:1 ff.; Exod. 20:2 ff.; Jer. 31:29 f.; Ezek., chap. 18.**

better adapted to individual or national life? (*b*) What, so far as concerns relationship to the deity, would be the result for the nation, of a regular and sincere adoption of the ceremonial? How different would the effect of observing the ritual be from that of attending church in more modern times? Would it, in some sense, bring them into touch with God, and under His influence? Was it, after all, a very natural expression of man's relation to God? (*c*) Are we to suppose that sacrifice (which may here be taken as representing the priestly system) from the beginning was something established by God himself and suggested by him directly to man?
Lev., chaps. 1-7. Is this not the way in which the Priest Code everywhere
Cf. § 216, (4). regards sacrifice? In other words, as something given by God to man through Moses? Does the Priest Code recognize the existence of a priestly system before Moses's day? or among other nations? How, then, is this presentation of the subject to be understood? (*d*) But in what way are we to account for the universal prevalence of sacrifice among the nations? What is to be said for and against the hypothesis of a primitive revelation to which all this points back? Is it easier to understand this common form of worship, viz., sacrifice, as a natural expression, on the part of man, of the relation which he believes himself to sustain to the higher powers? In this case what was the nature of the feeling which originally prompted the action, and controlled the devotee in the process of the action?
Lev., chap. 16; 4: 35; 9: 3; 10: 16 ff.; Numb. 15: 22-31; 19: 1-9. (*e*) Was it his sense of God's holiness and his own sin? his feeling that he deserved death? Did he therefore present animals in sacrifice as his own substitute? What is meant in this connection by the use of the words "piacular," "propitiation?" But can we suppose that the men of primitive times, savages, had reached so advanced a point of philosophical reflection? May we perhaps suppose that this act, which constitutes so large an element in all priestly systems, had its origin and abiding function in a desire to acknowledge dependence upon the higher power and to render to it homage? Would it be far removed from this to say that the chief

purpose of the worshiper, whether nation or individual, was to gain the favor of the god, or to avert his displeasure? (*f*) What is involved in that other explanation which finds the essence of sacrifice in the meal which followed, a communion of man and God in food? Did not eating together constitute a covenant or bond of friendship? God and the tribe being one, would not this union be strengthened, or, if temporarily strained, be restored by eating food in common? And did not the god receive his share in the blood poured upon the altar? In this case how explain the whole burnt offering, all of which was given to the god? How much change in this conception of sacrifice was involved in the advance from nomadic life, when all property was held in common by the tribe, to the agricultural life, when men began to hold personal property? (*g*) In any case, is it not true that in Old Testament times the idea most in vogue is that the priestly system, with the act of sacrifice as its central feature, represented the means by which a man might make a *gift* to God? Is it anywhere suggested that the giving of *gifts* to God is something displeasing to him? Is there great difference of opinion, on the other hand, as to the particular thing which shall be given?

Lev. 4:20, 26, 31, 35; 5:5f., 13, 18f.; Numb. 19:13.
Gen. 18:1-8; 31:54; Exod. 18:12; Numb. 22:40; Deut. 27:6*b*, 7; 1 Sam. 1:3ff.; 9:12f.; 16:2, 5; 20:29; Ezek. 39:17-20.
Lev. 8:15, 24; 9:18; 17:6.
Lev. 1:3-9.
Numb., chap. 28; Exod. 30:7f.
Mic. 6:6-8; Amos 5:21-24; Hos. 6:6.

4. *Its function in connection with the messianic idea.*—(*a*) In what sense is the word "messianic" to be taken? What are some of the more important elements of which it is constituted? In how far may the word "eschatological" be used as a synonym? Who are indicated as the conspicuous representatives of this movement or element, (1) during the existence of the kingdom; (2) during the Babylonian exile? (*b*) When Jerusalem is rebuilt and the second temple is erected—that is, at the time of the restoration—what official figure comes into especial prominence? At the same time what feeling becomes uppermost in the minds of the people? As a consequence of this overwhelming sense of *sin*, what new importance attaches to the idea of *atonement?* (*c*) Were the people of the restoration disappointed in their failure to see the fulfilment of the prophetic

Isa. 9:6f.
Isa. 49:1-6; 52:13-53:12.
Hag. 1:1, 12, 14; 2:2, 4; Zech., chap. 3.
Lev., chap. 16; 10:16ff.; Numb. 19:1-9.
Hag. 2:6-9, 20-23; Zech. 6:15; chap. 8.

promises concerning the re-establishment of the king-
dom and the coming of the Messiah? How did they,
Mal. 1:1–14; 2:1–17. after awhile, account for the refusal or failure of God to
Cf. §§ 38, 15; 92, 11. fulfil these promises? Regarding themselves as respon-
sible, what steps were taken to force God to bring these
Mal. 3:1–6. things to pass? How did this affect the priestly system?
In what way, also, the further development of the
messianic idea?

5. *Its function in relation to the introduction of Greek thought.*— What, in general, was the effect upon the eastern world of the fall of the Persian empire and the supremacy of the Greeks, attained through Alexander the Great? How was Greek influence exerted upon these eastern nationalities? To what extent was the
Cf. § 51. Jewish nation affected by Greece? What were the
essential contributions received by Judaism from Greece? To what extent did Judaism successfully resist the movement which exerted so strong an influence upon all other nations with which it came in contact? What enabled Judaism to withstand this influence? What were the elements in the priestly system that enabled it to render this very striking service?

Cf. § 197, 3. § 283. **The Essential Thought of the Priestly Element** may be grouped around three or four subjects. These are, God, Man, Sin, and the Church.

1. *God.*—(*a*) Does not the priestly thought of God, after all, represent the whole Old Testament, except the portions known as Wisdom?

(*b*) How, and in what sense, does the priestly element include the prophetic?

(*c*) Can a distinction be made between the priestly and the prophetic conceptions of God in the periods that precede the captivity in Babylon? in the periods that follow the captivity?

(*d*) What stages of growth may be discovered in the
Cf. §§ 18, 38, 49. priestly conception of God before its incorporation of
the prophetic? likewise, after the incorporation? Was the later conception more strongly priestly or prophetic?

(*e*) What distinct conceptions, if any, are to be found in the Wisdom element? Are they older than the priestly, or later? higher or lower?

(*f*) Are *holiness* and *majesty* perhaps the two predominant conceptions of God in the priestly element? What others might be mentioned as almost equally prominent? Was either of these attributes a part of the primitive Semitic conception of God? At what time in Greece's history did they begin to be recognized? How is the *holiness* of God symbolically represented in the Levitical ritual? How is the *majesty* of God indicated, especially in the Priest Code? Upon what aspects of deity do the Psalms dwell most earnestly? Lev., chaps. 8, 9, 16. Exod. 24:15*b*–18*a*; 34:29–35. Pss. 23, 90, 91, 103, 136, 46.

2. *Man.*—(*a*) In what way is the priestly element especially concerned with man? (1) as an individual? or (2) as representing the human race? or (3) as he appears, earlier, in the Israelitish nation and later, in the Judaistic church? What is the position of the individual, in contrast with that of the nation, as represented in the Levitical ritual? in the Psalter? *Cf.* § 283, 2, 3.

(*b*) Is it through Israel alone that God will meet the world? What will be Israel's relation to the world at large? Does the materialistic conception continue to the end in spite of the prophetic teaching? Exod. 19:6; Deut. 26:19; 32:8 f.

(*c*) Is the *sinfulness* of man's nature more definitely and frequently expressed than any other quality? What is the form of expression most common in the ritual? in the Psalter? Lev. 4:35; 9:3; 10:16 ff.; chap. 16; Numb. 19:1–9; Pss. 51; 90:8; 41:4; 38:3; 32:1–5.

3. *Sin.*—(*a*) Have there been different stages in the growth of the priestly idea of sin? What, for example, was the prevailing idea in the patriarchal time under the primitive Semitic worship? What, later, when the prophets have given their message? What, still later, when the fulness of the monotheistic conception has come to be realized? Josh., chap. 7; Deut. 7:25; 8:19; 9:5 f.; 11:16; 25:13–16. Lev. 4:1 f., 13, 27; 6:1 ff.; chap. 16; Numb. 15:22 ff.

(*b*) Is it true that the idea of *sin* is always and everywhere simply a corollary of the idea of God? What connection may be traced in the development of the priestly system between these two ideas? How shall we explain the growth, among the Hebrews, of the intensity of feeling concerning *sin?* *Cf.* § 92, 11.

(*c*) Is it true that the different Hebrew words for *sin* express various phases of the idea as they were recog- Lev. 4:3; 16:16; 20:20; Numb. 15:28; Deut. 17:2.

nized by the Hebrews? What are the more important of these words (in English), and what is the distinctive meaning of each? What, as a matter of fact, is the meaning of the word (*ḥaṭṭath*), commonly translated *sin?*

Amos 5:7, 10 ff., 15; Hos. 2:13; 4:6; 6:6 ff.; Lev. 18:1–5; 15:31; 6:1 ff.; 5:14 ff.

(*d*) Can a distinction be made between the priestly and the prophetic conceptions of *sin?* Does Wisdom furnish any varying ideas? Wherein consists the difference between the priestly conception of sin, as expressed in the Psalter and the ritual, and that which is found in the Assyrian penitential psalms and corresponding ritual?

Pss. 51; 36:1–4; 39:1; 53:1.

Lev., chap. 16; 5:5 f. Numb. 19:1–10.

(*e*) How may *forgiveness* of sin be secured? What is the essential idea in the teaching concerning atonement as it appears in connection with the ritual?

Exod. 12:3; 16:1; Lev. 4:13; Numb. 35:24; Ps. 74:8.

4. *The Church.*—(*a*) Does this word really belong to Old Testament thought of any school? What is the usage of the terms "congregation" and "synagogue"? Is "Zion" a priestly or a prophetic word? What general significance does it have aside from its literal meaning? What is the distinctive meaning of two other common phrases, "the Covenant people," and "the theocracy"?

Pss. 2:6; 9:11; 48:12; 51:18; 53:6; 126:1; Isa. 1:8; 14:32; 28:16; Jer. 26:18; 50:5. Amos 1:2. Lev. 24:8; 26:42.

(*b*) Was it with the inner or outer sense of the terms cited above that the priestly element had most to do? Was there a time after which the inner sense received greater consideration?

Gen. 1:27–30; 9:8–17; 17:1–14; Exod. 31:16 f.

(*c*) Did the great priestly narrative [P] lay stress upon certain covenants, viz., with Adam, Noah, Abraham, and Moses? What bearing did these covenants have upon the later conception of the church?

Ezra 9:1–4; chap. 10; Neh., chaps. 9, 10; Lev. 4:13 ff.; chap. 25.

(*d*) Was Judaism a kingdom or a church? Was the ruling power a monarchy or a hierarchy? Did the priestly element, therefore, really become a church system? and were the institutions of worship precursors in *thought* as well as in *form* of the idea of the church?

Isa. 8:16–18.

(*e*) Was the company made up of Isaiah and his disciples the first step away from the national community to the church community? Did Isaiah's teaching of the *remnant* prepare the way for Jeremiah's teaching of individualism, and the two together thus furnish the basis for the church idea? Did Ezekiel continue to develop this thought in the direction of a church community

Isa. 7:3; 10:20–22. Jer. 31:29 f.

Ezek., chaps. 18, 33, 40–48.

made up of those who were circumcized of heart? Were Jeremiah and Ezekiel priests as well as prophets? Jer. 1:1; Ezek. 1:3.

(*f*) In what way did the period of the exile during which *worship* in the usual sense was impossible contribute to the development of the church community? Did this period also make more prominent the observance of the sabbath and the service of prayer? Did Ezekiel gather together the people for exhortation? What indications are found, in Ezra's times and later, of the growing habit of assembling for prayer and for the reading and interpretation of Scripture? *Cf.* §§ 118 and 137, 3. Ezek. 8:1; 14:1; 20:1. Ezra 10:1 ff.; Neh. 9:1 ff.

(*g*) If we may understand that back and under all institutions *thought* is to be found, and if we measure the importance of the thought by the number of the institutions involved, as also by the acknowledged character of the institutions, is it not true that the *church*, with all that it represented before the times of the Christian church, was one of the most essential subjects of thought in the priestly element?

§ 284. **Many of the Ideals of Modern Church Life and Worship** are the direct contribution of the priestly element found in the Old Testament. The word "inheritance" is perhaps a better word in this connection than "contribution." Some of these ideals are institutions; and some, aspirations of the most holy character. Consider and formulate in some detail the following propositions:

1. That the Christian church goes back directly to the synagogue community.

See: J. A. SELBIE, art. "Congregation," HASTINGS'S *Dictionary of the Bible;* S. C. GAYFORD, art. "Church," *ibid.;* BACHER, art. "Synagogue," *ibid.;* J. A. ROBINSON, art. "Church," *Encyclopædia Biblica;* I. J. PERITZ, art. "Synagogue," *ibid.;* SCHÜRER, *History of the Jewish People in the Time of Christ*, Division II, Vol. II, pp. 52–89, 243–52; ZAHN, *Forschungen zur Geschichte des Neuetestamentlichen Canons*, Vol. II (1883), p. 165; IDEM, *Einleitung in das Neue Testament*, Vol. I, pp. 66 f.; HATCH, *The Organization of the Early Christian Churches.*

2. That the Christian service of song, prayer, and exhortation goes back to the Jewish temple ritual and the exercises of the synagogue.

See: chap. xviii; WEISZÄCKER, *The Apostolic Age of the Christian Church*, Vol. II, pp. 246, 254, 258.

3. That the beginning of the modern Bible in form and idea dates from the priestly reform of Josiah's times when Deuteronomy was published.

See: CORNILL, *Prophets of Israel*, pp. 89 f.; F. H. WOODS, art. "Old Testament Canon," HASTINGS'S *Dictionary of the Bible;* WILDEBOER, *The Origin of the Canon of the Old Testament*, pp. 22–25.

4. That the conception of the clergy as distinct from the laity goes back to the Levitical priesthood.

See: §§ 62 f.; and HATCH, *The Organization of the Early Christian Churches*, pp. 141 f.; CORNILL, *Prophets of Israel*, pp. 87 f.

5. That the idea of the mission of the church to the world at large goes back to the commission of Israel to be a priest nation.

See: Exod. 19:6; Isa. 42:1–7; 61:6; 1 Pet. 2:5, 9, and HOLZINGER, *Exodus*, p. 67; DILLMANN, *Handbuch der alttestamentlichen Theologie*, pp. 457 f.; G. A. SMITH, *The Book of Isaiah*, Vol. II, pp. 237 ff.

6. That the thought of bringing God into the world comes from the determination of the Jewish saints, under priestly influence, to live lives of such purity and holiness as to make God introduce the messianic times, of which there had been dreams, but as yet no realization.

See: CHEYNE, *Jewish Religious Life after the Exile*, pp. 80 f.; MONTEFIORE, *The Religion of the Ancient Hebrews* (Hibbert Lectures, 1892), pp. 321 f.

7. That the highest ideals of mankind touching the soul's contact with God have come from the experiences of Jewish saints expressed in song for purposes of Jewish worship (*i. e.*, the Psalms).

See: §§ 275–277; and PEROWNE, *The Book of Psalms* (8th ed.), Vol. I, pp. 25–40; KIRKPATRICK, *The Book of Psalms* (Cambridge Bible), Vol. I, pp. lxxviii ff.

8. That the Lord's Supper is the continuation of the Jewish Paschal feast.

See: PLUMMER, in HASTINGS'S *Dictionary of the Bible*, Vol. III, p. 145; J. A. ROBINSON, in *Encyclopædia Biblica*, col. 1419.

9. That the Lord's day, Sunday, is the offspring of the Jewish sabbath.

See: HESSEY, *Sunday, its Origin, History, and Present Obligation* (Bampton Lecture, 5th. ed., 1889); H. R. GAMBLE, *Sunday and the Sabbath* ("Golden Lectures" for 1900–1901); N. J. D. WHITE, art. "Lord's Day," HASTINGS'S *Dictionary of the Bible;* ZAHN, *Geschichte des Sonntags vornehmlich in der alten Kirche;* G. A. DEISSMANN, art. "Lord's Day," *Encyclopædia Biblica.*

10. That the Christian Easter celebration is the continuation of the spring feast which has come down to us through the Jewish Passover feast.

See: HITZIG, *Ostern und Pfingsten* (1837–38); DUCHESNE, *La question des origines du culte chrétien* (1889), pp. 226 ff.; CANON VENABLES, art. "Easter," *Encyclopædia Britannica.*

11. That Thanksgiving day is the modern representative of the Feast of Tabernacles.

See: Deut. 16:13–15; and A. T. CHAPMAN, art. "Feast of Tabernacles," HASTINGS'S *Dictionary of the Bible;* BENZINGER, art. "Feast of Tabernacles," *Encyclopædia Biblica.*

12. That the more widely accepted theories of the atonement (whether right or wrong) rest fundamentally upon the Old Testament doctrine of sacrifice.

See: J. O. F. MURRAY, art. "Atonement," HASTINGS'S *Dictionary of the Bible;* DALE, *The Doctrine of the Atonement;* WILSON, *Hulsean Lectures on the Atonement* (1899); SCHULTZ, "The Significance of Sacrifice in the Old Testament," *American Journal of Theology*, Vol. IV (1900), pp. 257–313; ARCHIBALD SCOTT, *Sacrifice, its Prophecy and Fulfilment* ("Baird Lecture," 1892–93).

13. That the New Covenant, a more accurate expression for the New Testament now commonly used, was first conceived and expressed in its fundamental principles by an Old Testament priest (who was also a prophet).

See: Jer. 31:31 ff.; and A. B. DAVIDSON, art. "Covenant," HASTINGS'S *Dictionary of the Bible;* MCCLYMONT, art. "New Testament," *ibid.*

14. That the Christian practice of fasting had its direct origin in the usage which grew up in later Judaism.

See: §§ 152–154; and J. S. BLACK, art. "Fasting," *Encyclopædia Britannica;* BENZINGER, art. "Fasting, Fasts," *Encyclopædia Biblica;* C. J. BALL, art. "Fasting and Fasts," SMITH'S *Dictionary of the Bible* (2d ed. 1893).

15. That the Christian rite of baptism is historically (through John the Baptist) and logically (moral uncleanness taking the place of ceremonial uncleanness), the successor to the Jewish rite of baptism, practised as a means of restoration from a state of ceremonial uncleanness, and employed in the case of proselytes.

See: PLUMMER, art. "Baptism," HASTINGS'S *Dictionary of the Bible;* J. A. ROBINSON, art. "Baptism," *Encyclopædia Biblica;* W. ELWIN, art. "Baptism," SMITH'S *Dictionary of the Bible* (2d ed. 1893).

§ 285. **Permanent Truth** of a most precious kind was wrought out through this long laboratory process, along with much which, of course, was temporary and ephemeral. Consider and formulate, among other great and fundamental truths of an eternal character, those relating to—

1. The Holiness of God, especially from the point of view of the Levitical system, in which it occupies a fundamental position.

See: J. SKINNER, art. "Holiness in the Old Testament," HASTINGS'S *Dictionary of the Bible;* BAUDISSIN, *Studien zur Semitischen Religionsgeschichte*, Vol. II, pp. 3–142; SMEND, *Lehrbuch der alttestamentlichen Religionsgeschichte* (2d ed.) pp. 325 f.; A. B. DAVIDSON, *Old Testament Theology*, pp. 144–60; SCHULTZ, *Old Testament Theology*, Vol. II, pp. 166 ff.

2. The filthiness of sin, especially as symbolized in certain details of the Levitical system, which undoubtedly were, however, only the tangible representation of previous prophetic thought.

See: KÖBERLE, *Sünde und Gnade im religiösen Leben des Volkes Israel bis auf Christum* (1905), pp. 325–57, 415–571; BERNARD, art. "Sin," HASTINGS'S *Dictionary of the Bible;* DAVIDSON, *Old Testament Theology*, pp. 203–34; TENNANT, *The Origin and Propagation of Sin;* IDEM, *The Sources of the Doctrine of the Fall and Original Sin;* CLEMEN, *Die Christliche Lehre von der Sünde.*

3. The forgiveness of sin, as illustrated by the ceremonial of the priestly system.

See: KÖBERLE, *op. cit.*, pp. 597–638; BETHUNE-BAKER, art. "Forgiveness," HASTINGS'S *Dictionary of the Bible;* SMEND, *Lehrbuch der alttestamentlichen Religionsgeschichte* (2d ed. 1893), pp. 394–403; DAVIDSON, *Old Testament Theology*, pp. 315 ff.

4. Vicarious suffering, as involved in the doctrine of sacrifice.

See: BAIRD, *Sacrifice, its Prophecy and Fulfilment;* SCHULTZ, "The Significance of Sacrifice in the Old Testament," *American Journal of Theology*, Vol. IV (1900), pp. 257–313; DRIVER, art. "Offer, Offering," HASTINGS'S *Dictionary of the Bible;* TH. NAVILLE, *Les sacrifices lévitiques et l'expiation* (1891).

5. The ecclesiastical state, as pictured by Ezekiel.

See: Ezek., chaps. 40–48, and the commentaries on these chapters, especially those of DAVIDSON (*Cambridge Bible*), KRAETZSCHMAR (*Hand-Kommentar zum Alten Testament*), BERTHOLET (*Kurzer Hand-Commentar zum Alten Testament*), and SKINNER (*Expositor's Bible*).

§ 286. **The Ethical Influence of the Priestly Element** is one which can be felt more easily than it can be described. (1) Analyze this element and point out the various individual factors in it which, one may believe, would tend to an ethical uplifting of those who conscientiously followed the rules and regulations of the priestly ceremonial. (2) Consider, on the other hand, the factors which might be expected to prove injurious ethically. (3) Would some of these factors for good vary in their influence, producing one result in certain cases, and a different result in still other cases? (4) What, upon the whole, would be the general ethical influence of the system?

§ 287. **Pre-natal Christianity and the Priestly Element.**—Much of that which was later called Christianity really existed before the coming of Jesus. This is true of teachings and ideals which were distinctively prophetic, and of those which were characteristic of the sage, as well as of those which were peculiarly priestly in their origin and character. All these elements, as they existed together in Judaism, may figuratively be called pre-natal Christianity. Endeavor to reconstruct this embryonic Christianity, and decide what part or portion of the whole was this priestly element, as separated from the other elements of prophecy and wisdom.

Appendixes

A. The Vocabulary of Worship; Lists of the More Important Words.

B. Classified Lists of Important Books.

C. New Literature on the Priestly Element.

APPENDIX A.

THE VOCABULARY OF WORSHIP.

The following list, though not designed to be exhaustive, aims to include all the more important words relating to worship and to the great ideas that find expression in the ritual. The list of Greek equivalents contains the various renderings employed in the Septuagint with the exception of some of the rarer ones, and of those evidently based upon different readings from those now found in the Massoretic Text.

Hebrew	Greek	English
אֹהֶל מוֹעֵד	*ἡ σκηνὴ τοῦ μαρτυρίου*	tent of meeting
אוּרִים	*δήλωσις, δηλοί*	Urim
אוּרִים וְתֻמִּים	*φωτίσων* (Neh. 7:65)	Urim and Thummim
אָלָה	*ἀρά, ὁρκισμός, ὅρκος, ὁρκωμοσία, κατάρα*	oath, curse
אֱלֹהִים	*θεός, κύριος*	God
אָסִיף	*ἑορτὴ συντελείας*	ingathering, harvest
אֱסָר	*ὁρισμός*	binding oath, vow
אֲפֻדָּה, אֵפוֹד	*ἐφούδ, ἐφώδ, ἐπωμίς* (or *ἐπωμίδες*, Exod. 28:8; 39:5), *ἱερατεία* (Hos. 3:4), *στολή* (2 Sam. 6:14; 1 Chron. 15:27)	ephod
אֵפֶר	*σποδός, σποδία, κοπρία* (Job 2:8)	ashes
אֲרוֹן	*κιβωτός*	ark
אִשֶּׁה	*θυσία, θυσίασμα, κάρπωμα, κάρπωσις, ὁλοκαύτωμα*	an offering made by fire
אָשַׁם	*πλημμελεῖν, ἁμαρτάνειν, ἀγνόειν*	offend, be guilty
אָשָׁם	*πλημμέλεια, ἄγνοια, πλημμέλημα, πλημμέλησις, ἁμαρτία*	offense, trespass, guilt, trespass offering
אָשֵׁם	*πλημμελεῖν, ἐν ἁμαρτίαις εἶναι* (Gen. 42:21)	guilty
אַשְׁמָה	*ἄγνοια, ἁμαρτία, πλημμελεῖν, πλημμέλεια*	wrongdoing, guilt
אֲשֵׁרָה	*ἄλσος, Ἀστάρτη* (2 Chron. 15:16; 24:18)	Asherah (A. V., "grove")
בַּד	*βάδ, βύσσινος, ἅγιος* (Ezek. 10:6, 7)	white linen

בִּכּוּרִים	*τὰ πρωτογεννήματα, τὰ πρωτόγονα*	first-fruits
בָּמָה	*ὑψηλόν* (*ὑψηλή*), *βαμά, ἀβαμά* (Ezek. 20:29), *βωμός, στήλη, ὕψος, βουνός,* (Ps. 78:58; 1 Kings 10:13), *εἴδωλον* (Ezek. 16:16)	high-place
בָּרִיא	*ἰσχυρός, ἀστεῖος* (Judg. 3:17), *ἐκλεκτός, παχύς* (Ezek. 34:3)	fat
בְּרִית	*διαθήκη*	covenant
בְּרָכָה	*εὐλογία, εὐλογεῖν, εὐλογητός*	blessing
בֹּשֶׂם } בֶּשֶׂם }	*ἥδυσμα, θυμίαμα, ὀσμὴ ἡδεῖα*	spice, balsam
בִּשֵּׁל	*ἕψειν*	boil, seethe
גּוֹרָל	*κλῆρος, κληρονομία, ὅριον, ὄνομα*	lot
גֵּר	*ξένος, πάροικος, γηώρας, προσήλυτος, γείτων*	sojourner, stranger
גִּלּוּלִים	*εἴδωλα, ἐπιτηδεύματα, βδελύγματα, διανοήματα, ἐνθυμήματα*	idols
דְּבִיר	*δαβείρ, δαβεῖρ, δαβίρ, ναός*	shrine, innermost room in Solomon's temple
דָּם	*αἷμα*	blood
דֶּשֶׁן	*πιότης, τὰ ἀγαθά, σποδός, σποδία, κατακάρπωσις*	fatness, fat ashes
הֵיכָל	*ναός, οἶκος*	temple
זָבַח	*θυείν, θυσιάζειν, σφάζειν, θυμιᾶν, θυμιάζειν, προσφέρειν* (Deut. 17:1), *ἐκζήτειν* (2 Chron. 28:23)	slaughter for sacrifice
זֶבַח	*θῦμα, θυσία, θυσίασμα, θυμίαμα, σφάγιον* (Am. 5:25), *ὁλοκαύτωμα* (Exod. 10:25)	sacrifice
חָג	*ἑορτή*	feast, pilgrim-feast
חָגַג	*ἑορτάζειν*	make a pilgrimage, celebrate a feast
חֹדֶשׁ	*μήν, νεομηνία, νουμηνία, ἑορτή*	new moon, month
חָזֶה	*στηθύνιον, ἧπαρ* (Lev. 7:30)	breast of animals
חָטָא	*ἁμαρτάνειν, ἐξαμαρτάνειν, ἀδικεῖν, ἐννοεῖν κακά, διαμαρτάνειν, ἐκκλίνειν, ἐφαμαρτάνειν, μιαίνειν, ἐξάγειν*	to sin
חִטֵּא	*ἀφαγνίζειν, ἁγνίζειν, ἐξιλάσκεσθαι, καθαρίζειν, ῥαντίζειν*	to atone, make expiation for

חֹטֶא	ἁμαρτωλός, ἄνομος, ἀσέβης, ἁμαρτάνων	sinful, sinner
חֵטְא	ἁμαρτία, ἀνομία	sin
חַטָּאת, חֲטָאָה	ἁμαρτία, ἁμάρτημα, ἀνόμημα, ἀσέβεια, ἀνομία, ἀσέβημα, ἀδικία, μετακίνησις (Zech. 13:1), κακία (Jer. 15:13), καρδία (Ps. 32:5), μάταιος (1 Kings 16:2)	sin
	ἱλασμός, ἐξιλασμός, ἁγνισμός, ἅγνισμα	sin-offering
חֵלֶב	στέαρ, μυελός (Gen. 45:18), γαλά (Ps. 119:70; Ezek. 34:3), ἀπαρχή (Numb. 18:29, 30, 32), θυσία (1 Kings 8:64), σάρκας (Ezek. 44:7)	fat
חֹק, חֻקָּה	νόμος, πρόσταγμα, δικαίωμα, τὸ νόμιμον, ἐντολή, κρίμα, διαστολή, τροπή, σύνταξις, δόσις	a statute
חֵרֶם	ἀνατεθεματισμένον, ἀνάθεμα, ἀνάθημα, ἀφόρισμα, ἀπώλεια, ἀπολλύειν, σαγήνη, ἐξολόθρευμα (1 Kings 15:21), ὀλέθριος (1 Kings 20:42)	devoted thing, ban
חֹשֶׁן	λογεῖον, λόγιον, περιστήθιον, ποδήρης	breast-piece, or sacred pouch
טָבַל	βάπτειν, μολύνειν	to dip, immerse
טָהֵר	καθαρὸν εἶναι, ἄμεμπτον εἶναι, καθαρίζεσθαι, ἁγνίζειν, ἀφαγνίζεσθαι	be clean, pure
טָמֵא	ἀκάθαρτον εἶναι, ἀκάθαρτον γίνεσθαι, ἐκμιαίνεσθαι, μιαίνειν (to defile), βεβηλουν (to defile), ἀκαθαρσία, μίανσις	be or become unclean
טֻמְאָה, טֻמְאָה	ἀκαθαρσία, ἀκάθαρτος, ἀποκαθημένη, μίανσις (Lev. 13:44), μιαίνειν	uncleanness
יוֹבֵל	ἄφεσις, ἀφέσεως σημασία, σημασία, σάλπιγξ, ἀφαίρεσις (Numb. 36:4)	ram, ram's horn
כָּבֵד	ἧπαρ	liver
כֹּהֵן	ἱερεύς	priest
כָּלִיל	ὁλοκαύτωμα, ὁλόκαυτος	holocaust
כְּמָרִים	χωμαρίμ (2 Kings 23:5), οἱ ἱερεῖς (Zeph. 1:4)	idol-priests

כִּפֶּר	ἐξιλάσασθαι, ἱλάσκεσθαι, ἀφιέναι (Isa. 22:14), ἱλάζειν, καθαρίζειν (Exod. 30:10), περικαθαρίζειν (Isa. 6:7), ἐκκαθαρίζειν (Deut. 32:43), ἀθῳοῦν (Isa. 18:23), ἁγιάζειν (Exod. 29:33)	to atone
כֹּפֶר	ἄλλαγμα, ἐξίλασμα, περικάθαρμα, λύτρον	atonement, ransom
כַּפֹּרֶת	ἱλαστήριον, ἐξιλασμός	propitiatory
כְּרוּב	χερούβ, χερουβίμ, χερουβείν, χερουβείμ, χερουβεῖν, χερουβίν	cherub
כְּתֹנֶת	χιτών, στολή (Isa. 22:21)	tunic
מוֹעֵד	καιρός, ἑορτή, ὥρα, συνταγή (Judg. 20:38), πανήγυρις, μαρτυρία, ὅρος (Exod. 9:5)	appointed time, meeting-place
מִזְבֵּחַ	θυσιαστήριον, βωμός	altar
מִזְמוֹר	ψαλμός, ὕμνησις, αἴνεσις, τέρας (Isa. 24:16), ᾠδή	melody, psalm
מִזְרָק	φιάλη, ἐσχάρα (2 Chron. 4:11), καλυπτήρ (Numb. 4:14)	bowl, basin
מִלֵּא אֶת־יָד	τελειοῦν τὰς χεῖρας, ἐμπιπλᾶν τὰς χεῖρας (Exod. 28:41), πληροῦν τὰς χεῖρας, πιμπλάναι τὰς χεῖρας (Ezek. 43:26), τετελειωμένος (Lev. 21:10)	install, consecrate consecrated
מִלֻּאִים	τελείωσις, πλήρωσις, γλυφή	installation
מֶלְקָחַיִם	λαβίδες, ἐπαρυστήρ (Exod. 25:38), ἐπαρυστρίς (1 Kings 7:49)	tongs
מִנְחָה	θυσία, δῶρον, θυσίασμα, ξένιον, προσφορά	gift, offering, grain-offering
מַסֵּכָה	τὸ χωνευτόν, χώνευμα, συνθήκη (Isa. 30:1)	molten image
מַעַל	πλημμέλεια, ἀδικία, ἀθέτημα, ἀθεσία, ἀνομία, ἀποστασία, ἀπόστασις, ἀσυνθεσία, λήθη, παράπτωμα, παραβαίνειν (Lev. 26:40)	transgression
מַעֲשֵׂר	δεκάτη, τὸ δέκατον, ἐπιδέκατον, ἐκφόριον (Mal. 3:10), ἀπαρχή (Deut. 12:6)	tenth part, tithe
מַצֵּבָה	στήλη, στήλωσις (2 Kings 18:18), στῦλος (Jer. 43:13), ὑπόστασις (Ezek. 26:11), θήκη (Isa. 6:13)	pillar, sacred stone

מַצָּה, מַצּוֹת	*ἄζυμος, τὰ ἄζυμα*	unleavened bread
מִצְוָה	*ἐντολή, ἔνταλμα, πρόσταγμα, νόμος* (Prov. 6:20), *δικαίωμα* (1 Kings 2:3), *κρίσις* (Deut. 11:1), *ῥῆμα* (Prov. 3:1), *φωνή* (Deut. 28:9, 13), *ὁδός* (Ps. 119:151)	commandment
מִקְדָּשׁ	*τὸ ἅγιον, ἁγιαστήριον, τὸ ἱερόν, τὸ ἡγιασμένον, ἁγίασμα, ἁγιασμός, τελετή*	sacred place, sanctuary
מְרִיאִים	*ἄρνες, ἐστεατωμένοι*	fatlings
מָשַׁח	*χρίειν, ἀλείφειν, διαχρίειν*	anoint
מִשְׁחָה	*χρίσμα, χρίσις, χριστόν*	anointing
מִשְׁכָּן	*σκηνή, σκήνωμα, κατασκήνωσις, οἶκος, συναγωγή*	tabernacle
מִשְׁמָר	*φυλακή, προφυλακή, προφύλαξ, ἐφημερία, πρόσταγμα, φύλαγμα, διατήρησις, ἀποθήκη, παρεμβολή*	watch, charge
מִשְׁפָּט	*κρίσις, κρίμα, κριτήριον, σύγκρισις, δικαίωσις, δικαίωμα, δικαιωσύνη, δίκη, ἐκδίκησις, διάταξις, σύνταξις, πρόσταγμα*	judgment
מַתָּנָה	*δῶρον, δόμα, δόσις*	gift
נְדָבָה	*ἑκούσιον, δόμα, αἵρεσις, ἀφαίρεμα* (Exod. 35:29), *ὁμολογία, ὁμολόγως* (Hos. 14:5), *σφάγιον* (Lev. 22:23)	voluntary offering
נִדָּה	*χωρισμός, μετακίνησις, μετακινούμενος, ἀποκαθημένη, ἀκαθαρσία, ὀνείδισμα, ἄφεδρος, ῥαντισμός, ἁγνισμός*	impurity
נֶדֶר	*εὐχή, ὁμολογία, δῶρον*	vow
נָזִיר	*εὐξάμενος, Ναζίρ, ἡγιασμένος, ναζιραῖος, ἁγνεία, ἅγιος, ἁγιασμός*	one consecrated, devoted, a Nazirite
נֵזֶר	*εὐχή, ἁγνισμός, ἁγνεία, ἅγιος, ἁγίασμα, καθαγιάζειν*	consecration, Naziriteship
נְחֻשְׁתָּן	*Νεεσθάν*	the bronze serpent
נֶסֶךְ	*σπονδή*	drink-offering
נְתִינִים	*Ναθινίμ, Ναθανίμ, Ναθιναῖοι, Ἀθινείμ* (Ezra 8:17), *οἱ δεδομένοι*	Nethinim
סְאָה	*μέτρον, μετρητής, οἰφί*	a measure of flour or of grain

סוּךְ	ἀλείφειν, χρίειν	anoint
סֹלֶת	σεμίδαλις	fine flour
עָבַר	παραβαίνω, παρέρχομαι, ἐγκαταλείπειν, παραπορεύεσθαι	transgress
עֵדָה	συναγωγή	congregation
עוֹלָה	ὁλοκαύτωμα, ὁλοκαύτωσις, κάρπωσις, ὁλοκάρπωσις, κάρπωμα, ὁλοκάρπωμα, θυσία, ἀναφορά, ἀνάβασις	whole burnt-offering
עָוֺן	ἀδικία, ἀδίκημα, ἁμαρτία, ἁμάρτημα, ἀνομία, ἀνόμημα, παρανομία, (Prov. 5:22), κακία (1 Chron. 21:8; Jer. 13:22; 16:18), ἀσέβεια (Ezek. 33:9), αἰτία (Gen. 4:13).	iniquity
עָצָב	εἴδωλον, γλυπτόν	idol
עֲצָרָה עֲצֶרֶת	ἱερεία (2 Kings 10:20), θεραπεία (Joel 1:14; 2:15), ἀργεία (Isa. 1:14), σύνοδος, ἐξόδιον, πανήγυρις	assembly
עָרַךְ	παρατάσσειν, στοιβάζειν, ἐπιστοιβάζειν, ἑτοιμάζειν, παρασκευάζειν(Isa. 50:42), προτιθέναι, προστιθέναι (Exod. 40:23; Lev. 24:8), ἐπιτιθέναι (Gen. 22:9), κοσμεῖν (Ezek. 23:41), αἴρειν (1 Chron. 12:8), παριστάναι, ἰσοῦν, ὁμοιοῦν (Ps. 40:5; Isa. 40:18), βοηθεῖν (1 Chron. 12:36), ἀναλαμβάνειν (Jer. 43:3), ἐπιτρέπειν (Job 32:14), καίειν (Exod. 27:21; Lev. 24:2, 3), κέντειν (Job 6:4), τιμᾶν, τιμογράφειν (2 Kings 23:35)	arrange, set in order (the parts of a sacrifice)
עָשַׂר	δεκατοῦν	to tithe
עִשָּׂרוֹן	δέκατον	tenth part
פִּגּוּל	μίασμα, ἄθυτον, βέβηλος, μεμολυμμένος	unclean thing, refuse
פֶּסַח	πάσχα, φασέκ	passover
פֶּסֶל	γλυπτόν, εἴδωλον, ἄγαλμα, περιβώμιον, γλύμμα, εἰκών	idol, image
פַּעֲמֹן	κώδων	bell on high priest's robe

פָּרֹכֶת	καταπέτασμα	curtain (in tabernacle before Most Holy Place)
פָּשַׁע	ἀθέτειν, ἀσέβειν, ἀφιστάναι ἀνομεῖν, ἀδικεῖν, ἁμαρτάνειν, πλανᾶν, ἄνομος, παρόνομος, ἁμαρτία, παραβαίνειν	to rebel, transgress
פֶּשַׁע	ἀσέβεια, ἀδικία, ἀδίκημα, ἁμαρτία, ἁμάρτημα, ἀνομία, ἀνόμημα, παράπτωμα, πλάνη, ἄγνοια	transgression
צוֹם	νηστεία	fasting, fast
צוּם	νηστεύειν, ἀσιτεῖν	to fast
צֶלֶם	εἰκών, ὁμοίωμα, εἴδωλον, τύπος	image
קָדֹשׁ	ἅγιος, καθαρός, ἡγιασμένος	sacred, holy
קִדֵּשׁ	ἁγιάζειν, ἁγνίζειν, καθαρίζειν (Job 1:5), δοξάζειν (Isa. 5.16), διαστέλλειν (Jos. 20:17), καθαγιάζειν, ἀναβιβάζειν (Jer. 51:28)	set apart, consecrate, dedicate
קֹדֶשׁ	ἅγιος, ἁγιωσύνη, ἁγίασμα, ἁγιάζειν, ἁγιασμός, ἁγνίζειν	sanctity, holiness
קְדֵשָׁה	πόρνη	temple-prostitute
קָהָל	ἐκκλησία, συναγωγή, ὄχλος, συνέδριον (Prov. 26:26), σύστασις (Gen. 49:6), πλῆθος (Exod. 12:6; 2 Chron. 31:18), λαός (1 Kings 12:3)	assembly, congregation
קִטֵּר	θυμιᾶν, θυμιάζειν, ἐπιτιθέναι, θύειν, ἀναφέρειν, προσφέρειν, ἐπιθύειν, θυσιάζειν (Exod. 40:27)	offer burnt-offering, offer incense
קְטֹרֶת	θυμίαμα, σύνθεσις	smoke, odor, incense
קֶסֶם	μαντεία, μαντεῖον, οἰώνισμα	divination
קָרְבָּן	δῶρον, κλῆρος (Neh. 10:34)	offering, oblation
רֵיחַ	ὀσμή, ὀσφρασία (Hos. 14:7)	scent, odor
רֵיחַ נִיחֹחַ	ὀσμὴ εὐωδίας	soothing odor
שְׁבוּעָה	ὅρκος, ἐνόρκιος (Numb. 5:21), ἔνορκος (Neh. 6:18).	oath
שַׁבָּת	σάββατον, σάββατα, ἑβδομάς, ἕβδομος, ἀνάπαυσις	sabbath
שׁוֹפָר	σάλπιγξ, κερατίνη	trumpet
שֶׁלֶם	σωτήριον, εἰρηνικόν, θυσία σωτηρίου, σωτηρία, τὸ τοῦ σωτηρίου	thank-offering, peace-offering

שֶׁמֶן	ἔλαιον, ἄλειμμα, πίων	fat, oil
שְׁנַת הַשְּׁמִטָּה	ἔτος τῆς ἀφέσεως (Deut. 15:9), ἐνιαυτὸς ἀφέσεως (Deut. 31:10)	year of release
תְּהִלָּה	αἴνεσις, ἔπαινος, ὕμνος, γαυρίαμα, καύχημα, ἀρετή, δόξα, ἔνδοξος, ὕμνησις	praise, song of praise
תּוֹדָה	ᾆδων, αἴνεσις, εὐχή χαρμοσύνης, ἐξομολόγησις	thanksgiving, praise
תּוֹעֵבָה	βδέλυγμα, ἀκαθαρσία, ἀκάθαρτος, ἀνομία	abomination
תּוֹרָה	νόμος, ἐντολή, τὸ νόμιμον	direction, instruction, law
תְּפִלָּה	προσευχή, ἐυχή, δέησις, ὕμνος	prayer
תְּרוּמָה	ἀπαρχή, ἀφαίρεμα, ἀφόρισμα, ἀφορισμός, εἰσφορά	gift-offering
תְּרָפִים	εἴδωλα, θεραφίν, δηλοί (Hos. 3:4), τὰ κενοτάφια (1 Sam. 19:13), τὰ γλυπτά (Ezek. 21:21), οἱ ἀποφθεγγόμενοι (Zech. 10:2)	Teraphim
תַּחֲנוּנִים	οἰκτιρμός, δέησις, παράκλησις	petition
תְּחִנָּה	δέησις, ἔλεος, προσευχή, βοή	favor, request
תֻּמִּים	ἀλήθεια, τὰ τέλεια (Ezek. 2:63)	Thummim
תְּנוּפָה	ἀπαρχή, ἐπίθεμα, ἀφαίρεμα, ἀπόδομα, ἀφόρισμα, δόμα	wave-offering

APPENDIX B.

IMPORTANT BOOKS FOR THE STUDY OF THE PRIESTLY ELEMENT.

I. Dictionaries and Encyclopædias.

J. Hastings, *A Dictionary of the Bible*, Vols. I–IV (1898–1902), with an extra volume, containing supplementary articles, indexes, and maps (1904).

T. K. Cheyne and J. S. Black, *Encyclopædia Biblica*, Vols. I–IV (1899–1903).

W. Smith, *A Dictionary of the Bible* (2d ed. 1893).

Herzog-Hauck, *Realencyklopädie für protestantische Theologie und Kirche* (3d ed. 1896 ff.; fourteen volumes have now been published).

II. Introductions to Old Testament Literature.

S. R. Driver, *An Introduction to the Literature of the Old Testament* (6th ed. 1897).

J. E. Carpenter and G. Harford-Battersby, *The Hexateuch*, 2 vols. (1900).

J. E. Carpenter, *The Composition of the Hexateuch* (1902).

C. A. Briggs, *The Higher Criticism of the Hexateuch* (2d ed. 1897).

W. E. Addis, *The Documents of the Hexateuch*, 2 vols. (1893, 1898).

W. R. Smith, *The Old Testament in the Jewish Church* (2d ed. 1892).

C. H. Cornill, *Einleitung in das Alte Testament* (3d ed. 1896).

H. Holzinger, *Einleitung in den Hexateuch* (1893).

W. von Baudissin, *Einleitung in die Bücher des Alten Testamentes* (1901).

E. König, *Einleitung in das Alte Testament* (1893).

A. Kuenen, *Historisch-critisch Onderzoek naar het ontstaan en de verzameling van de boeken des Ouden Verbonds*, 3 vols. (2d ed. 1885–89). German translation, *Historisch-kritische Einleitung in die Bücher des Alten Testamentes* (1887–92); English translation of Vol. I, *The Hexateuch* (1886).

G. Wildeboer, *De Letterkunde des Ouden Verbonds naar de tijdsorde van haar ontstaan* (1893; 3d ed. 1903). German translation, *Die Litteratur des Alten Testaments* (1895).

C. Steuernagel, *Allgemeine Einleitung in den Hexateuch* ("Handkommentar zum Alten Testament," 1900).

III. Hebrew Institutions and Archæology.

W. H. Green, *The Hebrew Feasts in Their Relation to Recent Critical Hypotheses Concerning the Pentateuch* (1885).

A. Scott, *Sacrifice, Its Prophecy and Fulfillment* ("Baird Lecture," 1892–93).

W. von Baudissin, *Die Geschichte des alttestamentlichen Priesterthums* (1889).

W. Nowack, *Lehrbuch der hebräischen Archäologie* (1894).

I. Benzinger, *Hebräische Archäologie* (1894).

IV. Semitic Institutions and Archæology.

W. R. Smith, *Religion of the Semites* (1889; 2d ed. 1894).

G. A. Barton, *A Sketch of Semitic Origins—Social and Religious* (1902).

W. R. Smith, *Kinship and Marriage in Early Arabia* (1885; 2d ed. 1903).

Morris Jastrow, Jr., *The Religion of Babylonia and Assyria* (1898). German translation, being a revised and enlarged edition of the English; Vol. I (1905).

L. W. King, *Babylonian Religion and Mythology* (1899).

A. H. Sayce, *The Religions of Ancient Egypt and Babylonia* (1902).

S. I. Curtiss, *Primitive Semitic Religion To-Day* (1902).

Wellhausen, *Reste des arabischen Heidenthums* (= *Skizzen und Vorarbeiten*, Vol. III, 1887; 2d ed. 1897.)

Lagrange, *Études sur les religions Sémitiques* (1903).

Schwally, *Semitische Kriegsaltertümer*, Heft I (1901).

Baudissin, *Studien zur semitischen Religionsgeschichte*, 2 vols. (1876, 1878).

Baethgen, *Beiträge sur semitischen Religionsgeschichte* (1888).

V. The Code of Hammurabi and Hebrew Legislation.

R. F. Harper, *The Code of Hammurabi* (1904).

C. H. W. Johns, *The Oldest Code of Laws in the World* (1903).

C. H. W. Johns, Article "The Code of Hammurabi," Hastings's *Dictionary of the Bible* (Extra Volume, 1904).

S. A. Cook, *The Laws of Moses and the Code of Hammurabi* (1903).

C. Edwards, *The Hammurabi Code and the Sinaitic Legislation* (1904).

C. F. Kent, "The Recently Discovered Civil Code of Hammurabi," *Biblical World*, Vol. XXI (1903), pp. 175–90.

A. H. Sayce, "The Legal Code of Babylonia," *American Journal of Theology* (1904), pp. 256–66.

D. H. LYON, "The Structure of the Hammurabi Code," *Journal of the American Oriental Society*, Vol. XXV (1904), pp. 248–65.
V. SCHEIL, *Memoires de la delégation en Perse*, Tome IV (1902).
V. SCHEIL, *La loi de Hammurabi* (1904).
H. WINCKLER, *Die Gesetze Hammurabis* (1903).
H. WINCKLER, *Die Gesetze Hammurabis in Umschrift und Uebersetzung herausgegeben. Dazu Einleitung, u. s. w.* (1904).
J. KOHLER UND F. E. PEISER, *Hammurabi's Gesetz*, Vol. I: *Uebersetzung, juristische Wiedergabe, Erläuterung* (1903).
D. H. MÜLLER, *Die Gesetze Hammurabis und ihr Verhältnis zur Mosaischen Gesetzgebung sowie zu den XII Tafeln* (1903).
H. GRIMME, *Das Gesetz Chammurabis und Moses* (1903).
S. OETTLI, *Das Gesetz Hammurabis und die Thora Israels* (1903).
J. JEREMIAS, *Moses und Hammurabi* (1903).
G. COHN, *Die Gesetze Hammurabi's* (1903).
A. ROSENBACHER, *Moses und Hammurabi* (1904).
ED. KÖNIG, "Hammurabis Gesetzgebung und ihre religionsgeschichtliche Tragweite," *Beweis des Glaubens* (1903), pp. 169–80.
LAGRANGE, "Le code de Hammurabi," *Revue biblique* (1903), pp. 27–51.

VI. Old Testament Theology and Religion.

H. SCHULTZ, *Old Testament Theology* (German, 1869; 5th ed. 1896; English, 1892).
C. G. MONTEFIORE, *The Religion of the Ancient Hebrews* ("Hibbert Lectures," 1892).
A. DUFF, *Old Testament Theology*, 2 vols. (1891, 1900).
A. KUENEN, *The Religion of Israel*, 3 vols. (Dutch, 1869–70; English translation, 1882–83).
A. B. DAVIDSON, *The Theology of the Old Testament* (1904).
J. ROBERTSON, *The Early Religion of Israel* ("Baird Lecture," 1889).
PIEPENBRING, *The Theology of the Old Testament* (1886; English translation, 1893).
K. BUDDE, *The Religion of Israel to the Exile* (1899).
T. K. CHEYNE, *Jewish Religious Life after the Exile* (1898).
R. SMEND, *Lehrbuch der alttestamentlichen Religionsgeshichte* (1893; 2d ed. 1899).
K. MARTI, *Geschichte der israelitischen Religion* (1897).
A. DILLMANN, *Handbuch der alttestamentlichen Theologie* (1895).

APPENDIX C.

NEW LITERATURE ON THE PRIESTLY ELEMENT.

P. 63, note 1—on **Hexateuchal Analysis**, etc.: H. G. MITCHELL, *The World Before Abraham* (1901); DRIVER, *Commentary on Genesis* (1904); C. F. KENT, *Beginnings of Hebrew History* (1904); TESCH, *Setzt der Prophet Amos autoritatives Gesetz voraus* (1895); PAUL VETTER, "Die Zeugnisse der vorexilischen Propheten über dem Pentateuch," *Theologische Quartalschrift* Vol. LXXXIII (1901), pp.94–112, 187–207.

P. 71, § 71—on **The Priest**: J. TAYLOR, art. "Nethinim," HASTINGS'S *Dictionary of The Bible* (1900); A. WALKER, "The Levitical Priesthood—a Study in Social Development," *Journal of Biblical Literature* Vol. XIX (1900), pp. 124–31; BENZINGER, art. "Nethinim," *Encyclopædia Biblica* (1902); W. R. SMITH AND A. BERTHOLET, art. "Priests," *ibid.;* W. R. SMITH AND A. BERTHOLET, art. "Levites," *ibid.;* GRAF VON BAUDISSIN, art. "Priests and Levites," HASTINGS'S *Dictionary of The Bible* (1902); FRANTS BUHL, art. "Hoherpriester," *Realencyklopädie für protestantische Theologie und Kirche* Vol. VIII, (3d ed. 1900).

P. 72, §72, topic 6—on **The Priest in other Semitic Nations**: W. H. BENNETT, art. "Molech, Moloch," HASTINGS'S *Dictionary of the Bible* (1900); G. F. MOORE, art. "Moloch," *Encyclopædia Biblica* (1902); IDEM, art. "Nature-Worship," *ibid.;* IDEM, art. "Tithes," *ibid.;* J. JEREMIAS, art. "Ritual," *ibid.;* M. J. LAGRANGE, "Les prêtres babyloniens d'après une publication récente," *Revue biblique*, 1901, pp. 392–413; SPIEGELBERG, *Der Stabkultus bei den Ägyptern* (1903); W. WRESZINSKI, *Die Hohenpriester des Amon* (1904).

P. 80, §81,—on **The Place of Worship**: L. W. BATTEN, "The Sanctuary at Shiloh and Samuel's Sleeping Therein," *Journal of Biblical Literature* Vol. XIX (1900), pp. 124–31; O. C. WHITEHOUSE, art. "Pillar," HASTINGS'S *Dictionary of The Bible* (1900); G. F. Moore, art. "High Place," *Encyclopædia Biblica* (1901); G. A. DEISSMANN, art. "Mercy Seat," *ibid.* (1902); G. F. MOORE, art. "Massebah," *ibid.;* BENZINGER, art. "The Brazen Sea," *ibid.* (1903); G. H. BOX; art. "Temple, Temple Service," *ibid.;* BENZINGER, art, "Tabernacle," *ibid.;* T. W. DAVIES, art. "Temple," HASTINGS'S *Dictionary of The Bible* (1902); A. R. S. KENNEDY, art. "Sanctuary," *ibid.;* IDEM, art. "Tabernacle," *ibid.;* J. T. MARSHALL, art. "Shekinah," *ibid.;* A. H. SAYCE, "Recent Biblical Archæology; Tree and Pillar Cult," *Expository Times*, Vol. XIII (1902) pp. 309 f.; W. E. BARNES, art. "Jachin and Boaz," *Journal of Theological Studies*, 1904, pp. 447–51; J. MEINHOLD, *Die Lade Jahves* (1900); IDEM, "Die Lade Jahves; ein Nachtrag," *Theologische Studien und Kritiken* Vol. LXXIV (1901), pp. 593–607; A. LOTZ, *Die Bundeslade* (1901); K. BUDDE, "Die Ursprüngliche Bedeutung der Lade Jahves," *Zeitschrift für die alttestamentliche Wissenschaft*, Vol. XXI (1901), pp. 193–7; W. RIEDEL, "Der Kultusort nach dem Bundesbuch, *Alttestamentliche Untersuchungen* (1902), pp. 48–51; M. VERNE, "Notes sur les sanctuaires de la region chananéenne qui furent fréquentés concurrement par les Israelites et les nations voisines," *Revue de l'histoire des religions*, Vol. XLIII (1901), pp. 352–54; P. TORGE, *Ascherah und Astarte* (1902); A. BÜCHLER, *Das Synedrium in Jerusalem und die grosse Beth-Din in der Quader-Kammer des Jerusalem-Tempels* (1902); J. PRESTEL, *Baugeschichte der jüdischen Heiligtümer, und die Tempel-Salomos* (1904).

Pp. 90 ff., §94—on **Sacrifice**: CHEYNE, art. "Incense," *Encyclopædia Biblica* (1901); W. P. PATERSON, art. "Sacrifice," HASTINGS'S *Dictionary of the Bible* (1902); S. I. CURTISS, "Discoveries of a Vicarious Element in Primitive Semitic Sacrifice," *Expositor*, 6th series, Vol. VI (1902), pp. 128–34; IDEM, "The Origin of Sacrifice among the Semites," *ibid.* (1904), pp. 461–72; S. R. DRIVER, art. "Propitiation," HASTINGS'S *Dictionary of The Bible* (1902); S. LANGDON, "History and Significance of Carthaginian Sacrifice," *Journal of Biblical Literature*, Vol. XXIII (1903), pp. 79–93; G. F. MOORE, art. "Sacrifice," *Encyclopædia Biblica* (1903); R. DE LA GRASSERIE, "Du rôle sociale du sacrifice religieux," *Revue de l'histoire des religions*, July–August, 1901; J. C. MATTHES, "Zoenoffers," *Teyler's Theologisch Tijdschrift*, Vol. II (1904), pp. 69–92.

Pp. 104 ff., §106—on **Feasts**: CHEYNE, art. "Purim," *Encyclopædia Biblica* (1902); BENZINGER, artt. "New Moon," "New Year," "Passover," "Pentecost," *Encyclopædia Biblica* (1902), and "Feast of Tabernacles," *ibid.* (1903); A. T. CHAPMAN, art. "Feast of Tabernacles," HASTINGS'S *Dictionary of The Bible* (1902); J. A. MCCLYMONT, art.

"Purim," *ibid.;* J. E. H. THOMSON, "The Samaritan Passover," *Palestine Exploration Fund*, Vol. XXXIV (1902), pp. 82–92; BELLELI, "The High Priest's Procession on the Day of Atonement," *Jewish Quarterly Review*, October, 1904; W. RIEDEL, "Die drei grossen jüdischen Feste," *Alttestamentliche Untersuchungen* (1902), pp. 52–63; FR. BUHL, art. "Laubhüttenfest," *Realencyklopädie für protestantische Theologie und Kirche*, Vol. XI (3d ed. 1902), pp. 303–6; HOCHFELD, "Die Entstehung des Hanukafestes," *Zeitschrift für die alttestamentliche Wissenschaft*, Vol. XXII (1902), pp. 264–84; S. HANOVER, *Das Festgesetz der Samaritaner nach Ibrahim ibn Ja'kub* (1904); B. D. EERDMANS, "De groote Verzoendag," *Theologisch Tijdschrift* (1904), pp. 17–41.

Pp. 114 ff., § 120—on **Sabbath**: TOY, "Earliest Form of the Sabbath," *Journal of Biblical Literature* (1899), pp. 191 ff.; W. R. SMITH AND BENZINGER, art. "Jubilee," *Encyclopædia Biblica* (1901); DRIVER, art. "Sabbath," HASTINGS'S *Dictionary of The Bible* (1902); G. HARFORD-BATTERSBY, art. "Sabbatical Year," *ibid.:* W. R. SMITH, MARTI, AND CHEYNE, art. "Sabbath," *Encyclopædia Biblica* (1903); T. G. PINCHES, "Šapattu, the Babylonian Sabbath," *Proceedings of the Society of Biblical Archaeology*, Vol. XXVI (1904), pp. 51–56; W. RIEDEL, "Der Sabbath," *Alttestamentliche Untersuchungen* (1902), pp. 74–89; BOHN, *Der Sabbat im Alten Testament* (1903).

Pp. 126 ff., § 134—on **Clean and Unclean**: A. MACALISTER, artt. "Leprosy" and "Medicine," HASTINGS'S *Dictionary of the Bible* (1900); A. R. S. KENNEDY, artt. "Food" and "Meals," *Encyclopædia Biblica* (1901); C. CREIGHTON, artt. "Leprosy, Lepers," and "Medicine," *ibid.;* A. S. PEAKE, art. "Unclean, Uncleanness," HASTINGS'S *Dictionary of the Bible* (1902); S. A. COOK, "Israel and Totemism," *Jewish Quarterly Review*, Vol. XIV (1902), pp. 413–48; FR. VINC. ZAPLETAL, *Der Totemismus und die Religion Israels* (1901); L. G. LÉVY, "Du totemisme chez les Hébreux," *Revue des études juives*, Vol. XLV (1902), pp. 13–26.

Pp. 133 f., § 139—on **Prayer**: J. A. SELBIE, art. "Praise," HASTINGS'S *Dictionary of the Bible* (1902); E. R. BERNARD, art. "Prayer," *ibid.;* CHEYNE, art. "Prayer," *Encyclopædia Biblica* (1902); JUSTUS KÖBERLE, *Die Motive des Glaubens und der Gebetserhörung im Alten Testament* (1901).

P. 135, § 142—on **Vows**: W. H. BENNETT, art. "Rechabites," HASTINGS'S *Dictionary of the Bible* (1902); A. S. PEAKE, art. "Vow," *ibid.;* W. R. SMITH AND T. K. CHEYNE, art. "Nazirite," *Encyclopædia Biblica* (1902); G. F. MOORE, art. "Vows, Votive Offerings," *ibid.*

Pp. 140 f., § 151—on **The Oath**: M. A. CANNEY, art. "Oath," *Encyclopædia Biblica* (1902).

Pp. 142 f., § 154—on **Fasting**: BENZINGER, art. "Fasting, Fasts," *Encyclopædia Biblica* (1901); J. J. P. VALETON, "Jets over Israelietischen Vastendagen," *Theologisch Tijdschrift*, Vol. XXXV (1901), pp. 521–29; M. TH. HOUTSMA, "Nog eenmal de Israelietische Vastendagen," *ibid.*, Vol. XXXVI (1902), pp. 334–41.

P. 145, § 157—on **Oracles, Ephod, etc.**: T. C. FOOTE, "The Ephod," *Journal of Biblical Literature*, Vol. XXI (1902), pp. 1–47; A. R. S. KENNEDY, art. "Urim and Thummim," HASTINGS'S *Dictionary of the Bible* (1902); G. F. MOORE, art. "Urim and Thummim," *Encyclopædia Biblica* (1903); ELHORST, "De Ephod," *Teyler's Theologisch Tijdschrift*, Vol. II, No. 2 (1904).

Pp. 146 f., § 160—on **Magic and Divination**: O. C. WHITEHOUSE, art. "Soothsayer, Soothsaying, Sorcery," HASTINGS'S *Dictionary of the Bible*, (1902); H. ZIMMERN AND

DAVIES, art. "Magic," *Encyclopædia Biblica* (1902); CHEYNE, art. "Serpent," §§ 3 ff., *ibid.;* G. F. MOORE, art. "Teraphim," *ibid.;* F. SCHMID, "Die Zauberei und die Bibel," *Zeitschrift für katholische Theologie*, Vol. XXVI, pp. 107–30; H. DUHM, *Die bösen Geister im Alten Testament* (1904).

Pp. 148 f., § 163—on **Mourning Customs, etc.**: MORRIS JASTROW, "The Tearing of Garments as a Symbol of Mourning," *Journal of the American Oriental Society*, Vol. XXI (1901), pp. 23–39; R. H. CHARLES, art. "Eschatology," *Encyclopædia Biblica* (1901); BENZINGER, art. "Mourning Customs," *ibid.;* M. JASTROW, "Baring the Arm and Shoulder as a Sign of Mourning," *Zeitschrift für die alttestamentliche Wissenschaft*, Vol. XXII (1902), pp. 117–20; J. A. BEET, "The Immortality of the Soul: Before Christ," *Expositor*, Sixth Series, Vol. III, pp. 50–61; J. GARNIER, *Worship of the Dead* (1904); J. C. MATTHES, "Rouw en doodenvereering in Israel," *Theologisch Tijdschrift*, Vol. XXXIV (1900), pp. 97–128, 193–224; Vol. XXXV (1901), pp. 320–49; J. WOHLGEMUTH, *Die Unsterblichkeitslehre in der Bibel* (1901); G. BEER, *Der biblische Hades* (1902); SARTORI, *Die Speisung der Toten* (1903); C. L. DELÉTRA, *Récherches sur les vestiges d'un culte des morts chez les anciens Hébreux* (1903); J. SCHREINER, *Elysium und Hades* (1903); F. ROUX, *Essai sur la vie après la mort chez les Israëlites* (1904); F. HROZNY, "Zur Höllenfahrt der Ištar," *Wiener Zeitschrift für die Kunde des Morgenlandes* (1904), pp. 323–30; G. WISSOWA, "Die Anfänge des römischen Larenkultes," *Archiv für Religionswissenschaft* (1904), pp. 42–57; A. LODS, "Les Israëlites croyaient-ils à la vie future?" *Revue chrétienne* (1904), pp. 283–300, 359–76.

Pp. 150 f., §166—on **Circumcision**: H. GUNKEL, "Ueber die Beschneidung im alten Testament," *Archiv für Papyrus-Forschung*, Vol. II (1902), pp. 13–21; P. WENDLAND, "Die hellenistischen Zeugnisse über die ägyptische Beschneidung," *ibid.*, pp. 23–31; ULRICH WILCKEN, "Die ägyptische Beschneidung," *ibid.*, pp. 4–13; KUTNA, "Studien über die Beschneidung, IV," *Monatsschrift für Geschichte und Wissenschaft des Judentums*, Vol. XLVI (1902), pp. 193–205.

Pp. 167 ff, § 181—on **The Deuteronomic Code**: CULLEN, *The Book of the Covenant in Moab* (1903); S. FRIES, *Der Gesetzschrift des Königs Josia* (1903).

Pp. 180 ff., chaps. xiv and xv—on **The Priestly Document**: DRIVER, art. "Law," HASTINGS'S *Dictionary of the Bible* (1900); G. HARFORD-BATTERSBY, art. "Leviticus," *ibid.;* IDEM, art. "Numbers," *ibid.;* G. F. MOORE, art. "Leviticus," *Encyclopædia Biblica* (1902); IDEM, art. "Numbers," *ibid.;* G. B. GRAY, *Commentary on Numbers* ("International Critical Commentary," 1903); J. HALÉVY, "Influence du Code Sacerdotal sur les prophètes," *Revue sémitique*, Vol. IX (1901), pp. 1–6; HOLZINGER, *Numeri erklärt* ("Kurzer Handkommentar," 1903); ERBT, *Die Sicherstellung des Monotheismus* (1903).

Pp. 225 ff., § 245—on **Ezra and Nehemiah**: W. H. KOSTERS AND T. K. CHEYNE, art. "Nehemiah," *Encyclopædia Biblica* (1902); A. E. COWLEY, art. "Samaritans," *ibid.* (1903); P. RIESSLER, "Über Nehemias und Esdras," *Biblische Zeitschrift*, 1904, pp. 15–27, 145–53.

Index

INDEX